The
Garland
Library
of
the
History
of
Western
Music

One hundred
eighty-five
articles in
fourteen volumes

General Editor
Ellen Rosand
Rutgers University

Contents
of
the
Set

Volume Twelve

*Opera
II:
Mozart
and
After*

*Garland Publishing, Inc.
New York & London
1985*

Library of Congress Cataloging-in-Publication Data
Main entry under title:
Opera.

   (The Garland library of the history of western music ; v. 12)
   Reprint of articles and essays originally published 1954–1982.
   Contents: Part 2. Mozart and after.
   1. Opera—Addresses, essays, lectures.   I. Series.
ML1700.063   1985   782.1   85-15983
ISBN 0-8240-7461-0 (v. 12)

The volumes in this series have been printed on acid-free,
250-year-life paper.

Printed in the United States of America

Contents

Acknowledgments

Heartz, Daniel. "Raaff's Last Aria: A Mozartian Idyll in the Spirit of Hasse," *The Musical Quarterly*, LX (1974), 517–43. Copyright © 1974 by G. Schirmer, Inc., reprinted by permission

Heartz, Daniel. "Mozart and His Italian Contemporaries: *La clemenza di Tito*," *Mozart-Jahrbuch 1978/79* (Kassel, 1979), pp. 275–93. Copyright © 1977 by the Internationale Stiftung Mozarteum, reprinted by permission

Cairns, David. "Les Troyens and the Aeneid," in Cairns, *Responses: Musical Essays and Reviews* (London: Secker and Warburg, 1973; repr. New York: Da Capo, 1980), pp. 88–110. Copyright © 1973 by David Cairns, reprinted by permission

Dean, Winton. "Donizetti's Serious Operas," *Proceedings of the Royal Musical Association*, C (1973–74), 123–41. Copyright © 1974 by Winton Dean and the Royal Musical Association, reprinted by permission

Bailey, Robert. "Wagner's Musical Sketches for *Siegfrieds Tod*," in *Studies in Music History: Essays for Oliver Strunk*, ed. Harold Powers (Princeton: Princeton University Press, 1968), pp. 459–94. Copyright © 1968 by Princeton University Press, excerpt, pp. 459–94, reprinted by permission of Princeton University Press

Dahlhaus, Carl. "Formprinzipien in Wagners *Ring des Nibelungen*," in *Beiträge zur Geschichte der Oper*, ed. Heinz Becker (Regensburg: Gustav Bosse, 1969), pp. 95–129. Copyright © 1969 by Gustav Bosse Verlag, reprinted by permission

Newcomb, Anthony. "The Birth of Music out of the Spirit of Drama: An Essay in Wagnerian Formal Analysis," *Nineteenth-Century Music*, V (1981–82), 38–66. Copyright © 1981 by The Regents of the University of California, reprinted by permission of The Regents

Petrobelli, Pierluigi. "Music in the Theatre (à propos of *Aida*, Act III)," in *Drama, Dance, and Music* (Themes in Drama, III), ed. James Redmond (Cambridge: Cambridge University Press, 1980), pp. 129–42. Copyright © 1980 by Cambridge University Press, reprinted by permission

Preface

The Garland Library of the History of Western Music, in fourteen
volumes, is a collection of outstanding articles in musicology that
have been reprinted from a variety of sources: periodicals, *Fest-
schriften*, and other collections of essays. The articles were selected
from a list provided by a panel of eminent musicologists, named
below, who represent the full range of the discipline.

Originally conceived in general terms as a collection of outstanding articles whose reprinting would serve the needs of students of musicology at the graduate and advanced undergraduate
level, the series took clearer shape during the process of selecting
articles for inclusion. While volumes covering the conventional
chronological divisions of music history had been projected from
the very beginning, several other kinds of volumes cutting across
those traditional divisions and representing the interests of large
numbers of scholars eventually suggested themselves: the volumes
on opera, source studies, criticism, and analysis.

Indeed, although the general objective of excellence remained
standard for the entire series, the specific criteria for selection
varied somewhat according to the focus of the individual volumes.
In the two on opera, for example, chronological coverage of the
history of the genre was of primary importance; in those on
source studies, criticism, and analysis the chief aim was the
representation of different points of view; and in the volumes
devoted to chronological periods selection was guided by an effort
to cover the various geographical centers, genres, and individual
composers essential to the understanding of a historical era.

The articles themselves were written over a period spanning
more than a half century of modern musicological scholarship.
Some are "classic" statements by scholars of the past or early
formulations by scholars still active today, in which musicological
method, intellectual vision, or significance for their time rather
than any specific factual information is most worthy of appreciation. Others represent the most recent research, by younger
scholars as well as more established ones. No general attempt has
been made to bring the articles up to date, although some authors

have included addenda and misprints have been corrected where possible.

Since no single reader could be fully satisfied by the selection of articles in his own field, the aims of this collection, by necessity, have had to be considerably broader: to provide not only a wide range of articles on a large number of topics by a variety of authors but to offer the student some sense of the history and development of individual fields of study as well as of the discipline as a whole. The value of these volumes derives from the material they contain as well as from the overview they provide of the field of musicology; but the series will fulfill its function only if it leads the student back into the library, to immerse himself in all the materials necessary to a fuller understanding of any single topic.

Ellen Rosand

Panel of Advisors

Richard J. Agee, The Colorado College

James R. Anthony, University of Arizona

William W. Austin, Cornell University

Lawrence F. Bernstein, University of Pennsylvania

Bathia Churgin, Bar-Ilan University

Edward T. Cone, Princeton University

John Deathridge, King's College, Cambridge

Walter Frisch, Columbia University

Sarah Ann Fuller, SUNY at Stony Brook

James Haar, University of North Carolina at Chapel Hill

Ellen Harris, University of Chicago

D. Kern Holoman, University of California at Davis

Robert Holzer, University of Pennsylvania

Philip Gossett, University of Chicago

Douglas Johnson, Rutgers University

Jeffrey Kallberg, University of Pennsylvania

Janet Levy, New York, New York

Kenneth Levy, Princeton University

Lowell Lindgren, Massachusetts Institute of Technology

Robert Marshall, Brandeis University

Leonard B. Meyer, University of Pennsylvania

Robert P. Morgan, University of Chicago

John Nádas, University of North Carolina at Chapel Hill

Jessie Ann Owens, Brandeis University

Roger Parker, Cornell University

Martin Picker, Rutgers University

Alejandro Planchart, University of California at Santa Barbara

Harold Powers, Princeton University

Joshua Rifkin, Cambridge, Massachusetts

John Roberts, University of Pennsylvania

Stanley Sadie, Editor, *The New Grove Dictionary of Music and Musicians*

Norman E. Smith, University of Pennsylvania

Howard E. Smither, University of North Carolina at Chapel Hill

Ruth Solie, Smith College

Maynard Solomon, New York, New York

Ruth Steiner, The Catholic University of America

Gary Tomlinson, University of Pennsylvania

Leo Treitler, SUNY at Stony Brook

James Webster, Cornell University

Piero Weiss, Peabody Conservatory

Eugene K. Wolf, University of Pennsylvania

Vol. LX, No. 4　　　　　　　　　　　　OCTOBER, 1974

THE MUSICAL QUARTERLY

RAAFF'S LAST ARIA:
A MOZARTIAN IDYLL IN THE
SPIRIT OF HASSE

By DANIEL HEARTZ

"Man muss aus der Noth eine tugend machen."

1

PRIOR to composing *Idomeneo* in 1780–81, Mozart had tailored his art to some of the greatest singers of the age, both in concert arias and in his several stage works. The castrato Giovanni Manzuoli comes to mind at once. For him Mozart wrote the title part of *Ascanio in Alba,* and he knew the voice well even earlier, from the singing lessons Manzuoli imparted when the Mozarts were in London in 1764–65. "Tailored" fits the case perfectly. It is the expression Mozart himself chose when expressing his function as composer. With regard to his *Mitridate,* written for Milan in 1770, he was reported by father Leopold as unwilling to compose much in the way of arias until he knew a voice firsthand, "so as to measure the garment exactly to the person."[1] Eight years later, when composing the

---

[1] "Um das Kleid recht an den Leib zu messen." Letter of November 24, 1770, No. 220, lines 6-7. Passages from Mozart's letters have been translated by the author from *Mozart Briefe und Aufzeichnungen. Gesamtausgabe,* ed. Wilhelm A. Bauer and Otto Erich Deutsch, 4 vols. (Kassel, 1962–63). Citations will be identified henceforth by date, number in this edition, and line, with the German text included where comparison with the original proves to be of particular interest.

aria "Se al labbro mio non credi" (K. 295) expressly to suit the voice and satisfy the taste of Anton Raaff (1714–1797), he used a similar formulation: "I like to measure an aria to a singer so accurately that it resembles a well-fitting garment."[2] Satisfying Raaff at this late stage of his long career proved no easy task. From his experience of Raaff in the theater at Mannheim, he knew exactly what he could and could not expect of the veteran tenor. He witnessed Raaff's performance in the title role of Holzbauer's *Günther von Schwarzburg* in November, 1777, and wrote to his father: "Whoever hears him begin an aria and fails to recall that this is Raaff, the old and once so famous tenor — he must certainly laugh wholeheartedly. For it is a fact, as I was thinking to myself, that if I didn't know it was Raaff singing, I'd double up with laughter; instead I take out my handkerchief and soil it. His life long, he was never anything of an actor, as people tell me even here, where they say he should be heard but not seen. He has no stage presence whatsoever. In the opera he has to die, and while doing so sing a /: long:/ slow aria; well, sir, he died with a grin on his face, and at the end of the aria his voice gave out so badly that one couldn't bear it any longer."[3] With this portrait in mind, it will be possible to appreciate all the more what a superb sartorial fitting Raaff both required and received in the role of Idomeneo.

Mozart left Salzburg for Munich in early November, 1780, in order to finish the composition of *Idomeneo* on the spot, in collaboration with the singers, players, dancers, and scenic artists. His first letter back to his father brings up the old problem anew: "Raaff is like a statue."[4] A week later it was a question of asking the librettist,

[2] Letter of February 28, 1778, No. 431, lines 26-27: "denn ich liebe dass die aria einem sänger so accurat angemessen sey, wie ein gutgemachts kleid." Compare also Mozart's words about "Non so, d'onde viene" (K. 294) written for Aloysia Weber, in a letter of December 3, 1778, No. 508, lines 44-45: "indemm sie ganz für sie geschrieben, und ihr so past, wie ein kleid auf den leib."

[3] Letter of November 14, 1777, No. 373, lines 61-68. I have preserved Mozart's use of repetition marks to emphasize a point. In the original he wrote in addition the word "ter" above "/: lang :/", i. e., "thrice-long."

[4] Letter of November 8, 1780, No. 535, line 46. In a subsequent letter (December 19, No. 565, line 53), Mozart referred to Raaff as a "schlechte acteur." There is no lack of corroborating evidence on Raaff's inadequacies as an actor. Metastasio referred to him as a "freddissimo rappresentante" as early as 1749; see Otto Michtner, *Das alte Burgtheater als Opernbühne von der Einführung des deutschen Singspiels (1778) bis zum Tod Kaiser Leopolds II. (1792)* (Vienna, 1970), p. 379, note 20. In the *Musikalisches Handbuch auf das Jahr 1782* ascribed to Carl Ludwig Junker there is another revealing picture of Raaff at the end of his career: "Nun hat er beynahe ausgedient

Abbé Varesco of Salzburg cathedral, to accommodate Raaff's request for a change at the end of the opera: "He is right moreover, and even were he not, some consideration should be shown his grey hairs. He was with me yesterday and I ran through his first aria, with which he was very content. Now the man is old and can no longer show himself to advantage in an aria such as he has in Act II, 'Fuor del mar, ho un mar in seno.' So, inasmuch as he has no aria in Act III, and his aria in Act I cannot be as cantabile as he'd like on account of the text, he wishes to have a pretty one to sing after his last speech, 'O Creta fortunata, O me felice,' instead of the quartet there. And thus another useless piece will be gotten rid of, and Act III will make a much better effect."[5] Only from these last remarks do we learn that the libretto originally included a second quartet, not to be confused, as is so often done, with the Great Quartet early in Act III, but a *licenza* of the perfunctory type that was so common, allowing the remaining principal singers to take their leave.[6] Raaff had a history of getting his way with composers and librettists when it came to final scenes. His death scene in *Günther* represented his fourth aria, as Mozart pointed out, noting the fact also that this gave him altogether some 450 bars of music to sing.[7] Earlier Raaff had the ending of one of Metastasio's most celebrated dramas altered so that he could sing an additional aria in place of the concluding *coro*. The case is instructive and warrants consideration here. In *Attilio Regolo,* which was Metastasio's own favorite among his dramas, the title hero is sent off the stage with a magnificent monologue, meant to be set as an obbligato recitative, without an aria.[8] This ending was so effective as composed by Jommelli for

3

und ist kalt. Ob er gleich mehr spricht als singt, oder obgleich sein Gesang meist singende Rede ist, so kann man doch aus den Ueberresten desselben und aus seiner meist guten Declamation schliessen, dass er ehmals gross müsse gewesen seyn. Von Action weiss er nichts." (This annual bears no place of publication and is not paginated; a copy exists in the Bavarian State Library, Munich, Mus. Th. 1654.)

5 Letter of November 15, 1780, No. 538, lines 9-20. The first-act aria in question is "Vedrommi intorno l'ombra dolente" (No. 6).

6 Confusion of the two quartet texts was made by Edward J. Dent, *Mozart's Operas: A Critical Study,* 2nd ed. (London, 1947), p. 37. and is encountered widely on Dent's authority.

7 Letter of November 14, 1777, No. 373, lines 59-60.

8 Metastasio expressed his preference to Casanova in a detailed and very informative interview accorded the latter in 1753, as related in Casanova's *Mémoires,* chap. 33 (Pléiade ed. [Paris, 1964], I, 713). Metastasio's instructions how to set *Regolo* were written to Hasse in a letter, which has been widely reprinted, dating from October 20, 1749.

Rome in 1753 that it was encored when sung at London the following year, according to Burney.[9] Perhaps Varesco had been em-
boldened to give Idomeneo a concluding monologue in recitative,
without aria, on precisely this model. Raaff intervened similarly in
both operas, at any rate. As given at Naples in 1761, Jommelli's
Regolo was a pasticcio "accomodato dal Sig. Nicola Sala con arie di
diversi," and the final aria for Raaff, composed by Domenico Alberti,
was borrowed in text from Metastasio's *Temistocle*.[10] Raaff may well
have suggested the text himself, as he was later to do with Mozart.

The new aria text requested of Varesco was quickly produced and
sent off to Munich on November 25. Leopold was already skeptical
as to its viability when he quoted the first two lines, which is the
only reason they have survived:

> Il cor languiva ed era
> Gelida massa in petto
> . . .

He objected specifically to the "ed era" at the end of the first line.
Infelicitous, to be sure, was a run-on line at this spot. In lyric arias
the first line was usually set as a discrete statement, either a phrase
or a half-phrase; it was also used at will in the subsequent course of
the piece where needed to provide text for transitions and the like.
Leopold sought to justify the verse with the rather lame remark:
"admittedly the same thing does occur often in Metastasio, where it's
up to the composer's skill; many dumb Italian composers would set
the first line to one melody and then make a different and separate
melody for the second."[11] Mozart replied to his father only four days
later: "the aria for Raaff which was sent pleases neither him nor me
at all. Concerning *ed era* I say nothing; for that is always an error
in this kind of aria. Agreed, Metastasio also has it sometimes, but

9 Charles Burney, *A General History of Music* (London, 1789), ed. Frank Mercer
(1935), II, 852: "It seems, however, worth recording, that a scene of *recitative*, in the
part of Serafini, was encored every night during the run of the opera, the only instance of the kind I can remember. . . . It was in the last scene of Jommelli's opera,
which ends without an air, that Regulus, determined to return to Carthage, addresses
the Roman people who endeavored to prevent his departure, in the recitative which
had so uncommon an effect, beginning: 'Romani, addio, Siano i congedi estremi degni
di noi' etc." The situation in Regolo's final monologue is not unlike that of Idomeneo,
and Metastasio's famed nobility of language here may have been exemplary for Varesco.

10 "Ah! frenate il pianto imbelle," Act II, scene 3, aria of Neocle. I am indebted
to my student Marita McClymonds for this information and for a detailed comparison
of the 1753 and 1761 versions of *Attilio Regolo*.

11 Letter of November 25, 1780, No. 543, lines 13-18.

extremely seldom, and those are not his best arias. And what is the need for it? Besides this the aria is not at all what we wanted, namely, it should express peace and satisfaction, and this it does not do until the second part. Of the misfortunes he has had to bear throughout the entire opera we have seen, heard and felt enough; now is the time for him to talk of his present condition. We don't need a second stanza anyway. So much the better if there is none. In the opera *Achille in Sciro* by Metastasio there is an aria of this kind, and in the style that Raaff would have liked:

> Or che mio figlio sei,
> Sfido il destin nemico;
> Sento degli anni miei
> Il peso alleggerir."[12]

Mozart erred in believing this aria to be of one quatrain only. It has two, like the great majority of Metastasio's arias, the second providing a typical nature simile, in this case a lovely image of new shoots springing from old wood:

> Cosi chi a tronco antico
> Florido ramo innesta,
> Nella natia foresta
> Lo vede rifiorir.[13]

Again on December 1, Mozart restated his needs after saying how pleased Raaff was with his second-act aria. He quoted Raaff as telling him and others: "I was always in the habit of changing my roles, in arias as well as in recitatives, but here all remains as written because I find not a note that is unsuitable to me."[14] The truth of the matter was quite otherwise, as we shall see. Mozart continues: "Raaff wishes, as do I, to have the aria you sent altered a bit; he also takes exception to the 'era.' And then we want here a peaceful, contented aria. Even if it has but one part, so much the better. The second part must be taken in the middle anyway, and that often gets in my way. In *Achile in Sciro* there is such an aria of this kind. . . ."[15] What is probably meant here is this: Mozart does not want to be obliged to have a contrasting musical section in the middle, which is almost mandatory if the textual content of the second stanza is very substantial. There are examples of this ternary

---

[12] Letter of November 29, 1780, No. 545, lines 1-17.

[13] *Achille in Sciro*, Act III, scene 7, aria of Licomede.

[14] Letter of December 1, 1780, No. 549, lines 42-45.

[15] *Ibid.*, lines 45-50. Mozart then quotes Metastasio's first quatrain again.

aria structure in *Idomeneo*. "Fuor del mar" is one; of the four others, two were cut before the première by Mozart himself.[16] The predominating aria form in the opera is binary, wherein the second stanza is distributed over the second key area, followed by a restatement in the tonic, without intervening middle section, of both parts.

Leopold sent Varesco's second attempt at a final aria for Raaff on December 11; Andreas Schachtner's German translation of it followed later, at an unspecifiable date. Both were printed in Libretto I, an Italian-German text for the opera that represented its state in the first part of January, 1781, before Mozart started making extensive cuts and revisions.[17] The new text and its translation read as follows:

Sazio è il Destino al fine	Nur erst nach ausgeprüften Leiden
Mostrami lieto aspetto.	Ertheilt die Fügung reife Freuden
Spirto novello in petto	Der Geist und Muth, den ich verlor,
Vien mi a rinvigorir.	Steigt doppelt frisch in mir empor.
Tal Serpe in frà le spine	So lassen auch die weisen Schlangen
Lascia le antiche spoglie,	Die Haut gestreift an Dörnern hangen,
E vinte l'aspre doglie	Um sich nach solcher blut'gen Pein
Torna à ringiovenir.	Verjüngt in neue Tracht zu freun.

Contrary to Mozart's wishes, Varesco provided a comparison aria in two stanzas, indebted somewhat to the proffered Metastasian model, from which it copies the end rhymes "alleggerir" and "rifiorir," turning them into "rinvigorir" and "ringiovenir." But now the comparison is to a rejuvenated snake that has hung up its skin on a thornbush. Raaff had compared himself with a deal of natural phenomena during his forty years of singing simile arias in opera seria. It is to be doubted that he had ever been asked to compare himself with an old snake. Schachtner's translation carries this bizarre image to another degree of tastelessness by rendering "aspre doglie" ("bitter sufferings") as "blut'gen Pein" ("bloody Pain"). The words of the first stanza may speak of joy and fulfillment, but

16 Arbace's "Se il tuo duol," No. 10a, and Idamante's "Non, la morte," No. 27a; the two ternary arias not cut were Ilia's "Zeffiretti lusinghieri," No. 19, and Arbace's "Se cola ne' fatti," No. 22. The numbers are those in my edition in the Neue Ausgabe sämtlicher Werke, of *Idomeneo*, 2 vols. (Kassel, 1972), referred to subsequently as the Neue Mozart Ausgabe.

17 On the two librettos for *Idomeneo* see the Vorwort to the Neue Mozart Ausgabe, section d, "Letzte Münchener Revision," pp. xii-xvi.

the sounds are far from being lovely. Five elisions occur in the first line alone. "Sazio è il" is hard to sing because the difficult "z" consonant explodes into a string of four vowels that must be pronounced as a single syllable — otherwise the line would not scan properly and yield the requisite seven syllables to match the other lines. Varesco could not have been thinking of musical setting when he concocted this harsh opening. How mediocre a poet he was when working without Mozart's direct guidance is nowhere more evident.

The reaction in Munich to Varesco's second effort can well be imagined. Raaff became increasingly hostile. Mozart tried at first to defend Varesco, with the result that Raaff began questioning the professional competence of composer and poet alike. This is the moment when Raaff raised objections to his part in the Great Quartet because it was not cantabile enough. He also objected to the text-setting in "Fuor del Mar." I have suggested elsewhere that the real problem with "Fuor del Mar" was Raaff's inability to sing it, and that the shortened version without coloratura (No. 12b) was in fact made at Munich for him.[18] Mozart at first attempted to weather the new storm without making further demands on Varesco, who was already irate with both Mozarts. In his letter of December 27 he only mentions the problem, after describing his other difficulties with Raaff: "just now he was totally indignant about the words in his last aria — rinvigorir — and ringiovenir, especially 'vienmi a rinvigorir,' five 'eee' sounds! It is true that at the end of an aria this is very unpleasant."[19] How far Mozart got with the composition of this aria cannot be determined. He may have showed the text to Raaff even before playing for him what he had in mind as to the music. The failure of Varesco's first text perhaps suggested such prudence. In his next letter three days later Mozart spelled out the dilemma in more detail: "I am now in an embarrassing situation with regard to Raaff's last aria and you must help me out of it; 'rinvigorir' and 'ringiovenir' he cannot stomach and because of these two words he hates the whole aria. It is true that 'mostrami' and 'vienmi' are also not good, but the two last words are the worst of all. In order to avoid putting the final trill on the *i* in the first 'rinvigorir' I have to take it on the *o*." Rarely does any composer of the time get down to cases regarding such matters as does Mozart here. The "o" is a possible sound for the melismas and cadenza that figured

[18] *Ibid.*, p. xv.
[19] Letter 570, lines 60-63.

7

by tradition at the end of the first section; even preferable to it was the open "a." But melismatic extensions could not occur on the "ee" sound of *"i"* or upon any other closed vowel. The "o" was also unlikely in this case because it was an unaccented syllable. Mozart continued the same letter with a proposal that is not his own: "Now Raaff has discovered, I believe in [Metastasio's] *Natal di Giove,* which admittedly /: is very little known:/ an aria that is suitable to the situation: I believe it is the *aria di licenza:*

Bell'alme al Ciel dilette,	Creta non oda intorno
Si, respirate ormai;	Non vegga in si bel giorno
Gia palpitaste assai:	Che accenti di contenti
E tempo di goder.	Che oggetti di piacer.

And this aria he wants me to compose for him. No one knows it, he says, and we won't tell. He is fully aware that it is hardly possible to ask the abbé to alter this aria again, and as it is, he will not sing it. I beg you for a quick answer. Wednesday I hope to have your reply, then I shall just have time enough to compose his aria."[20] Mozart sent this urgent request on Saturday the thirtieth of December, 1780. Act III had already been put into rehearsal a few days earlier. Leopold Mozart acted at once to wrest a new aria from Varesco. The result was in Mozart's hands by Wednesday, January 3, as he acknowledged in closing his letter the same day: "I am very happy to have received the aria for Raaff, for he was absolutely determined to have his own text substituted. I would have been forced /:NB with a man like Raaff:/to the solution of having Varesco's text printed and Raaff's sung."[21] It is ironic that Varesco's "Sazio è il destin" was in fact being printed at just this time, in Libretto I.

Raaff was a man who knew his Metastasio. Of course he had been singing the cantatas, operas, and oratorios of the Caesarean poet all his life, and when he finally died, he was reported as reading not only from the Bible but from his edition of Metastasio.[22] He possessed the sumptuous Paris edition that began to come out in 1780, as I was happy to ascertain from the list of subscribers at the end of Volume XII, where he is listed as "Signor Antonio Raaff di Manheim."[23] Perhaps he even had Volume I at the time of his

---

20 Letter of December 30, 1780, No. 573, lines 28-49.

21 Letter of January 3, 1781, No. 574, lines 52-55.

22 Heinz Freiberger, *Anton Raaff (1714–1797): Sein Leben und Wirken als Beitrag zur Musikgeschichte des 18. Jahrhunderts* (Bonn, 1929), p. 61.

23 *Opere del Signor Abate Pietro Metastasio* (Paris, 1780–82).

controversy with Mozart. It included *Il Natal di Giove,* from which Raaff extracted "Bell 'alme." Directly preceding this *aria di licenza* was a line of recitative that may have initially led Raaff to light upon the choice: "In di cosi felice e Creta, e il Mondo." Recall that Idomeneo's final words in recitative were: "O Creta fortunata o me felice." With this truly mellifluous aria text as a goad and a model, Varesco was able, probably with Leopold Mozart's prompting, to produce a truly viable piece of *poesia per musica.* It is short, consisting of only two tercets; each of the first three lines is a discrete thought; the imagery is beautiful and so is the language, which cannot be easily translated, except in a most literal fashion:

Torna la pace al core,	Peace returns to my heart,
Torna lo spento ardore	My exhausted ardor revives,
Fiorisce in me l'età.	Age is flowering within me.
Tal la stagion di Flora	Thus the season of Flora.
L'albero annoso infiora	Makes the ancient poplar bloom
Nuovo vigor gli dà.	And gives it new vigor.

For all its charm and grace the verse is but a composite of ideas and sounds from the previous ones, which agrees with Mozart's emphasis throughout the correspondence upon altering rather than inventing from nothing. Using "core" in the first line goes back to Varesco's earliest verse. The play on "Flora" and "fiora" occurs in the first Metastasian aria given him as a model, as does the simile of new shoots from old wood. Varesco salvaged "vigor" from the much maligned fourth line of his second text, and "torna" from its last line. And he finally learned from "Bell 'alme," it seems, the lesson that Metastasio had to teach all librettists: in a lyric aria the more open vowels and liquid consonants, the better.[24]

24 Other possible textual models include Metastasio's early and very popular Canzonetta *La Primavera* (Rome, 1719), which begins as follows: "Già riede primavera / Col suo fiorito aspetto; / Già il grato zeffiretto / Scherza fra l'erbe, e i fior. // Tornan le frondi agli alberi / L'erbette al prato tornano / Sol non ritorna a me / La pace del mio cor."

"Torna la pace al alma" figures as the final piece in *Ippolito ed Aricia* (Parma, 1759), the first "reform" opera based on Rameau, with text by Frugoni and music by Traetta — see Daniel Heartz, "Operatic Reform at Parma: *Ippolito ed Aricia,*" in *Atti del convegno sul settecento parmense nel 2° centenario della morte di C. I. Frugoni* (Parma, 1969), pp. 271-300. The opera was known to the circles that would eventually produce *Idomeneo;* Holzbauer set the same text, probably adapting some of Traetta's music (Mannheim, fall, 1759).

10

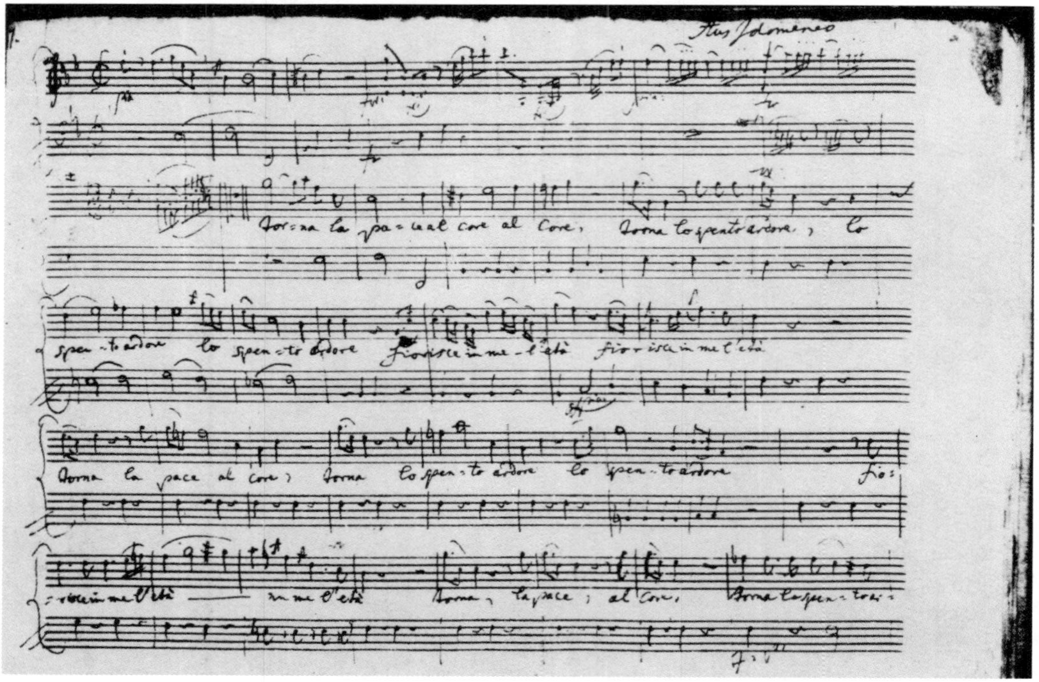

Courtesy of the State Library, Berlin.

Plate I.

Draft-sketch for "Torna la pace" in Mozart's hand; the first page.

Mozart set to work at once on the musical setting. He drafted a version in two voice-parts of the entire piece and it survives, by some miracle, along with the autograph of Act III at Berlin. It is reproduced here in facsimile for the first time. Plate I shows the first page, beginning with the nine-bar orchestral ritornello. On the top line Mozart writes in only what will become the first violin part, even though there are important motivic elements elsewhere, e. g., the introduction of the forte in measure 4 by a churning sixteenth-note figure in the second violins and violas, to which the first violins respond, and also in measure 6 the fluttering chromatic thirds of the clarinets and bassoons, against which the violins merely provide a pedal with their repeated F's. Omission of significant compositional detail like this suggests that Mozart is not sketching the piece for his own benefit, prior to scoring the orchestral version. This he does not need to do in any case: with him the whole piece is in his head, typically, as soon as the text is right. To what purpose, then, write out such a draft? Because Raaff needed something to study, and the time was short. Given the peculiar history of this case, it is also clear that Mozart was taking no chances on the possibility of another veto. From his earliest days he was loath to waste time or music paper until certain his efforts would meet requirements.

The fragile voice of Raaff required extraordinarily careful treatment. As the voice enters Mozart switched to the tenor clef, bringing him in on a sustained F, led up to by a little connecting passage in thirds by the clarinets and bassoons, which is in the vocal draft — Raaff needed to hear this. The F has no competition because all the strings, violins included, are scored under the voice. Later the violins climb up and help him by playing (no doubt very softly) in unison with the vocal line. His vocal part is confined to a very small range, from the fifth below middle C to the fifth above. What appears to be long and dull pedals in the bass line will be enlivened in the full orchestration by undulating thirds in the winds as already introduced in the ritornello — a lovely example of "Neapolitan zephyr music," and similar to what surfaces later in the terzettino "Soave sia il vento" of *Così fan tutte*.[25] But indeed Mozart had already used a similar texture and sonority for the middle section of Ido-

[25] For an example very similar to Mozart from a composer of the Neapolitan school, see Traetta's "Aure placide, che mormorate," illustrated in the article cited in the preceding note, p. 293.

12

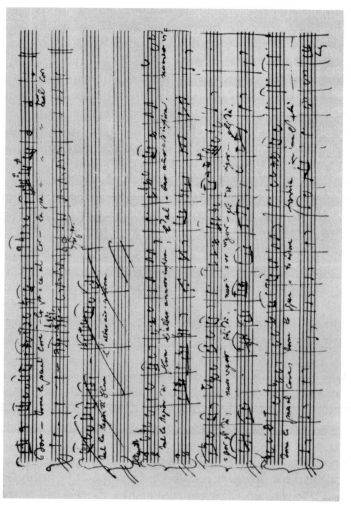

Plate II.

Draft-sketch for "Torna la pace"; the second page.

meneo's Prayer, "Accogli o ré del mar," and not by chance does this section, to the text "Torni Zeffiro," share the same clarinet key of B-flat.

Plate II shows the draft approaching the end of the first part. From the spacing it is clear that Mozart tucked in an extra measure as an echo in the lower line after the third measure; it is an afterthought that will appear in the full score an octave higher, for the winds. He brings the initial line of the text back for the fourth time here. The reason must be because he wants to take the concluding melisma on the "ah" of "pace." He does not bother to notate the ensuing ritornello.

Mozart first began drafting the middle section with the melodic idea of the falling fourth, which had been prominent throughout the main section, but derives specifically from what may be called the second theme (the second measure in Plate II). He got no further than four measures, complete with text and the precise articulation of the melody. Even before writing in the accompanying bass another idea displaced the first. He crossed out the four measures and started over by transforming the melodic motive into an Allegretto in 3/8 time. The change in meter and tempo allows him to get away from the foursquare phraseology of his first attempt and to arrive at two three-measure phrases — a delightful example of how seven-syllable lines in Italian are apt to generate non-square phrases. Upon repeating the second line of the middle section he draws it out to four measures and a cadence on F. The process repeats itself for the last line, "Nuovo vigor gli da," set to the leap of a sixth, which certainly radiates vigor after all the conjunct motion preceding it. Raaff's high note of G is reached as the three-measure phrase is repeated in a rising sequence. This time the concluding phrase, with cadence on G minor, is stretched to six measures by means of an interrupted cadence with leap up to the high G. What happens next is contrary to all the "rules." Mozart, having repeated the last line of text four times, resorts to the first stanza, even though the middle section is not over. The textual anticipation of the reprise is very effective nevertheless, because the beginning of the tonal return to B-flat is already felt when the voice enunciates "Torna la pace." Mozart reinforces this rather subtle point by reintroducing the winds, heretofore excluded from the middle section, at precisely this juncture, prior to the first "Torna." Their presence confirms tonal indications that the reprise is near.

13

The change of compositional plan evident on this page makes it necessary to modify what was said above concerning draft versus sketch. This is surely a working version of the aria for Raaff's perusal. At the same time it is a working sketch, because Mozart was still making compositional decisions while jotting it down, important decisions at that, such as those involving the whole character of the middle section. Furthermore, the decision to change meter and tempo betrays Mozart's relentless effort to do everything in his power to please Raaff. Allegretto 3/8 middle sections in a common-time aria represent a fashion that was long out of date. They were, in fact, a trademark of the great J. A. Hasse, although not his exclusive property, it goes without saying. An example, one from an incredible number of Allegretto 3/8 middle sections that could be adduced, will show many features in common with Mozart. The aria is "Per pietà bell'idol mio," from Hasse's third setting of Metastasio's *Artaserse,* for Naples in 1760 (see Ex. 1). The melodic-harmonic sequences, the ambling gait of the bass line, and the canonic conduct between the voice and bass at "Sallo amor, lo sanno i Numi" are all typical. Coming back to the middle section of "Torna la pace" we find a similarly ambling bass line and, moreover, a similar canonic dialogue at "Nuovo vigor gli dà." Mozart changed this canonic passage in the full score, making it more euphonious and more chromatic, which had the effect of masking its old-fashioned prototype, at least slightly. He made another small change in the

Ex. 1

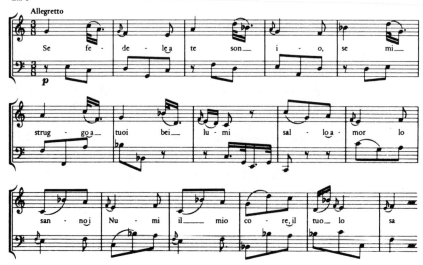

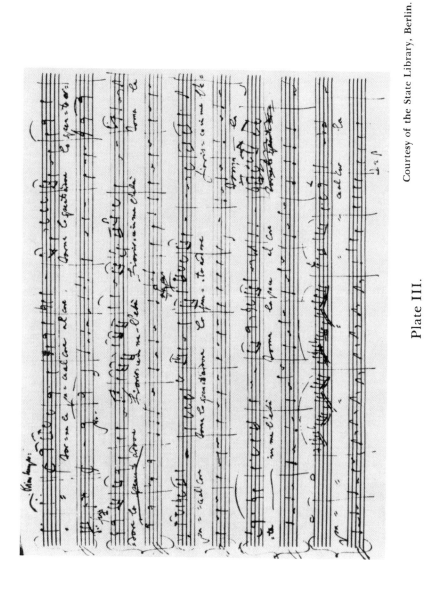

Plate III.

Draft-sketch for "Torna la pace"; the third page.

15

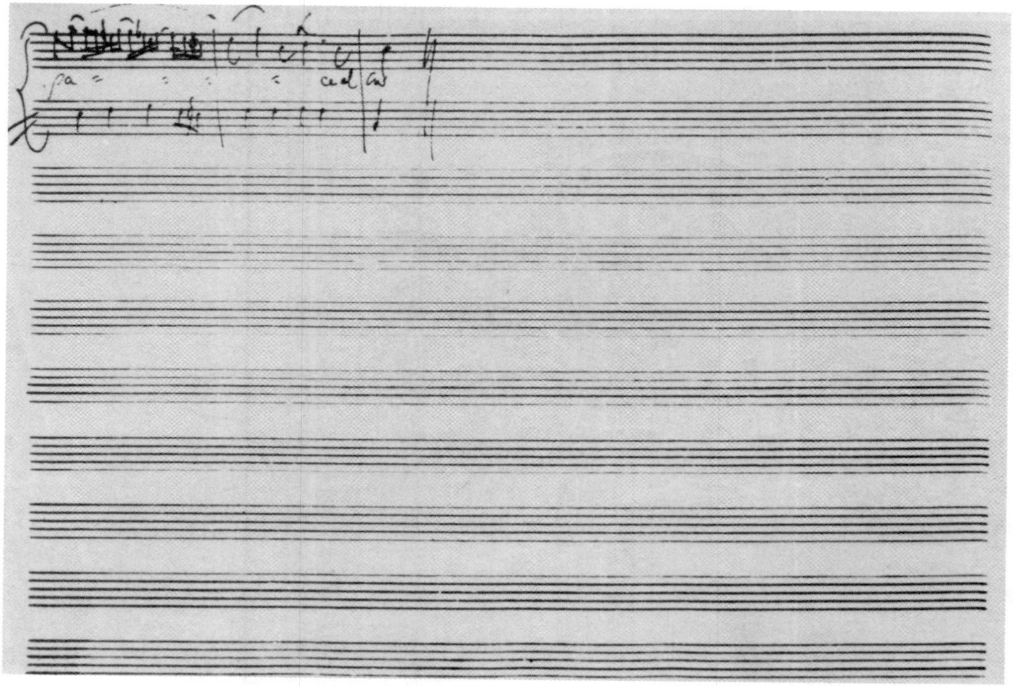

Courtesy of the State Library, Berlin.

Plate IV.

Draft-sketch for "Torna la pace"; the fourth page.

bass line here which allowed him to avoid arriving at an open fifth between outer voices on the third "Nuovo vigor."[26] The case well illustrates how he continued to refine and polish his part-writing while orchestrating. It did not affect Raaff's part, and thus did not invalidate the purpose of the vocal draft.

The return of the Primo Tempo at the top of Plate III offers nothing remarkable until the transition section, when Mozart started recomposing. Keeping Raaff's voice within its narrow range did not allow the solutions of transposing up a fourth or down a fifth. Beginning with the "Torna" at the end of line 2, Mozart enriches the harmony with a wonderfully rich-sounding secondary dominant, to accompany the expressive leap of a seventh in the voice, then resolving in the next measure to a dominant ninth chord. These are new colorings and shadings. In the final version Mozart changed the leap from G up to G so that the voice struggles up the chord tones to the high G (measure 109). This change must have been imparted to Raaff at the last minute. The voice part is completely rewritten for the subsequent material, which must now appear in the tonic instead of the dominant. At the end of the second staff from the bottom on Plate III there is evidence of another change of tactic in the course of composition. Mozart first used the second line of text, "Torna lo spento ardore," but when he got to the long held F, with melisma ahead, he reverted to his first line, "Torna la pace." The reason can only be that he wanted to display Raaff's voice under the most favorable conditions of all, with the "ah" of "pace" rather than the "oh" of "ardore." There remained only the approach to the cadence, via a strong emphasis on the subdominant E-flat and a final melisma, again taken on "ah." Mozart must have felt that the cadence came too soon in his original version, especially after the busy and syncopated interlacings of the first measure on Plate IV. Comparison with the final version in full score shows that he extended the precadential tonic six-four to dominant from one measure to two, each harmony receiving an entire measure. Again Mozart did not bother to notate the orchestral ritornello. And there is no suggestion here as to the cadenza that Raaff was expected to improvise fol-

17

[26] Mm. 72-73 of the score. It is the same kind of change that Mozart often suggested to his English student Thomas Attwood. See *Thomas Attwoods Theorie- und Kompositionsstudien bei Mozart*, Neue Mozart Ausgabe, Series X/30, Vol. 1 (Kassel, 1964), especially the minuets that Attwood composed in late 1786, during the final months of his sojourn at Vienna.

lowing the orchestral pause on the tonic six-four chord towards the end of the final ritornello (measure 140). That was the singer's prerogative altogether.

Raaff was pleased with his last aria, as well he should have been. So were those who heard it in rehearsal, according to Mozart's last letter from Munich to Salzburg, with its stunning news that "Torna la pace" was to be cut. Without indignation or the slightest sign of self-pity, Mozart reported why all the troubles taken were to go for naught: "The rehearsal of the third act went excellently and people judged it far superior to the first two acts. But the text is far too long, and consequently the music /: which I have maintained from the beginning:/. Thus we are cutting Idamante's aria 'Nò, la morte io non pavento,' which is inept where it stands in any case, but over the loss of which those who have heard it in music lament, and also Raaff's last aria, over which they lament even more. Still, one must make a virtue out of necessity."[27] The aphorism applies as well to the whole composition of "Torna la pace." When Libretto II was printed shortly before the première of *Idomeneo* on January 29, 1781, it confirmed the cutting of both arias and also the elimination of Electra's third-act aria. Idomeneo's monologue ended with his last words of recitative "O Creta fortunata, o me felice," precisely as it had in the original version, some three months earlier.

The extraordinary lengths to which Mozart went to please his lead tenor actually began three years earlier at Mannheim, with the earlier aria written for Raaff, "Se al labbro mio," K. 295. Mozart explained in the greatest detail why he picked this text in a letter to his father: "Yesterday I was at Raaff's and brought him an aria that I composed for him recently. The words are 'Se al labro mio non credi, bella nemica mia etc.' I don't believe that the text is by Metastasio. The aria pleased him enormously. Such a man one must treat very gingerly. I sought out the text with care, knowing he already had an aria on the same, and would consequently sing mine with more ease and pleasure. I told him to tell me frankly if something doesn't suit him or please him and that I would alter it as he wishes, or even write another one. God forbid, he said, the aria must remain as it is, for it is very beautiful, only please shorten it a bit for me, for I can no longer sustain my notes. Very gladly, I answered, as short as you want. I made it a little long on purpose because it is always easy to cut, but not so easy to lengthen [note the possibility

[27] Letter of January 18, 1781, No. 580, lines 9-16.

that Mozart used a parallel strategy when composing, then cutting "Fuor del mar" in *Idomeneo*!]. After he had sung the second part he took off his glasses and looked at me with wide-open eyes and said, Beautiful! Beautiful!, that is a beautiful *seconda parte,* then he sang it three times. When I left, he thanked me most politely and I assured him that I would arrange the aria so that he would sing it very gladly, for I like to measure an aria to a singer so accurately that it is like a well-fitting garment."[28] Presumably Mozart prepared for Raaff a vocal score similar to that for "Torna la pace." It does not survive as such, but, then, such scores are among the greatest rarities today. The earlier aria shares with "Torna la pace" the key of B-flat and much more. It also has a main section marked Adagio, in common time, *alla breve.* The contrasting middle section, the *seconda parte* that so pleased Raaff, is an Allegretto in 3/8. Moreover, the main theme for the voice plays on the same range, even the same melodic turn.

Ex. 2

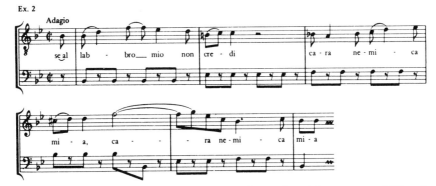

It could not have escaped Raaff that the cadential gesture of "Se al labbro" became the opening gesture of "Torna la pace" — an F prepared as a consonance, resolving as a suspension, by way of G, to E-flat. Even the spacing of the orchestral accompaniment is similar.

Mozart's inspiration for the beginning of "Se al labbro mio" raises an interesting question. The same text is set as an insert aria for Arbace in Hasse's 1760 setting of *Artaserse* for Naples.[29] Hasse

28 Letter of February 28, 1778, No. 431, lines 9-27, cited briefly in note 2, above.

29 Raaff sang at Naples in the 1760–61 season, as we saw above in connection with the mangled version of Jommelli's *Regolo,* but he did not sing in Hasse's *Artaserse.* The part of Arbace was written, moreover, for a soprano, Mozart's old friend Manzuoli. It was frequent practice at the time for soprano arias to be sung by tenors; see the Vorwort by Stefan Kunze to his edition of Mozart's concert arias, Neue Mozart Ausgabe, Series II/7, Vol. 2, pp. xx-xxi (Kassel, 1967). Kunze's edition of "Se al labbro

begins his melody by moving up the tonic triad to the fifth degree, then falling by stepwise motion (see Ex. 3). The correspondence with Mozart's opening (Ex. 2) may or may not be a coincidence, and the question is the more involved since we know Mozart was trying to capitalize on Raaff's affections for an older aria on the same text. For his middle section, that "seconda parte" by which Raaff evidently set such great store, Hasse reverted to his favorite 3/8 Allegretto style. He began in the parallel minor, no doubt prompted by a desire to express the words, "il cor dolente." After leaping via the triad to high A, the voice remains in a restricted ambitus and the leaping motion passes to the violins. Hasse's use of independent orchestral writing is remarkably fine throughout the Allegretto, which is quoted in its entirety (Ex. 4). By the time that the second line "ma d'ogni colpa privo" has begotten three phrases of three measures each, the long melodic extension on "innocente" comes as a surprise, a moment that is all the more intense for the long and partly chromatic rise in the voice, unaccompanied except by the violins in unison; the goal is the same high A of the initial measure. Canonic interaction between the voice and the bass begins at "ardor" but does not continue long; the descent of the bass line here seems to mirror the earlier ascent. After the cadence on F the voice intones the F major triad heard earlier in the first violins and the bass begins a chromatic rise that closes in on the pedal E of the voice and first violins. Or to put it another way, the E is reinterpreted several times, emotional intensity rising to a height with the diminished chord of the penultimate measure, before the release that comes with the cadential six-four chord and its resolution, with the fall of the voice through an octave to the lower E. It is not difficult to imagine that Raaff might have fallen in love with such a piece.

Mozart, not surprisingly, turned to an Allegretto in 3/8 for the middle section of his "Se al labbro." He chose G minor, the relative minor in this case, and began by outlining it triadically, while the bass jogs along in the old-fashioned style noted above in connection with "Torna la pace." A comparison with Hasse's middle section

---

mio non credi" is found in the same volume, No. 20, and his speculations as to the possible author of the text on pp. xiv-xv. Raaff sang Hasse to good effect on an occasion related in *Anecdotes du xviii* siècle (London, 1787) according to the article "Raaff" in *Enciclopedia dello Spettacolo*: the Principessa di Belmonte, inconsolable at the loss of her husband, was brought out of her torpor by Raaff's admirable execution of an aria by Hasse.

22

gives the impression that Mozart is trying to be different, but not too different, that is, not too unlike what Raaff was used to singing. When towards the middle of his Allegretto Mozart closes in on a cadence by a chromatically rising bass line, the suspicion arises again that he was paying the older composer the sincerest kind of flattery.

Ex. 5

23

A colored drawing of Raaff in stage costume has been preserved, along with some other mementos of the Mannheimer Kappelle, in the Theater Museum at Munich (Plate V).[30] His sartorial finery is bright red in the original, while his armor is colored silver. The drawing is sometimes referred to as Raaff playing the role of Idomeneo, but there is no basis for such an ascription. In fact, the drawing could represent Raaff in any of his numerous heroic roles,

[30] For details on this drawing, see Daniel Heartz, "Idomeneus Rex," *Mozart-Jahrbuch*, 1973, p. 9, note 6.

24

Plate V.

Raaff in heroic costume.

after his return to Germany and engagement at Mannheim in 1770. It could even represent his costume as Günther in Holzbauer's masterpiece — we do not know that the German subject of the opera entailed a corresponding departure from the conventional operatic costume, which was modeled, however loosely, on Roman antiquity. More likely, the costume is earlier still. Bustle, cloak, and feathers were already going out of style on advanced operatic stages by the 1760s. On the other hand, it is just possible that Raaff, as an honored relic from the fabled generation of mid-century singing "stars," obtained his way with costumers quite as much as he did with librettists and composers. He may have insisted upon wearing similar frippery at the first production of *Idomeneo*. If so, his appearance can hardly have matched the sets designed by Lorenzo Quaglio, an artist noted for his neoclassic sobriety and Piranesi-like somberness.[31]

A more impressive portrait of the old singer now graces the Beethoven House in Bonn, near which town Raaff was born (Plate VI). The painter, C.-A.-J. Philipart, rendered his likeness in oil at some time after 1777, date of *Günther*, a score of which Raaff holds in his hands. It is not a full score, to be sure, but only the "Tenor Arien," which were probably written in a two-part working version prepared for his benefit, such as Mozart made for "Torna la pace." Raaff looks out at us with the proud mien and noble stance of a Primo Tenore, his grey hairs dressed to a fault, his eyes unbedimmed by the years and unencumbered, moreover, by his eyeglasses, although we know these were necessary when he read music. Holzbauer's *Günther* preceded Mozart's *Idomeneo* by a scant few years, albeit the composers were separated by two generations in age. If Philipart's portrait was done later than 1780, a possibility that cannot be dismissed, Raaff's choice of music reveals in telling fashion where his sympathies lay: with the generation of Holzbauer and Hasse.

Mozart, too, venerated both older masters. In this respect he was quite unlike Leopold, who lost few opportunities to disparage music other than his son's. Witness his remark that *Ascanio in Alba* had

---

31 The gloom of Piranesi's "Carceri" weighs upon the massively framed harbor with ships designed by Quaglio, possibly for *Idomeneo*, Act II; see Daniel Heartz, "The Genesis of Mozart's *Idomeneo*," *The Musical Quarterly*, LV (1969), 1-19, Plate III. The well-known design by Quaglio representing Neptune's temple shows his more neoclassic side; although often ascribed to *Idomeneo*, it does not match what the libretto calls for at all, and must have been done for some other opera.

25

26

Plate VI.

Philipart's portrait of Raaff.

"quite beaten" Hasse's *Ruggiero* at Milan in 1771.[32] What a different attitude emerges from the words written by the young genius of the operatic stage! Unable to attend all the performances, as he would have liked, he was nevertheless present in spirit: "Today is Hasse's opera, but since Papa is not going out, I can't go; luckily I know all the arias by heart, and thus I can, even at home, hear them and see them in my mind."[33] Twenty years later, in November, 1791, Mozart would follow the performances of *Die Zauberflöte* from his deathbed with watch in hand. His heart was in the theater then as always. Cutting Raaff's last aria, in spite of its undeniable beauties, was wise in terms of theater, and Dent draws a proper comparison with Beethoven's unyielding stubbornness in such matters, writing of Mozart: "he thinks only of the stage and the general dramatic effect . . " and "is his own physician and surgeon."[34] For all that the two "Viennese" masters had in common, Mozart was in some ways more attuned in temperament to a grand old figure like Hasse, although separated from him in age by more than half a century. Like "il caro Sassone," he never questioned the fundamental Italian premise that an opera composer's first duty was to enhance the human voice, and treat it individually. In this respect Mozart was at one, in the deepest sense, with the spirit of Hasse.[35]

27

32 Letter of October 19, 1771, No. 250, lines 7-9: "mir ist Leid, die Serenata des Wolfg: hat die oper von Hasse so niedergeschlagen, dass ich es nicht beschreiben kann." Leopold's unabashed glee is all the more inexcusable because the commission for Mozart's Milanese operas was passed by way of Hasse.

33 Letter of November 2, 1771, No. 254, lines 23-26.

34 *Mozart's Operas*, 2nd ed., p. 63.

35 This paper was read at the Annual Meeting of the American Musicological Society, Dallas, Texas, 1972.

Mozart and his Italian Contemporaries:
"La clemenza di Tito"

BY DANIEL HEARTZ

Mozart's "La clemenza di Tito" is often dismissed with the summary remark that it is a mere Opera seria, the implication being that the genre per se rendered the work unworthy and moribund – beyond rescue even by Mozart. Such remarks are made in the bliss of ignorance. Truth is, the serious operas of the Neapolitan school between Vinci and Paisiello remain the greatest unknown field of eighteenth-century studies. So uncharted is this realm, that the very nomenclature remains nebulous. The designation "Opera seria" was not common at the time, and neither was "Opera buffa", although both terms occur in the correspondence of the Mozart family. The two qualifying designations referred to types of singers before they designated genres. Thus in the Goldoni librettos of ca. 1750 there are often "Parti buffi" and "Parti serie". The arrival of a troupe of "Buffoni" at Paris in 1752 and the works they played (such as Pergolesi's Intermezzo "La Serva padrona") gave rise to the celebrated "Querelle des Bouffons". As a result the expression "Opéra bouffe" became common in French. Rousseau, in his "Confessions", speaks of the "Opere buffe" he saw when in Italy, using the proper Italian plural form. In his "Traité du melo-drame" (Paris, 1772), Laurent Garcins contrasted "Opéras bouffes" with "Opéras serieux" as Italian genres. Yet Planelli's "Dell'Opera in musica", printed the same year at Naples, contains no reference to "seria" and "buffa" types of opera. The most influential writer on opera at the time, Algarotti, refers in his "Saggio sopra l'opera in musica" (Venice, 1755) to "Opere buffe" and "Opere serie" but in a context of the disputes at Paris in the early 1750s. Did the traditional distinction that everyone accepts without question actually get started in French criticism? It probably did. In Italy the comic genre was called "Operetta", "bernesca", "burletta", "ridicola", and a few other names, but rarely "buffa". Gianmaria Ortes in his "Riflessioni sopra i drammi per musica" (Venice, 1757) contrasted the comic and serious genres by using the terms "serio" and "burlette". In a letter that Jommelli wrote to the court of Lisbon in 1769 he promised to supply annually "un opera Seria, ed un altra grottesca". The same year, at Vienna, Gassmann brought out his comic parody opera called "L'Opera seria", suggesting that the term had become common by this time, at least outside Italy. By 1783, when Arteaga published the first volume of his "Le rivoluzioni del teatro musicale italiano dalle sue origini fino al presente", he accepted the terms "seria" and "buffa", but he broadens and weakens their significance by including under the former everything from the Florentine Camerata on, and under the latter, whatever is mainly comic, starting with Madrigal comedies. For him, the serious genre reached its height with Metastasio and his composers, the comic one with Goldoni and his composers. I propose that we accept these two paragons among poets as a way to define what we mean by Opera seria and Opera buffa. So defined, Opera seria betokens the kind of serious drama in Italian built up on the basis of exit arias. Metastasio perfected this type in the 1720s. It flourished with undiminished vigor right up to the end of the century, and lasted even somewhat beyond.

The problem of nomenclature is a practical one. It had to be faced when we brought out "Idomeneo" in the Neue Mozart-Ausgabe. Mozart himself never refers to the work in his letters as an Opera seria; he called it his Munich opera, or his "große Oper" (cf. "Die Zauberflöte"!). And the first printed score calls it "Drama Eroica" (sic). At our last general meeting, which I had the honor to lead off, I proposed calling "Idomeneo" by a still nobler name – tragedy[1]. In the printed edition we settled for the name by which it went in the two printed librettos, "Dramma per musica". This is the designation that all serious Italian librettos bear throughout the eighteenth century, almost without exception (not including the different category of occasional pieces designated "Serenata", "Festa teatrale" or the like). I resisted the suggestion that we call "Idomeneo" an Opera seria. With its connections to Mannheim and to the world of choral and balletic spectacle inherited from Tragédie lyrique, "Idomeneo" became an opera sui generis. In the case of "La clemenza di Tito" we are fortunate to have Mozart's own description of the work in his catalogue: "Opera seria . . . ridotta a vera opera dal Signor Mazzolà." So it is at once an Opera seria, and more than one, because of the revisions introduced by the librettist.

"La clemenza di Tito", like most of Metastasio's dramas, attracted dozens of settings. It was not set so often as his "Artaserse", or his "Olimpiade", yet some forty different composers took it up in one form or another between Caldara's original setting in 1734 and Arena's in 1839. No composer after Caldara ever composed the libretto exactly as the poet wrote it, that is with its twenty-five arias and thousands of lines of recitative. When Hasse set it for Verona in 1738 he substituted several aria texts, and the reason he did so was to achieve more metric variety than Metastasio offered. Hasse made at least three additional settings, in which he went back to some of the original arias, while making substantial cuts in the recitatives[2]. Cutting back the number of arias is a gradual process which can be observed in this and other Metastasian dramas throughout the century. Gluck at Naples in 1752 reduced the number of arias to twenty-three by diminishing the part of the seconda donna, Servilia[3]. He also eliminated the choruses in act 1 and act 3 because the San Carlo at that time did not provide choristers (the simple "coro" at the end, sung by the soloists, remained). Furthermore, he set a dialogue that was somewhat emasculated, by palliating the cruelty and cunning of the prima donna, Vitellia – as if the original character conceived by the poet were too strong for courtly

[1] See Daniel Heartz, Idomeneus Rex, in: MJb 1973/74, Salzburg 1975, pp. 7–20.
[2] Frederick Millner, The Operas of Johann Adolph Hasse (Ph. D. dissertation, University of California, Berkeley, 1976), pp. 241 ff. Mozart saw a "Tito" by Hasse at Verona in 1770.
[3] William Weichlein, A Comprehensive Study of Five Musical Settings of "La clemenza di Tito" (Ph. D. dissertation, University of Michigan, 1957), pp. 88–89.

sensibilities at Naples. Such changes were treated like a matter of state in the Kingdom of the Two Sicilies, as we know from the case in 1760 where the tenor Raaff wished to substitute a final aria by Domenico Alberti in Jommelli's "Attilio Regolo", a request that went to the Impresario, to the Prime Minister, and finally to the King, and back[4]. When Jommelli set "Tito" for Stuttgart the following year, the arias were reduced in number to eighteen, with cuts in all roles. By the time of Anfossi's setting for Rome in 1769 the arias numbered only seventeen, and they were further cut by Holzbauer at Mannhein in 1780. Thus there is a long trend at work providing the precedent by which Mozart and Mazzolà reduced the arias to only eleven. A certain amount of rewriting and substitution was the rule, not the exception, with this libretto. The local poet was called upon, although rarely named (out of deference to Metastasio) to adjust and "tailor" roles to the singers at hand, to the occasion, and perhaps lastly to the composer. At Turin in 1760 the court poet Vittorio Cigna provided four substitute arias, three for the part of Vitellia, sung by Caterina Gabrielli; it may be suspected that her wishes were being served by the alterations, as much or more than those of the composer, who was Galuppi[5].

The revisions of Metastasio's librettos made in the theater would provide material for several volumes. Few composers came close to setting the poet's every word. The elderly Hasse was the most faithful (but the young Hasse had been willing to set hastily and poorly contrived revisions). Jommelli was also devoted to the poet and complained only that he did not supply enough new works. He complained also when other composers set mangled versions of the original. Such was the case with the setting of "Adriano in Siria" by Carlo Monza that he witnessed at Naples in 1769, of which he wrote, "the drama has been despoiled and adorned not in heroic but in Harlequin's dress – blunders that would be avoided even by a born goatherd."[6] As the operas traveled from town to town, they gathered more accretions and ever more complicated relationships to the original. An instance is the "Demofoonte" set by Anfossi for Pavia in 1775, the printed libretto of which explains in a preface that the poem was taken partly from the libretto used at Milan in 1759, and partly from a Neapolitan production. One of the witnesses of the Pavia production took note of its circumstances: "L'Opéra qu'on a joué a été le 'Demophoon' de Métastase, (mais un peu changé comme c'est l'ordinaire) mis en Musique, par le celebre Pascal Anfossi, Maître de chapelle Napolitain."[7]

Through all the cuts and substitutions, Metastasio's original dramas generally remained a source of strength for composers. This is the case when Mozart set "La clemenza di Tito". Aside from being well made, and mellifluous in language, as always with Metastasio, "La clemenza di Tito" had the advantage of a fascinating character in Vitellia, who makes up in hauteur and sheer drive what she lacks in nobility of sentiment. No wonder that her partner, Sesto, bends to her headstrong lead. "La clemenza di Tito" is dominated by the prima donna from beginning to end. She sings first at the opening, setting the action in motion. She has the first aria in act 1, and the last, which Metastasio preceded by an impressive monologue, "Aspetta, Oh Dei!", set by most composers after Caldara as an elaborately accompanied orchestral recitative (or recitativo obbligato, to use the proper eighteenth-century term).

---

[4] Ulisse Prota-Giurleo, Alcuni musicisti d'oltralpe a Napoli, in: Analecta musicologica 2 (1965), pp. 136–37.

[5] Turin was one place that liked its operas on the long side, apparently. Galuppi wrote twenty-five numbers, including the Overture. As late as 1798, when Ottani set the libretto anew for the same court, Metastasio's original remained substantially intact; a concession to modern taste was made by turning the confrontation between Titus and Sextus in act 3 into a duet.

[6] Original letter in the Music Library of the University of California, Berkeley. This and many other unpublished letters of Jommelli are edited and translated in the Marita Petzoldt McClymonds, Niccolò Jommelli: The Last Years (Ph. D. dissertation, University of California, Berkeley, 1978). The passage in question is quoted on p. 625 A.

[7] Jean Bernouilli, Lettres sur différens Sujets écrites pendant le cours d'un voyage par l'Allemagne, la Suisse, la France méridionale et l'Italie en 1774 et 1775 (Berlin, 1777), vol. 3, p. 82.

Mazzolà transformed this scene into a Terzetto, using the same words, or rather into a solo aria for Vitellia, with occasional vocal accompaniment from Annio and Publio, who between them have exactly one line of text, expressing befuddlement at her erratic behavior ("Oh come un gran contento confonde un cor"). Metastasio also gave Vitellia the last aria in his act 2, and in act 3, that is to say, the last aria in the opera, which had to be the musical climax of the work, and certainly is with Mozart. After her final aria there is nothing left but the ultimate clemency of Titus, hardly unexpected, and therefore somewhat less than dramatically overpowering. It is Vitellia, finally, who confesses all, and manages thus to dominate even the pardon scene. Sesto, by contrast, is more sympathetic by virtue of his long-suffering abuse at her hands. He is not strong in dramatic terms even by the standards of Metastasio's often vacillating heroes. He leaves the stage twice without an aria, a distinct oddity for a primo uomo. His biggest dramatic scene is the head-to-head meeting with Titus, whom he has attempted to assassinate at Vitellia's instigation. Mozart relegated the confrontation to simple recitative, the way Metastasio intended[8]. It is indicative that in the sumptuous Paris edition of the poet's works (1780–82) this very scene, which Voltaire had praised was singled out for illustration (see Plate I on page 279).

The addition of ensembles, for which Metastasio characteristically made no provision, goes back to the beginning of the libretto's history. When setting "Tito" for London in 1737, Veracini composed two ensembles. For Verona the following year Hasse placed a Terzetto for Vitellia, Servilia, and Annio in place of the big solo scene for Vitellia in the last act. Ensembles found less favor in Italy, with the exception of love duets, than they did in the outposts of Italian opera like London and Vienna[9]. This situation did not change very much until towards the end of the century, when more and more operatic fashions from the outposts and from French opera begann to flow into Italy.

Mozart's last decade in Vienna was a constant struggle for domination in the world of opera. In the first part of the decade, before the German troupe disbanded in 1783, it was Opéra comique sung in translation that most pleased audiences at the Burgtheater, to judge from the number of performances, and not "Die Entführung aus dem Serail". Thereafter the most performed operas were by Italians like Paisiello, Cimarosa, Guglielmi, Martín, Sarti, and Salieri[10]. Mozart missed none of the comedies of his Italian contemporaries, nor did he fail to take stock, season by season, of what novelties and fashions most pleased the Viennese. This has been most clear, perhaps, up to now, in the case of Paisiello, whose "Barbiere di Siviglia" became the delight of audiences at the Burgtheater in 1783–84. (Count Almaviva's serenade "Saper bramate", as set by Paisiello, left a few traces, it is generally agreed, upon Cherubino's serenade "Voi che sapete".) Paisiello himself stopped at Vienna in mid-1784, on his way back to Naples after several years as music director at the Russian court. At the express wish of Joseph II, who held him in great esteem, he set Casti's "Il Re Teodoro in Venezia" (after Voltaire's "Candide"), which was composed in a matter of days and performed with success at the Burgtheater. Paisiello's subsequent career as Maestro di cappella at Naples will occupy us next, in order to provide some idea of the typical operatic climate during the years from 1785 to 1790. For Vienna was not typical.

Upon his triumphal return to Naples, Paisiello first showed himself to the public with Metastasio's "Antigono", given at the San Carlo for the Carnival season of 1785. Later the same year he brought out Palomba's comedy "La grotta di Trofonio" at the smaller Teatro dei

---

[8] Some composers set this crucial scene as a duet; see note 5 above.
[9] The most telling example of this is Galuppi's "Artaserse". As written for Vienna in 1748 the first act ends with a great dramatic quartet, the text of which is made by collapsing several arias and recitatives; as revived at Padua in 1751 the quartet gave way and the singers reclaimed their arias. For more detail, see D. Heartz, Hasse, Galuppi, and Metastasio, in: Venezia e il melodramma nel settecento (Venice, Cini Foundation, 1978), vol. 1, pp. 309–340.
[10] See the paper of Clemens Höslinger, pp. 149–153.

Plate I: J.-A. Martin, Vignette to Metastasio's "La clemenza di Tito", 1774.
From Opere del Signor Abate Pietro Metastasio, (Paris, 1780), III.
(Berkeley, Music Library of the University of California)

Fiorentini, which specialized in comic operas. In 1786 it was again the same – "Olimpiade" for the San Carlo during Carnival, and a comedy, "Le gare generose" (by Palomba), for the Fiorentini. In 1787 he set Gamerra's serious libretto "Pirro" for the San Carlo and Lorenzi's comedy "La Modista" for the Fiorentini. In 1788 Salvioni's serious libretto "Fedra" provided the Carnival opera for the San Carlo, and Palomba's "L'Amor contrasto ossia La molinara", a comedy for the Fiorentini. Meanwhile Paisiello was also filling commissions for other centers at the rate of about two a year. In 1789 he set Metastasio's "Catone in Utica" for Carnival at the San Carlo, and "I Zingari in fiera" by Palomba at the Teatro del Fondo, another of the smaller theaters at Naples. For the summer palace at Caserta this same year he set a pastoral opera that Carpani and Lorenzi arranged after a French libretto by Marsollier for Dalayrac, "Nina ossia La Pazza per amore". In 1790 he set Metastasio's "Zenobia in Palmira" for the San Carlo and Lorenzi's comedy "Le vane gelosie" for the Fiorentini. We could go on year by year through the 1790s, but the pattern remains the same – serious operas for the big theater, comic ones for the smaller houses. It is the same with Paisiello's chief rivals in Naples at this time, Guglielmi and Cimarosa. It is the same with Sarti, who worked at Milan and Venice before he left for Russia to replace Paisiello. It is the same all over Europe where Italian opera flourished, whether at London or St. Petersburg, at Dresden, Munich, or Berlin – everywhere, that is, except Vienna.

Mark Twain once cabled, upon reading his obituary in a newspaper, "Reports of my death have been greatly exaggerated". If Opera seria could speak, I should wish it to utter the same witticism. Far from dying out, as critics have reported its doing on any number of occasions (including "Idomeneo"), the genre remained in great demand all over Europe during the 1780s. Vienna did without because Joseph II disliked serious opera of any kind (Gluck's having given him a case of musical indigestion, apparently, when several were revived at the Burgtheater in 1781–82). Since music historians have tended to see everything, even opera, through the prism of Vienna, they believed that Opera seria, being out of fashion there, was out of fashion everywhere[11]. How do they then imagine that serious opera passed from the hands of Cimarosa and Paisiello to the young Italian composers coming to the fore about 1800? By way of Vienna? At issue partly is a blind spot in Mozart scholarship. We have presumed that Mozart by age twenty-five or so was immune to further outside "influences", at least in the field of opera. This presumed immunity has been taken as a license by scholars exempting them from paying much attention to his Italian contemporaries in the 1780s. My point is that precisely these contemporaries formed the part of Mozart's "Umwelt" needed to help explain the passage from "Idomeneo" to "La clemenza di Tito".

Sarti's "Giulio Sabino" offers a convenient point with which to begin an assessment of Italian Opera seria in the 1780's. It was written for the San Benedetto at Venice in 1781. This theater, like the San Giovanni Grisostomo before it, and the Fenice after it, was the large house for serious operas and the greatest voices, while comic operas played at the several smaller theaters. Unlike most Italian operas, "Giulio Sabino" was printed in full score (not at Venice but at Vienna). French operas were often printed then but not Italian ones. The printed score perhaps helps to explain why the work was very widely performed, while most operas of the kind travelled only where the composer travelled. One curious fact about the printed score is that the librettist is not mentioned, anywhere. He was Pietro Giovannini. However young he may have been, he was quite content to swim in the same stream charted by Metastasio three generations earlier. There are six characters: the hero Sabino (a role created for the castrato Pachierotti) who is in hiding on account of former offenses against the emperor Tito, who loves Epponina, not knowing she is the wife of Sabino; the three secondary characters only

---

[11] Henry Raynor offers a perverse switch upon the usual misinformation in his *A Social History of Music* (London, 1972), p. 292: "The German and Austrian courts kept opera seria . . . alive long after the Italian opera houses, in which opera seria grew up, had left the form to die."

complicate the central drama and stretch it out to the requisite length. Each singer receives one aria apiece in both acts 1 and 2, but in the last act only the three principals sing arias, accounting for a total of fifteen. There is no chorus and ensembles are restricted to a duet at the end of act 1, a terzetto at the end of act 2, and the traditional "coro" sung by the soloists to end the opera. Tonally, the keys are restricted to very few, never passing beyond three accidentals. There is some evidence of broad tonal planning. It emerges especially in the role assigned to A major, which sounds directly after the opening Overture in C major, and again for the most expressive piece in the opera, the Rondo sung by Sabino prior to the concluding "coro" in C major. Thus the tonal relationship of a major third is emphasized. Most of the arias are in binary form, and some of them are so short that they provide a marked contrast with the very long ones, just as in Mozart's "La clemenza di Tito". Multi-tempo arias occur several times. They progress from slow to fast, giving an overall stringendo effect that is the direct ancestor of the nineteenth-century cantabile-cabaletta combinations. The final Rondo is marked Largo–Allegro–Presto. Only the prima donna and primo uomo are allowed to sing Rondeaux, a type of piece which had quite clearly become the favorite showpiece of Italian opera. Arteaga, in his "Rivoluzioni del teatro musicale italiano" (1783–85) gives an apt definition of the sentimental Rondeau in two tempos: "those arias resembling in part the Rondeau are not all true Rondeaux, but sublime and grand airs containing two motives or subjects, one slow, the other spirited, each stated only twice, which arias are certainly better than what used to be called an Aria cantabile, because they are more natural, more true, and more expressive."[12] What Arteaga neglected to say was that the two subjects were often related by variation, also that Gavotte rhythms were characteristic of the slow or fast theme, or both. Sarti is no exception. By saving the hero's big Rondo for the penultimate scene of "Giulio Sabino", he made it truly the dramatic and musical high point of the work, just as is Vitellia's "Non più di fiori" in Mozart's "La clemenza di Tito". Sarti leads up to his piece by having the hero conducted to his death to the strains of a richly scored "Marcia lugubre" in c minor[13]. In the following obbligato recitative, fragments of the March break in upon Sabino's monologue, a distortion that prefigures the ending of the Marcia Funebre of the "Eroica" Symphony. With tension raised to a very high point, the tender and slow strains of the Rondo in A commence, with wonderfully poignant effects. After the two statements of the Largo theme, the Allegro ensues and its theme is also repeated; then comes what must have been a surprise to everyone in the opera house: Epponina bursts in and turns the same piece into a short duet, Presto, as she tries to join her husband in death. The inevitable clemency of Titus then saves the day and allows the opera to come to a happy end, as most critics, if not all, preferred at the time. An illustration accompanying the printed score of 1781 shows one of the distressful final scenes and the dungeon in Gaul where they took place; it probably gives a good idea of how operas on ancient Roman subjects were then costumed (see Plate II on page 282).

The sentimental Rondeau in two tempos became the most prominent feature of Italian opera only during the last third of the century. Traëtta, Galuppi, Piccinni, Anfossi, and Christian Bach[14] were all vying with each other during the 1770s in attempts to make this type of aria more expressive and appealing, so that it is difficult to say where the priority lay. Also unclear is the relationship of the type to French models. The Gavotte rhythms, the simple, rather folk-

---

[12] For the original Italian passage, see D. Heartz and A. Mann, Thomas Attwoods Theorie- und Kompositionsstudien bei Mozart (NMA. X, 30/1.), Kritischer Bericht (Kassel, 1969), p. 102; Attwood's later version of his two-tempo Rondeau written for Mozart forms the appendix of the same volume.

[13] Ernst Bücken, Der heroische Stil in der Oper (Leipzig, 1924), gives the funeral march in excerpt, pp. 56–57 and p. 33.

[14] Edward O. D. Downes in his study The Operas of Johann Christian Bach as a Reflection of the Dominant Trends in Opera Seria, 1750–1780 (Ph. D. dissertation, Harvard University, 1958) did not recognize that the two-tempo Rondeau constituted a special type, nor did he use Arteaga's explanation of the same.

36

Plate II: Anonymous illustration to Sarti's "Giulio Sabino" (Vienna, 1782).
(Berkeley, Music Library of the University of California)

like melodies, and the form itself (which resembles the old Rondeau, especially when the slow and fast themes are linked by variation, even if not identical with it) all point in the direction of France. The composer among the above who had the most to do with French-oriented courts was Traëtta (Parma, Turin, Vienna, St. Petersburg, at all of which contact with Opéra comique was inescapable); I suspect him of originating the vogue on these grounds and also because his lyric intensity and innovatory powers put him in a class apart, as the greatest of the neo-Neapolitans. Mozart himself took up the aria type rather late, in his operas only after "Idomeneo". While the first version of that masterwork had no piece of the kind, he took pains to include one for the performance at Vienna in 1786: Idamante's "Non temer amato bene" (K. 490) – a perfect specimen of its kind, and with an obbligato solo (violin) in addition. This was not the only example during the year of "Le nozze di Figaro". "Der Schauspieldirektor" received one; the garden aria of Susanna, "Deh vieni, non tardar", was first sketched as a Rondeau of the type, in E-flat, on the text "Non tardar amato bene". Prior to this Belmonte's "Wenn der Freude Tränen fließen" in "Die Enführung aus dem Serail" offers a good example of the type, and shows that it was equally at home in the Opéra comique/Singspiel kind of sentimentality. When writing to his father to describe Belmonte's aria, Mozart used the French spelling, Rondeau (letter of 20 July 1782). After "Le nozze di Figaro", both "Don Giovanni" and "Così fan tutte" received their Rondeaux, placed late in the opera as climactic pieces. In 1789 Mozart decided to add a Rondeau, "Al desio" for Susanna in "Le nozze di Figaro". Compared to Vitellia's "Non più di fiori" the two Rondeaux of 1789 ("Al desio" and Fiordiligi's "Per pietà") are as tame animals to wild ones; Vitellia's Rondeau is full of surprising turns, and so is Sesto's. The two Rondeaux in "La clemenza di Tito" make up for the lack of the same in its twin, "Die Zauberflöte".

When Cimarosa set "Olimpiade" for the opening of the new theater at Vicenza in 1784, Metastasio had been dead for two years. Had he been alive, and witnessed the event, he would have been surprised at what still passed under his name. Whereas the first act, ending with the great duet for Aristea and Megacle is left almost intact, acts 2 and 3 have been collapsed and combined into a single act, one in which a lot of text not found in the original was required. This represents a major structural change in Opera seria, one that was becoming widespread in the 1780s. Mazzolà, prior to putting "La clemenza di Tito" into two acts for Mozart, had written two-act serious librettos for Naumann at Dresden. In Cimarosa's "Olimpiade" there are eight numbers in act 1, not counting the splendid Overture for large orchestra, and eleven in the new second and final act. The economy is effected by cutting arias in every part. One part, Alcandro, has been eliminated altogether. Aminta and Licida receive only two arias apiece, and one of Aminta's is a little song of thirty measures. The other characters get three arias apiece, but only the prima donna, Aristea, and primo uomo, Megacle, are allowed Rondeaux. These are long pieces in two tempos, and the larger of the two goes to the hero in the penultimate scene of the opera, as in Sarti's "Giulio Sabino". Also like Sarti, Cimarosa's two Rondeaux are marked by Gavotte rhythm in both slow and fast sections. The two pieces are in A major and F major respectively, which seemed to have been favorite keys for this type, and remained so down to Mozart's Rondeaux for Sesto and Vitellia. Their main themes are as follows (see Musical Example 1 on pp. 283f.) Cimarosa had no chorus at his disposal in Vicenza, so the pastoral chorus in act 1, "Oh care selve" was turned into an aria, as often happened in Italy ever since Pergolesi's influential setting of 1735. The sacrificial chorus in the

Cimarosa: Themes of two Rondeaux from "L'Olimpiade" (1784)

Larghetto con moto

ARISTEA: Gran - - di, è ver, son le tue pe - ne: per - di, è

ver l'a-ma-to be - ne

Allegro giusto

Chi non sen - te il mio tor - men - to, chi non

sen - te il mio tor - men - to

Largo

MEGACLE: Nel la - sciar - ti, o pren - ce a - ma - to, mi si

spez - za in se - no il cor.

38

Allegro

Voi che un dol - ce a - mor pro - va - te, deh spie -

ga - te il mio do - lor; voi che un dol - ce a - mor pro -

va - te, deh spie - ga - te il mio do - lor.

last act Cimarosa replaced by a lugubrious orchestral March. Throughout the score he makes generous and telling use of the orchestra in many obbligato recitatives (just what Metastasio reproved in his well known letter to Hasse concerning "Attilio Regolo"). The anonymous poet at Vicenza administered the "coup de grâce" with his ending to "Olimpiade". He turned Metastasio's dénouement, intended to be set as recitative, into a complex Finale, that is to say an action Finale such as had grown up in Opera buffa starting with Goldoni and Galuppi around 1750. In setting it Cimarosa resorted to several different keys, tempos, and meters, and makes quite an imposing ensemble to end the opera. When he got through, he wrote in the autograph (preserved at the Naples Conservatory) the number of measures, as was his custom: "233 Finis Laus Deo".

284

Paisiello rejoined the operatic scene in Italy shortly after Cimarosa's "Olimpiade". The librettos of Metastasio he worked for the San Carlo had to be adapted in ways similar to what we have just observed, and there was no dearth of poets at Naples who could perform the operation. Calzabigi was there, among others, and he would eventually collaborate with Paisiello on his two final operas, "Elfrida" in 1792 and "Elvira" in 1794. In turning next to the non-Metastasian librettos, "Pirro" and "Fedra", as set by Paisiello, I hope to show some of the elements being added that helped diversify the stock of situations and devices available to serious opera just prior to 1790. "Pirro" of 1787 begins, after the Overture, with a lengthy ensemble involving the main characters in debate and dispute – in other words, an Intro-duzione, or use of the Finale techniques at the beginning of an act (such as is found in "Don Giovanni" of the same year). The origin of this device is again Opera buffa. Act 1 of "Pirro" ends with an enormous Finale involving all the singers. Here the librettist, Gamerra, went so far as to show an attempted assassination on the stage, an outrage precluded by the Metastasian niceties (which are none other than the "bienséances" of French classical tragedy). The grim event inspires some powerful and somber music from Paisiello, who chooses E-flat major, as one might expect, with contrasting episodes in g minor, and c minor among other places, and one memorable passage clothing the words "A morte!" in the flat submediant, C-flat major. Act 2 ends with an even longer Finale, by which time we have reached No. 17 in the score. No. 14 is a "Rondeau" in g minor for the prima donna. There is a third act, or rather, the vestigial remains of one, consisting only of some dialogue, a Terzetto, the dénouement (in recitative) and concluding "coro". In subsequent productions it was amalgamated with the second act.

Paisiello's "Fedra" of the following year is a different kind of opera altogether. What it shares with "Pirro" is a relatively high level of violence and anguish. Salvioni, in a preface to his libretto, mentions his indebtedness to Euripides and Racine, and a printer's note adds that he should have cited Frugoni as well. Indeed he should have, for the libretto was nothing other than an adaptation of Frugoni's "Ippolito ed Aricia" (after Racine and Pellegrin), produced at Parma with music by Traëtta [and Rameau][15] – the first attempt in Italy to effect a marriage between Opera seria and Ramellian Tragédie lyrique. What French opera texts offered, besides a generally high literary quality, was spectacle on the grand scale, such as had been typical of Italian seventeenth-century opera, before Zeno and Metastasio abolished it. The story of "Fedra" moves back and forth to Hades, the gods of which are much in evidence as is Diana, who descends from the skies to set things aright not once but twice. Besides this there is a grand hunting chorus, a very picturesque disembarcation scene, then a great storm, "un orrida tempesta", with thunder and lightning, plus a sea monster. The stage engineer at the San Carlo must have been busier than he had been in anyone's memory, for Metastasio had eschewed all this recourse to the "Merveilleux". In music, spectacle such as this required much orchestral tone painting, lots of pantomimic ballet music, and many choruses. With his demonic music for the underworld scene, Paisiello shows that he knew and respected Gluck's "Orfeo"[16]. The emphasis on the spectacular worked to reduce further the number of the arias. Not that the popular aria types are forsaken. Aricia sings a long Rondeau at the beginning of the second and last act. It begins with the words "Parti, ma pensa", directed to Ippolito. The force of the Italian aria tradition was such that her initial word "depart" had almost invariably called forth a melodic descent of a fourth or fifth as far back as Hasse's first setting of "Parto" in "Tito". Paisiello, like Mozart, proved no exception. He followed the tradition. The renewal of Opera

---

[15] See D. Heartz, Operatic Reform at Parma: Ippolito ed Aricia, in: Atti del convegno sul settecento Parmense nel 2° centenario della morte di C. I. Frugoni (Parma, 1969), pp. 271–300.

[16] In his earlier Opera buffa "Socrate immaginario" (Naples, 1775), Paisiello had parodied the same Gluck scene; the poet set this up by using the same "Quinari sdruccioli" that were characteristic for scenes of horror. See Wolfgang Osthoff, Die Opera buffa, in: Gattungen der Musik in Einzeldarstellungen: Gedenkschrift Leo Schrade, I (Berlin, 1973), pp. 702–03.

seria from the materials of Tragédie lyrique was such a general current at the time that it perhaps requires no further comment, except this one in the form of a question: are we dealing here with something that should still be identified under the rubric Opera seria? It applies to Mozart's "Idomeneo" as well as to Paisiello's "Fedra"[17]. The "Lärm und Getümmel" that was characteristic of Mannheim opera[18], and which achieved such terrifying results at the end of act 2 in "Idomeneo", stem ultimately from French opera. With regard to Mozart's "La clemenza di Tito", the point is that crowd scenes and tumultuous choruses such as enliven the Finale of act 1 come not from Metastasio, but from the hybrid operas blending French spectacle and Italian music.

The ending of Paisiello's "Fedra" makes up for the nearly unrelieved gloom of the tale. Rameau, like Racine, following Greek and Roman precedent, was content to let Ippolito perish. Frugoni and Traëtta had mitigated the calamity by having the Goddess Diana intervene to rescue him from the monster and restore him to Aricia. Salvioni and Paisiello went them one better by bringing the reunited lovers together in a final reconciliation with Teseo, who, enlightened by the truth at last, pardons their transgressions and blesses their union. To go beyond this it would be necessary to rehabilitate the self-convicted Fedra and explain her incestuous passion for Ippolito – so far as that no one went even during those most enlightened times. Clemency, urbanity, and placidity are the very virtues that Planelli proffered as the reason why modern opera with its "lieto fine" was superior to the carnage of ancient tragedy; to him these virtues represented certain proof that mankind had progressed: "Questo passagio fatto per la Tragedia dal tristo al lieto Fine è una pruova ben certa del progresso fatto dal genere umana nella placidezza, nella urbanità, nella clemenza, che che si dicano i nostri misantropi."[19]

The last clause, "che che si dicano ...", "whatever our misanthropes may say to the contrary", testifies to the conflicting claims upon drama by those who would go all the way towards restoring antique drama in all its starkness, and those who, like Metastasio and Voltaire, held back from accepting the atrocities of ancient tragedy as a comment on the human condition. The battle of the Enlightenment forces with those of the anti-Enlightenment plays upon all intellectual life of the time and of course touches opera. Pessimism and optimism clash nowhere more powerfully than within the work that synthesizes so much of eighteenth-century thought, and does so while focusing on the opera question, Diderot's "Le Neveu de Rameau".

Paisiello's serious dramas and those of his most important Italian contemporaries around 1790 received many productions up and down the peninsula, some even beyond. Did Mozart know them? The singular restrictions that Joseph II imposed on the Burgtheater made sure that only comedies were staged there. But concert performances of music from the latest Italian serious operas took place at Vienna, including substantial selections from Paisiello's "Fedra", given in the Burgtheater on 16–17 April 1786, a concert in which Mozart participated. The comedies that the Emperor and the Viennese public preferred were those of the Italian composers, as we have seen. Since the languages of comic and serious opera were merging more and more, the very distinction began to lose meaning; big, serious pieces like the sentimental Rondeau in two tempos could appear in comic operas and remarkably slight and song-like pieces could appear

[17] It is necessary to specify which composer of "Idomeneo" is meant here. Galuppi wrote an opera of the same name (Rome, 1756), as did several other Italian composers in the course of the period from ca. 1750 to 1810. Paisiello himself composed an opera "Il ritorno d'Idomeneo in Creta", qualified as a "Rappresentazione tragica" on a libretto of S. Salzi for Perugia in 1792.

[18] See the paper of Roland Würtz, pp. 163–171.

[19] Dell'Opera in musica (Naples, 1772), pp. 72–73. On the cultural-political ramifications of choosing a clemency theme in connection with the coronation of Leopold II, see Adam Wandruszka, Die "Clementia Austriaca" und der Aufgeklärte Absolutismus. Zum politischen und ideellen Hintergrund von "La clemenza di Tito", in: ÖMZ 31 (1976), pp. 186–193.

in serious operas, along with rousing ensemble Finales. Given Mozart's intense interest in everything to do with the world of opera, it would be surprising if he did not keep abreast of what his major Italian rivals were doing in their scores, just as he is reputed to have studied the French operas of Grétry, Gluck, Piccinni, and Salieri[20].

One work of Paisiello, among the several brought to the stage of the Burgtheater in the late 1780s, won a special place in the hearts of the Viennese. The pastoral opera "Nina", after several successes in Italy, was produced at Vienna in the fall of 1790. For Paisiello, this libretto was something out of the ordinary. It had almost no plot. An abandoned girl, driven mad by her despair, waits and waits until her lover Lindoro finally returns and gradually restores her to sanity. With no subplots, no incidents, no ornaments of any kind to enhance this drama of sentiment, it required a really heartfelt effort to bring it off. Paisiello sought after and found the means. The simple, almost naive melodic statement with which he clothes Nina's first song, "Il mio ben", represents a concentration of his expressive language to its essence (see Musical Example 2 on pp. 287ff.). The effect this almost legendary piece had upon contemporary sensibilities passed all bounds of moderation; audiences wept profusely and individuals were heard to shout their consolations to poor Nina. Formally the piece is a Rondeau in the old sense, with one tempo. It could also be called a Romance. Cultivated naiveté marked this epochal newcomer to the operatic stage (Rousseau started the fashion in his "Devin du village" of 1753) and archaic-sounding modal turns, such as the arrival at the cadence on the mediant in the middle of the Paisiello example, were among its special properties. Rousseau described the Romance in his "Dictionnaire de la musique" (1767) as follows: "Comme la Romance doit être écrite d'un style simple, touchant, et d'un goût un peu antique, l'Air doit répondre au caractère des paroles; point d'ornemens, rien de maniéré, une mélodie douce, naturelle, champêtre..." Given the amount of ornamental filigree characteristic of most Italian arias of the time (cf. Cimarosa in Example 1), Nina's song can be said to be without ornament or mannerism. Particularly expressive is the return to an absolutely straightforward melodic style at the beginning of the second half, on the words "di bei fior". Perhaps it is no coincidence that when Vitellia begins her last aria, which is also about garlands of flowers, or their absence, Mozart achieves a similarly elegaic mood – something that goes beyond the

41

Paisiello: Nina's Rondeau from "Nina" (1789)

[20] As reported by his student Joseph Frank. See Mozart. Die Dokumente seines Lebens, ed. Otto Erich Deutsch (Kassel, 1961), p. 476.

42

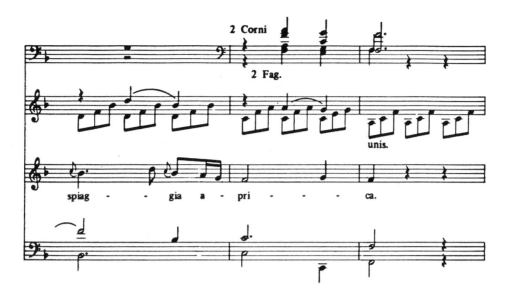

obvious similarity of key, meter, tempo, and the melodic turn of phrase that links "di bei fior" with "Non più di fiori". The resemblance is all the more striking when, upon the second statement by Vitellia of the slow Rondeau theme, the basset horn accompanies her in slow triplet figurations such as Paisiello gives his second violins.

Several other features of Paisiello's "Nina" suggest parallels in Mozart's last Italian opera. The Neapolitan master was known for the speed with which he wrote, which was incredibly fast, even by the then-prevailing standards in Italian opera. He could compose whole operas in a matter of a few days, partly because he relied on very few types of orchestral accompaniment and on a texture that was unusually thin, with lots of unison passages and rarely more than two or three real parts. His favorite accompanimental device in "Nina" is the alternating third, played by the basses in eight notes. An example is the aria of Susanna, Nina's governess (see Musical Example 3 on page 290). Charles Burney in his "History of Music" (vol. 4, 1789) called attention to this very accompaniment in connection with Italian opera; he labeled it "shorthand" (i.e. stenography) and showed its origins in Galuppi's serious operas as far back as the 1740s. Paisiello was not the only Italian of his time to use such an economical accompanying figure, of course, but he was so successful in generating catchy melodies above it that the device became one of his trademarks, as it were. Mozart uses the same "economy-style" orchestration in several places. Tito's second aria in act 1, "Ah, se forse intorno al trono" (No. 8), provides a particularly striking example, since much of the piece relies on the same bass. This piece is known to be among those written after Mozart's arrival at Prague a few days before the première[21], and hence under conditions that demanded utmost economy of time. Sometimes Paisiello foregoes using his "shorthand" bass during the first stages of a piece, so that he can bring it in near the end as a kind of rhythmic "punch", to generate excitement and incite applause; an example is the end of Lindoro's aria in act 2. Mozart turns

---

[21] Alan Tyson, 'La clemenza di Tito' and its chronology, in: Musical Times (March 1975), pp. 221–27; see p. 223. Tyson's conclusions supersede other recent work on the opera's chronology, which he cites in his Note 1. The most outstanding contribution to the earlier literature is Helga Lühning's Zur Entstehungsgeschichte von Mozarts "Titus", in: Mf 27 (1974), pp. 300–318, although it fails to mention relevant English articles published in 1969, 1970, and 1973. An unworthy altercation concerning her conclusions was subsequently allowed to see print in the pages of the same journal.

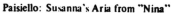

Paisiello: Susanna's Aria from "Nina"

to the device for a similar heightening of rhythmic drive towards the end of the Terzetto, No. 18; he resorts to it also for climactic effect in Vitellia's first aria (No. 2) and in Sesto's Rondeau (No. 19). When Paisiello wants to convey tension and struggle, he sometimes uses his "shorthand" bass together with a syncopated treble. In the Finale of act 2, for example, as Nina struggles to regain her memory, he combines these features with a modulatory passage, further enhancing the unsettled quality (see Musical Example 4 on pp. 291 f.). To find a similar

Paisiello: Excerpt from the Finale, Act 2, from "Nina"

291

LINDORO:

Sì Lin - do - ro, Lin - do - ro ec - co a tuoi

pie - di pien d'a - mo - re e fe - del - tà.

46

passage in Mozart's "La clemenza di Tito" we return to the cynosure of the work, Vitellia's Rondeau (No. 23). The syncopated treble against bass "shorthand" first come in as she utters the words "Infelice! qual orrore!" (mm. 49 ff.), a transition passage that provides a fluid and astonishing link between the slow and fast Rondeau themes, passing from F major to A-flat by way of f minor. The force of the syncopated passage then returns with even greater intensity at the dissonant orchestral shrieks interpreting the words "Stretta fra barbare" (mm. 86–90), another transition passage, just after Mozart has extended and deepened the piece by bringing back the slow theme and its text in the fast part of the Rondeau, an unprecedented departure in this genre so dependent upon precedents. The massive strokes of Mozart's orchestra here still do not exceed two real parts. In this economy of means and amplitude of effect Mozart is already using some of the orchestral sonorities that will become characteristic of Italian opera in the following two decades, with the generation of Simon Mayr, Spontini, and Weber (who held "Tito" in high regard). Had Mozart lived to rival the same, he would undoubtedly have shown them much more to admire along these lines.

That Mozart's "La clemenza di Tito" enjoyed more international success than any of his other operas during the last years of the eighteenth century and early years of the nineteenth century, should occasion no surprise. It was the most modishly up-to-date work he left. The simplified orchestral accompaniments were employed not only to save effort, which they did save, but because Mozart was trying, for a final time, to beat Paisiello and the Italians at their own game. And he succeeded. Moreover, "La clemenza di Tito", unlike their operas, is all of a piece in inspiration (exception made only for the simple recitatives which, lamentably, had to

292

be entrusted to another hand). The clue to its unity of style is Vitellia's great Rondeau, which, along with Sesto's equally fine Rondeau provided so much of the opera's essence, that Mozart resorted to them when, at the last minute, he had to write down the magnificent Overture. For musical reasons I believe that Vitellia's Rondeau must have been conceived in close connection with the rest of the opera, whatever our musicological misanthropes may say. If, as I believe, the very end of an opera by Mozart represents another crucial key to its essence, like the Overture, there is a certain resolution that resides in those final syncopated triads in the treble, rising above the "shorthand" of the bass, after the chorus has finished. Vitellia's anguish is extinguished, yet still remembered. C major has rarely sounded like such a beautiful and satisfying achievement.

Les Troyens and the Aeneid

Tristram Shandy's father, who knew the power of names, would have approved the notion—put forward by I forget which French critic—that, by calling him Hector, Dr Berlioz determined his son's fate: from the first the name marked him out for glory and tragedy, heroic deeds and the bitterness of failure and mutilation. The more one considers Berlioz's life, the more it seems almost mystically inevitable that his crowning work should be an epic on the Trojan war and its aftermath, the wanderings of Aeneas and the myth of the founding of Rome, and the more one comes to see his discovery of Virgil during boyhood and his precocious response to the passion and tenderness of the *Aeneid* as the most important single event of his imaginative existence. No less inevitably, such a work was bound to bring defeat and misery on its creator in the cultural climate of Second Empire Paris. As Gounod justly remarked, Berlioz, like his great namesake, died beneath the walls of Troy; for the final blow in a lifetime's struggles against a hostile musical environment was the rejection of the work that he knew to be his culminating achievement and artistic justification.

The conviction of its supreme significance in his life pervades the letters that he wrote during the two years of the work's composition. In their mood of exhilaration and their sense of destiny fulfilled, they recall the passage at the end of *The Gathering Storm* where Churchill describes his emotions on taking power in May 1940: 'I felt [...] that all my past life had been but a preparation for this hour and for this trial.' *Les Troyens* is a summing up of everything that Berlioz stood for. It marks the furthest point in the development of his musical style; and in it the characteristics of most of his previous works—the electric energy of the Fantastic Symphony, the ceremonial splendours and terrors of the Requiem, the exaltation and sensuous beauty of *Romeo and Juliet*, the massive grandeur of the Te Deum, the sweetness and archaic simplicity of *L'enfance du Christ*, the refinement of *Nuits d'été*—are united.

The determination to write a grand opera on the *Aeneid* crystallized in the early 1850s. In 1854 Berlioz confessed that the idea had been 'tormenting' him for the last three years. His writings around this time are full of allusions, comic and serious, to Virgil. In *Evenings in the Orchestra* (published in 1852) the narrator, asked by his friends to tell them about the Paris Opéra, answers in the ominous words with which Aeneas begins his account of the catastrophe of Troy: *Si tantus amor casus cognoscere nostros.** Later in the same book, modern music torn by conflicting ideologies is likened to Cassandra, 'prophetic virgin fought over by Greeks and Trojans, whose inspired words go unheeded, who lifts her burning eyes to heaven—her eyes alone, for chains bind her hands' (*Aeneid* II, 405–6). In a letter to Hans von Bülow written in 1854, Berlioz humorously attributes the bad luck suffered by *Benvenuto Cellini* to the workings of the 'Destiny of the ancients', and compares the opera's successive resurrections and collapses to the wounded Dido 'thrice raising herself upon her elbow, thrice falling back'; then, as if unable to contain his admiration, he bursts out, 'What a great composer Virgil is! What a melodist, what a harmonist! *He* could have made the deathbed remark *Qualis artifex pereo*, and not that humbug Nero, who was gifted with only one bright idea in his life, the night he had all Rome set on fire . . .' By this time, although he was still fighting against it, the ambition to write a Virgilian opera was fully acknowledged.

* 'If you are so eager to hear our misfortunes.'

49

It is hard to believe he had not dreamed of it much earlier. *Les Troyens*, planted in boyhood, casts its giant shadow over the years between. The conscious decision to compose it was like the emergence of an underground river to the surface. With hindsight we can see the work pursuing a secret subterranean course during the years when its composer is taken up with other, quite different preoccupations. Even in a jocular context it pops up, reminding us of its future existence—as when, describing his hurried departure from the island of Nisida under threat of a storm, Berlioz likens the Neapolitan fisherman in charge of their coracle to Aeneas cutting his vessel's cables and putting out from the port of Carthage on his destined journey to Italy (*Voyage musical*, 1844, later incorporated in the *Memoirs*). Earlier, in 1836, he looks back, with a quizzical eye, on his bouts of musical improvisation in the countryside near Rome, when under the stimulus of the landscape's Virgilian associations, guitar in hand and chanting 'a strange recitative to still stranger harmonies', he would hymn the great figures of the later books of the *Aeneid*, Pallas, Evander, Turnus, Aeneas, and yearn for 'those poetic days when the heroes, sons of the gods, walked the earth'.

In 1848 he began his *Memoirs* and wrote the chapters dealing with childhood and youth, including the famous second chapter which describes his discovery of poetry under the influence of Virgil and his profound distress at the death of Dido. The action of reliving such an experience must have helped to develop and define the still-shadowy, half-formed idea of a great Virgilian work that would bring his career full circle. 1848 was a watershed in Berlioz's life— the year of the Revolution (which threatened to make his daily existence even more precarious, and disenchanted him still further with Parisian musical life), the year of his father's death and of his return to the scenes of his adolescent awakening, of the first step in the bizarre pilgrimage that led him back to his boyhood infatuation with Estelle Dubœuf: the year when the nostalgia that is such an important aspect of his nature took decisive hold. But the period that immediately followed, though it produced the Te Deum and *La fuite en Egypte*, the second part of what was to become *L'enfance du Christ*—music steeped in a sense of the past—was not propitious for a major dramatic work. The lessons of the calamitous failure of *The Damnation of Faust* were too painfully recent; he was still resolved 'not to stake twenty francs on the popularity of [his] music with the Parisian public'. It was at about this time that in the same mood of defeatism he deliberately suppressed the inspiration for a new symphony that had come to him. *Les Troyens* continued to grow and take shape in his mind. But it needed help from without.

The impulse to commit himself unreservedly to a project of this kind and on this scale came from the changed circumstances of his external life, combined perhaps with an inward and reckless sense that the moment had come and that, whatever the likely consequences (the taste of Second Empire Paris being what it was), he must seize it before it was too late. If he finally—as he put it—succumbed to the temptation to write *Les Troyens*, one reason was simply that he could afford to. Since the death of his wife Harriet in 1854, he had no longer had the burden of two separate households to support. By the end of the same year *L'enfance du Christ* had been completed, and performed with a success that seemed to confound his earlier pessimism. The following year, 1855, apparently confirmed the new trend in his fortunes. His activities during that year kept him busy. Tours of Germany, publication of several major works, the Paris Exhibition and the first performance of the Te Deum, left no time for sustained composition. But the project was certainly discussed at Weimar with Liszt's mistress the Princess Wittgenstein, who urged him to undertake it. By this time he must have known that he would have to: he had no choice. His Virgilian passion must be satisfied; the great business of his life was upon him. And in 1856, after further encouragement from the Princess, he began. The first line of

51

the libretto was written on 5 May, the anniversary of Napoleon's death ('an epic date, if there ever was one,' Berlioz remarks in a letter to his uncle Félix Marmion, a veteran of the Grande Armée). Slightly less than two years later, despite illness and the distractions of journalism, the huge richly wrought work was essentially complete.

Such rapidity of creation was the fruit of a lifelong germination. Berlioz himself acknowledged it in a letter to the Princess which is the prime text for our understanding of the subject:

> As for the principal object of the work, the musical rendering of the characters and the expression of their feelings and passions, it was always the easiest part of my task. I have spent my life with this race of demi-gods; I know them so well that I feel as if they must have known me. And this recalls to me a boyhood experience which will show you how fascinated I was from the first by those splendid creatures of the ancient world. It was during the period in my classical education when I was construing, under my father's direction, the marvellous twelfth book of the *Aeneid*. My mind was possessed by the glory of its characters— Lavinia, Turnus, Aeneas, Mezentius, Lausus, Pallas, Evander, Amata, Latinus, Camilla and the rest. I was like a sleepwalker 'lost in my starry meditations' (to borrow Victor Hugo's phrase). One Sunday I was taken to Vespers. The sad persistent chant of the psalm *In exitu Israel* had the magnetic effect on me that it still has today, and plunged me deep in the most real and vivid daydreams of the past. I was with my Virgilian heroes again: I could hear the clash of their arms, I could see Camilla the beautiful Amazon running; I watched the maiden Lavinia, flushed with weeping, and the ill-fated Turnus, his father Daunus, his sister Juturna, I heard the palaces of Laurentium ring with lamentation—and I was seized by an overwhelming sadness. I left the church, sobbing uncontrollably, and cried for the rest of the day, powerless to contain my epic grief. No one could ever get me to tell the reason, my parents never knew nor had any inkling what sorrows had taken possession of my childish heart that day. Is that not a strange and marvellous manifestation of the power of genius? A poet dead thousands of years shakes a guileless, ignorant boy to the depths of his soul with a tale handed down across the centuries, and scenes whose radiance devouring time has been powerless to dim.

Forty years later, his 'Virgilian passion satisfied', Berlioz dedicated *Les Troyens* 'to the divine Virgil', *Divo Virgilio*. It was a repayment of his debt to 'the poet who first found the way to my heart and opened my budding imagination'. A special sense of affinity bound him to Virgil, an affinity only strengthened by the supreme artistic experience of transmuting his poem into music. Near the end of his life he wrote: 'I must be reconciled[. . .]to not having known Virgil —I should have loved him.' Earlier, standing on the site of Maecenas' villa at Tivoli, he could imagine he heard 'Virgil's melancholy voice reciting [. . .] some splendid fragment of the *Georgics*'. (It was a passage from the *Georgics*, invoked to fill out the bloodless rhymes of the official versifier, that had inspired one of his finest student pieces, the epilogue to the competition cantata *La mort d'Orphée*.) Not even Shakespeare occupied a more personal place in his Pantheon. Shakespeare, to Berlioz, was a kind of humanistic God the Father; artistically, he was the most far-reaching influence of all (an influence vitally felt in *Les Troyens* itself, which in Berlioz's words is 'Virgil Shakespeareanized', the libretto articulating the poem by methods learned from the history plays: open form and bold juxtaposition of genres, lofty soliloquy and vernacular conversation, private emotion expressed in a framework of public action). But with Virgil it was something more intimate, a companionship, a sense of identification. While composing *Les Troyens*, he felt that Virgil was alive again in him:

> The countryside [at Saint-Germain] seems to make my Virgilian passion more intense than ever. I feel as if I knew Virgil, as if he knew how much I love him[. . .]Yesterday I finished an aria for Dido which is simply a paraphrase of the famous line: *Haud ignara mali miseris succurrere disco* [My own troubles teach me to help the unfortunate].* When I had sung it through once I was naïve enough to say, out loud: 'That's it, isn't it, dear Master? *Sunt lacrymae rerum?*' just as though Virgil himself had been there.

* A misquotation for *Non ignara*, etc.

53

He was justified in feeling it. Studying the opera and the poem together, we cannot but become increasingly aware of deep correspondences between the two artists. If this high theme was (in every sense) Berlioz's fated goal, it is equally true that one of the poem's many destinies, 'across the centuries', was to be its musical incarnation in a work that is among the last great manifestations of the unique hold of Troy and its legends on the mind of Western man.

Les Troyens is Virgilian in many ways. There is the blend of romantic rhetoric and classical restraint, of monumentality and pictorial vividness; the fondness for mixing genres and in particular for using the lyrical to diversify the tragic and at the same time to bring it into sharper focus; the combination of an aristocratic aloofness with an awareness of the sufferings of ordinary humanity; the sense of fatality, of obscure inimical powers that lie in wait for man, and of the madness that can strike a people and drive it blindly to its own destruction. (The two men have also in common their fear of the collapse of civilization as they knew it, and the doubts that assailed them at the end about the value of their work.) As with the *Aeneid* in Virgil's life, *Les Troyens* grew from seeds planted in youth. As Virgil went back to Homer in order fully to realize himself, so Berlioz turned to Virgil. The opera's outward structure, too, shows Berlioz's fidelity to his model (he has shared the criticism sometimes levelled at Virgil that the character and fate of Dido are treated with such power that they dominate the epic and deflect it from its course). *Les Troyens* follows the *Aeneid* in making the tragic death of an individual the last action that the audience sees enacted on the stage. And just as the *Aeneid* is an epic constructed of two personal tragedies (Dido's and Turnus'), so is *Les Troyens*. Even in consisting of two distinct though interlocking halves the opera reflects the shape of the poem, which is divided into the wanderings of Aeneas, including his narrative of the sack of Troy, and the struggle to found a new Troy in Italy. And though the action of the opera does not take the Trojans as far as Italy, the poem's central idea of the founding of Rome runs through it; Italy is the leitmotiv of the drama.

A study of the libretto in relation to the poem reveals Virgil as its constant guiding spirit. It is not only that a great deal of it is direct translation or paraphrase of the Latin of the books from which the main action is taken—Books I, II and IV. The whole poem is pressed into use. Even the stage direction at the beginning of the opera, 'three shepherds playing the double flute'—represented in the orchestra by oboes—is derived from the *Aeneid*, echoing a passage in Book IX where the Rutulian warrior Normanus taunts Ascanius with 'Go and dance to the double-mouthed pipe on Mount Dindyma, that's all you're good for.' Where Berlioz adds to the poem for dramatic purposes, he nearly always goes to Virgil for his material or his inspiration, working in ideas taken from anywhere and everywhere in the poem. Thus the scene in Act I where Hector's widow Andromache and her son Astyanax, dressed in the ritual white of mourning, lay flowers at the altar and receive Priam's blessing, springs from two different sources, one in Book II, where Aeneas, getting out onto the palace roof through a postern gate during the sack of the city, remembers that through this gate Andromache used to bring her child to see his grandfather Priam, the other in Book III where Aeneas meets Andromache in the Epiran city of Buthrotum, performing the rites of the dead at an altar dedicated to the ashes of Hector. Virgil, in fact, has inspired both the visual content and the tragic irony of the scene.

The episode in Book V where the disgruntled Trojan women gaze out to sea, and groan at the thought of the endless voyaging that lies before them, is transmuted into the scene in Act 5 for the two sentries who march up and down by the Trojan ships, grumbling at the prospect of leaving Carthage, where they are comfortably billeted, and entrusting themselves to the sea's tedium and the rough mercies of the storm (a scene whose Shakespearean ethos is so contrary to orthodox dramatic ideas in France that it

is usually cut out when the work is performed there).
Cassandra, urging Corebus to fly from the wrath to come, is
answered with sentiments similar to those of Aeneas' reply
to Anchises in the burning house: *Mene efferre pedem,
genitor, te posse relicto/Sperasti?** Aeneas' words to his son,
spoken before he goes off to fight the Numidians, para-
phrases the hero's words in Book XII on the eve of the
final battle against Turnus and the Rutulians. The invasion
by Iarbas and his Numidian hordes, an interpolation made
in order to provide a climax for the third act and give
dramatic emphasis to Aeneas' arrival in Carthage, is a
development of an idea put forward by Dido's sister Anna
when she argues that Dido ought to marry Aeneas and
share her kingdom with him: Carthage is surrounded by
wild tribesmen, among them the Numidians and their chief
Iarbas, who is all the more dangerous since Dido humiliat-
ingly rejected his offer of a dynastic marriage.†

The process by which Berlioz fashioned his libretto is most
clearly illustrated in Acts 1 and 2. The opera follows the
main events of the sack of Troy.‡ But new material is
added by the development of hints in the poem, and a good
deal else has necessarily been subjected to compression or
expansion. Thus the one-and-a-half lines in which Virgil
tells of the cold fear that creeps over the Trojans at the news
of Laocoon's death are built into a full-scale ensemble which
shows the city poised at the fatal moment of decision. In

---

* 'Father, did you really expect me to run away and leave you behind?'

† A possible influence here is Piccini's *Didon*, which Berlioz had got to
know during his student days (though written in 1783, it remained in the
repertoire at the Opéra until 1826). Much of the action of Marmontel's
libretto is concerned with Iarbas and his unsuccessful wooing. There are also
verbal similarities between the two librettos in the later scenes, where Marmontel stays closest to Virgil.

‡ Originally Act 1 included the episode of the Greek spy Sinon. It was
later removed by Berlioz, though not until several years after the completion
of the score. The scene, 235 bars long, has survived (mostly in short score)
and is published, for the first time, in the New Berlioz Edition, vol. 2c,
pp. 875–86.

Act 2 Aeneas is made to succeed in his desperate attempt to
relieve the citadel (in the poem he merely conceives the wild
idea of doing so*); and he escapes with the royal insignia
of Troy. The motive for this change may partly have been
tidiness and coherence: Ascanius later presents a rich
selection of Trojan relics to Queen Dido (a scene which is a
conflation of two separate passages in Book 1). But the
main reason, as with the finale of Act 3, is one of dramatic
emphasis, to clinch the act with a decisive forward-looking
event. In this case the action is not shown. We hear of it,
from Cassandra, in the course of a scene which does not
figure in the *Aeneid* except by implication, in the cries of the
wailing women in Priam's palace (*plangoribus aedes femi-
neis ululant*), in the glimpse of Helen cowering by the
entrance to the temple of Vesta, and in the brief description
of Cassandra being dragged from Minerva's sanctuary.

The development of Cassandra into the protagonist of
Acts 1 and 2 is the biggest single change that Berlioz made.
But here too he went to Virgil, deriving the character from a
few lines in the *Aeneid*, just as Virgil derived Aeneas from
the merest hint in the *Iliad*. Cassandra fills the role taken
in Book II by Aeneas, who in the poem recalls Troy's downfall several years after the event. In the opera the tale comes
to us through the eyes of the prophetess cursed with second
sight. We see the catastrophe twice over: as it gradually
forms in her mind (from the vague fears of 'Malheureux roi'
to the fierce clarity of her vision in the following scene), and
when it comes. This double process has the dramatic
effect of heightening the sense of tragedy and doom. The
vehemence and certainty of her unheeded prophecies throws
the blindness of her fellow-countrymen into more merciless
relief—that of Corebus in particular; the young warrior is
mentioned briefly by Virgil as being 'on fire with desperate
love for Cassandra' and as refusing to listen to her warnings,
but in the opera he is betrothed to her: a lyrical addition

---

* If indeed we are to read *arcem* as 'citadel' and not simply 'strong point'.

57

which, by holding out the possibility of a happiness that will never be fulfilled, sharpens the cruel irony of Cassandra's personal tragedy. The text of Cassandra's scenes inevitably contains few direct Virgilian echoes; the prophecy to the Trojan women about the founding of a new Troy in Italy, based on Anchises' words in Book III, is a rare exception. Yet the whole character and her heroic, despairing utterances are in a sense simply a personification of Aeneas' tragic cry at the moment when he describes the entry of the Wooden Horse into Troy while Cassandra vainly prophesies:

O patria o divum domus Ilium et incluta bello
*Moenia Dardanidum!**

Cassandra is the first of the two tragic pillars which support the edifice of *Les Troyens*; across her fate, and Dido's, the epic of Roman destiny marches to its fulfilment. Berlioz had no choice but to kill her off in heroic circumstances at the end of his Act 2. The scene is not in Virgil; but its conception does not dishonour him.

In adapting the *Aeneid* to the totally different medium of opera, Berlioz also made some changes in the order of events as recounted by Virgil. The conversation (already referred to) between Anna and her sister Dido, with its tender urgings on one side and its barely suppressed emotion on the other, prompted the very similar duet in Act 3, 'Reine d'une jeune empire'. But whereas in the *Aeneid* the conversation occurs after the Trojans' arrival in Carthage and is very much concerned with them, Berlioz places it just before, as a means of projecting the state of Dido's heart at the moment of Aeneas' intervention in her life—her restlessness, her half-conscious yearning for love, her ripeness to yield. His dramatic judgment is correct. By doing so he is able partly to compensate for the fact that he has had to unfold the

* 'Oh my country! Oh Ilium, home of gods, oh walls of Troy renowned in war!'

events of the plot in straightforward chronological sequence
and therefore to start the Carthaginian part of his story cold,
where Virgil, by recounting the sack of Troy and its aftermath in flashback, through the mouth of Aeneas, with the
fascinated Dido devouring his words, can accumulate
tension over two or three thousand lines of verse and so
prepare gradually for the explosion of passion which comes
at the beginning of Book IV. (Yet such is music's power of
suggestion, and so vibrant the impression of a woman of
peculiar radiance and energy that Dido makes on us in those
early scenes of Act 3, that the disadvantage is partly overcome.) The opera also redistributes and telescopes the
sequence of events between Aeneas' decision to leave Dido
and her death—a sequence which in the poem occupies four
or five hundred lines, or well over half Book IV. A chart of
the various sources, line by line, of Dido's soliloquies in
Act 5—'Dieux immortels, il part', 'Je vais mourir', 'Adieu,
fière cité' and the final invocation from the pyre—would
show the text as woven of threads freely drawn from many
different points in the last 250 lines of the book. The result
is clear, logical and compelling, and does no violence to
Virgil's psychology.

The third and final category of change concerns the new
emphasis that Berlioz gives to certain events or ideas in the
poem, his intention normally being to make explicit and
theatrically telling what in the poem can afford to take its
time and grow by degrees in the reader's mind. To take one
of the most obvious instances: the theme of *fatum*, destiny,
which is fundamental to the *Aeneid*, has had necessarily to
be much more simply and directly set forth (a process in
which the traditional importance of the chorus in French
opera plays a vital part). This need applies also to the
specifically Italian direction of the destiny of the Trojan
survivors; not being native and instantly intelligible to
Berlioz's audience as it was to Virgil's, it had to be made
plain. In the *Aeneid* there is some doubt about the true
identity of the mysterious object of Aeneas' wanderings. The

59

ghost of his wife Creusa tells him, on Troy's last night, that
his goal is Latium; but after that, uncertainty descends and
it is only subsequently, several false scents later, that Italy is
defined as the destined site of Troy reborn. An opera composer cannot afford such inconsistency (if indeed it is not
deliberate and subtle poetic realism on Virgil's part) and, as
we see, Berlioz is at pains to state the theme clearly and re-
emphasize it at regular intervals, so that we shall be in no
serious danger of not recognizing it as the majestic impulse
of the epic, before which everything must ultimately give
way. Contrary to Virgil, he makes Hector's ghost specify
the object of Aeneas' wanderings. Later, he ends his picture
of the sack of Troy with the Trojan women's defiant repeated
cry of 'Italie'. Similarly, when the Trojans land at Carthage,
their spokesman Panthus is more emphatic about the god-
fated and only temporarily frustrated aim of their voyage
than is Ilioneus in the equivalent passage in the *Aeneid*.
In the opera, at the peak of the lovers' ecstasy, Mercury
appears in the moonlit garden and, striking Aeneas' shield,
intones three times 'Italie'. Mercury's larger role in the
Aeneid, as explicit messenger of the gods, is not sacrificed
but is filled, with the greater directness appropriate to
drama, by the spirits of the illustrious Trojan dead, who
rise up in turn to whet Aeneas' almost blunted purpose.
Again, Berlioz sees to it that Aeneas is fully awake and
conscious when Hector's ghost delivers his message; in the
Aeneid the apparition comes to Aeneas in a dream, through
the veil of sleep. All this makes for a necessary gain in
clarity and conciseness, inevitably at a slight cost in poetic
suggestiveness and truth to life.

In the same way, Aeneas' heroic role and his consciousness of his destiny as a hero have to be spelled out; the
point must be established quickly—it cannot be left to the
cumulative effect of epic verse. In *Les Troyens* the last words
uttered by Hector's ghost before the vision fades tell of the
death that Aeneas will meet in Italy; the final line, 'Où la
mort des héros t'attend', is not in Virgil. Later Panthus, in

his speech to Dido in Act 3, refers to it as an accepted fact. Aeneas himself, in his monologue in Act 5, says that he could not sway the outraged Dido even by reminding her of 'la triomphale mort par les destins promise'—the end awaiting him on Ausonian fields that is to crown his glory; and almost his last words to her, when she confronts him by the ships, speak of the death to which he is going.

It is sometimes objected that Virgil, concerned with the overriding theme of the epic of Rome, failed to make Aeneas sufficiently sympathetic. This is usually said by people who have fallen in love with his glorious Dido and who consequently regard any man capable of abandoning her as an unspeakable cad. Such indignant charges do more credit to the critics' chivalry than to their careful reading of the poem. Berlioz might appear to belong to their number, from the references in his *Memoirs* to the 'hypocrite', the 'perfidious' Aeneas. But the composer of *Les Troyens* understood the depth of passion hinted at in Virgil's resonant understatements and justly praised silences; and he was quite right, on Virgilian as well as on operatic terms, to make Aeneas' love for Dido whole-hearted and avowed and to dramatize the resultant conflict in the hero's mind. The famous duet in Dido's garden is not only obligatory for the composer of grand opera but also artistically essential to the drama as a whole. The words, adapted from the scene between Lorenzo and Jessica in the moonlit garden at Belmont in the fifth act of *The Merchant of Venice,** represent the one major textual innovation that is not Virgilian in origin. Its setting gave Berlioz the opportunity to lavish all his lyrical and orchestral art on a poignant evocation of the warmth and vast splendours of the starlit Mediterranean night. The *Aeneid* is not abolutely precise about the season of the Trojans' sojourn in Carthage. In *Les Troyens* it is, unequivocally, summertime; the great feasts with their bards and heroic tales and jewel-encrusted goblets take place out of doors under the open sky. Berlioz has also

61

*and suggested to Berlioz by its allusions to Dido and Troilus.

transferred the setting of the hunt and storm from open mountainous country to virgin forest, and has peopled his scene with the woodland satyrs, bathing naiads and glinting streams and waterfalls which help to make it the neo-classical masterpiece it is, a movement that has been compared to some great Claude or Poussin, and that combines attributes of both painters, Poussin's grandeur and universality and dynamic form, Claude's numinous clarity and sense of the golden moment.

An example of all three types of change—the interpolating of new material derived from Virgil himself, the re-ordering of the sequence of Virgil's narrative, and the making explicit what in the poem is implied—is the Quintet in Act 4, 'Tout conspire à vaincre mes remords'. Here we see Berlioz's dramatic imagination at work on the *Aeneid*, distilling from it a scene which, as such, is not found in the poem, but which is necessary to the scheme of a dramatic work based on it—in this case, the moment of Dido's change of heart, from lingering attachment to the memory of her dead husband Sychaeus to unreserved commitment to her new love. In the first place, the picture of Dido feasting Aeneas and begging him to repeat the tale of Troy's woes is moved on in time so as to follow the acknowledgment and consummation of their mutual passion; in Virgil it belongs to the preceding stage of their relationship (a part of the poem not included in the opera, except by implication). Then, Virgil's divine intervention (Venus and Juno in league) is discarded. In the *Aeneid* Cupid, in the likeness of Ascanius, fans the flame and 'gradually dispels from Dido's mind all thought of Sychaeus', while she, unaware of his true identity, 'fondles him and holds him close'. Berlioz retains the visual setting but replaces the supernatural with a dramatic idea developed from a reference, in Book III, to Hector's widow Andromache having married Pyrrhus. In the opera it is the discovery that Andromache is now the wife of the man whose father slew Hector that acts as a catalyst on Dido, severing the threads that bound her to her old life (and at the same time setting up in the spectator's mind a sudden resonance with the almost forgotten moment, three acts ago, when the desolate figure in white walked silently through rejoicing crowds by the walls of Troy). Finally, an echo of Cupid substituted for Ascanius survives in the stage direction which shows the boy 'leaning on his bow, like a statue of Eros', and in the smiling comment of the royal entourage that he resembles Cupid, as he slips Sychaeus' ring from the heedless Dido's finger. This last action is one of the very rare non-Virgilian ideas in the libretto; Berlioz took it from Guérin's painting, *Enée racontant à Didon les malheurs de Troie*.

Most of this examination has shown only the skill with which Berlioz reshaped the *Aeneid* into a fresh mould—a mould for the music that was waiting to pour out of him. It is the music that makes him a true descendant of the poet he loved. 'As for the principal object of the work, the musical rendering of the characters and the expression of their feelings and passions, it was always the easiest part of my task.' But not only the characters' passions, one wants to exclaim, but the Virgilian ambience itself, the whole environment of the epic, has been absorbed by the composer into his inmost being and given back reborn in his own language. A re-reading of the *Aeneid* with the music of *Les Troyens* in one's mind is a startling revelation of artistic correspondence. Feature after feature of the poem reappears in the score. Certain elements may be isolated. On the level of individual images, we find details such as the violin harmonics which in Act 5 suggest the electric effect of the apparitions on Aeneas, matching Virgil's graphic description of the hero rigid with fear, his hair standing on end (*arrectaeque horrore comae*). At the beginning of the opera the combination of shrill, rapidly pulsing woodwind chords, a texture devoid of bass, the absence of strings, and the curiously jaunty melodic material, at once trivial and possessed, conveying a sense of ritual madness, help to establish from the outset the idea of *fatum*, of a people rushing to ruin. An

63

ominous rhythmic figure,* 𝄽𝄽𝄽𝄽 first heard as part of the orchestral texture in the opening scenes and stated explicitly in the Octet 'Châtiment effroyable' which follows the death of Laocoon, recurs as a kind of reminder of fatality at moments where the action of destiny is most manifest or the tragic irony most intense—the apparition of Hector's ghost in Act 2 and of the spirits in Act 5, the tumultuous exit of Aeneas as king-elect at the head of combined Trojan and Carthaginian forces at the end of Act 3, the climax of the Royal Hunt, Dido's farewell—'ma carrière est finie'— and the solemnities which precede her immolation. But for the most part the correspondence needs no analysing. It leaps out at us. The Octet, for instance, once heard seems the inevitable setting of the dread words *Tum vero treme- facta novus per pectora cunctis/Insinuat pavor*—a whole people's blood running cold, panic spreading as an inkling of their doom 'works its way' into the back of their minds. How much of Cassandra's music directly echoes, in its piercing sadness, Aeneas' cry of anguish over the horror, the pity of it—*O patria o divum domus Ilium!*

Or what could be more Virgilian than the scene in Act 2 where Hector, 'recalled to life by the will of the gods', appears before Aeneas and lays upon him his sacred mission, then sinks back to nothingness, his task accomplished— the apparition materializing to the sound of stopped horns groping from note to note, accompanied by pizzicato strings, then uttering its message on the successive notes of a falling chromatic scale above a dim fabric of divided cellos and basses, with occasional interventions from the trombones, at once nightmarish and majestic; Aeneas staring and motionless, except for a sudden lurch in the orchestra, like a missed heartbeat, at the words—the most terrible in the

* Borrowed, perhaps, from Max's scena in *Der Freischütz*, via Herod's aria in *L'enfance du Christ*.

Aeneid—*hostis habet muros*: 'the enemy's within our walls'.
In the orchestral prelude to the same act the very sound and
feel of Virgil's lines are reproduced in the rhythm, texture,
colour and harmonic movement of the music—*clarescunt
sonitus armorumque ingruit horror*:* war and rumours of war,
the hideous confusion of battle. Again, how true to Virgil
are the music's insights into the effect of war and the great
national enterprises born of war on the ordinary human
being—poignant in the case of the Palinurus-like figure
of the young sailor Hylas, eaten with nostalgia for the
homeland he will never see again; humorous in the case of
the two grumbling sentries who would like to stay in Carthage and have done with the whole senseless idea of Italy;
tragic in the case of Andromache, whose grief, though it
pales before the cataclysm to come, remains the ultimate
comment on the misery of war. How deeply Berlioz has
absorbed the example of the humanity of the *Aeneid*—those
little touches that mark Virgil out among ancient writers,
like the picture of the women and children waiting in a
long line beside the piled-up loot in the courtyard of Priam's
blazing palace. Such sudden shifts of viewpoint give a new
dimension to the epic, in Berlioz's music as in Virgil's verse.

Dramatic effects of sharply contrasted colours, textures and
rhythms are a common feature of the two works. The
moment in Book I when the magic cloak shrouding Aeneas
is stripped away to reveal him in all his glory is paralleled by
the sudden change that occurs in the music when Aeneas
throws off his sailor's cloak and steps forward in shining
armour. Acts 1 and 2 of *Les Troyens* mirror Book II of the
Aeneid in their alternation of light and dark, their evocation
of flaring light amid surrounding blackness—the doomed
splendour of the great processional entry of the Horse
through the torchlit darkness, the smoky glare of the Temple
Scene shot through with gleams of martial trumpets. The
feeling we experience in the opera when the harsh, possessed

* 'The noise grew clearer and the roar of battle swelled.'

65

sound of Berlioz's Troy gives way to the lyrical and sensuous sound of his Carthage (flute and clarinet in octaves, piccolo trills, softer string sonorities), is just such as we experience in Book I of the poem when Virgil cuts abruptly from the clangorous description of the frescoes depicting the Trojan War in the temple of Juno to the delicate and luminous vision of Dido making her way through the throng, attended by young courtiers.

The criticism sometimes heard of Act 3, that the lengthy ceremonies in which Carthage celebrates its first seven years are a distraction from the main business of the drama and a concession to Meyerbeerian grand opera, is in effect a criticism of a too close fidelity to Virgil, for the plan of the opening scenes of the act is inspired by the intensely vital and brilliant first impression of Carthage that we receive in Book I. Berlioz's purpose in following Virgil, however, is a dramatic one, being both to provide an interval of repose after the concentrated fury of Act 2 and to emphasize the rising star of the new city so that the tragedy of its fall may be fully felt. To this end, and perhaps also borrowing an idea from Book VII (the picture of Latium as a kingdom of Saturn, still enjoying the blessings of the golden age), he has made his Carthage something of a matriarchal Garden of Eden, absorbed in the beneficent work of building and cultivation, fearful of the enemies surrounding it, yet defence-less until saved by the hero who is destined to be its destroyer (the limping, melancholy strains of the Trojan March in the minor mode telling not only of Trojan sufferings endured but of Carthaginian disasters to come). But in his development of this gentle pastoral state the composer is, as always, the disciple of the poet—especially the poet of the *Georgics*, who is heard through the mouth of the bard Iopas. In the *Aeneid* Iopas sings of the elements and the movement of the stars, but in *Les Troyens* of the shepherd and the farmworker and the fruits of the well-tilled earth.

In this fourth act, set in Dido's gardens at night within sound of the sleeping sea, Berlioz matches Virgil's mastery of verbal magic in music beneath whose beauties lies the same sense of the pathos of life and the brevity of human happiness. Yet the fifth and final act is in some ways the most profoundly Virgilian of all, both in its heroic sweep and in its classicism: on the one hand the great arches of extended melody in Aeneas' scena—the huge stride of the vocal line above the surge and stress of the orchestra, the powerful swing of the rhythmic movement between agitation and serene exaltation; on the other hand the simplicity of Dido's grief. In response to the tragic dénouement of Book IV Berlioz strips his art to an extraordinary economy of gesture. One thinks of the gentle swell of the sea cradling Hylas to a death-like sleep; the two-note semitone figure which suggests Aeneas rocking to and fro in the anguish of his indecision; the brief shudder in the strings, like a premonition of a life escaping into air (*in ventos vita recessit*), that abruptly breaks the trancelike calm of Dido's first words from the pyre; the bareness of the vocal line a moment earlier as Dido, speaking as if in a dream, gives the order for the last rites to begin—a passage whose broken phrases and slow chromatic descent through an octave recall the music of Hector's prophecy which was to be the cause of her grief. (Virgil would have recognized here a poetic device of his own, whereby resonances are set up between pairs of similar or ironically contrasted incidents located in different parts of the epic.) While at work on Dido's recitative 'Je vais mourir', Berlioz wrote of his conviction that the music he was composing had a 'heartrending truthfulness'. What is even more remarkable is the sense of a calm beyond suffering that he achieves in the aria, 'Adieu, fière cité' (*urbem praeclaram statui*),* which succeeds the torment of the recitative. Nothing in music is more expressive of utter finality than the aria's concluding bars—the voice dying away, a last flicker of agony (the cor anglais' flattened sixth), then a mysterious peace, with a rustle of pianissimo strings and, on trombones, the quiet beat of the rhythmic motif of

* 'I founded a noble city.'

destiny, stilled in a cadence of such purity and simplicity that the silence which follows is almost palpable: there is nothing more to be said. Dido accepts her fate.

In the tragic climate of the ancients, redemption is neither demanded nor expected. Alone among Romantic dramatists, Berlioz was able to re-create it because it was his own imaginative world. It had become his natural element. The memory of the emotional shock that Dido's death had been to him, forty years before, and of all that had followed in his adolescent imaginative life, remained with him, fresh and undiminished. To it was added long experience as a composer of dramatic music and a capacity for feeling, for pain, for regret, that life had sharpened to a fine point. He had been waiting for this. His musical style, with its long flexible melodic line and its use of timbre and rhythm as subtly varied means of poetic expression, was ideally suited to the task. So was his temperament. The call of Virgil's heroic world was irresistible. A concept of human existence as it might once have been in some possible dream of a golden age took root in boyhood and grew till it possessed his mind. The Virgilian vision—a vision of grandeur without illusions, of destruction lying in wait outside and within man, and life lived subject to the will of implacable fate but, while it lasts, lived fully and ungrudgingly even in the shadow of doom—answered his deepest longings. It is the heroic temper expressed in Hecuba's proud prophecy in the last scene of *The Trojan Women*:

> We sacrificed in vain. Yet if the god had not seized this city and trampled it beneath the earth, we should have disappeared without trace: we would not have given a theme for music and the songs of men to come . . .

the mood that is expressed in the ardent, exalted music to which Aeneas, drunk with his mission, already part of history, apostrophizes Dido in sublime farewell, before turning to embrace his fate and the knowledge of his death.

As with Aeneas, there could be for Berlioz no turning back
once he had begun. But like Aeneas he knew the outcome.
'What agonies I am storing up for myself by becoming so
passionate about this work!' Its likely fate had been one of
his strongest reasons against being drawn into composing it.
The indifference of the French musical establishment was
nontheless a crippling blow. He had schooled himself in a
proud stoicism, but his resolve broke down. 'I know that I
promised you I would resign myself to whatever might
happen,' he wrote to the Princess, 'and here I am, failing
completely to keep my promise. I feel a terrible bitterness of
spirit.' The bitterness was not relieved, even by the momentary pleasure of seeing the second part of the work staged and
rewarded with a *succès d'estime* despite poor performances and
numerous cuts. It is the sense of defeat that *Les Troyens*
engendered which, more than anything else, even his son's
death and his own painful and incurable disease, accounts
for the gloom of Berlioz's last years. At least he was spared
the tragi-comedy of the work's subsequent fortunes in
France: non-publication, non-performance, performance in
versions mutilated almost beyond recognition, critical dis-
missal, lawsuits, and the rest of the scene he knew so well.
To quote the late Claude Rostand, in an act of public
recantation of dramatic completeness:*

Relying purely on received opinions, with a wilful blindness
that has persisted, to be precise, for one hundred and seven
years, France has always refused to accept that *Les Troyens* is a
great masterpiece, the high point of its composer's genius [. . .]
According to the official view that we used to be taught, *Les
Troyens* was an operatic 'monster', fruit of the old age of an
artist in decline, its occasional beauties set in an ocean of feeble-
ness, and in any case humanly impossible to perform or to listen
to in one evening. These judgments, these summary convictions, repeated ad nauseam—till recently even by the most
enthusiastic Berliozians—were in fact based not simply on
incomprehension but first and foremost on a liberal measure

* Reviewing the Philips recording of *Les Troyens* in *Le Figaro Littéraire*,
21-27 September 1970.

of pure ignorance. What a confession![. . .] We have here one of
the most astonishing musical scandals of all time[. . .]

     In the seventh book of the *Aeneid* an indignant Juno looks down
on the Mediterranean and exclaims in wonder that the Trojans
have endured so many cruel vicissitudes: half-drowned,
blasted with fire, their might scattered; yet they are still
unbowed, and life lies ahead of them. She might have been
prophesying the destiny of Berlioz's opera. Despite all that
has and has not happened to it, it has survived. Its worth
is at last coming to be recognized. In a real sense life lies
ahead of it for, with the publication of the full score (in
1969, a hundred years after the composer's death), the work
may be said for the first time fully to exist. It can at last be
recognized for what it is, the vindication of its creator's faith
in his lifelong vision, and proof of the magic power of a great
poet working, two thousand years later, on the mind of a
kindred genius.

70

Donizetti's Serious Operas

WINTON DEAN

UNTIL RECENTLY Donizetti was not respectable enough for musicology. He was remembered for two or three comedies; yet he and Rossini both devoted their mature years almost entirely to serious opera. Of Donizetti's 70 stage works, a few of which are lost, exactly half belong to the *opera seria* class (that includes two French grand operas); three are early works on Classical subjects, nine are *opere semiserie*, and 23 are comedies or farces. But those figures do not give a true picture. In the first place, twelve of the comic operas but only one of the serious are in a single act. Second, if we take the end of 1828 as a dividing line—which is roughly when Donizetti reached maturity—we find that before that date he composed 29 operas, of which only six are serious, whereas after it he produced eight comedies (five in one act), four *semiseria* (one in one act), and 29 full-length serious operas. Clearly he regarded Romantic tragedy as his main line.

Traditional opinion assures us that, because Donizetti composed very rapidly, 'even allowing for the thinness and conventional character of the accompaniments, it is clear that such work can be no more than successful improvisation'. (Exactly the same could be said of *Messiah*.) '. . . Facile, sentimental melodies can no longer sustain the interest or be supposed to represent adequately dramatic action, and Donizetti seldom rises above that standard.'[1] That view was almost universal in England until perhaps the last ten years, and is still heard today despite the enterprising revivals of so many of Donizetti's forgotten operas—though at least half of the best have not yet been staged in this country. The prejudice derives partly from our peculiar brand of Philistinism that regards music written gratefully for the singing voice as *per se* trivial, if not immoral, and partly from the increasing reputation of German opera, especially Wagner. Donizetti was of course not the only casualty: Bellini, nearly all Rossini and a great deal of Verdi were likewise consigned to the garbage heap.

[1] *Grove's Dictionary of Music and Musicians*, 5th edn., London, 1954, art. 'Donizetti'.

Before considering Donizetti's achievement it is worth glancing at the origins of his style. His teacher, Simone Mayr, was a very important influence on Italian nineteenth-century opera. Mayr was a Bavarian, a younger contemporary of Mozart, who studied in Italy and soon decided to settle there, italianising his name. Between 1794 and 1824 he composed more than 60 operas, all in Italian; like Donizetti he tended to concentrate on comic operas in youth and serious in maturity, and he had many successes in both forms. In 1802 he established himself at Bergamo, Donizetti's birthplace, from which he refused to budge, despite invitations to London, Paris, Lisbon and Dresden. His operas, like those of Peter von Winter and Ferdinando Paer, give a very good idea of what may be called the routine style during the period of Beethoven's early maturity, the generation before Weber, Schubert and Rossini. They are thoroughly competent, but suffer from a bland tone and a lack of creative heat. They look back rather than forward, to Gluck, Cimarosa, Cherubini and above all Mozart; the demonic D minor element in *Don Giovanni*, which influenced so many composers of this period, brought out the best in Mayr, notably in *Medea in Corinto*, perhaps his most successful opera, which was produced at Naples in 1813. The novel feature of his music, from an Italian point of view, was his varied and subtle treatment of the orchestra, especially the woodwind instruments. He probably learned this from Mozart; he certainly bequeathed it to Rossini, who was much more his direct heir than Donizetti. There is very little Romantic feeling in Mayr. In his Leonora opera, *L'amor conjugale*, one is never aware of the darkness of the dungeon as a dramatic force, as one is in Beethoven and in earlier French Revolution composers like Méhul and Dalayrac. Nor was Rossini in this sense a Romantic composer, though the powers of nature do make themselves discreetly felt in his later operas, *William Tell* in particular. Romanticism in Italy was always a matter of pathos and politics rather than the supernatural that obsessed the Germans. The negative side of this emerges from Verdi's treatment of Joan of Arc's voices and the witches in *Macbeth*.

From Mayr, an excellent teacher, Donizetti acquired a sound operatic technique, a feeling for instrumental colour and a firm control of harmonic movement, especially in big concerted pieces. He was more profoundly and lastingly influenced by Rossini, whose bouncy rhythms, clattering orchestration, irrepressible crescendos, resounding thumps off the beat before the voice enters, and rare but decisive and cunningly judged modulations haunt Donizetti's early operas and reappear from time to time in the later ones, serious as well as comic. It was the digestion of the Rossini influence more than anything else that delayed Donizetti's maturity till beyond the age of thirty. What seems to have turned him from a follower of Rossini into a Romantic composer was his contact with Bellini, his junior by four years—'seems' because the matter requires more detailed investigation. The two were composing at the same time, often for the same theatres and with the same collaborators, and they were constantly in direct competition. Temperamentally they were very different. Donizetti was the most generous and open-handed of men; he admired Bellini and said so repeatedly. Bellini on the other hand was consumed by suspicion and envy, convinced that every other composer's hand was against him; Donizetti, as the most successful of his rivals, was most frequently accused of trying to damage his interests and his reputation. Bellini's character was as unlike his music as could be imagined; but it is his music that matters, and it can hardly be coincidental that Donizetti's sudden emergence as a composer of Romantic opera came soon after his encounter with Bellini. He wrote most enthusiastically of *Bianca e Fernando*, Bellini's second opera, at Naples in May 1826; but the decisive work was probably the very successful *Il Pirata*, produced at La Scala in October 1827. Bellini's individual brand of long-breathed elegiac lyricism was conspicuous here for the first time (along with much that was trivial and still immature), and Donizetti soon began to reflect it, combining it with his own stronger feeling for harmonic structure, orchestration and rhythmic energy. His later operas, especially those written for Paris and Vienna, show many signs that he studied Beethoven, Meyerbeer and Weber among others; and it is amusing to find him echoing 'Va, pensiero' from *Nabucco* in *Dom Sébastien*.

Before staking any claims for Donizetti one must allow some weight to the case against him. It is true that his work is uneven. He did write, if not too rapidly, at least without always exercising a due measure of self-criticism. Even his best operas are liable to regress without warning into footling little tunes more appropriate to a municipal bandstand than an imperial or renaissance court. The young Verdi was an even more glaring offender here, if only because he put more vim into them. It is also true that Donizetti's plots sometimes throw up

73

5*

dramatic absurdities. Two flagrant examples are the happy ends of *Adelia* and *Maria Padilla*; in the latter, after a splendid tragic build-up, all logic is suddenly abandoned: the heroine recovers her lover while he is in process of marrying someone else, fires off a brilliant rondo-finale, and dies of joy—or perhaps sheer surprise. This was due not to cynicism on Donizetti's part—he was thoroughly disgusted with what he had to do—but to the censorship's refusal to permit a suicide on stage. Librettists at this period could be slapdash and inconsequent, but some of their worst excesses were imposed on them by the censors. Everyone knows the trouble Verdi had over *Rigoletto* and *Un ballo in maschera* a decade or two later, and he was a tougher character than Donizetti.

There are three main reasons for looking closely at Donizetti's serious operas. First, though none is a flawless work of art, a great many are—or could be—extremely moving in the theatre. Second—though this may come as a surprise—Donizetti was not just content to accept things as they were; he was from the first a conscious innovator, eager to expand the range of operatic form, though hampered at every stage by factors over which he had little or no control. Third, he exercised a more decisive and fruitful influence on Verdi than is commonly recognized. These points of course are connected. Marco Bonesi, a fellow-student under Mayr, said that as early as 1820 Donizetti 'had many ideas how to reform the predictable situations, the sequences of introduction, cavatina, duet, trio, finale, always fashioned the same way. "But", he added sadly, "what to do with the blessed theatrical conventions? Impresarios, singers, and the public as well, would hurl me into the farthest pit"'.[2] He told Mayr in a letter of February 1828 that he wanted to break the yoke of the finales, an ambition he achieved with striking success. In 1832, long before Verdi, he was demanding brevity from his librettists. In 1839, when preparing *Poliuto* for production in Paris, he rejoiced in the chance to get rid of crescendos and cadenzas and in the emphasis laid by French taste on motivation between verses of cabalettas, so that they do not become mere repetitions. His letters are full of care for dramatic detail; again and again they refute E. J. Dent's suggestion[3] that he took little trouble to read the libretto he was setting.

[2] Quoted by William Ashbrook, *Donizetti*, London, 1965, p. 42.
[3] 'Donizetti: an Italian Romantic', *Fanfare for Ernest Newman*, ed. Herbert Van Thal, London, 1955, p. 92. The reference is to the early operas, but the implication is extended to the later.

It was not so easy to put this into practice, and Donizetti had to proceed cautiously; but proceed he did, loosening the forms by degrees from the inside. One characteristic feature was his treatment of recitative, in particular the relaxation and expansion of dialogue sections by means of short lyrical ariosos, often only a few bars long but intensely expressive of the emotion behind the words. Besides varying the design this helped to deepen the characterization. It is rare in Bellini and almost unknown in Rossini, even in *William Tell*, but common in Donizetti's operas from *Il paria* (January 1829) and *Anna Bolena* (December 1830). The final scene of *Anna Bolena*, his first great international success, is a masterpiece of dramatic pathos of a type personal to Donizetti, but quite unlike Bellini or for that matter Verdi (though it haunted Verdi's memory). The unhappy queen languishes in prison, her mind wandering, after being condemned to death by her brutal husband, whose marriage procession with her supplanter Jane Seymour is heard backstage. Instead of the conventional and far inferior mad scene he was to write in *Lucia di Lammermoor*, and which we meet in Bellini, Meyerbeer and elsewhere, Donizetti gives the queen a series of ariosos of varying length, interspersed with comments from the chorus (her ladies in waiting) and other characters. By expanding the recitative and at the same time breaking up the cavatina sections he produced a fluid texture that reflects the quickly changing moods—until the final cabaletta, which is more conventional. The last scene of *Maria Stuarda* is similar, though not quite on the same level; and so is much of Act IV of *La Favorite*. Vivid little ariosos that never return occur throughout Donizetti's serious operas. Sometimes, as with the first phrase uttered by Lucrezia Borgia or Tasso's 'Poco dunque ti pare' in Act II of *Torquato Tasso*, he seems to toss away material that could have formed a whole movement. There are beautiful ariosos for Emma in Act I of *Ugo, Conte di Parigi*, both Parisina and Duke Azzo in the bedroom scene of *Parisina*, Nello in Act II of *Pia de' Tolomei*, Pedro the Cruel at his first entry in *Maria Padilla* (and for Maria herself near the beginning of Act III) and countless others. Most of them are mere fragments, yet they haunt the memory and carry the individual stamp of the composer.

One of the notorious stumbling-blocks to appreciation of Italian opera of this period is the regularity of the aria plan. All too often an expressive cantabile is followed by a bouncy cabaletta over a standardized accompaniment that may bring

75

applause to the singer (which of course was one of its intentions) but causes the fastidious listener's heart to sink. It is
not easy to vary them, as Verdi complained later. Donizetti
wrote quite enough of the regular pattern, which he eventually
discarded; but he also evolved a new type—the slow cabaletta, generally marked 'andante' or 'moderato' or 'maestoso',
which pays more attention to the dramatic requirements than
to the pyrotechnical demands of the singer. If there is coloratura, it is expressive rather than spectacular; and that applies
to Donizetti's coloratura in general, much more than to
Rossini's. Perhaps the most familiar example of the slow
cabaletta is Edgar's 'Tu che a Dio spiegasti l'ali' at the end
of *Lucia di Lammermoor*. Quite a few other operas, including
Parisina, *Pia de' Tolomei*, *Torquato Tasso* and *Roberto Devereux*,
end with a movement of this kind. There are no fewer than
five in the score of *Pia de' Tolomei*, and almost as many in
Maria di Rohan and *Gemma di Vergy*. The cabaletta of Chevreuse's aria in Act I of *Maria di Rohan* is actually slower than
the cantabile before it. These are all dark tragic operas, in
which the hero or heroine is betrayed, condemned or killed
by someone he or she loves; more often than not it is a wife
despatched by her jealous husband. One response to this
threat is to hurl defiance in the face of destiny, as Anna
Bolena does; but other solutions can be more moving and revealing of character, quite apart from the variety they introduce into the musical design. Pia's final aria begins with a
Larghetto expressing love for her husband, who has already
poisoned her out of groundless jealousy, though she does not
know it; in the 'andante' cabaletta she forgives him, and prays
for peace between the warring factions. During the second
stanza the drooping vocal line and the accompaniment
gradually disintegrate as she grows weaker. Parisina is suddenly confronted with the corpse of her lover, who has been
executed by her husband; her cabaletta is a lament over his
body, and at the end she collapses. One of the most striking
examples is Queen Elizabeth's 'Quel sangue versato' at the end
of *Roberto Devereux*. If we can forget the historical absurdity
of her abdication in favour of James I, this makes a superb end
to a very impressive opera.[4] Her plans for rescuing Essex,
whose execution she has ordered but planned to circumvent,
have been frustrated by the jealous Duke of Nottingham, with

[4] See Winton Dean, 'Donizetti and Queen Elizabeth', *Opera*, iv (1953),
333–6; reprinted in *The Opera Bedside Book*, ed. Harold Rosenthal,
London, 1965, pp. 152–7.

whose wife Essex has been having an affair. The cannon from the Tower announces the execution, and the queen gives vent to a vision of blood and horror in a superb 'maestoso' melody nearly 30 bars long. This is not at all like Bellini's long tunes, but it is very similar in mood and outline to Lady Macbeth's 'Vieni t'affretta', in which another formidable queen has the the smell of blood in her nostrils.[a]

These slow cabalettas not only underline a tragic dénouement. They can set up a situation rich in dramatic irony at the first entrance of the principal character. The heroine of *Gemma di Vergy* sits at home longing for her husband's return from the wars. In the first scene of the opera we learn that he intends to divorce her and marry again. When she makes her entry she does not know this, but everyone else on stage does, though each views the prospect differently. Her cantabile expresses her horror of war, which has been disturbing her dreams. She is then told that her husband is returning that very day, and cries out in joy. By setting this cabaletta in slow tempo, while the chorus remarks that her happiness is doomed, Donizetti exploits the irony of Gemma's predicament to the full.[b]

So far as I know, Donizetti was not anticipated in this type of cabaletta. More surprisingly it was not seized upon by Verdi, perhaps because in his cabaletta days he was more concerned to release energy than express pathos. What is in no doubt is the contribution the slow cabaletta made to the flavour of Romantic melancholy, founded not in sentimentality but in dramatic irony, that pervades all the best of Donizetti's serious operas and is perhaps his most personal contribution to the form.

Other factors operated to the same end: choice of subject, vocal layout, harmony, orchestration and the shaping of individual scenes and movements. Donizetti was not interested only in swooning heroines. At least three operas, *Sancia di Castiglia*, *Lucrezia Borgia* and *Belisario*, have no love interest at all in the usual sense. They are concerned partly with politics and partly with relationships inside the family, especially between parents and children. The mutual love of father and daughter that is one of the central themes of *Belisario* was not lost on Verdi; the duet in which they set out for their lonely exile is paralleled and directly echoed in the last act of *Luisa Miller*, even down to the slow cabaletta (one of the very rare examples in Verdi). Both operas incidentally have librettos by Cammarano. There is another fine father-

daughter duet in Act III of *Maria Padilla*. In *Torquato Tasso*
Donizetti tried to combine a tragic theme, the love of the poet
for a woman above his station, with a *buffo* element represented
by a comic bass and a male chorus of courtiers who make fun
of him and also comment on the action. It is perhaps not a
complete success, but it shows enterprise, and one can almost
sense the courtiers in *Rigoletto*. This is even more evident in
Act III of *La Favorite*, where the courtiers mock Fernando
when he finds he has married the king's discarded mistress;
we think too of the laughter of Samuel and Tom in *Ballo*.
Torquato Tasso is not an *opera semiseria*, a type descending from
the French Revolution *opéra comique* with a bourgeois dom-
estic background, as in *Emilia di Liverpool* and *Linda di Chamou-
nix*, or for that matter *La sonnambula*, but an attempt to enlarge
the scope of Romantic opera by bringing together two things
much further apart, heroic tragedy on the one hand and
broad comedy on the other, as Verdi was to do in *La forza
del destino*.

The fact that Tasso, the lover-hero, is a baritone considerably darkens the vocal colour. This is very characteristic of Donizetti's serious operas, especially the later ones.
In *Belisario*, *Maria Padilla* and *Caterina Cornaro*, as well as *Tasso*,
the tenor is almost a peripheral figure; in *Maria Padilla* he is
the heroine's father who goes mad, thereby poaching the
conventional prerogatives of both baritone and soprano.
Again and again the soprano and baritone carry the main
burden of the plot, and there is often a prominent bass as well.
Marino Faliero has four basses and baritones, all important in
the action, two of them very substantial parts composed for
Tamburini and Lablache. In *Gemma di Vergy*, *Parisina*, *Pia
de' Tolomei* and *Maria di Rohan* the powerful figure of the jealous
baritone husband dominates the opera, vocally and dramatically. The magnificent scene in Act II of *Parisina*, where the
Duke is maddened by jealousy on hearing his sleeping wife
murmur her lover's name, inevitably suggests Othello—and
the grim concentration of the music is closer to Verdi's opera
than to Rossini's. *La Favorite* has a mezzo-soprano heroine,
another dominant baritone in the king, and a Grand-
Inquisitorial bass in the prior of the monastery. It was Donizetti
who established the type of dramatic baritone that Verdi was
to put to such splendid use.

As early as *Anna Bolena*, and much more later, Donizetti's
operas show a growing preoccupation with the darker emotions
of guilt, jealousy and remorse. They inspired some of his finest

music and, especially in the late works written for Paris and Vienna, are reflected in a greatly enriched harmony and orchestration, the result no doubt of contact with French Grand Opera. The bold, restless harmonic style of parts of *Dom Sébastien*, his last opera (1843), is closer to middle-period Verdi, even the Verdi of the Requiem, than to Bellini or Donizetti's own operas of a few years earlier. *La Favorite* shows how little justification there is for criticising Donizetti's accompaniments for their 'thinness and conventionality'. Not that the Italian operas lack either fulness or individuality in scoring: witness the trio in *Maria Padilla* accompanied by cor anglais alone, the long introduction for bass clarinet and harp to Act II of *Maria di Rudenz* and the original obbligato for glass harmonica in the *Lucia* mad scene.

The sombre orchestral introductions with which Donizetti liked to begin an act or important scene are often memorable in themselves and very effective in setting an atmosphere. The introduction to Act II of *Lucia* is a familiar example, and *Poliuto* and *Maria Padilla* each have more than one of outstanding quality. There is a hint of Florestan's dungeon in the C minor Andantino that begins Act III of *Torquato Tasso*. Some of these introductions suggest other Romantic composers, and not always earlier ones: for example the extended Schumannesque syncopations that begin Act II of *Sancia di Castiglia* or the startling anticipation of Mahler's First Symphony in the prelude to *Dom Sébastien*, which recurs as a funeral procession in Act III of the opera. The opening bars of Essex's scene in the Tower in *Roberto Devereux* were actually borrowed by Verdi; they might equally be early Wagner. One theme in the introduction to Act IV of *La Favorite* has a strong flavour of *Tannhäuser*; it may or may not be a coincidence that the first edition of the vocal score was arranged by Wagner. Donizetti's use of the horns, generally four of them, to evoke a sinister or Romantic atmosphere has not a little in common with *Der Freischütz*, for example in the prelude to *Maria Padilla*; it is worlds apart from *William Tell*, where Gessler's horns—an important element in the drama since for two acts they are all we hear of the tyrant—sound neither sinister nor romantic but merely jolly.

One feature in which Donizetti is nearly always at his best, and consistently superior to Bellini, is the construction of ensembles, especially the slow pieces that concentrate the action at the beginning of a finale. Everyone knows the sextet in *Lucia*, but there are plenty of others of equal quality, sextets

in Act I of *Belisario* and Act III of *Maria Padilla*, the quartet
in Act III of *La Favorite*, a magnificent septet in Act IV of
Dom Sébastien, and a complex trio-cum-quartet in Act II of
Gemma di Vergy. If a headlong stretta follows, which is not
always the case, it is sometimes arrested at the climax, by a
recitative in which the hero surrenders his sword in Act I of
Ugo, Conte di Parigi, by a death sentence and a drop from
'vivace' to 'maestoso' in Act III of *Dom Sébastien*. Towards the
end of his life Donizetti tended to abandon the stretta and
adopt unorthodox ends to acts and whole operas. In *Dom
Sébastien* again, an opera whose principal feature is its un-
compromising dramatic honesty, he concludes Act II with a
romance without cabaletta, its second stanza enriched by new
chromatic harmony, and the whole opera with a free recitative such as Verdi employed at the end of *Simon Boccanegra*.
The lovers are shot just when they think they are safe; instead
of giving them a duet of hope or farewell Donizetti cuts them off
before they can open their mouths, and the opera ends with
a defiant cry from the loyal poet Camoens. The whole scene
occupies three pages in the vocal score. This is nearly twice
as long as the astonishing last scene of *Maria di Rohan*. After
B flat has been established as the key, there is a violent plunge
into D major for the climactic recitative; B flat is regained
for a single bar, whereupon the tonality collapses into E flat
minor during the quick nine-bar coda, and only just gets
back in time for the curtain. An earlier and weaker opera,
Marino Faliero, also ends with a dramatic recitative, punctuated by the fall of an executioner's axe. The finale of *Belisario*
is on the face of it a big solo scene for the soprano, the com-
monest type of conclusion in Rossini and Bellini. But the
cantabile is separated from the cabaletta—another slow one—
by a beautifully managed episode, a conflation of funeral
march, ensemble and recitative during which Belisario is
carried in mortally wounded; the voices are superimposed
conversationally on the march rhythm without interrupting
it, and Belisario's death triggers off the cabaletta, sung by his
treacherous but now penitent wife. This opera also contains
a prime example of the patriotic *Risorgimento*-type aria,
'Trema, Bisanzio', which has the same accompaniment figure
as 'Di quella pira' in *Il trovatore*.

The big double arias and duets by no means always adhere
to the conventional plan of a cantabile followed by a two-
stanza cabaletta; in the late operas they very seldom do.
Almost all the set pieces in *Caterina Cornaro*, *Maria di Rohan* and

Dom Sébastien and many in earlier operas (the father-daughter duet in *Maria Padilla* is an outstanding example) are free and unpredictable in design, abandoning symmetry to follow the dictates of the plot. This is far too complex a matter to explore here, but Donizetti's duets and trios in particular, and a comparison of his methods with those of Verdi, would make a rewarding study. A very effective stroke that Donizetti made his own, though it was not peculiar to him, is the introduction of the second voice in a duet with a change of mode as well as new material. There are two beautiful examples in *Poliuto*. In Act II the baritone Severo has a regular sixteen-bar stanza in E minor with short agitated phrases, at the end of which Paolina (who formerly loved him but is now married to Poliuto) enters with a much broader melody in E major beginning on a long-held top E. The fact that her words are sad ('Ei non vegga il pianto mio') enhances the impact. A similar stroke, in the same key, distinguishes the duet for Paolina and Poliuto in the last act: she urges him, in the minor, to escape a horrible death by renouncing his Christian faith; he proclaims his belief in a happier afterlife in the major, again entering on the top E. One thinks inevitably of 'Ah! che la morte ognora' in *Il trovatore*, especially as the accompaniment changes to triplets at the same time. There is a similar moment in the duet for the two sisters in Act II of *Maria Padilla*. Other personal traits—again not unique—are Donizetti's habit of vacillating between major and tonic minor in the course of a melody, to produce an effect of plaintiveness or pathos, and of modulating unexpectedly just before the end of a paragraph. In Camoens's cavatina in Act I of *Dom Sébastien* he goes from F to A in the third bar of a nine-bar tune, regains F in the fifth and is in G flat by the seventh. In the same character's Act III romance, a much longer melody, he suddenly moves from E flat to G flat two bars before the cadence, and then after regaining the tonic adds a second paragraph in E flat minor. Neither of these arias has anything approaching a cabaletta.

Donizetti makes happy use of Rossini's trick of a running tune in the orchestra, sometimes repeated in different keys, while the voices carry on independently, but he invests it with a more powerful irony, for example in Act II of *Lucia*, where the almost flippant A major melody during the recitative before the signing of the marriage contract returns with mocking effect when Edgar learns of the wedding. There is a very striking instance of this sort of texture in the little duet

81

for two spies in Act I of *Lucrezia Borgia*, where a sinuous tune
winds its ironical way through the orchestra, punctuated by
pairs of staccato quaver chords, while the voices hatch a plot
in free parlando. This was almost certainly the inspiration for
the colloquy between Rigoletto and Sparafucile, which is
identical in layout and dramatic context and conveys the
same impression of dirty business afoot, and more remotely
for the entry of the Grand Inquisitor in *Don Carlos*.

Anyone who considers Donizetti's choruses may at once
recoil from the tiresome jauntiness of the wedding guests in
Lucia, one of the most prehensile tunes ever written. But he
can do much better than this. *Belisario* contains choruses of
puzzled senators in the first act and exiles in the second that
are not only impressive in themselves but go a long way towards establishing these bodies as living characters in the
drama instead of a mere background. The scene in Act II of
Roberto Devereux where the courtiers await the outcome of
Essex's trial, based on an ostinato figure and a long winding
melody in the orchestra, is a marvellous compound of lyricism
and suspense. The unison prayer for male voices, 'Divo
spirto', in Act II of *Pia de' Tolomei* is fully the equal of the
famous prayers in *Mosè* and *Nabucco*. *Lucrezia Borgia* has three
vivid choruses of ruffians, at once swashbuckling, furtive and
sinister, that play an important part in the plot, and *Caterina
Cornaro* a chorus of assassins so fraught with menace that it
reduces Banquo's murderers in *Macbeth* to the status of a child's
puppets.

The many direct anticipations of Verdi to be found in
Donizetti's operas are not confined to the chance resemblances
one would expect between two near-contemporaries using
the same idiom and writing for the same audience.[5] Of course
Verdi was influenced by Rossini, Bellini and Donizetti—
it could hardly be otherwise—and sometimes used them as
models. But I suggest that Donizetti was easily the most
important of the three, for two principal reasons. First, when
Verdi echoes him either literally (which is not to say deliberately) or in more generalized fashion, one constantly finds
quite intricate parallels, not only in mood and material but
in key and dramatic situation. Second, these echoes are far
less common in Verdi's early operas than in those of his growing and complete maturity. There are very few before the

82

---

[5] For a fuller account see my paper 'Some Echoes of Donizetti in Verdi's
Operas', *Atti del III° congresso internazionale di studi verdiani*, Parma, 1974,
pp. 122–47

first version of *Macbeth* (1847) but a great many in the operas
from then on, up to and including *La forza del destino*. It was
when Verdi began to individualize his characters and explore
their more complex emotions that he became most susceptible
to Donizetti's influence. This is not as surprising a conclusion
as it may sound. We are apt to look at the early Verdi with
hindsight, knowing what he was to achieve later, and scarcely
knowing Donizetti at all. But whereas the Verdi of the 1840s
was a composer of immense energy and spasmodic insight,
the Donizetti of the later serious operas was a more experienced
and in many ways a more subtle artist. The early Verdi was
simply not ready for him.

Direct echoes in the same keys are sometimes very striking,
as between the last scene of *Anna Bolena*, where the queen's
mind wanders into the past (Ex. 1a), and another queen in
the same situation, Lady Macbeth sleep-walking (Ex. 1b).

83

Ex. 1

The virtually identical melody, harmony, rhythm and key
in Exx. 2a and 2b correspond to their virtually identical
dramatic situations and even their position in the operas.
Both are ariosos of the characteristic Donizettian type,
mentioned earlier, the first sung by Percy in *Anna Bolena* after
he knows he has lost Anna for ever, the second by the duke
in Rigoletto when he thinks he has lost Gilda. Another
pregnant arioso is sung by Ghino in the first scene of *Pia
de' Tolomei* when he thinks Pia has betrayed his love (Ex. 3).
It is scarcely necessary to quote the parallel in *La traviata*.
The duets in *Belisario* and *Luisa Miller* in which father and
daughter decide to spend the rest of their lives in exile are
similar all through in mood and layout, and built around the
same keys, F major and minor and A flat major, though
Donizetti's cabaletta is in F, Verdi's in A flat. Each begins

84

with a falling seventh; Belisario sings it to the words 'O figlia!'
(Ex. 4a), Verdi leaves it to the orchestra (Ex. 4b). Or again,
two tenors cursing, both (as in the last pair of examples) to
words by Cammarano; Edgar in *Lucia di Lammermoor*, on

Ex. 4

Lucia's betrayal, and Rodolfo in the last act of *Luisa Miller*, cursing the day he was born, may sing in different keys, but rhythm, accompaniment and general shape are the same.

Il trovatore echoes at least five Donizetti operas—six if we count one melody that occurs in two works—of which three might be mentioned here. First, the duet for Elizabeth and Essex in Act I of *Roberto Devereux* (Ex. 5) is mirrored in the

Ex. 5

trio that ends Act I of *Trovatore*. Second, a prominent theme from the finale of Act II of *Poliuto* (Ex. 6), which also occurs

Ex. 6

in *Maria di Rudenz*, may have suggested part of the Count di Luna's 'Il balen'. And third, Riccardo's aria 'Alma soave e cara' in Act II of *Maria de Rohan* (Ex. 7), a late opera consistently prophetic of Verdi in mood, especially in the last two acts, has a parallel in Leonora's 'Mira, di acerbe lagrime', which has the same accompaniment figure and the same harmony, including the soulful diminished seventh in the third bar.

Ex. 7

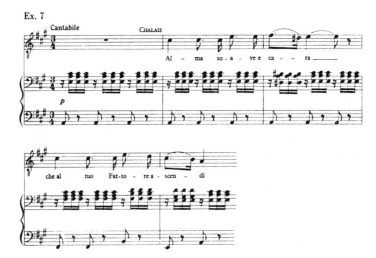

There are two remarkable reminiscences of *Roberto Devereux* in *Un ballo in maschera*. In key, harmony and both its principal phrases the introduction to Essex's scene in the Tower (Ex. 8a) was virtually taken over by Verdi for the opening of Ulrica's incantation (Ex. 8b). There is a more subtle relationship

Ex. 8

between the two big love duets, whose dramatic situation is identical: the tenor is keeping a secret assignation with the

wife of his closest friend, and this leads directly to the catastrophe. The closest thematic resemblance is between a
secondary idea—not the main theme—in the slow $\frac{6}{8}$ sections
near the beginning, bars 5-8 in Donizetti, 13–16 in Verdi.
Each composer repeats the phrase, but Verdi—now in full
maturity more than ten years after Donizetti's death—makes
more of it. There is an interesting tonal link here. Donizetti's
movement is in D flat, Verdi's in F; but when Amelia takes
the phrase over from Riccardo she steers it into Donizetti's
key with the harmony it had on its first appearance in his
opera but not in Verdi's.[c]

One might suppose that by 1862, the year of *La forza del
destino*, Verdi would have outgrown Donizetti. Far from it,
though he does of course enrich him. There are three surprisingly close parallels. One is the scene which occurs in
both *Forza* and *La Favorite* where the heroine (Leonora in
each case) comes to a monastery, hears monks praying
accompanied by an organ, and longs for sanctuary and forgiveness. The whole treatment of voices and accompaniment,
as well as one phrase sung by the soprano, is remarkably
similar. When Verdi's Leonora thanks the Father Superior
for giving her sanctuary and calls on the angelic choir to
welcome her, the music echoes the duet from *Poliuto* in which
hero and heroine claim the blessing of the Church in their
martyrdom (Ex. 9). The tune is not the same, but almost
everything else is; key, rhythm in the voice parts (steady $\frac{4}{4}$
crotchets), accompaniment with triplet arpeggios on the harp,
and even some of the words (a few bars later Verdi's Leonora
sings 'Plaudite, o cori angelici, mi perdonò il Signor' to a
variant of the same melody). And the overture to *La Favorite*,
produced in 1840, must surely have been at the back of Verdi's
mind when he wrote the overture to *Forza* more than twenty
years later. There are resemblances between all three themes in
both works, but the most notable feature is the similarity of
atmosphere and design: an agitated nervous main theme in
the minor, then a soaring melody with a climax in the major,
starting quietly against tremolo accompaniment and rising
higher at the second statement before falling back to a recall
of the opening. The climax of both overtures is a *fortissimo*
statement of the major melody at the end.[d]

There is one significant point about these examples. None
of them is musically trivial. They tend to show both composers
at their best and most characteristic, taking into consideration
the period when they were written. The conclusion to be

87

Ex. 9

88

drawn is that there was a quality in Donizetti's imagination that appealed to the maturing Verdi, who responded in much the same way to similar dramatic stimuli. His unconscious memory did the rest. From *Rigoletto* on of course he far out-stripped Donizetti. But the man who inspired Verdi in this way was a considerable artist in his own right.

The following recorded illustrations were heard during the lecture:

a Part of the cabaletta 'Quel sangue versato' from Act III of *Roberto Devereux*.

b The cavatina 'Una voce al cor d'intorno' and cabaletta 'Egli riede?' from Act I of *Gemma di Vergy*.

c The opening ⁶⁄₈ sections of the duets 'Dacchè tornasti, ahi misera!' from Act I of *Roberto Devereux* and 'Non sai tu che se l'anima mia' from Act II of *Un ballo in maschera*.

d Part of the overture to *La Favorite*.

WAGNER'S MUSICAL SKETCHES
FOR *SIEGFRIEDS TOD*[*]

ROBERT BAILEY

W AGNER originally planned to make just one opera from the Nibelung material with which he had become familiar during his years in Dresden. In 1848, according to his usual habit, he wrote an elaborate prose scenario and then a complete libretto for a "grand heroic opera in three acts" (and a prologue) called *Siegfrieds Tod*.[1] Later on, he expanded his material into a tremendous cycle for three days and a preliminary evening, and *Siegfrieds Tod*, after careful revision, assumed its position as the final opera in *Der Ring des Nibelungen*. The structure of the whole cycle thus parallels that of the first dramatic conception, eventually called *Götterdämmerung*,[2] which serves as "a recapitula-

[*] I appreciate this opportunity to offer my sincere gratitude to Professor Strunk who drew this subject to my attention and who, with characteristic generosity, turned over to me his own transcriptions and notes on the problem. Transcriptions from Wagner's sketches are printed here with the gracious permission of Mme Winifred Wagner, Bayreuth. Portions of this essay were delivered as a lecture at the annual meeting of the American Musicological Society in Washington, D.C., December 26-29, 1964.

[1] The scenario was published by Otto Strobel in *Richard Wagner: Skizzen und Entwürfe zur Ring-Dichtung, mit der Dichtung "Der junge Siegfried"* (Munich, 1930), pp. 38-55. This scenario, dated October 20, 1848, at the end, lacks the prologue for which Wagner later made an undated prose sketch, published *ibid.*, pp. 56-58. The poem, complete with prologue, was written between November 12 and 28, 1848, according to the dates at the beginning and end of the manuscript; it was revised during the first weeks of 1849 and, in this form, was incorporated into the German edition of Wagner's collected writings: *Sämtliche Schriften und Dichtungen*, 5th edn. (Leipzig, n.d.), II, 167-228. (The pagination is the same in the 6th edition.)

[2] The title remained *Siegfrieds Tod*, even in the cycle, for some time. Wagner changed it because of the conclusion of the work, which was not given its final form until after a considerable portion of the music had been composed. The first documented mention of the new title occurs in a letter to Franz Müller of Weimar, dated June 22, 1856, i.e., several months after *Die Walküre* was complete in full score. For the important passages of this letter and for further information on the problem of the ending, see Strobel, *Skizzen*, pp. 258-61, and his supplementary article, "Zur Entstehungsgeschichte der Götterdämmerung: Unbekannte Dokumente aus Wagners Dichterwerkstatt," in *Die Musik*, xxv/5 (February 1933), 336-41. Ernest Newman has summarized the essential facts in *The Life of Richard Wagner*, II (New York, 1937), 354-56.

tion of the whole, a prologue and three pieces."[3] It is now possible to trace almost every step of that complicated evolution of the poem to its completion at the end of 1852, thanks to the excellent publications of Otto Strobel,[4] archivist to House Wahnfried until his untimely death in 1953.

Shortly after Wagner had finished the initial revision of *Siegfrieds Tod*—during the first weeks of 1849[5]—he became involved with the revolutionary forces in the Dresden uprising and ultimately was forced to flee German territory. He devoted most of his time during the ensuing years to literary activity: this is the period not only of the *Ring* poem, but also of his longest and most famous prose treatises—*Art and Revolution, The Artwork of the Future, Opera and Drama*, and *A Communication to My Friends*. But he also began sketching music for *Siegfrieds Tod* in the summer of 1850. Accordingly, not only are these the first musical sketches connected with the *Ring* in any way,[6] but also they constitute Wagner's only dramatic music between the completion of *Lohengrin* in the spring of 1848 and the beginning of work on *Das Rheingold* in the late autumn of 1853. As far as *Siegfrieds Tod* was concerned, Wagner himself later wrote about this period as follows:

> During that period, in the autumn of 1848, I did not even think about the possibility of performing *Siegfrieds Tod*, but regarded the technical completion of its poem and isolated attempts at setting it to music as nothing more than a private satisfaction to which I treated myself at that time of disgust with public affairs and of withdrawal from them.[7]

[3] ". . . *eine Wiederholung des Ganzen, ein Vorspiel und drei Stücke.*" From the entry in Cosima Wagner's diary for September 9, 1876, published in *Bayreuther Blätter*, LIX/1 (Winter 1936), 5.

[4] For an English summary of Strobel's publications with critical commentary, see Ernest Newman, *Life*, II, 24-31 and 325-61, and "The Nibelung's Ring" in *The Wagner Operas* (New York, 1949), pp. 393-450.

[5] Strobel, *Skizzen*, pp. 59-60, and Newman, *Life*, II, 31.

[6] The first draft of the poem contains a musical fragment in the margin on the page with Siegfried's monologue and death in the second scene of Act III. This page was first published in facsimile by Houston Stewart Chamberlain, *Richard Wagner* (Munich, 1896), following p. 266. Chamberlain assumed that this fragment was related to *Siegfrieds Tod* even though it has the appearance of trombone parts for something else as yet unidentified. The page is also reproduced in Erich Engel, *Richard Wagners Leben und Werke im Bilde* (Vienna, 1913), p. 169.

[7] *Eine Mitteilung an meine Freunde*, in *Schriften*, IV, 331.

He had also been encouraged to proceed with the music by Liszt, who by the spring of 1850 was reporting favorably on the preparations under way at Weimar for the forthcoming production of *Lohengrin*. Liszt promised to use his influence to persuade the Grand Duke to commission *Siegfrieds Tod* for Weimar and to give Wagner a grant which would enable him to finish the opera within a year.

The commission never materialized, but Wagner nonetheless set to work with enthusiasm. As he tells us in his autobiography,

> I now felt very much attracted to accepting the Weimar proposal. Still worn out by my strenuous labor on *Opera and Drama* and exhausted by so much which weighed sorrowfully upon my heart, I sat down again—for the first time in a long while—at my Haertel piano which had been recovered from the Dresden catastrophe, in order to see how I might get started on the composition of my weighty epic drama. In a hasty sketch, I drafted music for the Norns' scene which had only been outlined in that first version [of the poem]; just as I was setting Brünnhilde's first address to Siegfried to music, however, all my courage failed me since I could not refrain from asking myself which singer should bring this heroine to life the following year.[8]

Wagner's reference to *Opera and Drama* is incorrect, for he did not begin work on the treatise until after he had abandoned his attempts to write the music for *Siegfrieds Tod*. He was indeed exhausted by a great deal which weighed sorrowfully upon his heart at that time, but it was not the strenuous labor of writing *Opera and Drama*; rather it was the disastrous love affair with Jessie Laussot in Bordeaux,[9] which Wagner apparently felt obliged to smooth over for the benefit of Cosima to whom he dictated the autobiography in later years. In *A Communication to My Friends*, written only a year or so after these events, his chronology is more accurate:

> After I had returned [to Zurich], I deceived myself once more with the thought of carrying out the musical setting of *Siegfrieds Tod*: half-despair was still at the root of this decision, for I knew I should now be writing this music only for paper. The intolerably

[8] *Mein Leben* ("Erste authentische Veröffentlichung," Munich, 1963), p. 541.
[9] For further biographical information on this episode, see Newman, *Life*, II, 136-58.

clear knowledge of this disgusted me once more with my project; in consciousness of the fact that in any case I should, for the most part, be ever so completely misunderstood in my endeavor, I again had recourse to literary work and wrote my book on *Opera and Drama*.[10]

In short, Wagner made sketches for the music of *Siegfrieds Tod* before he had written *Opera and Drama*, and the treatise is thus to some extent the result of at least some practical experience in working out a new manner of writing musical drama, rather than purely a presentation of theoretical ideas in advance, as we have always supposed. The two passages just quoted indicate some of the reasons why he gave up the project before completing even the prologue. But he must also have felt the need to organize his new ideas more concretely before attempting to apply them on a grand scale.

In 1933, an extended musical sketch for the prologue of this work was published in facsimile.[11] At the beginning, it bears the date August 12, 1850, and it contains a careful draft in ink of the Norns' scene and continues through the second speech in the ensuing duet of Brünnhilde and Siegfried. While Newman and Westernhagen both referred to it as a "Composition Sketch," Strobel[12] called it an "Orchestral Sketch," implying in his use of this term that there must also have been an earlier and less elaborate sketch for the same material.[13] The published sketch, in addition to being carefully

[10] *Schriften*, IV, 337.

[11] In *L'Illustration* (February 11, 1933), pp. 166-68. This sketch has been discussed by Newman in *Life*, II, 159-61, and in *Wagner Operas*, pp. 412-14, and also by Curt von Westernhagen, *Vom Holländer zum Parsifal: Neue Wagner-Studien* (Zurich, 1962), pp. 38-54, and "Die Kompositions-Skizze zu 'Siegfrieds Tod' aus dem Jahre 1850" in *Neue Zeitschrift für Musik*, 124/5 (May 1963), pp. 178-82. For a long time the sketch was in the possession of M. Louis Barthou, who left it to the Bibliothèque Nationale in Paris. It has since been sold and is now in France in private hands.

[12] *Richard Wagner. Leben und Schaffen: Eine Zeittafel* (Bayreuth, 1952), p. 41.

[13] Wagner's procedure in working out the music for a dramatic work perhaps requires some explanation. He ordinarily made at least two complete drafts: first, a very hasty and sketchy one in pencil, and secondly, a more detailed and elaborate one in ink. Strobel, in an attempt to put all the treasures of the Bayreuth archives into some kind of order, categorized these drafts with the names *Kompositions-skizzen* and *Orchesterskizzen*, and through the writings of Newman the terms have become familiar to English-speaking readers as "Composition Sketch" and "Orchestral Sketch." Wagner never referred to these drafts in any consistent way, and the terms are misleading, for the function and degree of elaboration of the drafts

written in ink with a minimum of corrections, contains detailed dynamic indications, tempo indications, and some stage directions, elements usually lacking in a Composition Sketch. Strobel's assumption was, of course, entirely correct: the Composition Sketch for *Siegfrieds Tod* is now in the Library of Congress, Gertrude Clarke Whittall Foundation.[14]

We can recognize at a glance that this sketch was made before August 12, when Wagner began the Orchestral Sketch, and we may assume that it was written some time after July 27, on which date

---

changed drastically during his career. As the orchestral fabric became more complicated, he naturally found it necessary to work out things more extensively in advance of the full score, so that the first draft of *Tristan*, for example, represents in many passages as advanced a stage as the second draft for *Tannhäuser*. And, similarly, for the last works of all, the first draft is nearly as complete as the more bare passages of the Orchestral Sketch of *Tristan*. The orchestral part gradually requires more staves, occasionally using as many as four in the latest works. The term "Orchestral Sketch" is particularly misleading because these drafts do not in any way approximate an orchestral score, and indications for the instrumentation are minimal. We must always bear in mind that anything actually noted down was much more meaningful to Wagner than it would be to us without our preliminary knowledge of the final version. In any event, all Composition Sketches have in common an emphasis upon the setting of the text, with the accompaniment for the moment relegated to the background; and the Orchestral Sketches have in common their attempt to bring the most essential details of the accompaniment into final focus. Once the Orchestral Sketch was complete, Wagner could consider his creative task at an end, for it sufficed to remind him of the music in detail, and all that remained for him was to work out the specific instrumentation in the definitive full score.

[14] The manuscript was formerly in the possession of a certain Gustav Herrmann of Leipzig. In 1913, he allowed it to appear in an exhibition whose catalogue contains the first known description. The entry begins as follows: "*Musical Sketches for 'Siegfrieds Tod,'* Wagner's first Nibelung drama, for which he worked out the libretto in November, 1848. It was to contain three acts and a prologue. The present musical sketches, made in 1849 [*sic*], are the sole evidence for the fact that Wagner in these early years was already thinking of even the musical realization of the Nibelung material, and at the same time proof that he found the main motives for the music of the Nibelung trilogy at that time." *Richard Wagner Gedächtnis-Ausstellung, aus Anlass des hundertjährigen Geburtstages Richard Wagners*, veranstaltet vom Komitee für das Leipziger Richard-Wagner-Denkmal und dem Stadtgeschichtlichen Museum zu Leipzig (Leipzig, May 1913), pp. 22-23. There follows a short paragraph (paraphrased in Westernhagen, *Wagner-Studien*, p. 39n) describing the sheet sufficiently well to identify it as the one now in the Library of Congress, which acquired it from an intermediate owner, Jerome Stonborough. Meanwhile, the first two lines of this sketch had been published in quasi-facsimile by Julius Kapp in *Richard Wagner: Sein Leben, sein Werk, seine Welt in 260 Bildern* (Berlin-Schöneberg, 1933), p. 50.

95

he made it clear in a letter to his friend, Theodor Uhlig, that he had not yet started composing the music for *Siegfrieds Tod* but was about to do so and that for this purpose he had procured a *Rastral* (a device for drawing musical staves).[15] The Washington Sketch is actually written on paper with staves drawn by such a device, and Wagner consistently uses lower case letters for the initial letters of common nouns,[16] a habit which he does not seem to have picked up until the winter of 1849-50. Like the published sketch, the earlier one is a single large sheet written on both sides. It, too, contains a setting of the prologue—the entire Norns' scene, with a few omissions which are added in the Orchestral Sketch, and the first part of the duet, which continues for an additional eleven lines beyond the later version. There are also sketches for music associated with the Valkyries. The lower portion of the second side of this sheet has been published in reduced facsimile.[17]

At this time, Wagner had not even thought of an opera which would correspond to the one we know today as *Die Walküre*, but the presence on this sheet of music for the Valkyries is not surprising. In the original versions of *Siegfrieds Tod*, he had planned to have all the Valkyries come to Brünnhilde in the third scene of Act I to plead with her to give up the ring which Siegfried had entrusted to her keeping during the duet. In the final poem for the *Ring*, however, it is only Waltraute who steals away from Valhalla on the hopeless mission. Wagner's first conception was a melody in two complementary phrases:

96

[15] *Richard Wagner's Briefe an Theodor Uhlig, Wilhelm Fischer, Ferdinand Heine* (Leipzig, 1888), Letter No. 14, p. 45. This publication gives no date for the letter since there is none on the original document. Glasenapp, in *Das Leben Richard Wagners*, II, 5th edn. (Leipzig, 1910), 434 dates it July 27 without a word of explanation. Nevertheless, this date proves to be correct, as can be seen in the dated letter of the same day to Julie Ritter, in which Wagner says that he has had "a rather lengthy letter to write to Uhlig" that very day. This letter to Julie Ritter leaves no doubt that the letter in question is the one to which Wagner refers. See Siegmund von Hausegger, ed., *Richard Wagners Briefe an Frau Julie Ritter* (Munich, 1920), Letter No. VI, p. 45.

[16] Wagner had planned to publish the poem in the spring of 1850, but this idiosyncrasy, together with his insistence upon the use of Roman type, had made the printer refuse his manuscript. For the projected publication, he wrote a preface which was published for the first time in Edgar Istel, "König Ludwigs 'Wagner-Buch,'" in *Die Musik*, X/1 (1910-11), 15-23. That preface was later incorporated into the 6th edition of *Schriften*, XVI, 84-85.

[17] Emanuel Winternitz, *Musical Autographs from Monteverdi to Hindemith* (Princeton, 1955), II, Plate 131.

Ex. 1 (from the Washington Sketch)

He soon hit upon the following continuation:

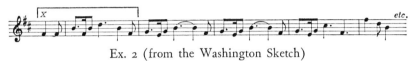

Ex. 2 (from the Washington Sketch)

The section marked *x* replaces the section so marked in Ex. 1. Because Wagner evidently wrote out the label "Walküren" before he noted down the theme, we are safe in assuming that he conceived the theme with the Valkyries in mind but without any specific textual association. Afterwards, he probably looked through the text of this scene and found that the lines of the concluding chorus could be adapted to the melody, and then wrote out the *incipit* above the first measure.[18]

As it stands, the melody differs rhythmically from its final form, in that the note on the second beat in each measure is sustained through most of the third. The second four-measure phrase begins in the dominant minor here and returns directly to the tonic, so that the melody as a whole lacks the vibrant color it later assumed. Wagner's next step was to elaborate a revised form of the melody *in ink*:

Ex. 3 (from the Washington Sketch)

[18] This kind of situation occurred frequently. See, for example, Wagner's letter of July 9, 1859, to Mathilde Wesendonk (Wolfgang Golther, ed., *Richard Wagner an Mathilde Wesendonk: Tagebuchblätter und Briefe, 1853-1871* [Berlin, 1908], p. 161), regarding a melody which he did not even know belonged in the final scene of *Siegfried* until after he had searched through the text!

Ex. 3 (cont.)

The first measure of the accompaniment is worked out, and Wagner has transposed the second phrase so that it now begins in the relative major, evidently in order to avoid the square feeling given by the immediate return to the tonic and to postpone the high f-sharp until the end. He has carefully adapted the text, and in addition, we find the call of "Hoiho!" associated with the Valkyries in the later work, but not part of the *Siegfrieds Tod* poem at all—a feature which has grown directly out of the *musical* conception. On the other hand, the adaptation of the text has necessitated some rhythmic changes in the earlier part of the melody.

The last two lines of this portion of the manuscript show the whole melody in B major and written out in octaves, presumably to indicate fuller instrumentation. Once again the third phrase is repeated, and except for two further details—the up-beat into the seventh measure and the c♮ (Neapolitan) in the eleventh—the melody has now assumed the final form in which it is used in *Die Walküre* and in the concert excerpt known as the "Ride of the Valkyrics."[19]

99

[19] The instrumental selection known as the "Ride of the Valkyries" is not simply the orchestral accompaniment of the beginning of the third act of *Die Walküre* with an appended "concert ending," but a new composition based on the material of that scene. Wagner made the excerpt in Biebrich during the autumn of 1862 for a series of concerts projected for the coming winter in Vienna. On October 14, he wrote to Wendelin Weissheimer, who was responsible for the preparation of the parts in Leipzig: "It was difficult to prepare the piece properly; I had to rearrange the order of various passages in the score ["musste in der Partitur bald vor, bald rückwärts greifen"]. Yet, as you will find, everything is unerringly put in order; I have even attached a special set of instructions." The text of the entire letter is printed in W. Weissheimer, *Erlebnisse mit Richard Wagner* . . . , 2nd edn. (Stuttgart and Leipzig, 1898), pp. 182-84. Glasenapp quotes only the first of these two sentences, and his ensuing account of the situation (in *Leben*, III, 4th edn., Leipzig, 1905, 397) is misleading in its implication that Wagner himself wrote out a full score of the new piece, from which Weissheimer could then get the parts copied. A later passage in Weissheimer's memoirs (pp. 209-210) makes it clear that this was not the case: "According to agreement I had remained in Leipzig in order to keep the copyists under my eye and to assist them with advice in their huge and very complicated task of writing out Wagner's scores. This was especially necessary in the case of the 'Ride of the Valkyries,' which had to be written out in an order different from that in which it stood in the score, because for concert use Wagner had excluded the vocal parts and had therefore undertaken changes in the arrangement of the piece. Close attention had to be paid to this and other circumstances so that nothing would go wrong." In other words, the parts were copied from the full score of the *third act of the opera*, Wagner having indicated the new ordering and supplied instructions about the ending and other necessary changes.

He conducted the premiere of the new piece at the first of the Vienna concerts

Newman has discussed two later drafts of this melody, the earliest known versions at the time he was writing.[20] The first, dated July 23, 1851, contains only the first four bars shown above in Ex. 3, and Newman correctly assumed that the motive had been conceived much earlier. The second sketch, made for an autograph album, is dated November 12, 1852, and continues for eight measures with a change in text in the last line, which eliminates the up-beat into the seventh measure. Detailed examination of the various versions of the last line of this quatrain illustrates Wagner's procedure in gradually working out text and music, each in relation to the other. The various versions of the text may be summarized as follows:

Prose Sketch (1848): nach Walhall erschlagene Sieger zu geleiten

Poem (1848/9): nach Walhall zu führen erschlagene Sieger

Washington Sketch (1850): zu führen nach Walhall erschlagene Sieger

Autograph Album (1852): wehrliche Sieger zu senden nach Walhall

on December 26, 1862, where it was an immediate and extraordinary success. He conducted it again at a concert in Munich given at the command of Ludwig II on December 11, 1864. In spite of the public's continuing interest in the work, however, Wagner was never satisfied with it. Several years later, the following notice—inspired, if not actually written by the composer—appeared in the *Musikalisches Wochenblatt* (11/44, October 27, 1871, p. 700): "For the purpose of settling various enquiries about the means of obtaining the score of the so-called 'Ride of the Valkyries' by R. Wagner, we herewith inform our readers that as yet, such a composition does not even exist, as there is no score at all for it from Wagner's hand. The orchestral parts for this piece were put together at one time by a capable Viennese copyist,—to be sure, according to Wagner's delineation of certain passages of the *Walküre* score (brought about, however, by special circumstances),—copied at some time or other, and later bought and used by B. Bilse, among others, behind Wagner's back and without his consent. Richard Wagner protests categorically against such a patchwork being presented to a concert audience as an actual piece of music,—a patchwork which he sanctioned only at a time of distress in making up a really 'attractive' concert program." The reference to a copyist in Vienna, rather than in Leipzig, undoubtedly resulted from a confusion in Wagner's mind later on, since the parts for most of the other selections played in the Vienna concerts had indeed been copied there. An interesting sidelight on this problem is the fact that among the copyists in Vienna was none other than Johannes Brahms! (See *Mein Leben*, p. 817.)

[20] *Life*, II, 240-42.

100

In Ex. 3, double alliteration is paralleled by rhythmic similarity in the first and second measures, and again in the fifth and sixth:

> nach *s*üden wir *z*iehen
> *s*iege zu *z*eugen
>
> and
>
> für *h*elden zu *f*echten
> *h*elden zu *f*ällen

If the version of the poem had been followed in the last line, the first syllable of the word "führen" would occur on the second beat in alliteration with "fechten" and "fällen," whereas no such alliterative parallel exists between the first two lines. Wagner therefore reversed the order of the first two phrases of the last line. The parallel structure is heightened by the new text of 1852: the initial "f" is eliminated altogether, as is the weak syllable at the beginning of the line, thus making the two couplets of the text and the two phrases of accompanying music exactly complementary in rhythm and placement of alliterative syllables.

When Wagner wrote *Die Walküre* later on, he used this melody only as an instrumental motive, and it is a striking characteristic of his unique imagination that this melody should have lingered in his memory in a form conditioned and changed by the gradual adaptation of texts with which it is nowhere associated in the opera. With this early conception in 1850 of an important musical motive, Wagner has established the tonality of a whole scene (*Die Walküre*, III/1) in advance of the composition of any of the music for the present *Ring*. This is also true of the Norns' scene, as has been pointed out by Newman.[21] The opening portion of that scene in *Götterdämmerung* is in E♭ minor, just as it is in these sketches for *Siegfrieds Tod*, made some nineteen years before, even though the two versions of that scene have entirely different texts.

A complete composite transcription of the music for the prologue is appended to this study. I have followed the reading of the Orchestral Sketch (the *L'Illustration* Sketch) as far as it goes (up through m. 166) and taken the remaining material from the earlier Composition Sketch (the Washington Sketch), supplying the text and a detail of the accompaniment in the last nine measures. The prologue does not run straight on from beginning to end in the earlier sketch, but the order of Wagner's procedure is not difficult to determine. He began in ink at the top of the sheet with the opening of the pro-

101

---

[21] *Ibid.*, p. 160.

logue; the use of ink may indicate that he was copying or elaborating a still earlier sketch of some kind. After making quite a few corrections, he broke off at m. 20. The remainder of the prologue is written in pencil and is thus probably the first draft. The passage in ink (see Ex. 4) extends onto the fourth staff. Beginning at the end of the fourth staff, Wagner continued in pencil through m. 41. He then turned the sheet over and started at the top with m. 56, continued through m. 77, and switched back to the first side to complete the Norns' scene (through the first major cadence of the instrumental epilogue at m. 108). The last four staves on the first side contain the beginning of the duet without the orchestral introduction, through the fourth line of Siegfried's first speech (m. 157). The duet continues at the bottom of the second side, the sketches for the music of the Valkyries having intervened, probably before Wagner began composing the duet. His work with the Washington fragment may be summarized as follows (measure numbers as in my composite transcription):

102

I. Recto, staves 1-4	Ink	(Mm. 1-20: elaborated version?)	Prologue/ Scene 1
II. Recto, staves 4-6	Pencil	(29-41: first draft, no text)	
III. Verso, staves 1-5	Pencil	(56-77: first draft)	
IV. Recto, staves 6-9	Pencil	(77-108: first draft)	
V. Verso, single staves 6 and 7	Pencil	(Valkyries: first draft; textual incipit only)	Act I/ Scene 3
VI. Verso, staves 8-11	Ink	(Valkyries: elaborated version; includes text)	
VII. Recto, staves 10-13	Pencil	(122-57: first draft)	Prologue/ Scene 2
VIII. Verso, staves 12-14	Pencil	(158-92: first draft)	

The declamatory style of the vocal lines and the harmonic style of the accompaniment are reminiscent of *Lohengrin*. But in some respects, Wagner has tried to get away from the more "regular" structure and the effect of squareness in his earlier works. In the

Norns' scene, for example, he has hit upon a new technique of tripartite organization. First of all, there are the three characters who sing of the past, the present, and the future. There are three occurrences of a refrain and three major narrative sections. Throughout, Wagner has consistently avoided traditional phrase lengths of four and eight measures. The overall tonal organization, with E minor used as the tonality contrasting with E♭ minor, is also a distinctly new feature. The formal structure of the scene may be diagrammed as follows:

Measures		First Norn (PAST)	Second Norn (PRESENT)	Third Norn (FUTURE)
1-9	*REFRAIN* 3 mm. (instrumental) + 6 mm. (vocal) 6/4 e♭ minor			
10-20	SECTION I: *Alberich and the Rheingold* 6/4 e♭ minor	3 mm.	3 mm.	5 mm.
21-29	*REFRAIN*			
30-47	SECTION II: *Gods and Giants: Grief* *of the Gods* **C** e minor	6 mm.	6 mm.	6 mm.
48-56	*REFRAIN*			
56-77	SECTION III: *Siegfried and Brünnhilde* **C** e♭ minor→E♭ major	6 mm.	6 mm.	9 mm.
78-80	*MODIFIED REFRAIN* 3 mm. (vocal) 6/4 E♭ major			
81-93	CODA (vocal) 6/4 E♭ major	2 mm.	2 mm.	2 mm. + 6 mm. *à 3*
94-108	*Instrumental epilogue* 6/4→ **C** E♭ major			

103

The sketch in ink at the top of the first side of the Composition Sketch represents a version of the first twenty measures (Refrain and Section I) even earlier than that shown in the complete transcription:

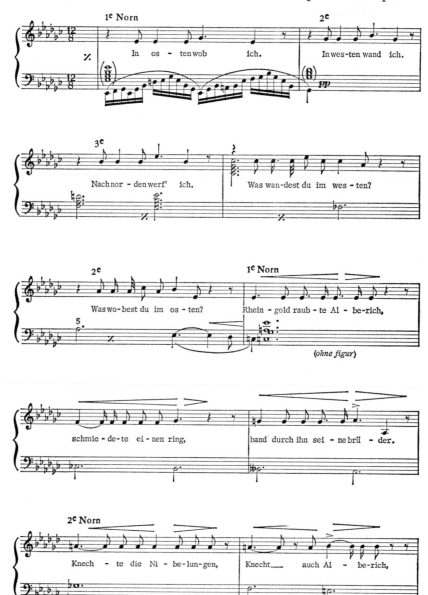

104

* For the sake of clarity, Wagner's corrections are not indicated.

Ex. 4

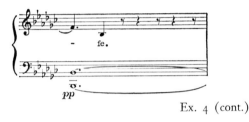

105

Ex. 4 (cont.)

Wagner must have seen that 6/4 would permit a less forced and
more natural manner of declamation, and he proceeded accordingly
from this point. When working out this section in the Orchestral
Sketch, he not only made the necessary change in the meter, but
also wrote a simpler bass figure in eighth notes, and introduced a
change to duple meter at the end of the section. In this context, it is
enlightening to glance at the beginning of the Composition Sketch
for *Das Rheingold*, in which Wagner again used a bass figure in
sixteenth notes, evidently planning already at this early stage to have
similar openings for the first and fourth operas of the cycle.

Ex. 5. *Das Rheingold*, Composition Sketch (original in the Archiv des
Hauses Wahnfried)

106

Ex. 5 (cont.)

Section II follows in pencil with no text, and the music for the third Norn's speech is missing. Wagner turned the sheet over to begin the music for Section III, and on the first staff is the following motive:

Ex. 6

The application of this material to the speeches of the first and second Norns follows, and it corresponds to mm. 56 through 68 in the transcription. Wagner expanded each of the first two measures of the original motive into a two-measure phrase for the first and second of the three lines, and then wrote a two-measure concluding phrase for the final line, which is similar in its scalar descent to the last two measures of the original motive. He then repeated the whole of the new phrase a third higher for the speech of the second Norn. In each of these speeches, the first two lines make one sentence, the third line a contrasting sentence, and this is reflected in his sequential setting of the first two lines in each case. Once again, as noted in the development of the theme of the Valkyries, the adaptation of the text has brought about changes in the initial musical conception: in this case, a conventional phrase of four measures has been expanded to six.

The most revealing section of the Norns' scene in the Composition Sketch is the setting of the first part of the third Norn's speech which follows immediately, for Wagner has two versions of it, with a correction in the fourth measure of the later version (see Ex. 7). Except for the word "treu," Wagner did not even bother to write out the text in the first version, but crossed out the whole passage and continued immediately with the new idea. In correcting the fourth measure of the latter, however, he wrote on top of his original thought, and this may have occurred at some later time, after he had tried it out at the piano.

Sequential treatment of this passage is present already in the earlier version. The sequential unit has two measures here, but only one in the corrected version, so that the musical line divides accord-

107

108

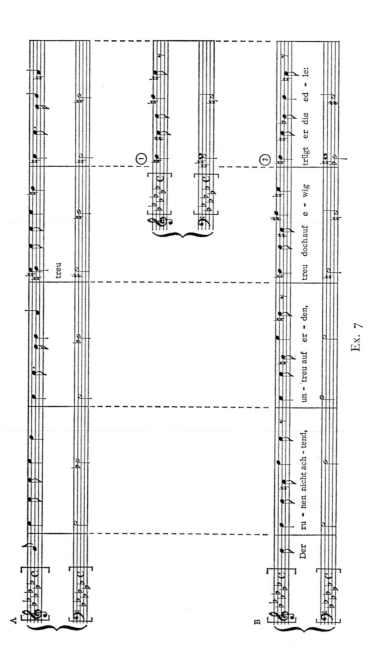

Ex. 7

ing to the structure of the text and thus follows the sense of the line. In addition, Wagner has eliminated the *Lohengrin*-like dotted rhythm in the second and fourth measures. The next two measures were originally alike in the later version, except for the contrast of the f♯ and f♮, this similarity evidently growing out of the double alliteration on the first and third beats:

*tr*eu doch auf *e*wig

and

*tr*ügt er die *e*dle.

But Wagner evidently felt that the sense of the line was improved if the whole of these two measures ran on as one melodic unit rather than being divided in half, since the two lines made a continuous clause. The juxtaposition of major and minor forms of a short phrase is a feature of Wagner's earlier style, and we see here a stage in its disappearance.

The poem of *Siegfrieds Tod* underwent extensive revision in 1852 so that it could serve as the final drama in the cycle. At that time, Wagner wrote an entirely new text for the Norns' scene, which he later considered "only outlined" in the earlier version.[22] But he left the text of the duet for Brünnhilde and Siegfried essentially unaltered. He did not begin composing the music for *Götterdämmerung* until the autumn of 1869, by which time he had written many of his most important works—*Tristan*, the new scenes of *Tannhäuser* for the ill-fated production in Paris, and the *Meistersinger*, in addition to the first three operas of the *Ring*—and his musical style had changed drastically. This is the only text for which Wagner made two independent settings, and they are separated by a crucial interval of nineteen years. As material for comparative study of stylistic change, they are as revealing as Alban Berg's two settings of Theodor Storm's *Schliesse mir die Augen beide* in 1900 and 1925.

Wagner's fundamental concern during the years following the completion of *Lohengrin* was the construction of a dramatic text that would be specifically and uniquely suitable for musical elaboration—a text constructed in such a way that, as Wagner later expressed it, the musical form is already completely prepared in the poem.[23]

[22] See the above quotation from *Mein Leben*.
[23] "*Zukunftsmusik*," in *Schriften*, VII, 123.

We have already seen some evidence of this concern in the Norns'
scene, with its threefold refrain and three-part structure growing
directly out of the dramatic material. In addition, however, Wagner
wanted to find means of avoiding long stretches of recitative-like
declamation in narrative texts, such as Telramund's accusation in
the first act of *Lohengrin*, or in most of the speeches of the king.
Part of the trouble lay in Wagner's almost complete avoidance of
triple meter, the central flaw in the music of *Lohengrin*: the only
passage in triple meter in the entire work is the short section in the
first act extending from the king's prayer to the duel.[24] This short-
coming in the music was undoubtedly a direct outgrowth of writing
poetic texts almost exclusively in iambs and trochees, also a characteristic of much German literary poetry of the early nineteenth
century in spite of tentative experiments in the direction of poetic
prose by men like Novalis.

Wagner's solution for the time being lay in *Stabreim*, or alliterative verse, and Westernhagen[25] has pointed out that this device
permitted a freer alternation of duple and triple meter. But there is
more to it than that. Wagner uses it to create a constantly shifting
pattern of stressed syllables, above and beyond the ordinary metrical
accentuation. Further, it enabled him to set up symmetries between
lines or groups of lines without using the same number of syllables.
And finally, there is the effective euphony of the device when the
lines are *sung*.[26] That Wagner found texts constructed along these

---

[24] The use of triple meter, particularly of the 3/4 signature, is an important
characteristic of Wagner's later musical style, for he seems to have avoided it
altogether before 1850. It is rare enough in *Rienzi*, and in *The Flying Dutchman*
it is used only for a short section in the choral scene of Act III. In *Tannhäuser*,
Wagner employs it only for the Pilgrims' Chorus in Act III and at the beginning
of the overture. It is hardly surprising that when he revised the first two scenes for
Paris in 1860-61, he used 3/4 for one of the newly composed speeches of Venus
and also for her big speech in the middle of the scene, taken over almost literally
from the Dresden version where he had composed it in 4/4. On a passage in the
poem of *Der junge Siegfried*, conceived originally for 2/4 meter but later (in the
final *Siegfried*) actually written in 3/4, see Newman, *Wagner Operas*, pp. 407-410.

[25] *Wagner-Studien*, p. 50.

[26] We must constantly bear in mind that these are texts to be *sung*. As poems
designed exclusively for *music*, they are unsurpassed, and nothing could represent
greater misunderstanding of Wagner's intentions or do him greater injustice than
to consider them apart from the music which accompanies them. In short, argu-
ments back and forth about their "*literary* quality" are both uninformed and
irrelevant. The fact that Wagner published the texts separately in no way negates
this: he often enough had cause to regret his action. On April 15, 1859, for example,
he wrote to Mathilde Wesendonk: "It occurred to me on that occasion [of reading

lines ideal for music, is indicated by the following passage of his letter to Theodor Uhlig of September 2, 1851, concerning *Der junge Siegfried* (later called simply *Siegfried*):

> I am now beginning the music, with which I really propose to enjoy myself. That which you cannot even imagine is happening quite of its own accord. I tell you, the musical phrases make themselves for these stanzas and periods, without my even having to take pains with them; it all grows out of the ground as if it were wild. I already have the beginning in mind, also some plastic motives such as Fafner.[27]

We have already seen some of these principles at work in his sketches for the music associated with the Valkyries, and we may now proceed to the duet itself. The earlier sketch is especially important here because it continues for eleven lines beyond the Orchestral Sketch. (It would be quite wrong to assume that Wagner had these sketches in his possession when he set to work at the composition of *Götterdämmerung* in 1869; in all likelihood, he had long since lost track of them, but they would have been of no use to him in any case.)[28]

Brünnhilde's first speech is organized in three stanzas and printed in this fashion in the final edition of the complete *Ring* libretto.[29] This permits yet another kind of tripartite musical organization

---

Goethe's *Tasso*] that it was ill-advised of me to publish [the poem of] *Tristan* after all. Between a poem entirely designed for music and a purely poetic stage-play, the distinction in design and realization must be so fundamentally different that the former, viewed with the same eye as the latter, must remain almost wholly incomprehensible as regards its essential meaning,—until it is completed by the music" (Golther, *Wagner an Mathilde Wesendonk*, p. 125).

[27] *Briefe an Uhlig, Fischer, Heine*, Letter No. 30, p. 99. This publication again has no date for the letter, but it is supplied, presumably from the envelope surviving with the copy made by Uhlig's widow, in John N. Burk, ed., *Letters of Richard Wagner: The Burrell Collection* (London, 1951), p. 620. It sounds as if Wagner may have made some musical sketches for *Der junge Siegfried* around this time, but aside from a few jottings in the margin of the poem, nothing of the kind has come to light so far. His statement about the beginning of the work seems sufficient evidence that he had at least decided upon the tonality of B-flat minor for the Nibelungs before the composition of the *Ring*, just as he had done in the case of B minor for the Valkyries.

[28] The very fact that these sketches survive but are not at Wahnfried is an indication that Wagner did *not* have them in his possession after 1864, from which time he gave all his musical manuscripts either to Cosima or to Ludwig II. The ones in Cosima's possession are at Wahnfried, while those given to Ludwig have been lost. On the latter group, see *Sänger-Zeitung*, xxxiv/10 (October 1958), p. 6.

[29] *Schriften*, vi, 182-83.

from that found in the Norns' scene. Both settings of the duet follow the same tonal plan: the first stanza begins in the tonic (A♭ major in 1850, E♭ major in 1869) and ends in the dominant, and both the second and third stanzas end in the tonic. In addition, the last lines of the first and third stanzas have the same metrical pattern, with the alliterative syllables in the same position. In 1850, Wagner gave each pair of lines approximately equivalent rhythmic patterns, arranged in such a way that the alliterative syllables always occur on the strong beat of a measure:

Ex. 8

In the later version, the phrase structure is much freer and thus the phrases for the two lines of each couplet are not of the same length. The important syllables now invariably coincide with the first beat of a measure:

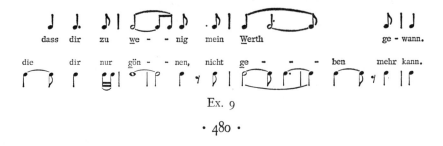

Ex. 9

Wagner has also emphasized the rhythmical similarity of "Ein einzig Sorgen" and "macht mich säumen" by setting each phrase to the same vocal line, a parallel which had not appeared in the earlier setting. And in the last line of each stanza, he has greatly increased the duration of the alliterative syllables, apparently to draw attention to the cadential function of these lines by setting them apart from the rest in style.

Westernhagen[30] has drawn attention to the similarity in treatment of "wie liebt' ich dich" in the two settings, with the rhythmic extension of the first word and the drop of a sixth in the melody; in addition, the melodic idea is the same in both settings of "liess' ich dich nicht." Each time, Wagner gave special treatment to this line, undoubtedly because of the symmetry of "liebt' ich dich" and "liess' ich dich."

In the second stanza, "heiliger Runen reichen Hort" stands in apposition with "Was Götter mich wiesen." In the earlier setting, Wagner has used the same rhythmic pattern on e-flat for the beginning of each line and supplied a different continuation. In 1869, however, he used sequence rather than simple repetition to enforce the grammatical relationship, and the melody of the entire first line is used again, continuation and all, for the second line, but a minor third higher. In both settings, the vocal line for "Was Götter mich wiesen" is the same, with the drop of a perfect fifth at the end. We encounter a similar situation in the third line of this stanza, "doch meiner Stärke magdlichen Stamm": Wagner seems to have felt on both occasions that the phrase "magdlichen Stamm" merited special treatment, and curiously, he devised the same melodic configuration, in spite of the different musical context, in each setting. The same figure, a third higher, is used for the first phrase of the following line, "nahm mir der Held," in 1850; in the later version, however, Wagner separated the two lines with a quarter rest and wrote a new figure for the phrase in question.

The first two lines of the third stanza are set up symmetrically; in 1850, Wagner gave the first half of each line, "des Wissens bar" and "an Liebe reich," the same figure, a third higher the second time. In addition, he used the same bass line for the second line as he had used for the first line, but a sixth lower. In 1869, however, he reinforced only the parallel between the two halves of the first line, "des Wissens bar" and "doch des Wunsches voll," by using the

113

[30] *Wagner-Studien*, pp. 46-47.

same figure a perfect fifth higher for the second phrase as he used for the first—and ignored the parallel situation in the second line.

Every line in the text of Brünnhilde's speech is divided into two phrases, each of which has two metrical feet, and alliteration connects the two halves of each line.[31] In Siegfried's speech, on the other hand, there are three feet to the line, and the alliteration serves to link two successive lines into couplets. This fundamental change in the structure of the text is reflected in the music of 1850 by a change to triple meter and by a change of key to C major. In 1869, the rhythmic structure of the music is so complicated that a change in meter is not necessary, and the modulation (also to C major) is postponed until the final couplet.

The first two couplets of this speech have essentially the same melodic lines in the 1850 setting, whereas in the later version melodic repetition is used only to support the parallel in the text between "Lehren" in the third line and "-lehret" in the fourth, a parallel which had received no consideration in the earlier setting. The last two couplets also have essentially the same settings in 1850, with a one-measure change of meter in the latter line of each couplet. Thus, in 1850, Wagner had set the speech in triple meter but had made an effort to contrast its duple structure with the three-part structure of Brünnhilde's preceding speech by using a twofold statement of one melodic line for the first two couplets and a twofold statement of another melodic line for the last two couplets. In the later setting, however, sequential treatment once again replaces repetition in the last two couplets, and the first line of each one has the same melody, but a semitone higher the second time. The second line of each couplet has a different vocal line, but the accompaniment continues the sequential parallel established in the first line of each couplet.

The last line of the speech serves, with a change in the verb, as a refrain after the next two speeches of Brünnhilde. The second and third occurrences of this refrain are essentially the same in the first setting, including the one-measure change to duple meter, but with the first syllable of the word "Brünnhilde" extended the second and third times. In the 1869 version, the parallel in the melodic lines is

---

[31] These remarks apply to the text of *Siegfrieds Tod* as printed in *Schriften*, ɪɪ, 170. In the later text of the complete *Ring* (*Schriften*, vɪ, 182-83), however, each phrase is printed as a separate line.

less exact, though here the first syllable of the word "Brünnhilde" is also lengthened in the second and third occurrences of the refrain. No metric change enforces the identification; instead, the orchestral accompaniment clarifies the function of this line as refrain.

Brünnhilde's next two speeches are organized in tercets, representing a return to the idea of tripartite structure in contrast to the duple structure of the intervening speech of Siegfried. The second and third lines both begin with the words "gedenke deiner," and Wagner has used a sequence in the vocal line in 1850. Later, however, he used the sequential idea only in the accompaniment, where it is carried one line further to support the parallel with the first line of the second tercet (also beginning with "Gedenke"). This symmetry had been ignored in 1850.

The second tercet has the same construction as the next speech, and each of the six lines uses the letter "f" as the alliterative consonant. Each tercet is followed by Siegfried's refrain. In 1850, the two units are set sequentially, refrain and all. In the 1869 version, the first lines and third lines correspond, but in different ways: the first are simply set to a repeated note a whole tone apart, while the third lines correspond in their use of the same characteristic motive, varied rhythmically and melodically the second time.

Wagner's setting of these lines in *Götterdämmerung* runs to 110 measures, whereas his earlier sketch contains only 71, so that the final version is half again as long as the earlier one. In several passages, he improved the declamation; by 1869, he had become a master of that art. In setting "Willst du mir Minne schenken," for example, he had placed the word "mir" on the first beat of m. 168, whereas the important stress of the line is placed more correctly and naturally on the first syllable of "Minne" in the later version.

In general, the vocal writing in 1850 emphasizes the smaller intervals except at a few important points, representing a continuation of the ingratiating lyrical style of such a passage as the bridal chamber scene in *Lohengrin*. The vocal lines are relatively independent, and one still has the feeling of melody plus accompaniment. In the later style, larger and more "characteristic" sixths, sevenths, and even octaves are regular features of the vocal writing. The role of the orchestra is expanded considerably, so that the vocal lines are overlaid on a more complicated orchestral fabric and thus serve as iso-

115

lated strands of a richer polyphonic texture. And Wagner's harmonic vocabulary in 1869 naturally represents a considerable advance beyond that of 1850.

We have seen that Wagner favored sequential treatment of various kinds to the mere repetition he had used in 1850. And where he had used sequences to underscore textual parallels in the earlier version, he found different means to do this later on. The two settings of the duet, in short, are alike more in their overall structural plan than in specific melodic, harmonic, or rhythmic details. The structure is certainly the important feature conditioned by the text, in which Wagner was careful to set up refrains and corresponding or contrasting lines and groups of lines, all of which might be reflected in the music.

By now it will be apparent that the central interest of the 1850 sketches does not lie in the more or less coincidental resemblance of an early turn of phrase to one in the later *Ring*. Rather, they are invaluable for the light they shed on the problem of what Wagner had formulated before he began composing the music for *Das Rheingold*, and in the insights they provide about his compositional methods. In recent years, it has become a commonplace among students of Wagner's works to speak of the "simultaneous conception of words and music," yet careful comparison of the two versions of the duet provides convincing evidence that this idea needs modification. While at work on the music for the second act of *Siegfried*, Wagner summed up his own view of the matter in a revealing passage of his letter to Liszt on December 6, 1856: "Strange! Only during the act of composition does the real essence of my poem reveal itself to me: everywhere I discover secrets which had hitherto remained hidden even from me."[32] Wagner certainly wrote his libretto with a view to making it suitable for musical realization, but insofar as the libretto foreshadows the music at all, it foreshadows two decidedly different settings equally well.

[32] Erich Kloss, ed., *Briefwechsel zwischen Wagner und Liszt* (Leipzig, 1910), Part II, Letter No. 223, p. 138.

APPENDIX

Wagner's 1850 Setting of the Prologue to *Siegfrieds Tod*

117

Ex. 10

118

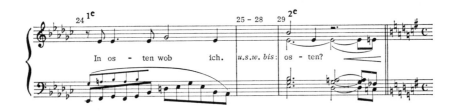

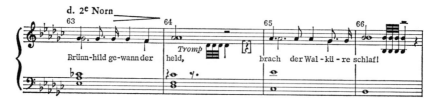

d. 2ᵉ Norn

Brünn-hild ge-wann der held,

Tromp

brach der Wal-kü-re schlaf!

120

d. 3ᵉ Norn *(bewegter)*

lie-bend lernt sie ihm ru-nen. Der ru-nen nicht ach-tend,

(langsamer) *(langsam)*

un-treu auf er-den, treu doch auf e-wig trügt er die ed-le;

dim.

(feierlich bewegt)

doch sei-ne that taugt sie zu deu-ten, frei zu voll-en-den, was

d. 2ᵉ

froh er be-gann. Win-dest du noch im wes-ten? We-best du

(immer mit d. figur)

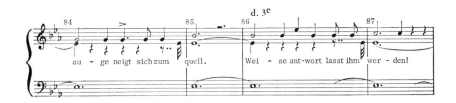

121

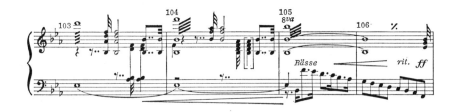

122

123

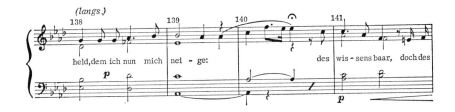

wun-sches voll, an lie - be reich, doch le-dig der kraft: mögst du die

(langs.)

ar - me nicht ver - ach - ten, die dir nur gön - nen, nicht ge - ben mehr

(lebhafter)   Siegfried

kann!   Mehr gabst du, wun-der-frau, als ich zu wah - ren

weiss!   Nicht zür-ne, wenn dein leh - - ren mich un - be-leh - - ret

liess!   Ein wis - sen doch wahr ich wohl: dass mir Brünn - hil-de

124

125

126

Addendum

The "special set of instructions" [*Conductor*] that Wagner sent to Weissheimer was sold at an auction held on 29 and 30 November 1966, by J. A. Stargardt in Marburg, *Katalog Nr. 77*, Lot 855. A small portion of the document is reproduced in the catalogue on p. 189.

Carl Dahlhaus

Formprinzipien in Wagners »Ring des Nibelungen«

I

Der Vorwurf der Formlosigkeit, der ein halbes Jahrhundert lang gegen Wagners »unendliche Melodie« erhoben worden ist, war ebenso zwielichtig wie borniert. Er richtete sich zwar, kaum anders als später das Schlagwort »atonal«, gegen einen greifbaren Sachverhalt: gegen die Negation der Form als Schema, zielte aber darüber hinaus auf eine Verdächtigung des gesamten Werkes, dessen musikalisch-theatralischer Gewalt sich sogar die Gegner nicht zu entziehen vermochten, der sie jedoch mißtrauten, als wäre sie illegitim.

In dem Vorurteil, dem Wagner begegnete, flossen der Formbegriff der musikalischen Formenlehre und der ästhetische Formbegriff trübe ineinander. Die Schemata der Formenlehre, Typen wie Liedform, Rondo und Sonatenform, sind — pointiert gesagt — Hilfskonstruktionen; sie gleichen Gerüsten, mit denen man ein Werk umstellt, um es einer Erkenntnis durch Begriffe zugänglich zu machen, und die man abreißt, wenn sie ihren Zweck erfüllt haben. Die Typen sind zwar von manchen Analytikern zu Normen erklärt worden, denen das einzelne, individuelle Gebilde sich unterwerfen müsse, um formale Prägnanz zu erreichen. Es liegt jedoch näher, sie als Idealtypen aufzufassen, die weniger das Maß der musikalischen Wirklichkeit bilden als ein Mittel zu deren Beschreibung. Die Schemata werden gleichsam als Versuchsanordnungen benutzt; und das Ziel der Analyse ist nicht die Darstellung eines Werkes im Hinblick auf eine Norm, der es gerecht wird, sondern gerade umgekehrt die Aufhebung des allgemeinen Schemas in der Deskription des Einzelfalls.

Erfüllt demnach die Form als Schema der Formenlehre eine eher heuristische als normative Funktion, so ist mit dem Formbegriff der Ästhetik eine Qualität gemeint, die einem Stück Musik nicht mangeln darf, wenn es nicht aufhören soll, Musik zu sein. Formlose Musik wäre demnach ein Widerspruch in sich; fehlt die Form, so ist von der Musik nichts übrig als der Anspruch oder leere Schein. Und es war das Quid pro quo divergierender Formbegriffe, das die Kritik an Wagners »unendlicher Melodie« vergiftete. Die Aufhebung der Schemata, die Leugnung ihres normativen Charakters, wurde verdächtigt, ein Sakrileg an der Form im ästhetischen Sinne zu sein.

Polemik und Apologie aber sind voneinander abhängig; die eine ist die Reversseite der anderen. Wer eine Sache verteidigt, neigt unwillkürlich — und zwar gerade dann, wenn er sich um äußerste Redlichkeit der Argumentation bemüht — zu dem Fehler, sich die Thematik und die Kategorien vom Gegner vorschreiben zu lassen und bloß zu negieren, was der andere behauptet, oder zu behaupten, was er negiert. Dem Begriff der Atonalität, der als kränkende Kritik an Schönberg gemeint war, aber zugleich einen Sachverhalt traf, setzte

Josef Rufer [1] eine erzwungene Deutung der Dodekaphonie als Tonalität entgegen: eine Deutung, die kaum weniger schief war als der Einwand, den sie entkräften sollte. Und dem ähnlich verqueren Vorwurf, Wagners Musik sei formlos, begegnete Alfred Lorenz [2] mit einem Versuch, den »Ring des Nibelungen« mit den Kategorien der traditionellen Formenlehre zu analysieren, also gleichsam in der Theorie rückgängig zu machen, was Wagner in der kompositorischen Praxis vollzogen hatte: die Emanzipation vom Schema. So borniert die Polemik gewesen war, so gewaltsam und zugleich unfrei war die Apologie, die nach Jahrzehnten die Herausforderung aufgriff.

Lorenz erweiterte zwar den Begriffsbestand der Formenlehre, übernahm aber deren Prinzipien, obwohl sie von Werken abstrahiert worden waren, die mit Wagners Musikdramen kaum vergleichbar sind. Form erscheint als Schema, darstellbar durch eine Buchstabenfolge, die nicht den Ausgangspunkt der Analyse, sondern deren Resultat bildet. Und das räumlich-symmetrische, architektonische Moment der musikalischen Form wird von Lorenz [3], im Widerspruch zu Wagners Formgefühl, sogar nachdrücklicher hervorgehoben als von Adolf Bernhard Marx oder Hugo Riemann. [4]

Daß die Sonatenform, der repräsentative Formtypus des 19. Jahrhunderts, sich einer Darstellung durch ein Buchstabenschema entzieht, hätte mißtrauisch machen sollen gegen den Versuch, Schemata zu entwerfen, in denen Wagners Musik restlos aufgeht oder aufzugehen scheint. Wären die Lorenzschen Analysen triftig, so würden sie bedeuten, daß Wagner hinter die »Kultur« der Sonatenform, um mit August Halm zu sprechen, auf eine gleichsam archaische Stufe des musikalischen Formbewußtseins zurückgefallen sei. Was als Apologie gemeint war, läßt polemische Konsequenzen zu, die denn auch von Theodor W. Adorno [5], der am Sach- und Wahrheitsgehalt der Lorenzschen Analysen nicht zweifelte, gezogen worden sind.

Würde eingewendet, daß es verfehlt sei, das Wort-Ton-Drama am Maß der Sonate oder Symphonie zu messen, so wäre zu entgegnen, daß gerade Lorenz mit besonderem Nachdruck von einem »symphonischen Gewebe« spricht [6], also Wagners These, daß die Symphonie im Musikdrama aufgehoben sei, beim Wort nimmt.

[1] J. Rufer, *Die Komposition mit zwölf Tönen*, Berlin und Wunsiedel 1952, S. 27.
[2] A. Lorenz, *Das Geheimnis der Form bei Richard Wagner*, Band I: *Der musikalische Aufbau des Bühnenfestspieles »Der Ring des Nibelungen«*, Berlin 1924; auf die Untersuchungen von Lorenz stützen sich C. von Westernhagen (*Richard Wagner*, Zürich 1956, S. 81 ff.) und H. von Stein (*Dichtung und Musik im Werk Richard Wagners*, Berlin 1962, S. 58 ff.).
[3] »... vom musikalischen Standpunkte aus sind die Leitmotive doch nichts als kleine Steine, durch deren Zusammensetzung erst die Wunderbauten der Wagnerschen Musik entstehen« (a. a. O., S. 9). »Der Vergleich des tönenden Geschehens mit räumlichen Verhältnissen ist durchaus angebracht und belebend, er gestaltet alles anschaulich, was ja der Zweck jeder wissenschaftlichen Verständlichmachung ist« (a. a. O., S. 121).
[4] A. B. Marx, *Die Lehre von der musikalischen Komposition*, Band II, 5. Auflage Leipzig 1864, S. 6 ff.; H. Riemann, *Große Kompositionslehre*, Band I, Berlin und Stuttgart 1902, S. 424 ff.
[5] Th. W. Adorno, *Versuch über Wagner*, Berlin und Frankfurt a. M. 1952, S. 48.
[6] A. a. O., S. 73.

128

Die Relevanz der Buchstabenschemata, deren Symmetrie für Lorenz den Inbegriff musikalischer Form bedeutet, ist aber sogar in der älteren Oper, nicht nur in der Symphonie, nicht selten zweifelhaft. Sowohl in der Kavatine der Gräfin aus *Le nozze di Figaro* (Nr. 10) als auch in der Tamino-Arie aus der *Zauberflöte* (Nr. 3), in Sätzen also, deren formale Festigkeit zu leugnen absurd wäre, ist die Reprise so schwach angedeutet, daß ein Buchstabenschema die Form nicht träfe; es ginge ins Leere. Und wollte man den Formen, die keiner Regel folgen, auch keiner selbstgesetzten, analysierend gerecht werden, so müßte man nach den Bedingungen suchen, unter denen sich musikalisches Gleichgewicht ohne Stütze an einem Schema verwirklichen läßt.

II

1. Nach Lorenz, der sich, offenbar ohne es zu wissen, auf eine bis zu Schelling zurückreichende musikästhetische Tradition stützte, ist musikalische Form Rhythmus im Großen.[7] *»Die Frage nach der musikalischen Form gehört in das Gebiet der Rhythmik ... Der einfache Wechsel von schwer und leicht, der das Wesen der Rhythmik ausmacht, wird zum Formgefühl, wenn zu diesem eine höhere Ordnung von Doppelt, Dreifach, Vielfach schwerer Akzente gebracht wird. Diese Akzente müssen, wenn sie rasch aufeinanderfolgen, in rationalem Verhältnis zueinander stehen, wie der Pulsschlag des Menschen. Je länger die Zeit ist, die zwischen ihnen verstreicht, desto irrationaler können sie gestaltet werden, da das Gedächtnis der Menschen für Zeitdauer unausgebildet ist.«*[8] Daß längere Zeitstrecken nur ungenau wahrgenommen werden, ist demnach für Lorenz kein Grund, die Bestimmung der Form als Rhythmus einzuschränken, sondern dient zur Rechtfertigung großzügiger Analysen, in denen auch bei auffällig verschiedener Taktanzahl der Teile von rhythmischer Korrespondenz die Rede ist. Die melodisch-thematische Struktur, die *»Wiederholung von Motiven, die als gleich oder ähnlich erkannt werden«*, soll nicht als Substanz der Form, sondern als eines der Mittel gelten, die eine *»rhythmische Gliederung«* bewirken oder unterstreichen.[9]

Im Gegensatz zu Lorenz betonte Schönberg in seinen Analysen, deren Methode durch Schönbergs Schüler überliefert wurde[10], die melodisch-diastematischen Zusammenhänge, nicht die rhythmischen Korrespondenzen. Gemessen an dem Verfahren der entwickelnden Variation, das gleichsam die Logik

---

7 *„Der Rhythmus ist die Musik in der Musik"*, schrieb Schelling 1802 in der Philosophie der Kunst, die posthum 1859 erschienen ist (Nachdruck Darmstadt 1960, S. 138); und bei Friedrich von Hausegger heißt es: *»In ihrer Lebendigkeit ist die Form Rhythmus ... Auch die Form der Sonate muß, wenn sie Anspruch auf Gültigkeit machen will, Rhythmus sein«* (Die Musik als Ausdruck, 2. Auflage Wien 1887, S. 201). Auch E. Hanslick sprach von *»Rhythmus im Großen«* als *»Übereinstimmung eines symmetrischen Baues«* (Vom Musikalisch-Schönen, Leipzig 1854, S. 32).

8 A. a. O., S. 13.

9 A. a. O., S. 13 f.

10 A. Berg, *Warum ist Schönbergs Musik so schwer verständlich?* (W. Reich, *Alban Berg*, Wien 1937, S. 142 ff.); E. Ratz, *Einführung in die musikalische Formenlehre*, Wien 1951; E. Stein, *Musik — Form und Darstellung*, München 1964.

des musikalischen Diskurses darstellt, ist nach Schönberg das räumlich-symmetrische Moment eine sekundäre Eigenschaft der Form oder sogar ein Rückstand musikalischer Primitivität.

Als Vermittlung zwischen den Extremen erscheint die These Hugo Riemanns, daß die Struktur der einzelnen Teile anderen Regeln und Kriterien unterworfen sei als die Gesamtform. Innerhalb einer Periode, eines Abschnitts von acht oder sechzehn Takten, sei die rhythmische Korrespondenz der Teile — der Takte, Phrasen und Halbsätze — das entscheidende Moment. Dagegen beruhe der Zusammenhang zwischen den Perioden, also der Konnex über weite Strecken, auf thematischen Beziehungen: auf der Übereinstimmung, Ähnlichkeit oder Verschiedenheit des melodischen Inhalts der Perioden. [11]

Die Triftigkeit eines methodischen Ansatzes zeigt sich am Resultat der Analysen, deren Ausgangspunkt er bildet. Ein begründetes Urteil ist nicht in abstrakter Allgemeinheit, sondern nur im Hinblick auf bestimmte Werke möglich. Mag also die Vorstellung eines Rhythmus im Großen der Struktur mancher Stücke gerecht werden: daß sie die Formen, aus denen sich der *Ring* zusammensetzt, verfehlt, ist unschwer zu demonstrieren.

Ein Zusammenhang zwischen Motivkomplexen, die sich über zwanzig, dreißig oder gar hundert Takte erstrecken, ist als rhythmisches Phänomen, wenn überhaupt, so nur dann faßlich, wenn das Prinzip der rhythmischen Korrespondenz — die Übertragung des Wechsels zwischen Schwer und Leicht von Zählzeiten auf Takte, Phrasen, Halbsätze und ganze Perioden — innerhalb der einzelnen Komplexe deutlich und unmißverständlich ausgeprägt ist. Ein Gesamtrhythmus setzt, sofern er existiert, Prägnanz des Rhythmus der Teile voraus. Rhythmische Korrespondenz auf engem Raum, der Zusammenschluß von Motiven und Phrasen zu Vorder- und Nachsätzen, ist jedoch im *Ring* eher eine Ausnahme als die Regel. Und wenn die Voraussetzung brüchig ist, muß die Konsequenz, die Deutung der Form als Rhythmus im Großen, preisgegeben werden. Sogar in Partien mit gleichmäßiger und beinahe schematischer rhythmischer Gliederung — einer Reihung von Zweitakten, die im *Ring* noch begegnet, wenn auch seltener als im *Lohengrin* — ist es nicht die rhythmische Korrespondenz, die der Gruppierung der Motive inneren Zusammenhalt gibt. Die Phrase Takt 15—20 aus der zweiten Szene des *Rheingold* wirkt unmißverständlich als Schluß der lang ausgesponnenen Exposition des Walhallmotivs, aber nicht, weil sie ein Nachsatz im Sinne eines rhythmischen Widerparts zum Vorausgegangenen wäre, sondern weil das Motiv, das ihr zugrundeliegt, eine Umkehrung des zweiten Taktes aus dem Walhallmotiv ist. Und daß in den Takten 23—30 ein Bruchstück des Walhallmotivs als einleuchtende, weder erzwungene noch mühsam angekittete Fortsetzung des Ringmotivs empfunden wird, beruht nicht auf rhythmischer Korrespondenz, sondern auf der melodischen Verwandtschaft der Motive, einer Ähnlichkeit, die eine Substitution des einen durch das andere erlaubt.

2. Die Vorherrschaft des Orchesters im Musikdrama, die primär instrumentale Prägung der Leitmotive, ist Wagner von seinen Kritikern immer wieder als Verstoß gegen die Natur der Oper zum Vorwurf gemacht worden. Man ver-

[11] H. Riemann, a. a. O., S. 50.

kannte, sei es absichtsvoll oder unwillkürlich, die Wechselwirkung des Vokalen und des Instrumentalen: den Sachverhalt, daß die Orchestermelodie ohne die Gesangsstimme, die über die Zäsuren hinwegträgt, oft genug auseinanderbrechen würde und daß umgekehrt der musikalischen Deklamation durch die Orchestermotive eine gleichsam indirekte melodische Qualität zuwächst. Ist demnach die Behauptung, daß die Gesangsstimme zu einem sekundären Moment herabgesetzt sei, polemisch gefärbt, so erscheint es um so seltsamer, daß Lorenz sie sich zu eigen macht und in den Analysen, die das »Geheimnis der Form bei Richard Wagner« enträtseln sollen, vom Vokalpart fast durchweg abstrahiert. Die Gesangsstimme sei nichts anderes als »ein Teil« der »Orchestersymphonie« [12]; und »je tiefer das innere Leben des Dramas im Orchester geschildert ist, oder je mehr sich die Dichtung der Umgangssprache nähert, desto mehr wird die Bedeutung des inneren Lebens den äußeren Schein der Worte überwiegen. Der Schwerpunkt der Melodie fällt dann ins Orchester und hier ist der Punkt, wo wir nun zur Betrachtung der großen Formen gelangen«.[13] So triftig aber die Beobachtungen sind, die der These vom Primat der Orchestermelodie zugrundeliegen, so fragwürdig ist die Verhärtung zu einem Dogma, das keine Abweichungen duldet. Die Konsequenz, mit der Lorenz den Vokalpart des Musikdramas, das von Wagner Wort-Ton-Drama genannt wurde, als quantité negligeable behandelt, verstellt ihm manchmal sogar den Blick für einfache Formen, die er sonst auch dort entdeckt, wo sie nicht sind.

Die erste ariose Periode in Loges Erzählung aus der zweiten Szene des *Rheingold* ist unverkennbar in zwei Strophen gegliedert, deren zweite eine Variation der ersten ist (T. 1344—1375: »*So weit Leben und Weben ...*«). Lorenz [14] aber ignoriert, obwohl sie das von ihm entworfene Formschema nicht stören würde, die Wiederkehr vokaler Phrasen, die im Text begründet ist (»*So weit Leben und Weben, in Wasser, Erd' und Luft*« — »*Doch so weit Leben und Weben ... in Wasser, Erd' und Luft*«), und stützt seine Analyse einzig auf Wiederholungen des Freia-Motivs im Orchester. An einem ähnlichen Irrtum oder Mangel krankt die Analyse der Takte 1357—1375 (»*Der weiblichste Held ...*«) aus der Schlußszene der *Walküre*, dem Dialog Wotans mit Brünnhilde. Lorenz [15] erwähnt zwar, außer dem Siegfried-Motiv, eine begleitende Orchesterfigur, die auf den Anfang des Dialogs zurückgreift (T. 1110: »*Weil für dich im Auge das Eine ich hielt ...*«), übergeht jedoch das Entscheidende, die Übereinstimmung der Vokalphrasen »*Von dir geschieden, schied ich von ihm; vernichten mußt' ihn der Neid*« und »*In Schmerz und Leid, wie kein Weib sie gelitten, wird sie gebären, was bang sie birgt*« — eine Übereinstimmung, die aus dem Text zu begründen gewaltsam wäre; sie erscheint als Rückstand »absoluter Musik« im Wort-Ton-Drama.

3. Daß trotz dem Theorem von der »unendlichen Melodie«, in deren Kontinuum der Gegensatz zwischen Deklamation und Gesang aufgehoben oder zur kleinsten Differenz verringert sei, eine Gliederung in Rezitative und Ariosi in manchen Partien des *Rheingold* und der *Walküre* noch durchscheint, vor allem

12 A. a. O., S. 69.
13 A. a. O., S. 70.
14 A. a. O., S. 228 f.
15 A. a. O., S. 153.

in den Dialogen zwischen Wotan und Fricka, ist niemals geleugnet worden. Den Konsequenzen aber, die sich aufdrängen, weicht Lorenz aus. Statt die Stildifferenz als Formprinzip gelten zu lassen, zwingt er den Dialogen Schemata auf, die einerseits über die Zäsuren zwischen Rezitativ und Arioso hinweggehen und andererseits in sich haltlos sind.

In den Takten 827—913 aus der zweiten Szene des *Rheingold* umgeben und unterbrechen Rezitative (*»Nur Wonne schafft dir«*, *»Doch bei dem Wohnbau«*, *»Liebeloser, leidigster Mann«*) ein arioses Duett (*»Was ist euch Harten«*). Und die abstrakte Form, der *»vollkommene Bogen«* (a b c d e d c b a), den Lorenz [16] als Schema des Dialogs konstruiert, ist eine Fiktion. Nur ein einziges Motiv aus dem ersten Rezitativ, das Vertragsmotiv, kehrt im zweiten wieder; und die ariosen Partien (c d und d c) sind durch nichts miteinander verbunden als durch eine viertaktige Phrase (*»Herrliche Wohnung«*), die von Fricka exponiert und von Wotan mit ironischem Akzent aufgegriffen wird.

Ähnlich gewaltsam ist die Deutung der Dialoge, die im zweiten Akt der *Walküre* einem formal geschlossenen Arioso, Frickas Klage, vorausgehen und folgen. Das Schema der Barform, das Lorenz [17] den Takten 154—252 überstülpt, stützt sich auf nichts als die Wiederkehr eines Motivs von vier Takten Länge (*»Heilig ist mein Herd«*): eine Analogie, die Lorenz genügt, um von zwei »Stollen«, die 21 und 18 Takte umfassen, zu sprechen. Andererseits ist unter dem Begriff des »Abgesangs« Heterogenes zusammengezwungen: ein Rezitativ Frickas (*»Achtest du rühmlich«*) und ein Arioso Wotans (*»Heut hast du's erlebt«*). Noch brüchiger ist die Konstruktion einer Barform bei den Takten 345—414. [18] Die beiden »Stollen« (15 und 17 Takte) haben nichts gemeinsam als eine wenig charakteristische Akkordfolge (Subdominante-Tonika-Dominante), die sich über zwei Takte erstreckt. Mit gleichem Recht hätte Lorenz auch — unter Berufung auf die Wiederkehr des Schwert- und des Vertragsmotivs — von einem *»vollkommenen Bogen«* (a b c b a) sprechen können. Die Vertauschbarkeit der Schemata ist das Zeichen der Willkür, mit der sie dem Text aufgezwungen werden.

Daß Rezitative die »unendliche Melodie« unterbrechen, ist nach Lorenz ästhetisch, als Konsequenz eines kompositorischen Ökonomieprinzips, zu verstehen: *»Natürlich durfte die symphonische Arbeit in einem Werke, welches sich durch zehn Akte lang immer steigern sollte, nicht von Anfang an mit ganzer Fülle einsetzen (ein Hauptfehler der neueren Komponisten). So mußten also besonders im Rheingold lange Stellen bloß durch den Adel der Gesangsdeklamation ohne starke Orchesteruntermalung bestritten werden.«* [19] Einfacher und näherliegend, wenn auch banaler wäre es, an die Entstehungsgeschichte zu denken, um den Unterschied zwischen *Rheingold* und *Walküre* einerseits, *Siegfried* und *Götterdämmerung* andererseits zu erklären. Daß in den früheren Teilen der Tetralogie noch Spuren des Opernstils, von dem Wagner das Wort-Ton-Drama abzuheben suchte, zu finden sind, ist beinahe selbstverständlich; erstaunlich

[16] A. a. O., S. 138.
[17] A. a. O., S. 158.
[18] A. a. O.
[19] A. a. O., S. 62 f.

wäre eher das Gegenteil, die restlose Aufhebung der Differenz zwischen Rezitativ und Arioso in sämtlichen Szenen. Und sogar einem orthodoxen Wagnerianer, der auf ungetrübter Übereinstimmung von ästhetischer Theorie und kompositorischer Praxis beharrt, muß es schwerfallen, den geschichtlichen, also in sich widersprüchlichen Charakter von Wagners Werk zu leugnen.

Aus der Entstehungsgeschichte ist aber auch der Rückgriff auf traditionelle Satztypen in den späteren Teilen des *Ring* zu verstehen: das Duett am Ende des *Siegfried* und das Terzett, mit dem der zweite Akt der *Götterdämmerung* schließt. Daß Stimmen von ausgeprägt verschiedenem oder sogar gegensätzlichem Charakter [20] ein Duett oder Terzett bilden, also zu einem zwei- oder dreistimmigen Satz zusammengezwungen werden, war von Wagner im *Rheingold* und in der *Walküre* vermieden worden, weil es dem Dialogprinzip des gesprochenen Dramas, das auch in der Oper gelten sollte, widerspricht oder zu widersprechen scheint. Und daß Wagner sich im *Siegfried* und in der *Götterdämmerung* über die eigene Ästhetik hinwegsetzte, ist kaum anders als aus der Tatsache zu erklären, daß die Dichtungen der beiden Teile früher entstanden sind als die des *Rheingold* und der *Walküre*. Die traditionellen Satztypen waren im Text zu deutlich vorgezeichnet, als daß eine Vertonung nach dem Dialogprinzip sinnvoll möglich gewesen wäre. [21] Zu fragen wäre allerdings, was es besagt, daß Wagner eher eine Rücksichtslosigkeit gegenüber der eigenen Theorie auf sich nahm, als daß er rigoros die Textfassungen antastete, die in die Jahre um 1850 zurückreichten. [22] War es Scheu, in die eigene Dichtung einzugreifen, weil Änderungen, die das Dialogprinzip forderte oder nahelegte, vermutlich andere nach sich gezogen hätten, so daß Wagner bei der Umarbeitung ins Unabsehbare geraten wäre? Oder soll man von einer Souveränität sprechen, die nicht davor zurückschreckt, selbstgesetzte Regeln zu mißachten und den Vorwurf der Inkonsequenz auf sich zu nehmen, einen Vorwurf, der den subalternen Geist dessen, der ihn erhebt, verrät?

133

[20] Daß die Rheintöchter oder die Walküren, die kaum individualisiert sind, sich zu musikalischen Ensembles zusammenschließen, ist mit dem Dialogprinzip des Wort-Ton-Dramas vereinbar.

[21] In der Schlußpartie des *Siegfried*, die fast ohne Änderung aus dem *Jungen Siegfried* (Juni 1851) übernommen wurde, ist der rhythmische und in den letzten Zeilen auch semantische Parallelismus von Brünnhildes und Siegfrieds Worten (*»Fahr hin, Walhalls leuchtende Welt...«* und *»Lachend erwachst du Wonnige mir...«*) zu auffällig, als daß sich Wagner bei der Komposition der Szene über die traditionelle Duettstruktur der zweimal 22 Zeilen hätte hinwegsetzen können. Und Analoges gilt für das Terzett am Ende des zweiten Aktes der *Götterdämmerung* (*»So soll es sein...«*). Daß die zweimal acht Zeilen, auf die sich in *Siegfrieds Tod* die Terzettpartie beschränkte, in der *Götterdämmerung* zu zweimal 18 Zeilen erweitert wurden — und zwar durch Parodierung einer Segensbitte (*Siegfrieds Tod*, sechste Szene: *»Allvater! Waltender Gott!«*) in einen Racheschwur (*Götterdämmerung*, fünfte Szene: *»Allrauner! Rächender Gott!«*) —, ist durch die Streichung der sechsten Szene der ursprünglichen Fassung motiviert: eine Streichung, durch die das Terzett an den Schluß des Aktes rückte, so daß es, um als Finale gewichtig genug zu sein, gedehnt werden mußte.

[22] Die erwähnte Parodierung von Bruchstücken aus *Siegfrieds Tod* macht deutlich, daß Wagner sogar dann, wenn Änderungen unumgänglich erschienen, von dem ursprünglichen Text zu bewahren suchte, was irgend zu bewahren war, sei es auch um den Preis einer Verkehrung der Bedeutung ins Gegenteil.

4. In dem Aufsatz *Über die Anwendung der Musik auf das Drama* beschreibt Wagner den »musikalischen Satzbau« des Wort-Ton-Dramas als Analogon zum »Symphoniesatz«, wenn er auch »*zu seiner Entfaltung unendlich reicherer Formen bedarf, als sie auf der Basis des Symphoniesatzes, nämlich der Tanzmusik, naturgemäß sich darbieten können. Dennoch muß die neue Form der dramatischen Musik, um wiederum als Musik ein Kunstwerk zu bilden, die Einheit des Symphoniesatzes aufweisen, und dies erreicht sie, wenn sie im innigsten Zusammenhange mit demselben über das ganze Drama sich erstreckt, nicht nur über einzelne kleinere, willkürlich herausgehobene Teile desselben. Diese Einheit gibt sich dann in einem das ganze Kunstwerk durchziehenden Gewebe von Grundthemen, welche sich, ähnlich wie im Symphoniesatze, gegenüberstehen, ergänzen, neu gestalten, trennen und verbinden: nur daß hier die ausgeführte und aufgeführte dramatische Handlung die Gesetze der Scheidungen und Verbindungen gibt, welche dort allerursprünglichst den Bewegungen des Tanzes entnommen waren*« [23] Daß »*einzelnen kleineren, willkürlich herausgehobenen Teilen*« einer Oper eine Motivtechnik zugrundelag, die man symphonisch nennen konnte, war nichts Ungewöhnliches. Wenn also Wagner betont, daß sich im Wort-Ton-Drama der Motivzusammenhang über das ganze Werk erstrecke, so hebt er hervor, was an seinem kompositorischen Verfahren neu war. Und die Beschreibung, in der er die eigene Methode an die Tradition anknüpft und zugleich von ihr abhebt, schließt nicht aus, daß auch einzelne Teile des Wort-Ton-Dramas, nicht nur das Ganze, eine symphonische Form ausprägen. [24] Die »Einheit des Symphoniesatzes« ist das Modell der Perioden, Periodengruppen und Szenen.

Die Walkürenszene, die den dritten Akt der *Walküre* eröffnet, kann ohne Gewaltsamkeit als symphonischer Satz beschrieben werden, der nach dem Schema der Sonatenform — allerdings einem modifizierten — in Hauptthema (T. 1—44), Seitenthema (T. 45—59), Durchführung (T. 79—98), Reprise (T. 99—161), zweite Durchführung (T. 162—205) und Coda (T. 205—215) gegliedert ist. Daß zwischen Seitenthema und Durchführung eine Wiederkehr des Hauptthemas eingeschoben ist (T. 59—78), erinnert an den Satztypus, den die Formenlehre als Sonatenrondo rubriziert. Und auch der tiefer in das Schema eingreifende Formgedanke, der Reprise eine zweite Durchführung folgen zu lassen, die sogar die erste an Ausdehnung und Bedeutung übertrifft, ist nicht ohne geschichtliche Vorbilder und stellt weniger eine Verzerrung des Satztypus als vielmehr ein Zeichen dafür dar, daß die Reprise, die als gleichsam statisches Moment in die dynamische Sonatenform des 19. Jahrhunderts hereinragt, zum Problem geworden ist: Einer der Lösungsversuche ist die Umdeutung der Reprise zum Ansatz oder zur Voraussetzung einer zweiten Durchführung. Zudem hat die Coda, als Zusammenfassung oder Rekapitulation der Themen,

[23] R. Wagner, *Gesammelte Schriften und Dichtungen*, herausgegeben von W. Golther, Berlin o. J., Band X, S. 185.

[24] Die Worte »*nicht nur*« in dem Satz, daß die Form »*über das ganze Drama sich erstreckt, nicht nur über einzelne kleinere, willkürlich herausgehobene Teile desselben*«, sind in einschließendem, nicht in ausschließendem Sinne gemeint: auch für kleinere Teile gilt, daß sie »*die Einheit des Symphoniesatzes aufweisen*«, was zu betonen jedoch überflüssig war, da es sich von selbst verstand.

134

Reprisencharakter, ist allerdings zu kurz, um als räumlich-symmetrischer, architektonischer Widerpart der Exposition zu wirken. Lorenz [25] deutet die beiden parallelen Verläufe, die Exposition mit Durchführung einerseits und die Reprise mit zweiter Durchführung andererseits, als Stollen und Gegenstollen einer Barform: eine Interpretation, die zwar — abgesehen von der gewaltsamen Zusammenfassung der Coda mit der folgenden Periode zu einem »Abgesang« — nicht irrig ist, aber eine Begründung der doppelten Durchführung aus der Entwicklungsgeschichte der symphonischen Form schuldig bleibt. Die Analyse, die in einem Buchstabenschema terminiert, bedarf, um nicht leer und nichtssagend zu sein, der Ergänzung durch eine genetische Erklärung.

Sind demnach außer dem ganzen Drama auch manche Teile als Analoga eines »Symphoniesatzes« beschreibbar, so erscheint es als terminologische Willkür, die nicht ohne sachliche Konsequenz bleibt, wenn Lorenz [26] einzig das erste Hervortreten eines Motivs in der gesamten Tetralogie als Exposition gelten läßt. Im dritten Akt der *Walküre* fällt das Walkürenmotiv, obwohl es unleugbar als Hauptthema eines Abschnitts in Sonatenform fungiert, für Lorenz unter den Begriff der »Themenverarbeitung«, weil es bereits früher, *»zuerst als Codagedanke der Einleitung zum II. Walkürenaufzuge«*, erschienen ist. [27] Die »Themenaufstellungen« werden den »Themenverarbeitungen« abstrakt — ohne daß die Trennung musikalisch-konkret, aus der Stellung und Funktion der Motive im Kontext, zu begründen wäre — entgegengesetzt. Und die Fragwürdigkeit der Methode zeigt sich an der Irrelevanz des Resultats. *»Es kann nun nachgewiesen werden, daß dieselben Formen, die bei der Aufstellung der Themen zutage getreten sind, auch in der Gruppierung der Motive in verschiedensten Ausmaßen wiederkehren«.* [28] Der »Nachweis« der Indifferenz, der Nicht-Unterscheidbarkeit von Aufstellung und Verarbeitung ist ein Ergebnis, das die Methode, aus der es resultiert, ad absurdum führt. Denn wenn Exposition und Durchführung, die *»Zeiten der Form«*, um mit August Halm zu sprechen, sich nicht mehr voneinander abheben, büßt der Begriff der symphonischen Form seine Substanz ein und wird zur leeren Vokabel. Entweder ist also von dem »Symphoniesatze«, auf den sich Wagner berief, nichts als das »Gewebe« der Motive — ohne Differenzierung der formalen Funktionen — übrig geblieben; oder aber die Kategorien, die Lorenz seinen Analysen zugrunde legte, sind der symphonischen Form des Wort-Ton-Dramas inadäquat.

Lorenz ist in dem Vorurteil befangen, daß eine musikalische Form, um plastisch zu sein, einem einfachen Buchstabenschema entsprechen müsse; und fast scheint es, als verbürge ihm das einprägsame graphische Bild einer Analyse deren musikalische Triftigkeit. Sein Formbegriff, für den Neologismen wie »Bogen« und »Strebebogen« bezeichnend sind, ist statisch: an räumlichen Vorstellungen orientiert. Ein »Bogen« mit rückläufiger Anordnung der Motive bei der Wiederkehr (a b c d e d c b a) soll als »vollkommener Bogen« gelten, obwohl der strenge Symmetriebegriff, der die Rückläufigkeit einschließt, als

---

[25] A. a. O., S. 245 ff.
[26] A. a. O., S. 75 ff.
[27] A. a. O., S. 78.
[28] A. a. O., S. 120.

musikalische Kategorie fragwürdig ist: Übertragen auf einen Vorgang in der Zeit mangelt es der Symmetrie — dem Krebsgang — an Prägnanz, so daß es ein terminologischer Mißgriff ist, sie als das musikalisch-formal »Vollkommene« zu rühmen. Lorenz aber ist unbeirrbar davon überzeugt, daß die Architekturmetaphern, die er benutzt, das Wesen der musikalischen Form ausdrücken. Veränderungen der Motive erscheinen darum nicht als Zeichen einer Entwicklung, die zu analysieren wäre, sondern als bloße Modifikationen der Buchstabenschemata, deren einfache Symmetrie sie stören. Das Entscheidende wird behandelt, als wäre es akzidentell. Die »entwickelnde Variation«, in der Schönberg das charakteristische Moment der symphonischen Technik erkannte, ist bei Lorenz gerade umgekehrt das, wovon er abstrahiert, um die Schemata entwerfen zu können, die für ihn den Inbegriff musikalischer Form darstellen.

Der Anfang der zweiten Szene aus dem ersten Akt des *Siegfried*, die Herausforderung Mimes durch Wotan, wurde von Lorenz [29] als »*Aufstellung von Wotans Wanderermotiv*« rubriziert und — nicht ohne Gewaltsamkeit — in vier Strophen gegliedert. [30] Lorenz verkannte, daß die »Aufstellung«, die sich über nicht weniger als 82 Takte erstreckt, bereits eine Verarbeitung — also nach Lorenzschen Begriffen ihr eigenes Gegenteil — in sich schließt und daß die Veränderung eines Motivs von nicht geringerer Bedeutung als die Wiederkehr ist, an die sich Lorenz klammert. Das Wanderermotiv erscheint auf wechselnden Stufen, wird parodistisch diminuiert (T. 27: »*nennt dich ›Wand'rer‹ die Welt*«), in Fragmente zerspalten (T. 34—39: »*denn Unheil fürchtet*«) und mit sich selbst verschränkt (T. 55—61: »*Einsam will ich und einzeln sein*«): Der dritte Akkord der Aufstellung ist zugleich der erste der Sequenz. Und daß die Varianten als solche kenntlich sind, setzt voraus, daß das Motiv zu Beginn der Szene nachdrücklich exponiert worden ist. Die Szene, Periode oder Periodengruppe stellt — analog einem Symphoniesatz oder Satzteil — den Kontext dar, innerhalb dessen die Modifikationen eines Motivs aufeinander bezogen werden.

Andererseits bildet im *Ring* außer der einzelnen Szene, Periode oder Periodengruppe auch die Tetralogie insgesamt einen Zusammenhang oder ein Bezugssystem, von dem die Bedeutung und Funktion der Motive abhängt. Ein Drama im Ganzen ist zwar nicht Form im Sinne der musikalischen Formenlehre — wenn Lorenz die drei Akte der *Meistersinger* als Stollen, Gegenstollen und Abgesang einer Barform apostrophiert, gebraucht er eine bloße Metapher und nicht einmal eine treffende —, wirkt aber zurück auf die Formen der einzelnen Teile: Daß die Motive doppelt bezogen sind, sowohl auf das ganze Drama als auch auf die einzelne Szene, erlaubt im engeren Kontext Verknüpfungen und Dispositionen, die in einem symphonischen Satz nicht möglich wären.

Waltrautes Erzählung, das Zentrum der dritten Szene aus dem ersten Akt der *Götterdämmerung*, ist insofern ein Gegenbild zur Wandererszene aus *Siegfried*, als die Varianten der Motive den Modellen, von denen sie abgeleitet sind, vorausgehen. Das Walhall- und das Rheingold-Motiv erscheinen zunächst in

---

[29] A. a. O., S. 84 ff.
[30] Die Gliederung in vier »Strophen« ist willkürlich, denn die Abweichungen sind auffälliger und relevanter als die Übereinstimmungen.

verzerrter (»*Jüngst kehrte er heim*« und »*Seine Raben beide*«), dann in ursprünglicher Gestalt (»*Der Götter Rat*« und »*dann noch einmal*«). Die »natürliche« Reihenfolge ist umkehrbar, weil sich die Motive durch ungezählte Wiederholungen in den früheren Teilen der Tetralogie dem Hörer fest eingeprägt haben. Daß sie, um verständlich zu sein, an weit Zurückliegendes angeknüpft werden müssen, besagt jedoch nicht, daß der unmittelbare, engere Kontext nicht auch in sich sinnvoll wäre. Der Übergang von der getrübten zur originalen Version der Motive ist als musikalischer Verlauf nicht weniger einleuchtend als das Gegenteil. Der Motivzusammenhang, der das ganze Drama umfaßt, ist also, ohne selbst Form zu sein, eine der Voraussetzungen für die Formen der einzelnen Teile; sie isoliert zu analysieren, wie es Lorenz versucht, ist inadäquat. Und umgekehrt müssen in den einzelnen Teilen überschaubare symphonische Formen ausgeprägt sein, wenn nicht das Motivgewebe, in dem alles mit allem verknüpft ist, als wirrer Knäuel wirken soll. Das Formproblem in Wagners *Ring* ist das Problem der Vermittlung — der mittleren Stufen — zwischen dem einzelnen Motiv und dem ganzen Drama.

5. An dem Begriff der »*dichterisch-musikalischen Periode*«, den Wagner in *Oper und Drama* entwickelte, pointierte Lorenz [31] einseitig das Moment der tonalen Geschlossenheit. Doch ist die Deutung der Periode als Abschnitt, der durch Einheit der Tonart gekennzeichnet ist, sowohl philologisch als auch sachlich haltlos. Sie verzerrt das von Wagner Gemeinte [32] und führt zu der fragwürdigen, als Maxime einer Theorie der musikalischen Form geradezu absurden Konsequenz, daß die Ausdehnung der Perioden an keine Norm, auch keine ungefähre, gebunden sei und zwischen Extremen wechseln könne: Die kürzeste der Perioden, in die Lorenz den *Ring* gliedert, umfaßt 14 Takte [33] und verhält sich zur längsten, die sich über 840 Takte erstreckt [34], wie 1:60.

Die Gleichgültigkeit gegenüber der Größenordnung, auf die sich ein Formbegriff bezieht, ist charakteristisch für das analytische Verfahren, mit dem Lorenz zu zeigen versuchte, daß der *Ring* als musikalische Architektur zu begreifen sei. Dieselben Formprinzipien, die im einzelnen herrschen, sollen auch über weite Strecken wirksam sein, ohne daß es notwendig wäre, die Begriffe zu modifizieren, wenn sie von kurzen Phrasen auf ganze Szenen übertragen werden. Die Frage, ob jedes der Schemata, mit denen Lorenz operiert, in jeder Größenordnung denselben Sinn habe, wird nicht einmal gestellt; das Fragwürdigste wird behandelt, als sei es selbstverständlich.

Der Begriff der Barform, den Lorenz ins Zentrum seiner Thorie der musikalischen Form rückte, ist von Liedstrophen, die aus Zeilen von vier oder acht Takten bestehen, abstrahiert. Und man kann zweifeln, ob es sinnvoll ist, einerseits ein Motiv von einem Takt Länge [36] und andererseits einen Komplex, der

---

31 A. a. O., S. 18 ff.
32 C. Dahlhaus, *Wagners Begriff der »dichterisch-musikalischen Periode«*, Beiträge zur Geschichte der Musikanschauung im 19. Jahrhundert, Regensburg 1965, S. 179 ff.
33 A. a. O., S. 152.
34 A. a. O., S. 223 f.
35 A. a. O., S. 9 und S. 121.
36 z. B. a. a. O., S. 241 (Übergang Gd. III).

Hunderte von Takten ausfüllt [37], als »Stollen« eines »Bar« zu klassifizieren. Die quantitative Differenz bedeutet einen qualitativen Sprung. Die Wiederholung einer Zeilenmelodie stiftet Form im räumlich-symmetrischen, architektonischen Sinne; dagegen ist die Sequenzierung eines kurzen Motivs ein bloßes Fortspinnungsverfahren, kein Formprinzip. Und der Begriff des Bar, der beides einschließen soll, schrumpft zu einer Abstraktion, so nichtssagend wie das Buchstabenschema a a b, dessen Etikett er ist.

Der Substanzlosigkeit des Formbegriffs entspricht die Willkür, mit der er benutzt und den Phänomenen aufgezwungen wird. Die 14taktige »Periode«, Hagens Erzählung von Brünnhilde aus dem ersten Akt der *Götterdämmerung* (»*Ein Weib weiß ich*«), ist nach Lorenz [38], der allerdings Zweifel an seiner eigenen Analyse andeutet, »barförmig« in 2+2+10 Takte gegliedert. Es ist jedoch durch nichts gerechtfertigt, aus einem Komplex von vier Motiven, die nach dem Schema

a^1	a^2	b	b	c	c	d^1	d^2
2	2	2	2	1	1	2	1

wiederholt oder sequenziert werden, das erste als »Stollen« und »Gegenstollen« herauszulösen und die übrigen zu einem »Abgesang« zusammenzufassen.

Gegenüber Fehlgriffen in der Größenordnung, in der ein Formprinzip wirksam zu werden vermag, Irrtümern also, die einen Mangel an Reflexion über das Wesen der musikalischen Form verraten, sind bloße Mißverhältnisse zwischen den Teilen, die Lorenz aufeinander bezieht, von geringerer Bedeutung; doch sind sie als Indizien nicht ohne Relevanz. Die Barform, die nach Lorenz [39] dem Anfang von Brünnhildes Monolog in der Schlußszene des zweiten Aktes der *Götterdämmerung* zugrundeliegt (»*Welches Unholds List*«), repräsentiert eine Proportion, 1:1:4, die verzerrt wirkt: »Stollen« und »Gegenstollen« umfassen je 7, der »Abgesang«, dessen Übergewicht erdrückend ist, 28 Takte. Und der äußere, scheinbar geringfügige Mangel ist das Zeichen und Resultat eines Irrtums in der Methode: des Fehlers, heterogene Stücke, die durch eine unüberhörbare Zäsur voneinander getrennt sind, unter der Bezeichnung »Abgesang« zusammenzuzwingen. Der Begriff der Barform ist zwar der Durchführungstechnik, ein Modell zu sequenzieren und einzelne Motive abzuspalten, nicht adäquat, würde aber, mit Vorbehalt gebraucht, immerhin dem Sachverhalt gerecht werden, daß die ersten 22 oder 26 Takte des Monologs zusammengehören: Ein Komplex von drei Motiven, der sich über sieben Takte erstreckt, wird zunächst in Halbtontransposition wiederholt, um dann durch Abspaltung und isolierte Sequenzierung eines der Motive, des Motivs der Todesverkündigung, fortgesponnen zu werden. Und die folgende Phrase (»*Ach Jammer*«) knüpft melodisch — durch den Halbton abwärts in punktiertem oder synkopiertem Rhythmus — an den Motivkomplex an. Der Rest des »Abgesangs« aber ist in Wahrheit eine zweite Periode (»*All mein Wissen*«), in der eine kantable Phrase den prägnanten Vordersatz einer sequenzierenden Fortspinnung bildet. Und sie

[37] z. B. a. a. O., S. 184.
[38] A. a. O., S. 152.
[39] A. a. O., S. 153.

wurde von Lorenz nur darum mit der ersten zusammengefaßt, weil ihre Form, für die Wilhelm Fischer den Terminus »Fortspinnungstypus« prägte, in dem Repertoire der Schemata, über die Lorenz verfügt, nicht enthalten ist.

Ähnlich fragwürdig ist die »Bogenform« a b a mit der schiefen Proportion 40:54:10, die Lorenz [40] aus Siegfrieds Erzählung in der zweiten Szene des dritten Aktes der *Götterdämmerung* herauslas. Eine Reprise von zehn Takten ist zweifellos zu kurz, um als Widerpart einer Exposition, die sich über 40 Takte erstreckt, fühlbar zu sein. Und gerade einen Analytiker, der Form als tönende Architektur begriff, hätte das Mißverhältnis stutzig machen müssen. Außerdem beruht die Bezeichnung »Reprise« auf grober Übertreibung: Mit dem Hauptsatz (*»Mime hieß ein mürrischer Zwerg«*), als dessen Wiederkehr er gelten soll, hat der dritte Abschnitt (*»Mit tödlichem Tranke«*) nichts gemeinsam als ein einziges Motiv, das Schmiedemotiv, das vier Takte ausfüllt. Eine flüchtige Reminiszenz wird also zur fiktiven Reprise aufgebläht, umgekehrt aber ein realer Zusammenhang unterdrückt, so unüberhörbar er sich aufdrängt: Daß das Waldweben, das über weite Strecken (43 von 54 Takten) die Substanz des »Mittelteils« bildet, nach 29 Takten wiederkehrt, wird als irrelevant abgetan; Lorenz nimmt zwischen Exposition und Reprise, obwohl sie sogar in derselben Tonart stehen, eine Periodengrenze an, zerschneidet also, ohne daß ein Grund ersichtlich wäre, einen Zusammenhang, den er andererseits nicht leugnet. [41]   Die Konstruktion schiefer äußerer Proportionen, die einen Irrtum im Ansatz der Analyse verrät, ist bei Lorenz nicht selten mit einer Verkennung des inneren Gewichts der miteinander verglichenen Teile verbunden: mit einer Fehleinschätzung also, die durch den Entschluß des orthodoxen Wagnerianers motiviert sein dürfte, sich blind zu machen gegenüber den Differenzen zwischen deklamatorischen und ariosen Partien.

Der »vollkommene Bogen« (a¹ b¹ c¹ ... c² b² a²), den Lorenz [42] im Anfangsteil der ersten *Rheingold*-Szene (*»Weia! Waga!«*) zu erkennen meint, erweist sich als Fiktion. Der Motivzusammenhang der Teile b¹ (T. 182—211: *»Hehe! Ihr Nicker!«*) und b² (T. 408—420: *»Wehe! Ach wehe!«*) ist, sofern er überhaupt existiert, zu schwach, als daß b² über Hunderte von Takten hinweg als Reprise von b¹ kenntlich wäre. Daß in den Takten 182—183 das Fronmotiv der Takte 408—409 vorgeformt sei, ist ebenso schwer einzusehen wie die Verknüpfung der Takte 202—203 und 412.

[40] A. a. O., S. 219.

[41] A. a. O., S. 202: *»Einschaltung der dritten Strophe des Vogelsangliedes aus der vorigen Periode.«* Die Abspaltung von der *»vorigen Periode«* ist um so unbegreiflicher, als der *»Einschaltung«* nichts als eine *»Einleitung«* vorausgeht.

[42] A. a. O., S. 166. Lorenz charakterisiert die Teile a b c, obwohl er eine Umkehrung zu c b a annimmt, als Hauptthema, Seitenthema und Schlußsatz.

Vollends haltlos aber ist die Behauptung, daß die Teile c¹ (T. 211—230: »*Mit uns will er spielen?*«) und c² (T. 331—407: »*Was zankst du, Alb?*«) sich »entsprechen«. Denn zwischen den beiden Abschnitten besteht weder ein melodischer Konnex noch eine Analogie auf Grund gleicher äußerer Ausdehnung. Und die Disproportion — das Mißverhältnis 1:4 — ist das Korrelat einer Differenz der musikalischen Bedeutung, wie sie schroffer kaum vorstellbar ist. Wird der Teil c¹ mit deklamatorischen Phrasen bestritten, die sich nirgends zu eigentlicher Melodik verfestigen, so ist c² ein beinahe konventionell kantables Duett, das dadurch, daß es parodistisch pointiert ist, nichts von der Prägnanz verliert, durch die es sich aus dem Kontext heraushebt. Von einem »vollkommenen Bogen«, in dem c² das Gegenstück zu c¹ wäre, kann also nicht die Rede sein.

An einem ähnlichen Irrtum, der Verkennung einer melodischen Kulmination als »Entsprechung« einer unscheinbar deklamatorischen Partie, krankt Lorenz' Analyse [43] des Anfangs der dritten *Rheingold*-Szene (Takt 1878—2035).

Um das Schema

a¹	b	c¹	d¹	e	d²	c²	f	a²
16	14	22	11	12	16	15	30	21

zu einem »vollkommenen Bogen« umdeuten zu können, ist Lorenz gezwungen zu der Behauptung, daß f eine »Entsprechung« zu b sei. Das Fronmotiv aber, auf dessen Wiederkehr sich die These stützt, ist zu schwach und flüchtig angedeutet, als daß es eine Analogie zwischen weit voneinander entfernten Abschnitten zu begründen vermöchte.

Entscheidend ist allerdings erst die von Lorenz verkannte oder unterdrückte Tatsache, daß ein unauffälliges Dialogstück (b) unmöglich als formaler Widerpart zu Alberichs pathetischem »Herrscherruf« (f), dem Höhepunkt, dem die Szene zustrebt, gelten kann.

6. Gemessen an der kaum absehbaren Menge denkbarer Schemata ist die Anzahl derer, die als sinnvoll gelten und von der musikalischen Formenlehre registriert werden, äußerst gering. Und die Beschränkung auf wenige Typen hat ihren Grund in der Sache, so billig andererseits der Triumph mancher Analytiker ist, die Wesentliches entdeckt zu haben glauben, wenn es ihnen gelingt, alle Musik, derer sie habhaft werden, auf die gleichen Schemata zu reduzieren: Daß das Wiederkehrende das Entscheidende sei, ist ein Aberglaube einer auf bloße Klassifikationsbegriffe zielenden Wissenschaft.

Die Auswahl der Schemata, die in der Formenlehre beschrieben werden, beruht, wenn auch unausgesprochen, auf der Einsicht, daß Formtypen von Strukturprinzipien abhängig oder mit ihnen durch Wechselwirkung verbunden sind.

43 A. a. O., S. 164.

So beruht etwa das Rondo, im Unterschied zu der Sonatenform, auf deutlicher, gleichsam architektonischer Abhebung der Teile; und es verliert seine raison d'être, sobald die »entwickelnde Variation«, um mit Schönberg zu sprechen, zur herrschenden Kompositionstechnik wird.

Ob die Schemata, mit denen Lorenz operiert, die Sache treffen oder verfehlen, ist also nicht ohne Berücksichtigung der Strukturprinzipien, die das Korrelat der Formen bilden, zu entscheiden. Und ein einfaches Exempel, an dem sich das Problem deutlich machen läßt, ist die von Lorenz zwar niemals ausgesprochene, aber in den Analysen praktizierte Maxime, daß der »Bar«, die Gliederung nach dem Schema a a b, das Strukturgesetz der Wagnerschen Sequenztechnik darstelle. So hartnäckig jedoch Lorenz an seinem Prinzip festhält, so irrig ist es. Um das Schema a a b zu erhalten, ist Lorenz immer wieder gezwungen, die reale Gliederung a a a b zu verleugnen und entweder die dritte a-Phrase zum »Abgesang« zu zählen [44] oder die erste als bloße »Ankündigung« von den übrigen abzutrennen. [45] Die Barformen, die Lorenz mit der Genugtuung eines Analytikers registriert, der seine Vorurteile bestätigt findet, sind zu einem nicht geringen Teil das Resultat willkürlicher Abgrenzungen und Zusammenfassungen; Lorenz setzt die Zäsuren, wo er sie brauchen kann. Die Notwendigkeit aber, Verbundenes zu trennen und Getrenntes zu verbinden, ist nichts anderes als eine Konsequenz des bereits früher erwähnten Irrtums, daß auf engem Raum dieselben Strukturgesetze gelten wie bei Formen, die sich über Dutzende oder Hunderte von Takten erstrecken, daß also das Schema a a a b nur darum, weil es in längeren Sätzen widersinnig wäre, auch bei Gebilden geringen Umfanges verfehlt sei — und verleugnet werden müsse, wenn es dennoch erscheint. So lästig und inadäquat es jedoch wäre, wenn die Anfangszeile eines Liedes oder die Exposition eines Sonatensatzes zweimal repetiert würde, so angemessen ist die doppelte Sequenzierung der Struktur mancher Wagnerschen Leitmotive.

Auch andere Abweichungen von den gewohnten Formtypen erweisen sich als legitim, sobald man die Voraussetzungen berücksichtigt, von denen sie getragen werden. Die dritte Szene des zweiten Aktes der *Walküre*, die Flucht Siegmunds und Sieglindes, stellt nach Lorenz [46] eine einzige lang ausgesponnene Periode dar, deren Anfang in eine Einleitung von 32 und einen Hauptteil von 142 Takten zerfalle.

I:	a^1	b^1	a^2		II:	a^3	b^2	a^4	c^1	d^1	a^5	f	c^2	b^3	d^2	a^6
	12	9	11			11	8	12	7	9	20	9	23	20	16	7

Die Zäsur zwischen a^2 und a^3 ist jedoch eine willkürliche, durch nichts gerechtfertigte Festsetzung, denn a^3 ist eine Transposition von a^2, und zwar eine Transposition von einer Genauigkeit der melodischen Übereinstimmung, wie sie im *Ring* bei Motivkomplexen, die sich über nicht weniger als 11 Takte erstrecken, selten ist. Das Ziel der Gewaltsamkeit, mit der Lorenz analysiert, ist die Konstruktion von zwei »Bögen«: a^1 b^1 a^2 und a^3 b^2 a^4. Statt in der Gliederung

[44] A. a. O., S. 153 (Gd. II, P. 14: 3+3+6 ist eine Umdeutung von 3+3+3+3) und S. 250 (Gd. I, P. 4: 4+4+7 ist eine Verzerrung von 4+4+3+4).
[45] A. a. O., S. 202 (Gd. III, P. 6).
[46] A. a. O., S. 168 ff.

109

a^1 b^1 a^2 a^3 b^2 a^4 eine Form eigenen Rechts zu erkennen — die Sequenztechnik, die im Detail herrscht, setzt sich in der Transposition von a^2 gleichsam auf höherer Stufe fort —, zerschneidet Lorenz den Zusammenhang zwischen a^2 und a^3, weil einerseits die unmittelbare Repetition vom traditionellen Rondoschema (das er sonst zweifellos dem Abschnitt zugrundegelegt hätte) abweicht und weil sich andererseits durch Abtrennung einer »Einleitung« der Schein eines doppelten »Bogens« hervorbringen läßt.

Kaum weniger fragwürdig ist es, daß Lorenz die Abschnitte d^1 und a^5, die zusammen einen kantablen Mittelteil bilden, durch eine Zäsur voneinander trennt: d^1 soll als Schluß eines Hauptsatzes gelten, der mit a^3 beginnt und dessen Reprise Lorenz in den Abschnitten b^3 d^2, der modifizierten Wiederkehr von b^2 und d^1, zu erkennen meint. Sofern aber d^2, Diminution von d^1, eine Reprise darstellt, kann dasselbe auch von a^5, einer Augmentation von a^3 und a^4, behauptet werden; die Hypothese, daß zwar a^5, aber nicht d^1 als kontrastierender oder mindestens abgehobener Mittelteil aufzufassen sei, ist hinfällig, weil sie in Widerspruch zur satztechnischen Struktur gerät.

7. Die Gewaltsamkeit, mit der Lorenz der »unendlichen Melodie«, die von Wagner als Gegensatz zum Lied konzipiert wurde, Schemata der konventionellen Formenlehre aufprägt, bewegt sich, als Methode betrachtet, zwischen Extremen. Einerseits löst Lorenz aus einem dichten Themengeflecht einzelne Motive — nicht selten sogar unscheinbare — heraus und erklärt sie zu konstitutiven Merkmalen einer Strophen- oder Reprisenform. Andererseits zwingt er einer ungegliederten Reihe von Repetitionen desselben Motivs eine symmetrische Form auf — das zweite Verfahren ist dem ersten, mit dem es nichts als die Willkür teilt, schroff entgegengesetzt.

Der Dialog zwischen Hagen und Brünnhilde in der Schlußszene des zweiten Aktes der *Götterdämmerung* (*»Vertraue mir, betrog'ne Frau«*) zerfällt nach Lorenz[47] in vier Strophen von ungleicher Länge (18, 9, 23 und 23 Takte). Die Übereinstimmung der Strophen, die keine sind, beschränkt sich jedoch auf wenige Takte — die zweite und dritte haben sogar nur einen einzigen, in dem das Siegfriedmotiv zitiert wird, gemeinsam: eine Tatsache, die angesichts der Vielzahl von Motiven, die in dem Dialog auf engem Raum zusammengedrängt sind, eher auf eine Tendenz, Wiederholungen zu vermeiden, als auf einen Zug zu räumlich-symmetrischen Formen schließen läßt. Wagners Motivgruppierungen sind der »musikalischen Prosa« Arnold Schönbergs näher als den Liedformen, auf die Lorenz sie reduzieren möchte. (Die Neigung des Historikers, im Neuen und Ungewohnten Altes und Vertrautes wiederzuerkennen, wird von Lorenz ins Extrem getrieben.)

Dasselbe Resultat, eine Strophenform, die sich bei näherem Hinsehen als Fiktion erweist, erzwingt Lorenz[48] auch bei umgekehrten Voraussetzungen, wie sie etwa in dem Dialog zwischen Alberich und Loge in der dritten Szene des *Rheingold* gegeben sind (*»Nach Nibelheim führt euch der Neid«*). Einem Rezitativ, das durch ein ostinat wiederkehrendes Motiv, das Logemotiv, gestützt

47 A. a. O., S. 130.
48 A. a. O., S. 226.

und unterbrochen wird, prägt Lorenz eine vermeintliche Strophenform auf, die sich auf nichts anderes gründet, als daß das Orchestermotiv in jeder der beiden Strophen dreimal — allerdings in unregelmäßigen Abständen und in wechselnder Länge — zitiert wird.

Es dürfte beinahe überflüssig sein, weitere Beispiele für die Willkür zu häufen, mit der einem widerstrebenden musikalischen Text Formprinzipien aufgedrängt werden, die ihm von Grund auf fremd sind. Das »Geheimnis der Form« bei Richard Wagner besteht zu einem nicht geringen Teil in der Hartnäckigkeit, mit der Lorenz darauf insistiert, es entdeckt zu haben. Wenn er[49] etwa den Schluß von Siegfrieds Erzählung im dritten Akt der *Götterdämmerung* (»...*bis den feurigen Fels ich traf*«) mit der Ermordungsszene und dem Sterbegesang (»*Brünnhild! Heilige Braut!*«) zu einer »Bogenform« zusammenfaßt, so ist die Gewaltsamkeit des Verfahrens unverkennbar: Der Sterbegesang, eine tönende Erinnerung an Brünnhildes Erwachen im dritten Akt des *Siegfried*, hat mit der Erzählung, als deren Reprise er gelten soll, nicht das Geringste gemeinsam. Und fast scheint es, liege der Konstruktion einer Bogenform unbewußt ein Moment zugrunde, das Lorenz verleugnet hätte, wenn es ihm bewußt geworden wäre: die Differenz zwischen Arioso (Erzählung und Sterbegesang) und Rezitativ (Ermordungsszene).

Wenn Lorenz behauptet[50], Hagens Erzählung von Siegfried im ersten Akt der *Götterdämmerung* (»*Ein Zwillingspaar, von Liebe bezwungen*«) sei in eine Bogen- und eine Strophenliedform gegliedert, so genügt ein zweiter Blick, der sich von bestechenden Tabellen nicht über musikalische Sachverhalte hinwegtäuschen läßt, um zu erkennen, daß weder die Reprise der Bogenform eine Reprise noch die Gegenstrophe der Liedform eine Strophe ist. Daß von drei Motiven eines — und nicht einmal das erste — wiederkehrt, begründet keine Entsprechung ganzer Komplexe; und daß zwei Abschnitte, die nicht ein einziges Motiv gemeinsam haben, zu Strophen erklärt werden, bleibt unbegreiflich, solange man nicht das Prinzip der »Stellvertretung« der Motive akzeptiert, auf das Lorenz immer dann zurückgreift, wenn alle übrigen versagen. Um aber in der Rheingoldfanfare einen Ersatz des Ringmotivs zu erkennen, bedarf es eher allegorischer als musikalischer Anstrengungen. Und da im *Ring*, mindestens in den späteren Teilen, schließlich alles mit allem zusammenhängt, hindert nichts den Interpreten, die Allegorese, von der die »Stellvertretung« der Motive abhängt, ins Unabsehbare ausschweifen zu lassen.

»*Auch bei Wagner werden uns neben Teilen, die einander sehr ähnlich, ja fast gleich sind, Strecken begegnen, die sich nur in der Stimmung entsprechen ... Es entstehen dann Symmetrien ohne nachweisbare Gleichheit, in denen sich nur der geistige Niederschlag wiederholt. Es tritt also hier für die Melodik das Prinzip der ›Stellvertretung‹ in Wirksamkeit, ein Prinzip, das in der Harmonik längst anerkannt ist und mittels dessen man tiefe Einblicke in die dominantischen und subdominantischen Funktionen der Harmonien gewonnen hat ... Diese ›freie Symmetrie‹ kann sich bis zur ›Gegensatz-Symmetrie‹ stei-*

49 A. a. O., S. 202.
50 A. a. O., S. 254 f.

gern, wenn ... *direkt gegensätzliche Motive durch ihre Anordnung als Entsprechungen sich erweisen und so eine ebenmäßige Großrhythmik erfühlt wird.*« [51]
Der Vergleich mit der Harmonik — in der es übrigens die von Lorenz postulierte »Gegensatz-Symmetrie« nicht gibt — ist trügerisch. Die Stellvertretung von Akkorden ist durch eine Theorie der harmonischen Funktionen erklärbar, die auch Einschränkungen vorschreibt; so ist etwa die IV. Stufe zwar in der Kadenz IV-V-I, aber nicht in dem Plagalschluß IV-I mit der II. Stufe vertauschbar. Dagegen ist eine analoge Theorie der melodisch-formalen Funktionen, eine Theorie, die zu begründen hätte, warum ein Motiv a zwar in Verknüpfungen mit x oder y, aber nicht in der Verbindung mit z durch b ersetzbar ist, kaum vorstellbar; sie wird denn auch von Lorenz nicht einmal skizziert.

Die Behauptung [52], daß in Siegmunds Erzählung aus dem ersten Akt der *Walküre* der Kontrast zwischen »*hastigem Hörnergetöse*« und »*unheimlicher Stille*« als »Gegensatz-Symmetrie« zu verstehen sei, die es rechtfertige, von zwei Stollen einer Barform zu sprechen, wäre nichts als ein bedeutungsloser Irrtum, über den man hinweggehen könnte, wenn sie nicht, ähnlich wie die Analyse von Siegfrieds Sterbegesang, ein halb unterdrücktes Bewußtsein von der gliedernden Wirkung des Unterschieds zwischen Arioso und Rezitativ verriete. Gerade die gewaltsamsten Analysen sind manchmal indirekte Zeugnisse für Einsichten, die Lorenz verleugnete, weil sie seine Konzeption gestört hätten

Andererseits sei nicht verkannt, daß der prekäre Begriff der »Gegensatz-Symmetrie« manche Sachverhalte wenn nicht trifft, so doch vage und andeutend umschreibt. Wenn Lorenz [53] die Perioden, in denen Siegfried den toten Mime in die Höhle wirft und den Leichnam Fafners vor deren Eingang wälzt, zusammenfaßt und als ergänzenden Kontrast interpretiert, so kann er sich einerseits auf die szenische Analogie und andererseits auf eine kurze Coda berufen, in der Wagner das Mime- und das Fafnermotiv unmittelbar nebeneinanderstellt.

Daß dichterisch-szenische Momente in die musikalische Form eingreifen und Analogien oder Gegensätze bewirken, ist eine Hypothese, die im Zusammenhang einer Theorie des Wort-Ton-Dramas begründet werden müßte, die aber Lorenz nur benutzt, um Mängel in der Symmetrie seiner musikalischen Formschemata auszugleichen. Was als Prinzip zu entfalten wäre, wird als Rettung aus Verlegenheiten mißbraucht. Es wirkt denn auch wie eine parodistische Pointierung der eigenen Interpretationsmaxime, wenn Lorenz [54] in seiner Analyse der zweiten Szene des *Rheingold* eine »freie Symmetrie« dadurch begründet, daß sich am Anfang einer Periode Fasolt und an deren Ende Freia »verlassen fühlt«. Und kaum weniger entlegen, um das Mindeste zu sagen, ist der Ge-

144

[51] A. a. O., S. 123. Um des Prinzips der »Stellvertretung« willen modifiziert Lorenz die Kennzeichnung der Musik als tönende Architektur: *»Oftmals paßt also der Vergleich mit der Baukunst nicht, man muß vielmehr eine andere Raumkunst heranziehen, die Malerei. In den Werken der Malerei gibt es eine Symmetrie höherer Ordnung, die nicht auf absoluter Gleichheit der Teile beruht, sondern nur auf Ähnlichkeit«* (a. a. O., S. 122).
[52] A. a. O., S. 157.
[53] A. a. O., S. 128.
[54] A. a. O., S. 139.

danke[55], Fafners Worte *»So sehr mich's reut«* und das Entsagungsmotiv, das vierzig Takte später zitiert wird, als zwei *»sentimentale Stellen«* einander gleichzusetzen.

Die von Lorenz zwar nicht ausgesprochene, aber in manchen Analysen praktizierte Maxime, daß die Übereinstimmung oder Verschiedenheit musikalischer Teilmomente, der Dynamik oder der Farbe, bereits genüge, um Formen zu begründen, bedarf der historischen Reduktion; sie ist nicht zu allen Zeiten gültig. So borniert es wäre, sich blind gegenüber dem Phänomen zu machen, daß die Funktion der Reprise von den sekundären, peripheren Merkmalen des Tonsatzes übernommen werden kann, so verfehlt ist es andererseits, die Bedingungen zu verkennen oder zu verleugnen, an die es geknüpft ist: Bedingungen, die Wagners Musik nicht erfüllt. Dynamik und Farbe wirken erst dann konstitutiv und nicht bloß akzessorisch, wenn rhythmische und melodische Wiederholungen vermieden werden: also in atonalen Werken wie Schönbergs *Erwartung*. In einer Wagner-Analyse ist die Behauptung, daß Analogien und Differenzen der Dynamik eine Form begründen[56], eine Übertreibung aus Verlegenheit. Und Ähnliches gilt von dem Verfahren, Partien auf Grund abstrakter satztechnischer Merkmale — *»absteigende Melodik«*[57], *»Akkordik«*[58], *»Unisono«*[59] oder *»plötzliches Abreißen«*[60] — einander gleichzusetzen. In einer Musik, die so sinnfällig ist wie die Wagners, sind abstrakte Analogien irrelevant.

III

Musikalische Formkategorien wie Periode und Strophe, Lied und Rondo können beschreibende, aber auch regulative Begriffe sein. Entweder registrieren sie, was vom Notentext ablesbar ist und sich in ein Schema bringen läßt, oder sie geben Gesichtspunkte an, unter denen die Motive und Phrasen, aus denen ein Satz besteht, zusammengefaßt und zueinander in Beziehungen gesetzt werden sollen.

Der Schlußteil von Brünnhildes Sterbegesang aus dem dritten Akt der *Götterdämmerung* (*»Grane, mein Roß«*) repräsentiert, grob vereinfacht, das Formschema

a^1	b^1	a^2	b^2	a^3
12	6	7	18	12

das aber, um keine nichtssagende Abstraktion zu bleiben, der Interpretation bedarf. Lorenz[61] sprach von zwei Strophen ($a^1 b^1$ und $a^2 b^2$); die letzte Wiederkehr des a-Teils, die zwölf Takte umfaßt, reduzierte er auf drei, die sich als bloßer Anhang abtun lassen. Die Verkürzung, durch die das Schema a b a b a

[55] A. a. O., S. 188.
[56] A. a. O., S. 136 (Gd. II, P. 7).
[57] A. a. O., S. 138 (Rh., P. 5).
[58] A. a. O., S. 135 (Wk. I, P. 9).
[59] A. a. O., S. 243.
[60] A. a. O., S. 193 (Gd. III, P. 4).
[61] A. a. O., S. 206 (Gd. III, P. 10, Schluß).

zu a b a b schrumpft, ist allerdings gewaltsam oder scheint es wenigstens zu sein. Und so wäre zu fragen, warum Lorenz eine Deutung der Periode als Doppelstrophe erzwang und auf die Interpretation als Rondo verzichtete, eine Interpretation, die nahegelegen hätte und die er in anderen Perioden aus schwächeren Andeutungen herauslas.

Sofern der Rondobegriff ein Formprinzip bezeichnet und nicht als bloßer Name für ein Buchstabenschema oder eine Gruppe von Buchstabenschemata gebraucht wird, impliziert er, daß das Ritornell den Hauptsatz darstellt, auf den der Akzent fällt; der wiederkehrende Teil soll als der entscheidende, als Gerüst der Form empfunden werden. In Brünnhildes Sterbegang ist jedoch gerade umgekehrt das Ritornell nichts als ein Ansatz für das Folgende oder eine Folie, von der es sich abhebt; und die Partie, die in der Sprache der Formenlehre als Episode zu etikettieren wäre, erscheint als Höhepunkt, dem die Entwicklung zustrebt. Der primäre Formteil des Rondos ist also zum sekundären geworden und der sekundäre zum primären: eine Akzentverlagerung, die in den Sinn der Form eingreift.

Deutung und Abgrenzung aber sind bei den Formen, in die sich die „unendliche Melodie" gliedert oder die man aus ihr herauszuhören meint, voneinander abhängig. Die Typen oder Modelle, an denen man sich orientiert, beeinflussen die Setzung oder Vermeidung von Zäsuren und umgekehrt. Ist der b-Teil des Sterbegesangs eine Kulmination und nicht eine Episode, so liegt es nahe, die Periode nach der Reprise des b-Teils — einer Wiederkehr, welche die Exposition noch überbietet — rasch, also mit einer kurzen Coda abzuschließen, statt sie in ein Ritornell einmünden zu lassen, das sich über nicht weniger als zwölf Takte erstreckt und als Abschwächung empfunden werden muß. Man könnte einwenden, der Motivzusammenhang, den Lorenz zerschneidet, sei so eng, daß sich einem unbefangenen Hörer die Vorstellung eines Schlußritornells geradezu aufdränge. Nach der Maxime, daß unter mehreren möglichen Interpretationen diejenige, die ein Werk am geglücktesten erscheinen läßt, die einzig triftige ist, sind jedoch ästhetisch-kompositionstechnische Normen wie die Regel über die Stellung von Höhepunkten für die Deutung und Abgrenzung musikalischer Formen keineswegs irrelevant, mag auch der erste Eindruck ihnen zuwiderlaufen. Und die Zäsur, die Lorenz setzte, eine Zäsur, die zunächst als willkürliche Zertrennung eines Motivzusammenhangs erscheint, wäre demnach in einem empfindlichen Formgefühl begründet, das nach dem Höhepunkt einer Periode deren Ende erwartet, also dazu neigt, das Folgende abzuspalten und als Neuansatz aufzufassen.

Es ist allerdings unwahrscheinlich, daß es ästhetisch-kompositionstechnische Gesichtspunkte waren, die Lorenz daran hinderten, die Periode als Rondo zu klassifizieren. Die Reduktion zur Doppelstrophe, die Verkürzung des Schlußritornells zum bloßen Anhang, war offenkundig anders motiviert: Lorenz[62] wollte der folgenden Periode, der eine räumlich-symmetrische, architektonische Disposition der Motive und Motivgruppen fehlt, wenigstens ein einfaches harmonisches Modell — Subdominante-Dominante-Tonika — zugrunde legen und konnte auf das Schlußritornell des Sterbegesangs, das die Subdominante aus-

[62] A. a. O., S. 186.

prägt, nicht verzichten, wenn sich das Schema eines tonal fundierten „Bar", in dem die Subdominante und die Dominante die beiden Stollen darstellen, ergeben sollte. Der Motivzusammenhang der einen Periode wurde der prägnanten Tonartenordnung der anderen — oder der Fiktion einer prägnanten Tonartenordnung — geopfert. Daß es demnach wenig einleuchtende Gründe waren, aus denen Lorenz die Periodenzäsur verschob, ändert jedoch nichts daran, daß es auch triftigere gibt, sie anders zu setzen, als es der Motivzusammenhang nahelegt. Eine Deutung, die vom Sinn musikalischer Formen ausgeht, ist manchmal gezwungen, von der Interpretation der Buchstabenschemata zu deren Modifikation fortzuschreiten.

Der Begriff der »dichterisch-musikalischen Periode«, den Wagner in *Oper und Drama* benutzte, bezeichnet Gebilde von ungefähr dreißig, seltener von fünfzig oder sechzig Takten, nicht aber, wie Lorenz vermutete, ganze Szenen oder Szenenteile, die Hunderte von Takten umfassen. [63] Daß Siegfrieds Abschied von Brünnhilde, Waltrautes Erzählung oder Brünnhildes Sterbegesang Perioden darstellen, die als geschlossene Formen, als »Bogen« oder »Bar«, begriffen werden sollen, ist eine Hypothese, die als Interpretation von Wagners Terminus irrig und als Zumutung an den Hörer utopisch sein dürfte.

Noch verwirrender als die Dehnung des Periodenbegriffs ins Monumental-Monströse ist jedoch die Unsicherheit über die Größenordnung der Formen, in der Lorenz den Hörer läßt. Ein Wechsel zwischen 14 Takten als unterem und 840 als oberem Extrem, wie ihn Lorenz annimmt, macht auch bei angestrengtester Aufmerksamkeit die musikalische Formwahrnehmung zunichte, die zu stützen doch gerade das Ziel war, das sich Lorenz gesetzt hatte. Wenn sich in einem so dichten Motivgeflecht, wie es die Musik der *Götterdämmerung* darstellt, Perioden mit deutlichem Anfang und Ende abzeichnen sollen, darf über die ungefähre Ausdehnung der Abschnitte, die als Perioden gemeint sind, kein Zweifel bestehen. Die formale Prägnanz der Perioden und die Festigkeit der Größenordnung, auf die sich ein um Formwahrnehmung bemühter Hörer einrichten muß, sind wechselseitig voneinander abhängig. Die Deutlichkeit der Periodengrenzen beruht auf der Faßlichkeit der Formen, zu denen sich die Motive gruppieren, aber auch umgekehrt die Einprägsamkeit von Motivgruppierungen auf Erwartungen des Hörers über die Länge der Perioden.

Waltrautes Erzählung im ersten Akt der *Götterdämmerung*, nach Lorenz [64] eine einzige Periode von mehr als 200 Takten, ist in Wahrheit ein Komplex von sieben Perioden, deren Zäsuren in der Dichtung deutlich vorgezeichnet sind. [65] Der Periodenbegriff verweist denn auch bei Wagner weniger auf die Komplementärrhythmik des Tanzes als auf die Syntax von Prosadichtungen, zu denen

[63] Dahlhaus, a. a. O., S. 179 f.
[64] A. a. O., S. 249 ff.
[65] Charakteristisch für die Tendenz zu gleichmäßiger Periodengliederung ist eine unscheinbare Änderung der Interpunktion. Bei der Komposition von Waltrautes Erzählung teilte Wagner den Abschnitt »*Jüngst kehrte er heim*...“ nicht in 4+8+8 Zeilen, wie es der Text nahelegte, sondern — zur Vermeidung einer kurzen Periode von nur vier Zeilen — in 8+12 Zeilen. Und um die musikalisch ausgeprägte Zäsur auch äußerlich kenntlich zu machen, vertauschte er am Schluß der achten Zeile (»*die Weltesche zu fällen*«) das Semikolon, das im gedruckten Textbuch steht, mit einem Punkt.

der *Ring* trotz des Stabreims, der für die Vertonung von geringer Relevanz ist, gezählt werden muß. Die ersten fünf Perioden sind relativ kurz; sie umfassen 17, 18, 17, 24 und 16 Takte, sind also so gleichmäßig, daß sich die Größenordnung, die der Gliederung zugrunde liegt, nachdrücklich einprägt. Die letzten beiden erreichen, mit 33 und 31 Takten, eine ungefähr doppelte Länge, ohne daß man die Dehnung als qualitativen Sprung, der zur Vertauschung des Periodenbegriffs mit einer übergeordneten Formkategorie zwingen würde, empfände. Um anzudeuten, wie willkürlich es ist, die sieben Perioden in ein zusammenfassendes Formschema zu pressen, mag der Hinweis genügen, daß die Barform a a b, die Lorenz der Erzählung überstülpte, unter seinen eigenen Voraussetzungen — die zu teilen allerdings schwerfällt — durch die Bogenform a b a ersetzbar wäre.

Die einzelnen Perioden sind durch Hauptmotive charakterisiert und voneinander abgehoben, die in entfernter Analogie den Situationsmotiven in älteren Opern, vor allem den großen Opern Spontinis, entsprechen. Der ersten Periode (*»Höre mit Sinn, was ich dir sage«*) liegt als Periodenmotiv das des Unmuts zugrunde, der zweiten (*»Jüngst kehrte er heim«*) das verzerrte und verdüsterte Walhallmotiv, der dritten (*»Des Stammes Scheite«*) das Motiv des Scheiterhaufens, der vierten (*»So sitzt er«*) das Todesmotiv und der fünften (*»Seine Raben beide«*) das Rheingoldmotiv in chromatisch getrübter und in ursprünglicher Fassung.

148

Die musikalische Entwicklung der Hauptmotive wird unterbrochen — und vor Monotonie bewahrt — durch eingesprengte Nebenmotive, die weniger durch den Gesamtcharakter der Periode als durch Details der Dichtung, zu deren Illustration sie dienen, hervorgerufen sind. Nicht selten stechen sie aus dem musikalischen Kontext befremdend hervor, wenn auch Wagner sich bei abrupten Motivzitaten, die gleichsam von außen in den musikalischen Zusammenhang hereinragen, manchmal um eine formale Rechtfertigung a posteriori bemüht.[66] Man könnte, mit nur geringer parodistischer Übertreibung, von Motiven sprechen, die auf ihr Stichwort erscheinen. Das Rittmotiv in der ersten, das Speer- und das Welteschemotiv in der zweiten und das Motiv der goldenen Äpfel in der vierten Periode von Waltrautes Erzählung sind nichts anderes als musikalische Verdoppelungen einzelner Vokabeln des Textes: weniger Symbole als Tautologien. Sogar vor Madrigalismen im verrufenen Sinne des Wortes scheut Wagner nicht immer zurück: daß von des *»Speeres Splittern«* die Rede ist, hindert ihn nicht, das unversehrte Speermotiv zu zitieren, sich also über die Negation hinwegzusetzen. Gerade die Nebenmotive aber knüpfen an die Tradition der Erinnerungsmotive an, eine Tradition, auf die sich sämtliche Versuche, eine Vorgeschichte der Leitmotivtechnik zu entdecken oder zu konstruieren, einseitig — unter Vernachlässigung der Situationsmotive in der älteren Oper — berufen.[67] Das sekundäre, ergänzende Verfahren wurde bei der historischen Reduktion behandelt, als sei es das primäre und charakteristische.

[66] A. Halm, *Musikdrama und Sonatenform*, in *Von Grenzen und Ländern der Musik*, München 1916, S. 49 ff.
[67] E. Schmitz, *Richard Wagner*, Leipzig 1909; K. Wörner, *Beiträge zur Geschichte des Leitmotivs in der Oper*, ZfMw XIV, S. 151 ff.; S. Goslich, *Beiträge zur Geschichte der deutschen romantischen Oper*, Leipzig 1937, S. 223 ff.

Die Konstruktion musikalischer Formschemata, in die sich die Nebenmotive einfügen, ist eine vergebliche Mühe, die eine Verkennung des Wesens der Stichwortmotive einschließt. In den Barformen, die zu entdecken Lorenz nicht müde wurde, erscheinen die Nebenmotive als Zusätze zu einem der Stollen, also als Störungen der Symmetrie (Ritt- und Speermotiv), oder aber als Teile eines Abgesangs (Welteschemotiv und Motiv der goldenen Äpfel), ohne daß der konstruierten Differenz ein realer Unterschied entspräche: Stets handelt es sich um Unterbrechungen, die nicht musikalisch-funktional, sondern dichterisch-assoziativ motiviert sind.

IV

Der Versuch, die Musik des *Ring* einem verengten Formbegriff zu unterwerfen, der aus der Gleichsetzung von Form und Schema resultiert, ist ebenso vergeblich wie gewaltsam. Wagner, ein Verächter der Regel, auch der selbstgesetzten, wechselte zwischen verschiedenen Verfahrensweisen, über deren auffällige und manchmal extreme Differenzen das Dogma von der »unendlichen Melodie«, die alle Unterschiede einschmilzt, nicht hinwegtäuschen sollte. Geschlossene Formen, die den Rückgriff auf die verschlissene Architekturmetapher — auf die räumliche Abbildung des musikalischen Zeitverlaufs — begreiflich erscheinen lassen, werden abgelöst von Perioden, deren Motivgeflecht sich den Buchstabenschemata entzieht, die für Lorenz den Inbegriff musikalischer Form darstellen.

Der Abschnitt »und wie im Traume« aus Waltrautes Erzählung im ersten Akt der *Götterdämmerung* (T. 1329—1344) scheint auf bloßer Reihung von Motiven zu beruhen, deren Aufeinanderfolge der Text diktierte. Aus dem Satz »...*des tiefen Rheines Töchtern gäbe den Ring sie wieder zurück, von des Fluches Last erlöst wär' Gott und Welt*« stechen einzelne Worte — Rhein, Ring, Fluch und Gott — hervor, die ihre musikalischen Äquivalente — das Rheingold-, das Ring-, das Fluch- und das Walhallmotiv — geradezu herbeizwingen. Die Motive stehen jedoch, obwohl die Zusammensetzung primär im Text begründet ist, nicht als bloße musikalische Zitate beziehungslos nebeneinander: Vielmehr ist das Fluchmotiv, wenn es dem Ringmotiv unmittelbar folgt, als dessen Umkehrung kenntlich, und von den Walhallmotiven wählte Wagner nicht das erste und prägnanteste, das sich in den musikalischen Kontext schwerlich eingefügt hätte, sondern das abschließende, das als Variante des Rheingoldmotivs, mit dem es verkettet ist, aufgefaßt werden kann. So eng aber die Motive aufeinander bezogen sind, so verfehlt wäre es andererseits, den Zusammenhang durch ein Buchstabenschema abzubilden. Das scheinbar Amorphe erweist sich als geformt, ohne jedoch den Kategorien der musikalischen Formenlehre zugänglich zu sein.

Einfache Formen, die sich ohne Zwang durch Schemata wie a b a und a a b bezeichnen lassen, sind im *Ring* eher eine Ausnahme als die Regel. Und als Ausnahmen sind sie aus besonderen Bedingungen erklärbar. Wotans Begrüßung Walhalls in der zweiten Szene des *Rheingold*, der Anfang der Todesverkündigungsszene im zweiten Akt der *Walküre* oder Brünnhildes Erwachen im dritten

Akt des *Siegfried* verdanken die prägnante Strophen-, Bar- oder Bogenform, die von Lorenz als exemplarisch gerühmt wurde, der Tatsache, daß am Beginn einer Szene dem Vokalteil eine Orchesterintroduktion vorausgeht. Die Geschlossenheit der Perioden beruht — anders als in symphonischen Formen — nicht auf dem Verfahren, einen zu Anfang exponierten Hauptsatz, auf den der Akzent fällt, entweder unmittelbar oder nach einem Zwischensatz zu wiederholen, sondern auf der Antizipation einer vokalen Partie durch eine instrumentale. Und die Differenz zwischen dem Prinzip der Repetition oder Reprise und dem der Vorausnahme ist zweifellos, obwohl sie vom Buchstabenschema einer musikalischen Form nicht ablesbar ist, für deren Sinn von eingreifender Bedeutung.

Anders motiviert, trotz äußerer Ähnlichkeit, ist die Form des Rheintöchter-Terzetts im dritten Akt der *Götterdämmerung*. Die Gliederung in zwei Strophen ist im Text begründet, der aus *Siegfrieds Tod* in die *Götterdämmerung* übernommen wurde, also in eine Zeit zurückreicht, in der sich die Musik des *Ring* — eine musikalische Prosa, aus der eine einfache Liedform befremdend hervorsticht — noch nicht einmal in vagen Umrissen abzeichnete. Der ursprüngliche Entwurf wurde von Wagner zugleich modifiziert und bewahrt: Die Strophenform wurde einerseits durch den Einschub melismatischer »Weialala«-Partien aufgehoben, um andererseits durch eine Orchesterintroduktion wiederhergestellt zu werden. In dem Schema (T. 50—145)

a¹	a²	b¹	a³	a⁴	c	b²
10	12	22	10	10	7	24

sind die ursprünglichen Strophen als b¹ und b² chiffriert; die a-Teile sind instrumentale (a¹ und a²) oder melismatische Partien (a³ und a⁴).

Der Anfang der Todesverkündigungsszene, der immer wieder als Muster einer geschlossenen Form unter den Bedingungen des Wort-Ton-Dramas gerühmt worden ist [68], wurde von Lorenz [69] in das Schema eines »potenzierten Bar« gepreßt; eines Bar in drei Größenordnungen, die in einer Buchstabenskizze durch griechische sowie durch kleine und große römische Buchstaben zu bezeichnen wären.

A^1:	a¹			a²			(b¹)
	α	α	β	α	α	β	γ
	4	4	4	4	4	4	5
A^2:	a³		a⁴				b²
	α	α	β	α	α		γ
	4	4	4	3	3		8

So unleugbar es jedoch ist, daß aus der Vorausnahme der ersten Periode (T. 30—55 = A²) durch eine Orchesterintroduktion (T. 1—29 = A¹) eine Doppelstrophe — nach Lorenz der Doppelstollen eines Bar — resultiert, so fragwürdig

---

[68] Lorenz, a. a. O., S. 176 f.; W. Serauky, *Die Todesverkündigungsszene in Richard Wagners »Walküre« als musikalisch-geistige Achse des Werkes*, Mf XII, S. 143 f.
[69] A. a. O., S. 179 ff.

sind die Details der Analyse, durch die Lorenz den Begriff des potenzierten Bar zu fundieren sucht.

Daß es sinnvoll ist, die Aufstellung und Sequenzierung eines Motivs, ergänzt und abgeschlossen durch ein anderes, manchmal gegensätzliches Motiv (ααβ), als »Barform« zu charakterisieren, leuchtet nicht ein. Denn die Motivgruppierung ist eher eine syntaktische als eine architektonische Einheit; sie entspricht der Verbindung eines Vordersatzes mit einem Nachsatz oder einer Fortspinnung, nicht einer Zusammenfügung von Zeilen zu einer Liedform.

Ein weiterer Mangel, an dem die Lorenz'sche Analyse krankt, ist die Verwirrung der Größenordnungen. Das Fragment des Walhallmotivs, mit dem die Instrumentaleinleitung schließt (γ), soll als »Abgesang« (b^1) gelten; die Phrase gehört jedoch zweifellos zu den Einzelmotiven, nicht zu den Motivgruppen, wäre also als γ, nicht als b^1 zu chiffrieren. In der zweiten Strophe (A^2) ist allerdings γ zu einem achttaktigen Komplex erweitert, kann also als b^2, als Widerpart zu a^3 und a^4, aufgefaßt werden. Andererseits fehlt aber β, das ergänzende Motiv zu $\alpha\alpha$; und man kann zweifeln, ob γ als »Abgesang« auf $\alpha\alpha$ oder auf a^3 und a^4 zu beziehen sei. (Daß Lorenz die Phrase γ zerteilt und die Aufstellung des Motivs auf $\alpha\alpha$, die Sequenz dagegen auf a^3 und a^4 bezieht, ist ein willkürlicher Eingriff, der die enttäuschende Tatsache verbergen soll, daß der Kalkül des »potenzierten Bar« nicht aufgeht.)

Die Fortsetzung von A^2 hat Überleitungscharakter und ist zudem als Gruppierung von 3 + 3 + 8 Takten, die in die Größenordnung von a, nicht von A gehört, zu kurz, um als »Abgesang« zu den »Stollen« A^1 und A^2 gelten zu können. Andererseits ist jedoch der »Abgesang«, den Lorenz annimmt, mit 87 Takten unverhältnismäßig lang; er steht in einer Disproportion zu den Teilen, deren Ergänzung er bilden soll. Und der Irrtum im Ansatz der Analyse zeigt sich wiederum an der Tatsache, daß die Größenordnungen durcheinandergeraten. Der fiktive Abgesang ist nach Lorenz in sich »barförmig«; die beiden »Stollen« aber, die er enthält, gehören mit 22 und 24 Takten in die Größenordnung von A^1 und A^2, die 29 und 26 Takte umfassen, nicht in die von a^1 und a^2, in die Lorenz sie verweist.

V

Die Architekturmetapher, in der Lorenz das Wesen der musikalischen Form ausgedrückt fand, die These also, daß sich die Musik des Ring in räumlich-symmetrischen Strukturen entfalte, muß, um nicht unverständlich zu bleiben, als Erwiderung auf den Vorwurf der Formlosigkeit begriffen werden; sie ist Apologie, deren Übertreibungen das Reversbild zu den Pointen der Polemik gegen Wagner darstellen. Analysiert man den Sachverhalt, ohne sich einem Vorurteil oder einem Gegendogma zu verschreiben, so zeigt sich, daß zwischen den Extremen der geschlossenen und der offenen oder aufgelösten Form, die in der Kontroverse einseitig hervorgehoben worden sind, ungezählte Zwischenstufen vermitteln: Formen, die zwar nicht auf ein Buchstabenschema reduzierbar sind, aber noch weniger als bloße Klitterungen von Motiven, die sich an Stichworte des Textes heften, mißverstanden und abgetan werden dürfen.

1. Überlieferte Satztypen wie die Lied-, die Sonaten- und die Rondoform bildeten für Wagner zwar Voraussetzungen, auf die er sich auch dann noch stützte, wenn er über sie hinausging, verloren jedoch die normative Bedeutung, die ihnen in der musikalischen Formenlehre zugeschrieben worden war. Statt sie als Muster zu respektieren, benutzte Wagner sie als Mittel oder Gerüste, die manchmal, aber nicht immer tauglich waren. Die Traditionsbestände wurden weniger bewahrt als vielmehr verbraucht. Und so sind im *Ring* — und zwar je nach den Forderungen des musikalisch-dramatischen Augenblicks — nicht selten verschiedene Formtypen miteinander verschränkt, so daß in einer Analyse, auch einer bloß skizzenhaften, versucht werden muß, einerseits die Formen, die in eine Szene oder einen Szenenteil eingeschmolzen sind, zu rekonstruieren und andererseits die Veränderungen zu beobachten, denen sie durch die Verquickung miteinander ausgesetzt sind.

Der Hauptteil des Dialogs zwischen Siegfried und Mime in der ersten Szene des *Siegfried*, ein Komplex, der sich über nicht weniger als 840 Takte erstreckt (T. 342—1181: *»Da hast du die Stücken«*), ist von Lorenz[70] als geschlossene Periode, der das Schema eines Rondo zugrunde liege, charakterisiert worden. Lorenz unterdrückt jedoch die Tatsache, daß nicht ein einziges Ritornell, sondern vier Refrains die Klammer bilden, welche die heterogenen Teile der Szene zusammenhält. Die Behauptung, daß der vierte Refrain (T. 715: *»Mein Kind, das lehrt dich kennen«*) — ein Motiv, das von pedantisch poetisierenden Kommentatoren als Motiv der »Liebessehnsucht« oder aber des »Lenzeszaubers« etikettiert worden ist — den ersten »vertrete«, ist sowohl unbegründet als auch in ihren Konsequenzen absurd, denn Lorenz ist gezwungen, dasselbe Motiv abwechselnd als Ritornell und als Episode zu erklären: Um sein Interpretationsschema nicht preisgeben zu müssen, um es vor einer Widerlegung durch die Fakten zu bewahren, läßt er Wagners Formgefühl als verwirrt erscheinen.

Die Refrains werden in geschlossenen Formen — den einzelnen Perioden der Szene, die von Lorenz insgesamt als Periode begriffen wurde — entwickelt oder ausgebreitet: der erste als Ritornell eines Rondos (T. 342: *»Da hast du die Stücken«*), der zweite und der vierte als Liedritornelle (T. 500: *»Das ist nun der Liebe schlimmer Lohn«*; T. 773: *»Es sangen die Vöglein«*), der dritte als Liedzeile (T. 512: *»Als zullendes Kind«*). Und daß sie während einer längeren Strecke beherrschend hervortreten, unterscheidet sie von den sporadisch aufgegriffenen Leitmotiven und gibt ihnen einen Nachdruck, durch den sie überhaupt erst aus einer Reminiszenz oder einem Zitat zu einem Refrain werden. Auch für die Leitmotive gilt die banale Regel, daß die Funktion, die ein Motiv erfüllt, nicht nur von seiner Beschaffenheit, sondern in kaum geringerem Maße von der Ausführlichkeit abhängt, mit der es dargelegt wird.

Musikalische Formen sind nicht bloße Schemata, sondern Charaktere: geprägt durch die Inhalte, die in ihnen verwirklicht worden sind. Nicht jede Form fügt sich zu jedem Inhalt; Verwickeltes und Entlegenes in Lied- oder Rondoformen auszudrücken, wäre widersinnig. Deren unauslöschlicher Grundzug ist Simplizität. Und so ist es kein Zufall, sondern zeugt von Wagners Formgefühl, daß sich gerade im Siegfried, der weniger ein Heroenmythos als

[70] A. a. O., S. 223 f.

eine Märchenoper ist, der Dialog immer wieder zu Liedformen verfestigt, auch ohne daß diese im Text deutlich vorgezeichnet wären. Aus der Szene zwischen Siegfried und Mime lassen sich nicht weniger als fünf Lieder herauslösen, deren Naivität zwar artifiziell ist, aber dadurch nicht das Geringste einbüßt — man ist im Gegenteil in Versuchung, von der zweiten Unmittelbarkeit zu behaupten, daß sie »echter«, treffender sei als die erste (T. 434: *Was ich ihm Gutes schuf*; T. 512: *Als zullendes Kind*; T. 739: *Jammernd verlangen Junge*; T. 773: *Es sangen die Vöglein*; T. 854: *Wie die Jungen den Alten gleichen*).

Den Widerpart und äußersten Gegensatz zu den Liedern, die einen großen Teil der Szene ausfüllen, bilden Reste oder verblaßte Umrisse der Sonatenform, einer Form also, die als Ausprägung des Gedankens der »entwickelnden Variation«, um mit Schönberg zu sprechen, ein drittes Prinzip neben der Formidee des Liedes und der des Ritornells repräsentiert. Hauptsatz (T. 342—433) und Seitensatz (T. 434—500), bestimmt durch die Motivik Siegfrieds und Mimes, heben sich deutlich und beinahe schroff voneinander ab; die Durchführung (T. 608—631), von der Exposition allerdings durch hundert Takte getrennt, spielt die kontrastierenden Motive in raschem Wechsel gegeneinander aus; die Reprise (T. 631—676) ist zwar modifiziert, aber dennoch als solche unverkennbar.

Die Motive haben jedoch — als Ausdruck der verlegenen Annäherungen Mimes und der rüden Abwehr durch Siegfried — eher gestischen als melodischen Charakter; von Themen oder Zeilen zu sprechen wäre verfehlt oder mindestens inadäquat. Die Vermittlung zwischen der sperrigen Prägnanz der Motive und den Forderungen des Sonatensatzes oder des Liedes war denn auch das eigentliche Strukturproblem, das Wagner bei der Einschmelzung traditioneller Formprinzipien in das Wort-Ton-Drama zu lösen hatte. Und man braucht sich nicht zu verhehlen, daß der Ausgleich nicht immer im selben Maße glückte. So unvergleichlich es in Mimes Partie *Was ich dir Gutes schuf* gelang, Liedmelodik und Orchestermotivik in einem psychologisch begründeten Kontrapunkt einander entgegenzusetzen, so fragwürdig ist, trotz äußerer Ähnlichkeit des Verfahrens, der Verschleiß des ursprünglich gestisch geprägten Mimemotivs als ostinate Begleitfigur in dem Lied *Als zullendes Kind*.

Manchmal ist es der Dramatiker Wagner, der einlöst, was der Symphoniker schuldig bleibt. So ist etwa die Durchführung der angedeuteten Sonatenform, der Wechsel zwischen parodierten Mime-Phrasen und abrupten Gesten des Ekels, von einer szenisch-musikalischen Drastik, die über den Mangel an absolut musikalischer Entwicklung hinwegträgt und ihn nicht fühlbar werden läßt. Daß die Symphonie im Wort-Ton-Drama aufgehoben sei, gilt, wenn überhaupt, so nur in dem eingeschränkten Sinne, daß Wagner der Durchführungstechnik gestisch-dramatische Züge aufprägte, die ihm dann, in seltsamer Vertauschung des Primären und des Sekundären, als das verborgene Wesen der Symphonie erschienen.

2. Die Unterscheidung zwischen Deklamation und Arioso oder Rezitativ und Cantabile ist zu grob und schematisch, als daß sie der Vielfalt von Satztypen gerecht würde, über die Wagner verfügt. Und die Gruppierung von Satztypen unter den Gesichtspunkten des Kontrasts, der Steigerung und des Ausgleichs ist denn auch — und zwar in höherem Maße als die Verkettung oder Mischung von Formen wie Lied, Sonatensatz und Rondo — ein Mittel, um im

Wort-Ton-Drama, das nicht als Symphonie mit vokalem Kommentar mißdeutet werden sollte, Zusammenhänge über weite Strecken zu stiften.

Der Hauptteil der ersten Szene aus dem dritten Akt der *Walküre*, Brünnhildes Flucht mit Sieglinde, ist in neun charakteristisch verschiedene Perioden gegliedert:

(I) »Mauerschau« von Brünnhildes Flucht (T. 216: »*Nach dem Tann*«)
(II) Walkürenruf (T. 253: »*Hojotoho*«)
(III) Bitte um Schutz (T. 267: »*Schützt mich, und helft*«)
(IV) Brünnhildes Erzählung (T. 310: »*Sieglinde ist es*«)
(V) Dialog mit den Walküren (T. 354: »*Wehe der Armen*«)
(VI) Sieglindes Todesbitte (T. 380: »*Nicht sehre dich Sorge*«)
(VII) Dialog Brünnhildes und Sieglindes (T. 409: »*Lebe, o Weib*«)
(VIII) Erzählung der Walküren (T. 453: »*Nach Osten weithin*«)
(IX) Duett Brünnhildes und Sieglindes (T. 475: »*Fort denn, eile*«).

Die Satztypen: Erzählung, »Mauerschau«, in sich geschlossene Rede (Sieglindes Todesbitte), dramatischer Dialog und kantables Duett — sind mit untrüglichem Sinn für dramatisch-szenische Gruppierung und Gewichtsverteilung gegeneinandergesetzt und miteinander verbunden, so daß sie einen Komplex bilden, der das Epitheton »architektonisch« eher verdient als die Formen, die Lorenz aus der Disposition der Leitmotive herauslas.

Das auffälligste Gruppierungsgesetz der Szene ist der gleichmäßige Wechsel zwischen weitertreibenden und retardierenden Partien, ein Wechsel, der in entfernter Analogie dem Rezitativ-Arie-Schema der älteren Oper entspricht:

»Nach dem Tann«
          »Hojotoho«
»Schützt mich, und helft«
          »Sieglinde ist es«
»Wehe der Armen«
          »Nicht sehre dich Sorge«
»Lebe, o Weib«
          »Nach Osten weithin«
          »Fort denn, eile«.

Gegenüber den dramatischen Dialogen, zu denen auch die Wechselrede der Walküren bei der »Mauerschau« zu zählen ist, erscheinen Ensemble, Erzählung, geschlossene Rede und Duett als ariose Unterbrechungen, obwohl die Rastlosigkeit, die den Grundcharakter der Szene bildet, in ihnen weiterwirkt.

Daß der solistischen Rede *(»Schützt mich, und helft«)* eine Ensemblepartie, das *»Hojotoho«* der Walküren, vorausgeht, entspricht einer Regel der Opernintroduktion, der sich Wagner ebensowenig entzog wie der Norm, daß ein dramatischer Dialog *(»Lebe, o Weib«)* in einem kantablen Duett *(»Fort denn, eile«)* kulminiert. (Daß das Duett den Höhepunkt darstellt, dem die Szene zustrebt, wurde von Lorenz[71] verkannt: Er erklärte es zur »Coda«, weil es aus dem Formschema, das er der Szene aufzuzwingen suchte, herausfällt.)

[71] A. a. O., S. 266 f.

Das Verfahren, charakteristisch verschiedene Satztypen sinnfällig zu gruppieren, ein Verfahren, dem die Szene ihre Geschlossenheit verdankt, ist demnach von der Operntradition und deren Handwerksregeln nicht so unabhängig, wie es Wagner von den Prinzipien des Wort-Ton-Dramas behauptete. Und umgekehrt ist der symphonische Zusammenhang, den Wagner als das entscheidende Moment hervorhob, so schwach ausgeprägt, daß Lorenz bei dem Versuch, eine symphonische Form zu entdecken oder zu konstruieren, in nicht geringe Verlegenheit geriet.

Das primäre Motiv der Szene, das deren Gesamtcharakter musikalisch andeutet oder ausprägt, ist das Götternotmotiv, von manchen Kommentatoren auch Unruhemotiv genannt. In der ersten Periode, die Expositionscharakter hat, wird es breit entfaltet (T. 216—234 und T. 243—251), in der dritten noch einmal aufgegriffen und nach dem Modell der Beethovenschen Durchführungstechnik verarbeitet und schließlich in Fragmente zerspalten (T. 282—285 und T. 295—306). Mit der Auflösung in kleinste Partikel oder Motivreste ist die eigentlich symphonische Entwicklung abgeschlossen, was nicht hindert, daß sich ein aus ihr herausgebrochenes Stück (T. 295—298) zu einem selbständigen Gebilde verfestigt, das als Refrain noch mehrfach wiederkehrt (T. 343—347, T. 426—430 und T. 449—453).

Lorenz erklärte den Refrain trotz dessen Kürze zur tragenden Substanz der Szene: In dem Schema A¹ B¹ C B² A², das er den Takten 267—474 — unter Ausschluß der ersten beiden Perioden — zugrundelegte, bildet der Refrain das einzige gemeinsame Moment der »analogen« Teile A¹ und A² sowie B¹ und B², und zwar als Hauptsatz von A (= a b a) und als Zwischensatz von B (= c a c). Er hat jedoch eher den Charakter einer Unterbrechung oder Interpolation, als daß er als Gerüst der Szene empfunden würde. (Zu einer übertreibenden Betonung des Motivzusammenhangs, der die Teile der Szene miteinander verklammert, ist Lorenz gezwungen, weil er die Gruppierung von Satztypen nicht als Formprinzip erkennt oder gelten läßt.) Und der musikalisch-formalen Funktion des Refrains entspricht es, daß die beiden Walküren, deren Gesang er stützt, von den übrigen getrennt »auf der Warte« stehen. Das szenische a parte ist das genaue Korrelat des musikalischen.

Die erste Periode, die Exposition und ausführlichste Entwicklung des Götternotmotivs, wurde von Lorenz aus dem Zusammenhang, dem er das Schema einer Bogenform überzustülpen suchte, ausgeschlossen: ein Irrtum, der paradox anmutet; denn einerseits übertreibt Lorenz den Refrain- und Gerüstcharakter des Götternotmotivs, und andererseits verkennt er, daß die symphonische Ausbreitung des Motivs die Voraussetzung für dessen Primat ist, dafür also, daß es aus dem Kontext der übrigen Motive als Refrain auffällig hervorsticht, statt eine bloße Reminiszenz neben anderen zu sein.

3. Der Formbegriff, der von der musikalischen Formenlehre geprägt worden ist, bezieht sich primär auf die Gliederung ausgedehnterer Zusammenhänge. Deren Begründung aber liegt in den Einzelmomenten, den Charakteren und Funktionen der Themen und Motive. Eine Form, die nicht aus den Details — dem »Inhalt«, wie Hanslick sie nannte — verständlich gemacht werden kann, bleibt bloßes Schema, der Musik von außen übergestülpt. Und die Stütze eines Typus, dem sich das individuelle Werk angleicht, wird nicht selten sogar

überflüssig: dann nämlich, wenn die Motive oder Phrasen in ihren formalen Funktionen prägnant und sinnfällig genug sind, um sich von sich aus und gleichsam unwillkürlich, ohne vorgezeichneten Grundriß, zu plastischen Formen zusammenzuschließen. Es gibt, und zwar nicht erst bei Wagner, Motivgruppierungen, deren Geschlossenheit unleugbar ist, ohne daß sie auf Schemata, wie sie die Formenlehre bereithält, reduzierbar wären.

Das Finale (Nr. 15) des zweiten Aktes der *Nozze di Figaro* ist oft als Paradigma eines Ensemblesatzes gerühmt worden. Arnold Schönberg — der als Revolutionär mit traditionalistischen Instinkten einen untrüglichen Sinn für das Unschematische in der musikalischen Klassik entwickelte — zitierte den dritten Teil des Finale, Allegro B-dur, zur Demonstration der These, daß ein Opernkomponist in Ensemblesätzen über Motive und Phrasen verfügen müsse, die eine den Wendungen und Verwicklungen des Textes entsprechende Mannigfaltigkeit von Kombinationen zulassen. *»In pieces of this type a composer must be capable of turning within the smallest space. Mozart anticipating this necessity; begins such a piece with a melody consisting of a number of phrases of various lengths and characters, each of them pertaining to a different phase of the action and the mood. They are, in their first formulation, loosely joined together, and often simply juxtaposed, thus admitting to be broken asunder and used independently as motival material for small formal segments.«* [72] So unleugbar es jedoch ist, daß die veränderliche Zusammenstellung der sechs Phrasen, mit denen Mozart nicht weniger als 160 Takte bestreitet, dem Wechsel der Aktionen und Stimmungen folgt, so verfehlt wäre es andererseits, in der Reihenfolge der Phrasen nichts als eine Spiegelung des Textes und musikalisch ein Zufallsergebnis zu sehen.

Die einzelnen Phrasen sind vielmehr musikalische Charaktere, die bestimmte formale Funktionen erfüllen: a ist ein Anfangsmotiv ohne Kadenz, das in sich selbst zurückläuft oder in andere Phrasen einmündet; e und f sind gerade um-

[72] A. Schönberg, *Style and Idea*, New York 1950, S. 68.

gekehrt Schlußmotive, die nur als Fortsetzungen denkbar sind und nicht am Beginn eines Abschnitts stehen könnten; c erscheint als abrupter Einwurf, der die musikalische Entwicklung unterbricht; b und d vermitteln den Übergang zwischen Anfangs- und Schlußmotiven — allerdings kann b durch eine angehängte Kadenz zum Schlußmotiv umgeprägt werden.

Von den formalen Funktionen der Motive ist die Gliederung des Satzes in Perioden, die 15 bis 30 Takte umfassen, abhängig. Hermann Abert [73] deutete die Form im Hinblick auf die häufige Wiederkehr der Phrase b, die »als einziges Motiv wirklich, und zwar nach allen Regeln der Kunst, durchgeführt« werde, als »völlig freies Rondo«. Die Reduktion auf ein Schema verdeckt jedoch, obwohl sie nicht unbegründet ist, den Sachverhalt, daß der Satz ein Formprinzip ausprägt, dessen Existenz und raison d'être der Formenlehre entgangen ist: das Prinzip wechselnder Gruppierung innerhalb der Grenzen, die durch die Charaktere und Funktionen der Motive gezogen sind. Die funktionale Prägnanz der Motive ist die Bedingung unschematischer und doch fester Formen.

Wagner bewunderte an den Nozze di Figaro ein Moment, das er als Dialogisierung der Musik bezeichnete [74] und das mit dem Prinzip der immer wieder wechselnden und doch plastischen Motivgruppierung eng zusammenhängt. Und es scheint, als habe Mozarts Verfahren in manchen Teilen des Ring, etwa in der Wanderer-Szene aus dem ersten Akt des Siegfried, Spuren hinterlassen. Dem ersten Abschnitt der Szene liegen vier Motive zugrunde, die sequenziert und auch abgewandelt, diminuiert und zerlegt werden (T. 1—76): die Wanderer-Akkorde (a), die Sequenzen zu Wotans Näherschreiten (b), ein Motiv, das Mimes erschrockenes Gestikulieren malt (c), und schließlich Wotans Phrase »Gastlich ruht' ich bei Guten« (d), die eine Gemütlichkeit demonstriert, der nicht zu trauen ist. Die formalen Funktionen der Motive sind unzweideutig. Die Wanderer-Akkorde stellen ein Anfangsmotiv dar, obwohl sie, nach einem Ausdruck von Schönberg, »vagierende Harmonien« sind. Zwar ist der Schluß tonal unschwer zu deuten (IV — IIn — V); der Anfang aber ist tonartfremd und seltsam ungreifbar und zwielichtig, so daß die Harmonien zu einem musikalischen Abbild Wotans werden, der als Geist seiner selbst umgeht. Die Phrase b, die mit einem über anderthalb Takte gedehnten Dominantseptakkord beginnt, hat Fortsetzungscharakter; und c, ein gestisch geprägtes Motiv, erscheint, ähnlich wie die dritte Phrase im Figaro-Finale, als Einwurf. Motiv d ist, obwohl es die Kadenz I-V-I umschreibt, weder am Anfang noch am Schluß eines Abschnitts vorstellbar; obwohl es kantabel und melodisch in sich geschlossen ist, scheint es nicht in sich selbst zu ruhen, sondern andere Motive vorauszusetzen, denen es sich in der Funktion einer Neben- oder Zwischenphrase anfügt.

Die formalen Charaktere der Motive sind so prägnant, daß die Gruppierung unschematisch sein kann, ohne amorph zu wirken. Und der Versuch von Lorenz [75], unter Ausschluß »störender, trübender Einwürfe« ein Strophenschema zu konstruieren, ist ebenso verwickelt und verwirrend wie überflüssig.

[73] H. Abert, W. A. Mozart, Band II, Leipzig 1924, S. 328.
[74] Wagner, a. a. O., Band X, S. 154.
[75] A. a. O., S. 84 ff.

4. Mit dem Terminus Durchführung ist in der Theorie der Sonatenform ein Abschnitt, aber auch eine Technik gemeint, die sich im 19. Jahrhundert über den ganzen Satz auszubreiten begann. Und ein charakteristisches, vielleicht das auffälligste Merkmal der Durchführungstechnik ist die Bildung von prägnanten, aus Motiven der Exposition zusammengesetzten Modellen, die sequenziert und dann in immer kleinere Partikel zerspalten und schließlich zerstäubt werden.

Das Verfahren wurde von Wagner adaptiert und den Bedingungen des Wort-Ton-Dramas unterworfen. In die Todesverkündigungsszene aus dem zweiten Akt der *Walküre* fügte er gegen Ende, nach Siegmunds Klage, als Ansatz zu einer Schlußsteigerung eine Periode unverkennbar symphonischen Gepräges ein (T. 1716: *»So jung und schön erschimmerst du mir«*). Zwei Motivkomplexe (a und b) werden als Modelle exponiert und in einen Entwicklungs- und Auflösungsprozeß hineingezogen, der sich von dem Durchführungsteil eines symphonischen Satzes durch nichts anderes unterscheidet, als daß die Dialogstruktur des Textes, die Gliederung in Rede und Gegenrede, die Interpolation einiger kantabler Kadenzphrasen (c, d und e) erzwang, die den symphonischen Fluß unterbrechen. (Die Indices x, y und z bezeichnen die Abspaltung von Doppel-, Einzel- und Halbtakten, die dann sequenziert werden.)

$$\begin{array}{cccccccccc} a & b & a^x & b & a^y & c & a & b & b^{x+y} & d \\ 3 & 4 & 2{+}2 & 4 & 1{+}1 & 3 & 3 & 4 & 2{+}1{+}1 & 2 \end{array}$$

$$\begin{array}{ccccccc} a^x & a^z & & a^y & b^z & & e & a^y \\ 2{+}2 & 1/2{+}1/2{+}1/2{+}1/2 & & 1 & 1/2{+}1/2{+}1/2 & 1/2 & 4 & 1 \end{array}$$

Daß Wagners Behandlung der Leitmotive im strengen Sinne symphonisch sei, oder genauer: daß man von »entwickelnder Variation« sprechen könne, wurde von Theodor W. Adorno geleugnet. »Gesten« — als welche die Motive von Adorno gedeutet werden — »können wiederholt und verstärkt, aber nicht eigentlich ›entwickelt‹ werden«.[76] Der Hinweis auf Ausnahmen mag, als bloße Einschränkung, aber nicht Widerlegung der pointierten These, pedantisch oder sogar müßig erscheinen, sei jedoch dennoch nicht verschmäht.

Der Anfang der Wandererszene aus *Siegfried* ist satztechnisch durch die Kontrastierung und Vermittlung von Diatonik und Chromatik bestimmt, die als Prinzipien und treibende Momente des musikalischen Verlaufs, nicht als bloße Färbungen der Harmonik begriffen werden müssen. Zu den chromatischen Wanderer-Akkorden (T. 1) stehen die diatonischen Sequenzen, das musikalische Ebenbild von Wotans Näherschreiten (T. 5), zunächst in ausschließendem Kontrast; die Prinzipien werden einander schroff und unvermittelt entgegengesetzt. Die Umwandlung der tonalen Sequenz in eine reale (T. 21) ist dann als Andeutung von Chromatik in der Beziehung der Sequenzglieder zueinander zu verstehen, einer Chromatik, die schließlich auch in das Motiv selbst eindringt (T. 25). Einer analogen Chromatisierung wird das Seitenthema, die Phrase *»Gastlich ruht' ich bei Guten«* (T. 28), unterworfen, und zwar durch Angleichung an die Wanderer-Akkorde, deren Harmonieschritt IV-IIn auf die ursprünglich diatonische Phrase übertragen wird (T. 64).

---

[76] Adorno, a. a. O., S. 41.

Die Umwandlung ist nicht »psychologisch«, im Text der Dichtung, sondern »symphonisch«, in der musikalischen Wechselwirkung der Motive, begründet, so daß sich der Begriff der »entwickelnden Variation« geradezu aufdrängt.

5. Die »*Kunst des Überganges*«, deren sich Wagner in einem Brief an Mathilde Wesendonck vom 29. Oktober 1859 als der »*feinsten und tiefsten Kunst*« rühmte, über die er verfüge, erschöpft sich nicht in technischen Merkmalen wie der Vermeidung von Zäsuren durch Trugschlüsse oder durch Verschränkung der Gesangs- und der Orchesterphrasen. Und mit Recht hob Ernst Kurth [77] die »*Verkettungen von Einzelmotiven*« hervor: das »*Ineinanderleiten der Motive*«, das oft auch als »*Ineinanderfließen der Ideen ohne weiteres verständlich*« sei. Es ist zwar unleugbar, daß Wagner, da Klitterung die Gefahr der Leitmotivtechnik ist, um so empfindlicher gegen Einschnitte und deutliche Absätze war. Er versuchte jedoch nicht nur, sie äußerlich zu überbrücken oder zu verdecken, sondern bemühte sich zugleich, der Beziehungslosigkeit der Motive von innen heraus Herr zu werden: durch rhythmische und melodische Angleichung, die es manchmal schwierig oder unmöglich macht, ohne Willkür zu entscheiden, ob Heterogenes einander angenähert oder aber umgekehrt Divergierendes aus demselben Ursprung entwickelt worden ist.

Das Verfahren, durch innere Beziehungen zwischen den Motiven musikalischen Zusammenhang zu stiften, ist manchmal für ganze Szenen charakteristisch, und die Suche nach einem räumlich-symmetrischen Formschema ist dann vergeblich und verfehlt, weil die Form, um eine Unterscheidung Jacques Handschins aufzugreifen, primär »logisch« und nicht »plastisch« bestimmt ist. Die Takte 170—380 aus der ersten Szene der *Walküre* (»*Sie neigt sich zu ihm herab und lauscht*«) wurden von Lorenz [78] als »potenzierter Bar« gedeutet. Doch ist bereits die Setzung einer Zäsur in Takt 170 willkürlich und gewaltsam; die Takte 170—180, die als »Stollen« gelten sollen, könnten mit gleichem Recht auch als »Abgesang« eines »Bar«, der von Takt 162 bis Takt 180 reicht (4 + 4 + 10 Takte), rubriziert werden.

Wesentlicher als die Gruppierungen der Motive sind deren Verknüpfungen, die oft unscheinbar sein mögen, sich aber zu einem Gesamteindruck von musikalischer Geschlossenheit summieren, der sich auch dann aufdrängt, wenn man die Gründe, auf denen er beruht, nicht durchschaut. Zur Demonstration des Verfahrens genügt es, aus den ungezählten Beziehungen, die Wagner zwischen den Motiven herstellt, ein einziges Moment, das der Diminution oder Augmen-

77 E. Kurth, *Romantische Harmonik und ihre Krise in Wagners »Tristan«*, Bern 1920, S. 422 f.
78 A. a. O., S. 269; vgl. auch S. 155 und S. 260 f.

tation, herauszugreifen. Die Häufung des Phänomens legt es nahe, von einem Zug zur Methode zu sprechen, der von Pedanterie nicht frei ist; der musikalische Kartonmaler ist zugleich ein Miniaturist (a = T. 171—172; b = T. 214—216; c = T. 237—238 und T. 248—249; d = T. 247, T. 270, T. 315 und T. 320—321; e = T. 340—341 und T. 344—346).

6. Sachverhalte, die so selbstverständlich sind, daß es überflüssig erscheint, sie zu erwähnen, geraten manchmal gerade darum in Vergessenheit. Daß die Dialogstruktur das Formgesetz des Dramas, auch des Wort-Ton-Dramas, darstellt, ist eine Trivialität, an die zu erinnern man sich scheuen würde, wenn sie nicht in den Analysen von Lorenz vernachlässigt worden wäre. Sowohl die Gliederung der Szenen in Perioden als auch die Gruppierung der Motive im einzelnen bleiben jedoch unkenntlich oder werden verzerrt, wenn man sich über die Dialogstruktur hinwegsetzt, sei es stillschweigend oder mit philosophisch auftrumpfenden Argumenten wie der Behauptung, daß die »innere Handlung« — die musikalische — die einzig entscheidende und die äußere ein bloßer »Widerschein« sei. [79]

In der Schlußszene der *Walküre* wären die Takte 73—102 (*»Deinen Befehl führte ich aus«*) — Lorenz [80] rubrizierte sie als »Zwischensatz« eines (schwach ausgeprägten) »Rondos«, ohne eine Gliederung im Detail zu versuchen — nichts als eine Häufung und Klitterung heterogener Motive, wenn nicht der Wechsel von Rede und Gegenrede als eine auch musikalisch relevante Artikulation empfunden würde: als Umwandlung einer amorphen Motivreihung in eine plastische. Und umgekehrt unterstreicht die deutliche Abhebung der Motive voneinander — die Sinnfälligkeit der Differenzen zwischen dem Walküren-, dem Todes- oder Schicksals-, dem Sturm-, dem Zorn- und dem Unmutsmotiv,

[79] A. a. O., S. 5: Die Leitmotive *»werden zum Spiegelbild der inneren Handlung oder besser gesagt, zur inneren Handlung selbst, welche ihren Schein auf die Bühne wirft, sich in dem sichtbaren Spiele der handelnden Personen objektiviert«.*
[80] A. a. O., S. 225.

128

um die Nomenklatur der Kommentatoren zu benutzen — die Gliederung des Textes. Dialog- und Motivstruktur stützen und profilieren sich gegenseitig. Daß vom manifesten Dialog manchmal ein latenter zu unterscheiden ist: eine innere Gliederung, die mit der äußeren nicht übereinstimmt und von der die Motivgruppierung abhängt, modifiziert zwar die Entsprechung, hebt sie jedoch nicht auf. Und das Manifeste und Äußere ist zudem nicht so gleichgültig, wie es den Verächtern des Sinnfälligen unter den Theoretikern des Dramas erscheint. Was im Theater zählt, ist das nachdrücklich Gegenwärtige; und so braucht das Wort vom Theatraliker Wagner nicht als der Vorwurf verstanden und abgewehrt zu werden, als der es gemeint war.

161

The Birth of Music out of the Spirit of Drama
An Essay in Wagnerian Formal Analysis

ANTHONY NEWCOMB

Music for Wagner was born out of dramatic image or idea. This is a commonplace. It is less commonplace to be reminded of the other side of the coin: dramatic idea cannot be communicated in music without speaking through the traditional musical forms and procedures known to the composer and his audience. If even today relatively little attention has been paid to the formal aspects of Wagner's music dramas, Wagner himself is partly responsible. Though he wrote voluminously about his own music, he was explicitly reluctant to go into specific technical detail—partly because he subscribed to the prevailing anti-mannerist view that art should conceal artifice; partly because he subscribed vigorously to an aesthetic oriented toward feeling and expression as opposed to an aesthetic oriented toward formal

concerns (for which Hanslick became the chief spokesman); and partly because a thick veil of mystery thrown around technique helped to project the flattering image of the artist as magician. On the rare occasions when Wagner wrote about specific passages in his own music, he tended to write about their dramatic and expressive content as embodied in the thematic ideas, their combinations and evolutions. Only in a much-cited passage written toward the end of his life did he regret that the thematic idea, by now called the leitmotiv, seemed to have absorbed all the attention of his commentators, while none was spent on his formal procedures.[1]

---

[1] *Über die Anwendung,* WAGNER-GS X, 185–86. A letter to Uhlig of December 1851 provides an early example of this concern, although here again the point of departure is thematic. Wagner seems concerned with the effect of his newly developing techniques of thematic elaboration on the formal aspects of his operas. See WAGNER-UHLIG, 142.

In some circles, at least, the twentieth century brought changing aesthetic attitudes, attitudes that became more dominant as the century progressed. As Carl Dahlhaus writes in the foreword to a recent book of essays on Wagner, "The idea that aesthetic access to a work is gained through understanding of technique has become the ruling maxim (as questionable as are many of the pedagogical consequences)" (DAHLHAUS 1970c, 8. See the List of Works Cited, at the end of this essay.) As a result of these changing attitudes, some of the Master's own followers felt that they had to defend him against growing accusations of formlessness—to defend him in terms which Wagner himself, with his hatred of applying the criteria of the visual arts to music, would likely have rejected.[2] This twentieth-century reaction away from an expressive aesthetic and toward a formal aesthetic culminates in the numbing mass of Lorenz's exhaustive exegesis, *Das Geheimnis der Form bei Richard Wagner* (4 vols., 1924–33). To Lorenz form meant large-scale arrangements of rhythmic-tonal units, deployed in time as architectural units are deployed in space, in patterns of complementarity and symmetry, patterns that can be held in the mind and appreciated there as a complete, static whole. With devastating diligence Lorenz divided all of the *Ring, Tristan, Meistersinger,* and *Parsifal* into tonally closed formal schemata of the sort representable by letters such as ABA, AAB, AABA, and so on. The "mystery" of Wagnerian form had been solved. Wagner had been promoted (or demoted) from magician to master-builder. Although few people, I suspect, read through all four volumes to learn how the mystery came out, few people had the temerity to question the conclusions of so massive and systematic a study.

Hard on the heels of Lorenz's excesses came Hitler's horrors, with their unfortunate expropriation of Wagner's music. That the works continued to be given in non-German opera houses and symphony halls during the 1940s and 50s is a tribute to their strong hold on the imagination. The musical public then wanted only to hear them, not to think or write about them.

Gradually the holocaust has loosed its hold on Wagner, and *Das Geheimnis der Form* has revealed itself as a product not of Wagner's but of Lorenz's diligent obsessions.[3] During the past twenty years Wagnerian formal analysis, though scarcely in full maturity, has at least come of age. For this we must thank above all the formidable Carl Dahlhaus and a group of German colleagues, who have struggled with the Wagnerian literary and musical corpus in a series of articles from the mid-1960s to the present day.[4] The seemingly indigestible lump of Lorenz has finally been broken down, its nutritious portions digested, its harmful ones expelled. The interpretations of other early twentieth-century writers on Wagner, less rigorous than Lorenz but richer in insight—ADLER 1904, HALM 1916, and especially KURTH 1923—have been re-read and used to raise new critical and analytical questions and to build new methods.

The remarkably sensitive, subtle, and erudite body of work done by Dahlhaus and his colleagues is to be faulted in one important aspect—an aspect probably caused by the cir-

163

---

[2] See, for example, Christian v. Ehrenfels, "Die musikalische Architecktonik," *Bayreuther Blätter* 19 (1896), 257–63.

---

[3] The most thorough single discussion of the theoretical defects of Lorenz's methods is DAHLHAUS 1969, 97–113. VOSS 1979 discusses the musical defects of specific analyses.

[4] See the writings by Dahlhaus in the List of Works Cited following this essay, plus especially STEPHAN 1970, KUNZE 1970, and BRINKMANN 1972. To look through WENK 1976 or through the index to American analytical writing during the years 1955–70 published in *In Theory Only* 3 (1978), 7–11, is to sense that Americans are unwilling to touch messy Wagnerian opera with their bright Schenkerian tools. MITCHELL 1967 studies the Prelude to *Tristan* as an independent instrumental piece. BORETZ 1972 mentions bits of the *Liebestod* and of the beginning of Act II as part of his analysis of the Prelude to Act I of *Tristan* as an atonal (what he calls "motivic") piece. But again, he never treats an entire musico-dramatic unit from a Wagnerian scene. BAILEY 1977 is principally concerned with large-scale structural patterns in the *Ring*, and BAILEY 1979 with changes in the method of composition across the years, as revealed in the sketch materials; neither article does close analysis of any individual musico-dramatic unit. BAILEY 1969 is the nearest that American (or English) writing comes to an analytic study of an entire Wagnerian musico-dramatic unit, although once again the sketch material is the principal focus of the study.

cumstances under which it came into being.
Just as Lorenz originated as a polemic against
the accusation of formlessness in Wagner, so
Dahlhaus's Wagnerian analyses originated as a
polemic against Lorenz, who viewed Wagner's
music dramas as an unbroken chain of tonally
closed and tonally defined formal schemata.
Perhaps as a result, Dahlhaus not only stresses
the flexible, anti-schematic nature of Wagner's
forms, he also regularly chooses to ignore the
tonal build of Wagner's units. This is a matter
to which I shall return below.

That this essay has its roots in the work of
these German scholars will be obvious from
the citations as the essay proceeds. Nonetheless, it is neither a summary of their work,
which is richer than any single essay can
suggest, nor a demonstration of their methods,
from which it departs in several respects. It is
not a short study, for I find it impossible to deal
shortly with music of Wagner's complexity and
amplitude. My method is to state general principles, referring to the current literature, but
also referring to three specific analyses—two
relatively short, one relatively long—which are
provided toward the end of the essay. In one
sense they illustrate my proposal, in another
sense they are its heart.

II

Behind many of the differences in approach
to Wagnerian formal analysis lie tacitly differing ideas of the meaning of the word *form* as
applied to music. Form is not equivalent to unity. Unity (for example, of thematic material)
may give coherence, but unity alone does not
give shape. Thus the studies of thematic inter-
relations in Wagner (the most recent of many is
COOKE 1979, 37–73) do not deal with Wagnerian form—a point which Wagner himself
made somewhat testily in *Über die Anwendung* of 1876 (WAGNER-GS X, 185–86). Form,
as I shall use it here, always implies *shape*.

Shape, in musical as in many other kinds of
material, can be thought of in several ways. It
can be thought of as static form in the architectural sense, as something one holds complete
in one's mind, as something one can, so to
speak, stand back from and view as a whole.
This view is represented for music by
Hanslick, Lorenz, and most purely formalist

analysts and aestheticians.[5] Wagner's music
dramas are by no means without this kind of
musical shape, although it is not the most
common kind there. (See the Rhinemaidens'
Songs in *Rheingold* 1: S 25/1–27/2, Eu 87–93,
and S 33/1–37/1, Eu 111–23. References to passages in Wagner's operas will locate the passages by page and, where relevant, system in
the Schirmer vocal scores [S], then the Eulen-
berg orchestral scores [Eu].)

Shape can also be thought of as musical
procedure. For example, the procedure of stepwise sequential repetition gives musical shape,
as does fugal procedure or the procedure of an
imitative-point motet. Shape conceived in
terms of procedure brings to mind those questions in intelligence tests where one is given a
series of numbers and asked to supply the next;
procedure arouses expectations about method
and direction of continuation, although it does
not always make clear where the series will
end.[6]

Shape can also be thought of not as traditional musical procedure, but as procedure
drawn from outside music. Music has long
drawn models for its own procedures from the
procedures of traditional rhetoric (see CONE
1967, 37 and DAHLHAUS 1971, 89ff. and analysis: *Walküre*, below). It may also draw on

---

[5]Schelling's famous characterization of architecture as fro-
zen music (see HONOUR 1979, 119, and fn. 3 for the history
of this *topos*), which freezes music as much as it does architecture, belongs to this school of thought. So does the
following passage from ROSEN 1971: "That which gives the
work an ideal existence as a simultaneous whole must be
called its structure. The rest is decoration." The eminent
literary critic J. Hillis Miller defines such a spatial conception of structure (whatever art form it may be referred to) as
"an assemblage of elements each with its own separate
meaning, all arranged in a fixed pattern to establish a total
significance" (MILLER 1968, 46).
The balance between static or spatial elements at the
one pole and dynamic or temporal elements at the other in
the experience of various artistic forms has received much
attention recently from critics of literature and of the visual arts, whose subtle thought on this matter has a good
deal to teach music critics. See the recent series of articles
on the subject by Joseph Frank, Eric Rabkin, William
Holtz, Frank Kermode, Rudolf Arnheim, and W. J. T.
Mitchell in *Critical Inquiry*, from 1977 to 1980. See also
CONE 1977, which I did not stumble upon until this essay
was completed.
[6]These two ideas of shape seem to be those called by Siegmund Levarie (borrowing from Ernst Lévy) "ontic" and
"gignetic" (LEVARIE 1979, 89).

dramatic or psychological procedure: on a series of moods, affects, or characteristics unfolding in a unidirectional dramatic procedure according to a model with which we are in some way familiar. Explicit appeal to this last kind of shape in music was fairly novel, though not unprecedented, in Wagner's time. Because of this relative novelty, Wagner insisted on this particular source for musical shape in his letters and prose writings, most often using the word *Entwicklung* (which is sometimes misleadingly translated as "development") for dramatic procedure in music, and opposing to it the word *Wechsel* for the self-contained patterns of the architectural forms of traditional musical *Formenlehre*.[7] The dramatic procedure appealed to should be a simple one that is both well known and capable of translation into musical terms. An example might be the presentation and modification of contrasting positions in dialogue (see analysis: *Siegfried*) or the passage from quietude to violent anger (ibid.). *Walküre* II, 2, a worrisome scene for both Wagner and his commentators, is an early attempt to structure a long musico-dramatic unit around a single such dramatic procedure, here the passage from utter dejection and stasis of the will through gradual activation of the will to anger and desperate decision. In one of his grandest achievements, Wagner uses dramatic procedure, now in two large complementary waves, to structure a large portion of *Tristan* III (up to the Shepherd's sighting of the boat).[8]

All three kinds of shape—the architectural, the musical-procedural, and the extra-mu-

sical-procedural—are important in Wagnerian music drama, which moves subtly back and forth among them, while tending to avoid completing the closed forms of the first and to stress the open-ended, always forward-moving elements of the second and third. In almost every Wagnerian unit, there is a tension among these various kinds of shape.

There is likewise a tension between the demands of shape or form on the one hand and those of theme or motive on the other—in particular, between the demands of dynamic procedure and those of arresting individual gesture, between the demands of *Entwicklung* and *Einfall*.[9] Expression of individual character in a theme, thematic combination, or thematic transformation speaks to the listener directly and immediately, and Wagner valued highly such directness of speech. It is especially in the thematic realm that the Wagnerian music drama is, as Thomas Mann has said, *"dieser exoterische Musik"* (MANN 1933, 80). In some units, particularly those in which a good deal of stage action takes place, the network of themes and motives may be the primary focus of the music. The result is a kind of *recitativo accompagnato*, or melodrama writ large, in which a series of short and highly individual musical formulations is hung on stage incident (as opposed to a dramatic procedure being projected through musical means)—a huge expansion of the techniques of the Wolf's Glen scene from Weber's *Der Freischütz*, a scene particularly beloved of Wagner. *Siegfried* II, for example, is almost entirely made up of such thematic-illustrative music; the demands of

165

[7]To me, Wagner's clearest expression of these formal concerns is in the essay of 1857 on Liszt's symphonic poems (WAGNER-GS V, 182–98, esp. 189ff.). Note that the famous letter of 29 October 1859 to Mathilde Wesendonck concerning the art of transition also presents musical form as dramatic procedure (WAGNER-WESENDONCK, 189–90), as does the interpretation of the *Coriolanus* overture in the Beethoven essay of 1870 (WAGNER-GS IX, 107–08). A wonderfully characteristic passage from *Das Braune Buch* (10 September 1865; WAGNER-BRAUNE BUCH, 84–85) describes a number of musical forms as various types of *Lebensläufe*.
[8]I believe it was the coordination between such dramatic or rhetorical procedures on the one hand and traditional musical forms and procedures on the other that occupied Wagner first of all, as he struggled with the original concep-

tion of a subject in his mind—readjusting the general procedures of the one to fit the traditional forms and procedures of the other. The specific embodiments and projections of the shapes and procedures could come later, as he fleshed them out with dramatic details and musical motives.
[9]See DAHLHAUS 1970[b], 140 and DAHLHAUS 1974/80, section III, 2. It is tempting to see the tension between Wotan and Erda in *Siegfried* III, 1 (see analysis: *Siegfried*) in this light. As procedure—here the procedures are those of tonal harmony and classical phrase-building—Wotan's material is highly directed, but as individual gesture it is quite restrained—for example, in harmonic or instrumental color. Erda's material is the opposite: undirected as procedure, but strikingly individual in thematic color.

striking, individual musical gesture rather bury the demands of larger musical shape. Although the balance never goes quite as far in the other direction—toward the demands of traditional musical shape and away from those of thematic gesture—the tension between the two poles is always present.

In Wagner's style, as in most others, there is also a tension between the projection of the overall form and the articulation of the smaller units of which it is built. To my ears, Wagner's style changed markedly in this respect during the late 1850s, especially in the course of his work on *Tristan*. After *Tristan* II, 1, he tended to minimize articulation on the smaller level in order to fix the listener's attention on the large time-span and the large musico-dramatic process. *Tristan* II, 2–3 seems to me the first of those large units in which one simply cannot understand the articulation of some smaller units without referring to the overall shape.[10]

III

Although Wagner often uses as the basis for his own forms the rich fund of traditional formal procedures and schemata he inherited from late eighteenth- and early nineteenth-century music, nonetheless in his techniques for *presenting* his forms to the listener he departs in several respects from older traditions.

The first important thing to understand is that within a single unit Wagner makes use of an extraordinarily wide variety of formal types, usually leaving each incomplete as he shifts from one to another.

Not even the most casual listener to the *Ring* will have missed that its range of formal types is wide, varying from the musically loosely structured, recitative-like, illustrative unit, such as much of *Siegfried* II or *Walküre* II,

1, to the musically highly structured and clearly articulated unit, such as *Siegfried* III, 1 or the Norn's scene from *Götterdämmerung*. Between these extremes lie manifold gradations, and the movement across these gradations may in itself be a source of shape. I have suggested above that *Walküre* II, 2, one of the freest of Wagner's forms before *Tristan*, tries to project a large-scale dramatic procedure through a similarly large musical procedure. The musical procedure in question is the gradual modulation from musically unformed recitative to a musically highly formed aria-like unit, the whole set off by two musically similar pillars of great intensity (from Wotan's *"O heilige Schmach!"* through his *"zernage ihn gierig dein Neid!"*—S 109/1–130/3, Eu 348/1–421/1).[11] One might be tempted to think that the relative musical looseness of the scene is due to the extreme length of Wotan's monologue, were it not that other long and talky sections from the early 1850s show more highly structured musical procedures. Loge's complex and circumstantial narrative in *Rheingold* 2 is built up of clearly articulated small musical units, and the long dramatic dialogue of *Walküre* I, 3 exhibits a still clearer musical procedure: varied repetition of parallel units, articulated by several kinds of interruption. That Wagner chose in *Walküre* II, 2 to concentrate on a single large progression from unstructured to highly structured formal types with minimal local articulation along the way must, I think, be attributed to a conscious and bold formal experiment on his part, rather than to a lack of other formal means for coping with the dramatic situation.

Instead of progressing gradually from one to the other, Wagner may juxtapose a musically highly structured and a loosely structured smaller unit (see analysis: *Siegfried*). Or he may move flexibly back and forth from the highly structured to the loosely structured within the single unit. *Walküre* II, 1, for example, is musically quite loosely structured as a

---

[10]Cf. ADLER 1904, 221–22: "Wir haben hier [in Wagner's later style] keine thematische Detailausführung, sondern eine Freskomalerei in der Tonkunst. Sie verhält sich zur symphonischen Musik im eigentlichen Sinne, wie die Dekorationsmalerei zur Landschaftsmalerei." Dahlhaus may also be making this point in his article on *Tristan* II, 2 (DAHLHAUS 1974), but if so, the point is blurred by the limitation of his discourse to the level of what he takes to be the *Periode* of 15 to 30 measures in length, a consistent trait of his analyses since the initial article of 1965 (cf. fn. 16 below).

---

[11]Wagner's awareness of the arrival of the aria type at Wotan's *"Nur einer könnte"* (S 120/2, Eu 381/1) is evidenced by his reportedly calling the music that follows the *Tonsatz*. See PORGES 1896.

whole, but it moves into and out of a number of clearly structured miniatures within itself (we shall look at one of these below). Variety and internal flexibility of musical form is the hallmark of Wagner's style, and an explicit aesthetic goal; dramatic variety and flexibility require it. He is constantly moving from the loosely structured, in this sense recitative-like, to the more highly structured, in this sense aria-like, and back.

When he uses the more structured style, Wagner must, of course, appeal to the traditional formal schemata and procedures that he and his audiences had inherited. But even in this more structured style, the formal schemes and procedures are usually left incomplete and are often constantly shifting in their implications.

Incompleteness of form, as a means of keeping the musical procedure open-ended and forward-moving, can be illustrated by sketching the outlines of a pair of examples developed more fully in the analysis of *Siegfried* III, 1, below. On the small scale, the first speech of Wotan (S 242/1–244/3, Eu 784–99) implies a closed ABA unit (an implication projected by the well-formed, closed first unit and by the clear contrast at the beginning of the second), but when the initial unit returns (S 244/1, Eu 796), it lacks its beginning, thereby losing some of its clarity and definition. The unit is then interrupted at its halfway point, leaving it both harmonically and melodically incomplete as it flows into the next unit of form. On a larger scale, the entire scene is left formally incomplete. The scene is roughly arch-shaped, and the moment of reprise is articulated with great vigor and definition. But not even the first phrase of this reprise is allowed to complete itself. Wagner first breaks the firm periodic structure of the phrase as originally stated by reflecting upon each chord under a fermata, so to speak. Then he takes advantage of an enharmonic implication in one chord to spring open the closed harmonic circle of the unit and move off into other regions, beginning a tonal transition to the next scene.

We have here not only formal incompletion but also a shift in formal implication. The passage seems at first to be a varied reprise, but in the process of variation the reprise is deflected to become a transition. Such shifts in implication are no less crucial than incompletion to Wagner's forms. An example on the smallest formal level is discussed in the *Walküre* analysis, below. On a somewhat larger scale, the "Spring Song" from *Walküre* I, 3 (S 53ff., Eu 150ff.) starts out with the clear periodic structures of the closed song form. The second section ("*Mit zarter Waffen Zier*") is introduced like a normal contrasting section in ternary song form. But it soon opens out into a different world, both emotionally and thematically, a world that Sieglinde enthusiastically accepts with a musically and dramatically parallel answer. What began as a contrasting section in an ABA form has become the initial unit in a process of continuing variation of parallel answering units. (The two implied forms are elided, so to speak, by the nod given the return of the initial section of the ABA form in the short instrumental postlude between Siegmund's first speech and Sieglinde's answer. It is as if Siegmund's initial intent to fashion a decorous song form had been derailed by his passion. The interlude may allude to the song form, but Sieglinde prefers to ignore the allusion and to follow Siegmund on his new path. Wagner developed his anti-conventionality of form precisely for its ability to embody such metaphorical, musico-dramatic meaning.)

Examples could be multiplied, in both small and large formal units. Wagner is continually making shifting allusions to the treasure of formal schemata and procedures that he had inherited from his predecessors: rondo, ternary song form, strophic and modified strophic form, ritornello procedure, sonata procedure, ricercar—yes, even *Bar* and *Bogen*. But he rarely lets any one of them work itself out to completion, and he alludes flexibly to one, then another, then yet another set of formal habits and implications as he moves along. Even his relatively closed, complete forms tend to be hybrids.

IV

A wide variety of formal types within a single unit, formal types left incomplete or transformed into something else as they unfold—these are characteristics of Wagner's novel methods of presenting traditional musical forms and procedures to his listener. Not only do his implied forms and procedures shift constantly, so too do the musical elements that define and determine formal contrasts and connections. Again, this musical flexibility is necessary to give Wagner the dramatic flexibility he desires.[12]

Thus motive and theme may be form-defining or merely referential. Likewise the divisions of the dialogue and the rhetorical structure of the text may parallel the musical form in an obvious way, or else they may contradict it locally, usually for the sake of the larger shape. Contrasts of style, too, may be formal or referential or locally expressive in function. On the other hand, instrumentation and tempo, which may be used for color and expression alone, are often used for formal definition as well. Only cadence can always be counted on as an indication of formal articulation—a large cadence is invariably an important formal articulation. In the interaction of all these form-defining elements, each individual formal unit must make clear its own rules.

1. Although tempo and instrumentation are not called upon alone to make clear a musical shape in Wagner, they are often the most powerful in a group of form-defining elements. This is especially true where form is conceived of less as traditional musical formal scheme than as dramatic process, and where the form-defining capacities of such traditionally powerful elements as theme and tonality have for some reason been called into question. The extraordinary stress laid by Wagner on choice and control of tempo in the correct projection of a piece of music is made clear in his essay on conducting and in his comments during the re-

hearsals for the first production of the *Ring* in Bayreuth (WAGNER-GS VIII, 274–308 and PORGES 1896).[13] The analysis below of the central section of *Siegfried* III, 1 gives an instance: here, in a section where tonality is unstable and much of the motivic content is referential, Wagner carefully indicates juxtapositions and modulations of tempo as a means of projecting a musico-dramatic process. Tempo is again an important communicator of the musico-dramatic shape in the long central dialogue between the two duets of Siegfried III, 3, or, as Brinkmann points out, in the *Wissenswette* of *Siegfried* I, 2 (BRINKMANN 1972).

In the brief section of *Walküre* II, 1, analyzed below, instrumentation (in this case not referential) plays a secondary role, but one that is certainly not negligible in reinforcing a primarily tonal shape of statement, contrast, and return. In a passage from Loge's narrative (*Rheingold* 2), instrumentation, together with chordal vocabulary, is not secondary but primary in structuring the progression from one cadence ("*lassen will nichts / von Lieb' und Weib,*" S 87/1, Eu 279) to another ("*und ewig bleibe ihr eigen,*" S 89/1, Eu 285/2). The passage is shaped by a clear progression toward the correct (that is, the original) harmonic and instrumental expression of the Rheingold Call.[14] From the troubled harmonies and double-reed woodwind instrumentation of the beginning of the passage, the motive proceeds toward its goal in a unidirectional series of carefully graded statements.

Yet instrumentation—like tempo, motive, even tonality—may be not structural but purely referential. To cite but one of many instances: the two striking appearances of the rich consort of brasses in *Walküre* II, 2—appearances particularly striking in the otherwise austere instrumental textures of the

---

[12]The following passage by Edward T. Cone (CONE 1961, 442) seems to summarize the Wagnerian ideal: "To say of a composition that it conveys sorrow or embodies agility or induces contemplation is to make a statement of only preliminary aesthetic importance. The artistic value arises from the coalescence of the abstract form and the expressive design in such a way that each can be interpreted as a consequence of the other. Every event demanded by the purely musical pattern must correspond to an event demanded at that point by the psychical pattern. If the composition is successful, the two streams, musical and psychical, of the mingled flow are felt as analogically fused—in effect as one."

---

[13]Egon Voss has recently stressed that tempo is a constitutive element in Wagnerian forms. See Voss 1977, 134.

[14]Harmony here means the chordal vocabulary used to state the motive, not the key in which it is stated. Although the motive is also moving toward the key of its original statement, the stages in this tonal progression, over a rather wandering series of pedals, are not as clearly shaped as are the instrumental and chordal stages. Wagner's letter to Uhlig of May 1852, quoted on p. 49 below, is relevant to this passage.

first part of Wotan's monologue—do not mark out places that are in any sense structurally analogous, nor do they point out anything concerning the overall musico-dramatic procedure of the scene. They are simply illustrative music called up by references to Valhalla.

2. The dramatic or rhetorical structure of the text, its division in dialogue, and the associated visual action on stage are used more consistently as form-defining elements. On the large scale they invariably project at least some aspect of the musico-dramatic form. The division of the scene in dialogue may simply provide an internal articulation for the scene, dividing it into sections without defining its procedure, or it may directly project the procedure of the scene. In *Walküre* II, 2, for example, Brünnhilde's questions to Wotan simply articulate what is in effect a monologue by Wotan (whose overall musico-dramatic procedure I have already suggested). On the other hand, the Wanderer's questions to Mime and Mime's to the Wanderer do determine and project the musical refrain structure of *Siegfried* I, 2.

On the detailed level there may be disagreements between the rhetorical or dialogue structure of the text on the one hand and the musical procedures on the other—disagreements due either to Wagner's changing his mind in the course of working out the passage in musical detail, or to his desire to help the continuity of the musical and dramatic flow by loosening slightly the synchronization of form-defining elements. The "Idyll" section of *Siegfried* III, 3 would appear to offer an example of the former situation (cf. NEWMAN 1949, 588–89), and Isolde's Narrative in *Tristan* I, 3 an example of the latter. The first section of Isolde's Narrative, before Brangäne's first interruption, is roughly speaking in arch form. Its verbal and dramatic design clearly implies a return to the opening musical material with the return of the opening image (Tristan lying helpless before Isolde) and phraseology ("*Von einem Kahn . . . ,*" "*Von seinem Lager . . .*"), and in pitch and tempo the return does in fact happen here. But the motivic material and figuration of the opening had returned a good deal earlier—in fact they began to in-

sinuate themselves almost immediately after the contrast had been established by the ironic quotation of Kurwenal's cocky, triadic Tristan-the-hero refrain. As for the tonal return, this does not come until close to the end of the unit. Such instances are not really disagreements between dramatic, rhetorical, or verbal structure and musical structure. They are rather (as Dahlhaus suggests in his 1974 article) blurrings of the formal articulations in order to enhance the musico-dramatic flow.[15]

The dramatic structure of a text, especially the large-scale dramatic structure, is not embodied solely in the divisions into dialogue, or in the antitheses, parallel members, repeated images, even the rational discourse of the text. For example, the broad contrast between differing styles of speech may itself help to structure a large section, as it does in *Tristan* II, 2, where the arch-shaped progression is from short, rationally incoherent exclamations to more sustained, rational discourse and back to short, incoherent exclamations. Indeed, the dramatic structure of a text may go beyond the dialogue altogether. Simple visual elements are powerful both in articulating a large musico-dramatic form (in *Walküre* III, 1, for example, the refrain-like action by one or other of the Valkyries in looking off-stage for the approaching Wotan, which is always accompanied by some form of the Need of the Gods motive), and sometimes even of tracing out its procedures (the Wanderer's progress toward the hearth in *Siegfried* I, 2; the rising and sinking of the fire in Siegmund's long first speech of *Walküre* I, 3). The structure of the dramatic action, however this may be expressed in the poem, is one of the most consistently used formal determinants in Wagner's musico-dramatic units.

3. The rhythmic structure of phrase and period does not always function formally in Wagner as it does in the Viennese classical

---

[15]Such formal blurring is not an invention of Wagner, of course. In the aria "Bäche von gesalz'nen Zähren" from Bach's Cantata No. 21, for example, the textual and musical contrasts of the central section of the *da capo* aria are synchronized and clearly defined, but the return is blurred—happening motivically, textually, and tonally at three different points.

style, or in Brahms.[16] Although Wagner may occasionally build a period or a series of periods using the cadential and motivic correspondences of the classical style (see analysis: *Siegfried*), he does not continuously maintain this style (or this syntax, as Dahlhaus calls it) to build larger units. In its pure form, it is in fact fairly rare even in smaller units. Instead, the rhythmic and harmonic structure of phrases and sections is often loosened for the sake of declamatory, dramatic, and illustrative flexibility, with the result that entire stretches of music are no longer heard against the background of regular periodic phrase structures.

This loosening of periodic structure does not mean, however, that periodicity is never a formal determinant in Wagner. It functions there in various ways, according to the procedures of the individual unit. Especially in some large instrumental sections, periodicity—that is, regularly recurring measure groups articulated by regularly recurring harmonic changes—is a strong factor in creating formal expectations and climax. To be sure, the harmonic patterns involved are usually not the simple functional tonal patterns of classical period structure, but are more likely to be taken from a previously established leitmotivic pattern, or may be a sequential pattern established newly within the section itself. Still, the cumulative metrical effect of the parallel units—and the concomitant effects of elision, truncation, and extension—are no less strong than in the classical style (where in fact this kind of harmonically open but metrically regular periodic structure occurs often in developmental and transitional sections). Examples of this kind of periodicity occur both in instrumental sections (see the preludes to *Siegfried* III and *Walküre* I) and in vocal sections (see analysis: *Walküre*). The end of the central dialogue in *Siegfried* III, 3 (from Siegfried's "*Ein herrlich Gewässer wogt vor mir*" S 322/3, Eu 1106) offers a sophisticated and particularly effective example of the manipulation of traditional periodicity as part of a large, dramatic vocal form.

Often, however, Wagner's style is not periodic in any sense; many Wagnerian formal units are not built up through regularly recurring accents of weight defined by harmonic change. They are in this sense recitative-like. Large sections of *Rheingold* 2 and *Walküre* II, 1 are clear examples. In fact, large-scale formal contrast may be projected by contrasting aperiodic with periodic phrase construction (see analysis: *Siegfried*).

By the time of the *Ring*, Wagner had developed a broad gamut of techniques of phrase and period construction, ranging from the metrically unstructured, dramatically flexible, illustrative style derived from recitative, through the hovering, aperiodic but rhythmically sustained style of the transition to *Siegfried* III, 3 or the prelude to *Parsifal* I or even the pantomimes of *Walküre* I, 1, through the harmonically anomalous periodicity of the prelude to

[16]Dahlhaus has discussed this matter in his writings from 1965 onward. Perhaps his most compendious exposition is in DAHLHAUS 1974/80, section III, 3; the most recent I have seen is DAHLHAUS 1978. KUNZE 1970 and DANUSER 1975 also discuss Wagner's phrase structures in some detail.

A considerable polemic has grown up around the precise meaning of Wagner's phrase, *die dichterisch-musikalische Periode*. PETERSEN 1977 opposed the interpretation proposed by Dahlhaus in 1965 and 1971; response by Dahlhaus and counter-response by Petersen followed in *Melos-NZ* (vol. 4, 1978, 224–25 and 403–04). I shall not enter into the question here, for it does not seem in itself to be of great importance to Wagnerian analysis. (Granted, it may be important to a detailed exegesis of *Oper und Drama*, part III.) As Rudolf Stephan has pointed out (STEPHAN 1970, 16), Wagner used the phrase only once. Thus, the concept would not seem to be a crucial one in his formal thinking; and one instance does not give us a firm basis for establishing or limiting his meaning when he uses the phrase.

Its most significant influence may lie in its having sidetracked the German analyses of recent years. Dahlhaus, following his interpretation of what Wagner meant by the phrase, stays in his analyses on the level of the 15- to 30-measure unit, which sometimes leads him to omit entirely the large-scale musico-dramatic shapes in the passage he is analyzing. (See his discussion of *Tristan* II, 2 in 1974 or of Brünnhilde's Immolation Scene from *Götterdämmerung* in 1971, 79–82.) Dahlhaus is not alone here; neglect of the large-scale formal context is a defect in most recent German analyses (BRINKMANN 1972 is an exception). FLECHSIG 1970, for example, groups together in minute comparative analysis two units near the end of *Tristan* II, 1. The units she compares, however, serve two very different purposes in the overall form of the scene, and the music that she isolates is falsified by looking at it alone. Especially the material at the end of her small unit ("*Zur Warte du . . .*,") the peroration and cadence to the entire scene) must be viewed in relation to the scene as a whole in order to be understood correctly.

Siegfried III, 1, to the harmonically more traditional periodicity of Wotan in Siegfried III, 1. These separate varieties of rhythmic-metrical style are easily distinguished by the ear. Hence they can be used in modulation or juxtaposition to project musico-dramatic form.

4. The function of motive in a Wagnerian musico-dramatic unit is potentially double: a motive may be form-defining or referential.[17] This potential dilemma is resolved by Wagner at the outset of a formal unit, where those motives that are to be form-defining are clearly laid out in an initial exposition. In addition, the principal form-defining motive is usually (although not always) a new one, or at least newly transformed. Unless care is taken to observe the distinction between form-defining and referential motives, the attempt to discern and describe Wagnerian forms by laying out the succession of motives—a method often used by Lorenz, with rich allowances for "motivic substitutions"—is bound to give unsatisfactory results.

As might be expected, the most clearly formed scenes offer the clearest examples of the differentiation between form-defining and referential motives. Siegfried III, 1 (see analysis: Siegfried) exposes its primary form-defining motive at the outset and with great clarity, in a repeated phrase formulated as an antecedent-consequent period (S 242/2–243/2, Eu 784–90). Although reference to this principal material later in the scene is never again so complete or self-contained, the strongly shaped exposition at the beginning leaves us in no doubt as to which material is invested with formal significance. The form-defining material of Siegfried I, 2 (Wanderer-Mime) is similarly placed before us at the outset of the unit. The leisurely exposition given the three sections of Wanderer Chords—an exposition complete with internal contrast (Mime's fright music) and internal sequential development—impresses this material thoroughly on our ears.

The rich web of motivic reference in the ensuing catechism never threatens its formal, articulating power.

Although the form-defining motives of a unit are often first introduced in that unit, this is not always the case. The motivic kernel of Wotan's refrain in Siegfried III, 1, is in fact a transformation of an old and much-used motive, as is the despairing outburst by Mime (developed from the Renunciation of Love motive) that stands as a massive formal pillar on each side of Siegfried I, 2. Here the very intensity of the formulation, both instrumentally and harmonically, makes it an example of what Rudolf Stephan (STEPHAN 1970, 13) has perceptively called an Attraktionszentrum, whose infrequent recurrence has the power to articulate large spaces.

Even a familiar and untransformed motive, when presented appropriately, can serve as a form-defining element within a unit. Thus, both the Valkyrie and Need of the Gods motives, the principal motives of Walküre III, 1, are familiar ones. The entire central section of the scene is articulated by the Need of the Gods motive, first introduced in Wotan's despairing monologue of Walküre II, 2 and associated in the present scene with the approach of the unhappy god. Here again, the nature of the initial exposition makes clear the motive's form-defining role in the ensuing section. This exposition of some thirty measures—whose beginning (S 203/1, Eu 724, before Waltraute's "Nach dem Tann lenkt sie / das taumelnde Ross") is articulated not only by change of motive, but also by change of instrumentation, tempo, register, and key—even has its own short passage of internal contrast (after "Das ist kein Held!"). After so long and clearly formed an exposition, brief references to the motive (visually reinforced by one of the brood's running to the back of the stage to follow Wotan's progress toward their mountain retreat) suffice both to articulate the musical form of the scene and to keep reminding us of the imminent approach of Wotan.

No one who has listened to a mature Wagner opera will have missed the virtuosity with which he draws one motive out of another, connecting them through a process

171

---

[17]DAHLHAUS 1969, section II, 4 and DAHLHAUS 1970ª, 38 both take account of this dilemma, without exploring it in the analysis of a scene.

similar to what Schoenberg called developing variation (cf. DALHAUS 1974/80, section III, 2). I shall leave aside here the extraordinary way in which Wagner uses this technique for psychological effects on a local level, for this is not strictly speaking a formal matter. The form-defining use to which the technique is put varies widely in Wagner (as, indeed, in Brahms). He may create local motive connections in order to smooth transitions and blur formal boundaries, thus maintaining the impression of continuous forward flow. Examples of this procedure are almost as numerous as the pages of the score. Dahlhaus points to a few in the *Tagesgespräch* of *Tristan* II, 2 (DAHLHAUS 1974, 478–79). At *"Gibt's eine Not, / Gibt's eine Pein"* (S 143, Eu 452) the Day motive is presented in a rhythmic and harmonic guise close to Kurwenal's Tristan Refrain, which then makes its first local appearance sixteen measures later. This example, especially, is not like the classical (and the Brahmsian) use of developing variation, since it does not lead anywhere, and has no logical implications; it simply smooths the flow back and forth in the motivic web. In other instances, Wagner uses the procedure to soften the potentially abrupt jolt at the introduction of a new motive. In the same scene, the Day motive, which is introduced at *"Dem Tage! dem Tage!"* (S 141, Eu 447) as the principal motive of the ensuing dialogue, is cannily previewed some thirteen measures earlier (*". . . Türe / dass nicht ich zu ihr führe"*); in the prelude to the same Act, the motivic joint at mm. 28–29 is smoothed over by placing the rising, expectant motive of the previous section as a tenor-voice counterpoint to the first presentation of the new, tumbling motive that will dominate the ensuing scene; in *Rheingold* 2 the chromatically sliding fourths (or fifths) of Loge's motive are foreshadowed several times before the complete motive itself appears,[18] so that when the motive is finally exposed in definitive form, we have the impression that we have heard it somewhere before, even though its musical characteristics are not drawn from any previous motive.

Wagner also uses the techniques of motivic connection and derivation to increase the impressiveness at an articulation of great formal weight, where he wants to bring forth a new motive with all the ceremony of a royal birth. On such occasions he makes the process of connection and derivation very clear, but he does not try to smooth the joint by hiding the importance of the arrival. A well-known instance is the gradual transformation in the transition between *Rheingold* 1 and *Rheingold* 2 of the harmonic, rhythmic, and instrumental characteristics of the Ring motive to produce the Valhalla motive. Another subtler instance discussed below is the bringing together, through insistence on certain rhythmic and melodic characteristics, of a family of motives, in order to give birth to the World Inheritance motive at the end of *Siegfried* III, 1 (see analysis: *Siegfried*).[19]

5. The form-defining function of tonality in Wagnerian music drama is perhaps the thorniest of all subjects to lay hands on. Although little scholarly blood has been drawn, the matter has received vigorously contradictory expositions in even the most recent literature; see BRINKMANN 1972, DAHLHAUS 1965 through

---

[18]E.g., m. 952 (S 65/4; Eu 214/2) and mm. 1036–39 (S 70/4–71/1, Eu 227/1).

---

[19]I should like to enter one personal caveat in the matter of motivic connection, a caveat that has more to do with musical hermeneutics than it does with formal analysis. Given the number of motive-defining elements with which Wagner worked, and given his virtuosity in using all of them, we must recognize that he could, if he wanted, discover and make us believe connections between almost any pair of motives. In commenting on the music, then, we must restrict ourselves to those connections that Wagner presents to us clearly and thus clearly wants us to believe. To place motives next to each other on the page and discover connections between them may be an amusing pastime, but in order for the pastime to have any relevance to the *Ring*, it must be demonstrated that Wagner draws these connections for us in the music—that he wants us to hear them and therefore places them before our ears. As a specific example: by isolating and drawing attention to rhythmic shape and instrumentation as motive-defining elements, one could easily assert a close connection between the Hunding motive of *Walküre* I, 2 and what Wolzogen calls the *Vaterfreude* motive associated with Wotan in *Siegfried* III, 2 (see ex. 4, below, for this motive). But Wagner never makes this connection, nor is there any reason to believe that it has any meaning in the *Ring*. There are scores of such connections waiting to be "discovered," but they must be made for us in the music in order to have relevance to the music.

172

1980, GEORGE 1970, JOSEPHSON 1979, and SERAUKY 1959, to cite but a few examples. I shall discuss some of these in a moment, after summarizing a fundamental tenet in my own position.

Traditional functional tonality—that is, the continuous observance of a syntax of chord connections through which all harmonic progressions can be related by function to a single central tonic—does not operate over large stretches of Wagnerian music drama. Many large stretches of Wagnerian music drama are not in this sense functionally tonal. Certainly returns to the original key are made after long spans of time—returns that do serve formally to round off large units. Nonetheless the *primary* element in defining the formal return and rounding-off is not tonality, but rather some other element or group of elements, such as motive, instrumentation, tempo, and dramatic situation. In these cases, unless the return to the original key is amply reinforced and explained by other elements, it is unlikely that this return will be perceived as such. Since the functional connections between chords—the syntax of functional tonality—will have been unclear over long stretches of the intervening music, we can no longer know where we are in relation to the original center. Only absolute pitch could tell us. Wagner was not an esoteric composer—that is the gist of Thomas Mann's comment quoted above—and it is inappropriate to maintain that perception of his forms depends on so esoteric a faculty as absolute pitch. In addition, internal musical evidence says that awareness of tonal return alone is not necessary to the perceptions of his forms, as I shall try to show in a moment. A passage from a letter of 31 May 1852 by Wagner to his friend Theodore Uhlig adds documentary weight to this musical evidence:

So, by clinging to the "individuality" of keys, one clings to a chimera, which anyhow formerly became as much of a dogma with us as the good God Himself. On the contrary, keys, like tones in general, only become characteristic in the instruments, and, finally, in the human voice with words. Thus, for example, the characteristic individuality of a key (E major or Eb major) stands out very prominently in a violin or a wind instrument, and it is, therefore, a piece of uncritical stupidity to consider the key by itself, and the instruments not at all, or else also by themselves. . . .—Whoever in judging my music divides the harmony from the instrumentation does me as much injustice as he who divides my music from my poetry, my song from the words![20]

Of course, we still understand all of Wagnerian opera as tonal music; we apply to it concepts such as tonic, dominant, prolongation, triad, and so forth, which belong to tonal music. I do not suggest that we hear, or should try to understand, Wagner as atonal music, as in BORETZ 1972. My point is that the tight, limited grammatical rules of chord connections, conventionally represented by the Roman numeral or letter designations that we assign to individual chords, are sometimes so far loosened as to lose much of their binding force.

Nor do I suggest that this extreme loosening of traditional functional tonality is, in historical terms, necessarily a progressive feature tending toward the avant-garde style of the

173

---

[20]"Hing man sich also an die 'Individualität' der Tonarten, so hing man sich an eine Chimäre, die allerdings früher bei uns eben so gut zum Dogma geworden war, wie der liebe Gott. Dagegen werden an den Instrumenten, und endlich an der menschlichen Stimme mit dem Worte, die Tonarten wie die Töne überhaupt, erst charakteristisch; so tritt z. B. die charakteristische Individualität einer Tonart (E-dur oder Es-dur) bei der Geige oder dem Blasintrument sehr entschieden hervor, und es ist daher eine kritiklose Halbheit, wenn ich die Tonart für sich und das Instrument wohl gar nicht, oder wiederum für sich nehme. . . .—Wer in einem Urtheil über meine Musik die Harmonie von der Instrumentation trennt, thut mir ein ebenso grosses Unrecht, wie der, der meine Musik von meiner Dichtung, meinem Gesang vom Worte trennt!—" WAGNER-UHLIG, 192–93; translation, slightly altered, from *Richard Wagner's Letters to his Dresden Friends*, trans. J. S. Shedlock (New York, 1890).

Admittedly, Wagner is talking here about the perception of individual keys in the abstract, not about the perception of their return in a large and tonally complicated form. But the two matters are closely related, a point that Wagner develops at greater length in the then recently completed *Oper und Drama*, part III, to which he has just referred in the letter to Uhlig (see especially WAGNER-GS IV, 148–49, 158–66). His point, in the letter as in the treatise, is that tonal form, especially in the music of someone eager to use the full resources of early nineteenth-century harmony—someone who, to use Wagner's metaphor, wanted to strike out from the shore and be a bold swimmer in the broad sea of harmony—such tonal form should be reinforced by instrumentation and by dramatic situation. At this point in his career, Wagner had not yet begun work on the music of the *Ring*, nor had he yet worked out the motivic techniques that would also play a large part in articulating his tonal forms.

early twentieth century (call the style atonal, contextual, motivic, or what you will). Most often this wandering tonality is Wagner's continuation of the *recitativo secco* style, and it is most evident in the talky passages of *Rheingold*, *Walküre*, and *Siegfried* I and II. The place of such talky passages in a large tonally determined form becomes clearer in the later acts of the *Ring*. For example, although local functional conventions are loose and distant at the height of the exchange between Wotan and Erda in *Siegfried* III, 1 (see analysis: *Siegfried*), this central section is held firmly bracketed in the tonally stable G minor form that surrounds it, and the place in G minor of the loosely connected harmonies is to some extent articulated by linear means.

Having said this, let me turn to one of the early operas of the *Ring* to exemplify the important distinction between a passage that is continuously tonal, in the sense of maintaining continuously the traditional connections of functional tonality, and one that returns repeatedly to the same key—a key which Wagner asserts by motivic, instrumental, or dramatic means to be the tonic—without maintaining continuously between these recurrences the syntax of functional chord changes. The concluding approximately 200 measures of *Rheingold* form one of the largest sections of continuously tonal music in the *Ring*. The stable block of the Thunderstorm maintains functional syntax in B♭, as does the ensuing G♭ block of the Rainbow, which is functionally related to the preceding B♭ through a deceptive cadence (S 207/3–208/3, Eu 682–84); the G♭ block is then related through a large plagal cadence (S 209/4, Eu 695–96) to the final D♭ section, which maintains contact with the tonic by using the functional Valhalla section from the beginning of scene 2 as a harmonic model, into which relatively short contrasting insertions are made. This entire section, then, can (and should) be heard as a massive, continuously tonal, cadential sentence in D♭.

Now there is also a sense in which the preceding 900-odd measures of music, from the transition to scene 3 to the above-mentioned deceptive cadence at the Rainbow motive, can be said to be in B♭ minor-major. But this section is not continuously tonal. Wagner main-

tains our contact with the original key by repeatedly touching back in a rondo-like fashion to a striking refrain defined by register, motive, and instrumentation—the material of the transition between scenes 2 and 3, later developed to include the motive of Servitude (Alberich's *Herrschersruf*). This refrain, Wagner tells us, identifies our tonic. He then makes the departures and returns to this tonic clear and clearly analogous. To pick an example inside this large B♭ unit: in the A minor-major contrasting section, during which Alberich is tricked (S 134/5–156/1, Eu 438/1–499/1), the initial move from an F dominant pedal (the key of the refrain) to an E dominant pedal (the key of the new section) is laid bare (at Alberich's *"Was wollt ihr hier?"*) and decked out in striking instrumental and motivic garb; this tonal move is later explicitly reversed, with the same instrumentation and motivic material, at the end of scene 3, when Alberich's downfall has been accomplished. Motive, instrumentation, and dramatic action round off the intervening section and tell us of return to the "tonic." Although the intervening material is not all tonally clear (it is not even held in relatively close control by the linear means present in the later acts of the *Ring*), the relationship of the section as a whole to the key of the refrain is made manifest. We leave by slipping down a half-step; we return by climbing up the same half-step.

This identity is asserted motivically, instrumentally, and dramatically—but we have to take Wagner on faith when he asserts it. For continuous functional tonality has not been maintained across the interim.[21]

V

I have already mentioned that recent analyses differ vigorously on the form-defining force of tonality over large stretches of Wagnerian music drama. GEORGE 1970, BRINK-

---

[21]The refrain is touched briefly within the A-minor-major section (at Alberich's *"Habt Acht"*—S 142/3, Eu 457/2), after which the falling half-step relation between this refrain material and the material of the contrasting section is again insisted on in a clear functional context (in the 30-measure section after Loge's *"dienen müssen sie dir"*—S 145/2, Eu 466), before functional syntax is again loosened in the second, larger part of the contrasting section.

174

MANN 1972, and JOSEPHSON 1979 hold in some degree to tonal patterns as defining large formal (or, in Josephson's case, symbolic) patterns in Wagner. On the other hand, Dahlhaus (DAHL-HAUS 1965, 181–82; 1974/80, section III, 4; 1975, 10–12 = 1977, 24–26), while recognizing in general the presence of both "expanded" (1974/80) and regular functional tonality in Wagner, does not develop this idea in analyses of specific scenes.

Concerning the first viewpoint, I do not see that one can attach formal or expressive weight to tonal relationships without giving careful attention to the crucial matter of how the keys in question are connected: whether tonal syntax is maintained in the interim, how tonal contrasts are introduced and how tonal returns are effected in the passage in question—in short, how the tonal moves *happen* in the music. With Wagner one can no longer simply assume the shaping and connecting power of functional tonality alone over sizeable stretches of time. It must be demonstrated in the music itself, and this demonstration must fulfill the same stipulations advanced by Dahlhaus in reference to Lorenz's view of form as the expansion of the local alternation of heavy and light beats to large-scale rhythmic correspondences (DAHLHAUS 1969, 97–98). If, says Dahlhaus, a formal element is to be felt on the large scale, it must be built up carefully through the small scale to the middle to the large. Similarly, if tonal connections are not maintained from phrase to period to section, the patterns of keys covering hundreds of measures that we make on paper may simply not be present to our ears.[22]

Among those presenting the case for tonality, Brinkmann is the most careful and convincing, and many of his points about local tonal connections are unexceptionable. Nonetheless, in his exposition of the tonal shape of the beginning of *Siegfried* I, 2 (BRINKMANN 1972, 145–48), he ignores the question of how non-traditional tonal connections between functionally unclear blocks of music some 15 to 25 slow measures apart are made clear to our ears. What happens in these 15 to 25 intervening measures cannot be dismissed as formal filler—a kind of polite musical tea-party conversation—as can some measures in highly traditional forms and processes. In fact, the measures contain some important motivic articulations, which confuse rather than clarify the tonal shape that Brinkmann would assert (e. g., the cadence at m. 13 of the scene and the strong contrast that follows it; the articulation made by the introduction of the new third phrase of Wanderer Chords at m. 28; or, a bit later in a similar situation, the push past D to E in some sense in mm. 73–77). I cannot help feeling that if Wagner had meant Brinkmann's tonal relationship to be form-defining for us, he would have clarified them rather than confused them with contradictory evidence.

George starts from an explicit commitment to a view of form as architectural, atemporal, static. We must, he insists, see the art work as a whole; we must be able to "gather it up into a meaningful unit." The only force that can accomplish this for us is tonality, because, unlike theme, it can be reduced to a few terms (GEORGE 1970, 15–17). George's single-minded adherence to these aesthetic convictions drives him to some strange acts. Not only does he forego any discussion of the musical or dramatic articulation of tonal patterns in his example from Wagner (*Meistersinger*), he goes so far as to describe Act II of this opera as a closed structure in G, even though it ends in E. Tovey's concept of "bright" and "dark" keys, to which George appeals, does indeed have formal and expressive power, but here again one must be able to follow one's way in order to feel this power—as Tovey would have been the first to insist. Keys, when disconnected from instrumental color or non-tempered tunings, are not bright or dark in some abstract sense. Their brightness or darkness depends on how they are approached and left tonally. Even A major, when approached from E major or B major, can seem dark.

Josephson's article, in spite of its title, does not discuss tonality as a form-defining element

---

[22]Guy Marco (MARCO 1979, 88) seems to miss Pevsner's point concerning Brunelleschi's Santo Spirito, which is exactly the one I have just made: the formal properties of the larger proportions in Brunelleschi's nave can be perceived by the onlooker because they have been carefully built up from the smaller levels.

175

in either the architectural or the procedural sense. It is concerned with the symbolic use of certain large-scale tonal relationships. Again, however, Josephson never seeks to demonstrate that the tonal relationships that he would assert are presented to us in the music in the way that he would have us hear them. Nor does he recognize that he should perhaps be expected to do so.[23] For example, he asserts that the Db major at the outset of *Rheingold* 2 is the symbolic top of a series of thirds piled up from Eb to G to Bb to Db. Ignoring for the moment his idea of the symbolic meaning of this tonal procedure, and ignoring the question of how the keys of G minor and Bb are reached within the first scene, I mention only that Db is approached not from Bb, but from a massive cadence in C minor (S 53/4, Eu 179). (The half-step tonal contrast between C minor and Db major, clearly exposed here, is indeed of great symbolic importance in the *Ring*.) Within the transition between C minor and Db (S 53/4–55/1, Eu 179–84), the local approach to Db is made downward by two fifths from Eb to Ab to Db. Nowhere is Db presented as the culmination of an upward-striving chain of thirds. One can see things this way only if one compares the keys of the first section of scene 1 with that of the first section of scene 2, ignoring the way things happen in between.

It is in 1974/80, section III, 4 that Dahlhaus expounds most clearly the view that functional

centers do not hold sway over considerable portions of Wagner's music dramas. In what Dahlhaus (borrowing from Schoenberg) calls "wandering" tonality, the keys or allusions thereto in Wagner are joined like links in a chain, without there being any connection between the first and the third, other than the second.[24] The importance rests in the local succession, rather than in any relation to a single governing tonal center.

In my view, this is certainly true both of many large Wagnerian units and of many small ones as well. (As I have said, such small units are almost always the ones most closely related to recitative.) But Dahlhaus's near rejection, in practice if not in theory, of the operation of functional tonality as a formal determinant in Wagner is too one-sided a view to deal adequately with the subject. Functional tonality was one of the strongest form-defining elements in the musical world where Wagner learned as a child and worked as a man. It should be no surprise that it still defines his forms, although it does so in various ways, some of which are quite different from those of a Beethoven symphonic movement—or a Mozart operatic finale. The ways in which Wagner uses cadence and tonal contrast, for example, may differ markedly from the methods of his Viennese predecessors.

Cadence, the birthplace of tonality, remains one of the most powerful and consistent articulative devices in Wagnerian music drama. But Kunze rightly points out that Wagner's cadences, although powerful as articulating devices, often do not group all that precedes them into a tonal unity, as classical cadences did (KUNZE 1970, 125, 128). The large cadence does not always put the period to a single long tonal sentence, because tonal syntax has not always been observed throughout the preceding section. Without this continuous observance, the coherence of the preceding unit as a single sentence, a coherence depending on the syntax of functional tonality, will have dissolved.

Still, large cadences, such as those at the end of Loge's narrative in *Rheingold* 2 (S 96/2–

---

[23]Key relationships can indeed have symbolic power, and their recall can have dramatic power enhanced by this. But the musico-dramatic point must be presented to us by the composer—and the presentation demonstrated by the critic or analyst. The juxtaposition of a dominant-chord-like E major with C minor toward the end of *Walküre* II, 2 (Wotan's "*Nur eines will ich noch: / das Ende! / das Ende!*"—S 127/3–4, Eu 210–12) and again toward the end of *Siegfried* III, 1 (Wotan's "*Weisst du, was Wotan—will?*"—S 256/2, Eu 845) is a case in point. In the original instance, the symbolic plunge from shrill light to extreme dark is laid bare and reinforced by tempo, instrumentation, register, and dramatic action; the recall in *Siegfried* III, 1 is connected to the original instance not only by absolute pitch, but also by all the above elements—most powerfully and obviously by instrumentation and dramatic situation (which includes the words). When key relationships function in a symbolic or dramatic way, the initial relationship is clearly presented and the connection between initial occurrence and recall never has to depend on key alone. These criteria must be fulfilled before one can assert a symbolic or dramatic function for the relationship.

[24]Kunze, too, talks of harmonic *Kettenstrukturen* in Wagner (KUNZE, 1970, 125–28).

176

97/5, Eu 308–14, after his *"das Gold wieder zu geben; / denn darum flehen sie dich"*) or at the end of the first duet in *Siegfried* III, 3 (S 301/2–3, Eu 1032–37), invariably mark important formal articulations. Indeed, the hierarchy of cadential strength, and especially the hierarchy of strength of cadential *preparation* within a unit, is one of Wagner's most powerful ways of projecting and articulating a form. But this may be more a harmonic than a tonal matter: it may be the harmonic formula of the cadence itself and its manipulation that creates closure, not the key of the cadence. In the cadence at the end of Loge's narrative, we recognize the formal closing function of the passage not by the return to D major, but by the force of the cadence itself—by its strong preparation and by the long, stable section of confirmation and the motivic peroration that follows it.

Wagner does, of course, sometimes write passages of conventional, functional tonality with tonally "summarizing" cadences. Likewise he sometimes makes us hear tonal contrast within a phrase or section in conventional ways, writing relatively simple, continuously functional tonal forms with contrasting key areas clearly related to the central tonic and using their own sets of continuously functional chords (see the Rhinemaidens' Songs from *Rheingold*). Usually, however, his local tonal procedures are more adventurous, the chordal vocabulary of his tonal contrasts wider and more colorful. In these cases the tonal contrast may be unified and related to the central tonic not so much by functional chord connections as by linear means.

It is not uncommon, for example, to find units using a wide-ranging, not continuously functional chordal vocabulary, which is related to a single central tonic by a clear linear prolongation of a primary tonal degree or of a strong functional progression. This linear prolongation is usually in the bass voice, whose primacy as a source of tonal control is never challenged in Wagner (see analysis: *Tristan*). A simple example is the passage from *Walküre* I, 3 beginning with Siegmund's *"Heiligste Minne. Höchste Noth"* (S 71/3–72/4, Eu 214–17). This small unit is clearly and centrally related to C minor-major, although the attempt to label all the chords within it would be as

difficult as it would be pointless. The structuring, skeletal line is here not the bass but the vocal part—a prolongation of the dominant, which climbs stepwise from g to g'. (Note that the metaphoric effort involved in attaining the high dominant is expressed by the increasing slowness of the process after the initial leap of g–e♭' has been filled in and surpassed.) Thus the internal tonal contrast of this unit is provided by a linear, not a functional harmonic prolongation of the dominant.

Wagner may also unify and shape a scene tonally by developing what one might call pitch reinterpretation—by returning insistently to and reinterpreting tonally a certain pitch or pair of pitches. He initially exposes the pitch or pitches in clear and close relation to the strong tonal degrees of the tonic scale—say, the flatted sixth degree as a local upper neighbor to the fifth degree. He then returns to the pitches, prolonging and reinterpreting them in harmonic language that may become so wide-ranging and various that our awareness of the central relation to the original tonic is preserved not so much through functional chord connections as through the insistent linear return to the pitches themselves, whose relation to the tonic was clearly defined at the outset. A fairly complicated example of this technique is discussed in the *Siegfried* analysis below. Here the friction between the flatted and the natural sixth degrees of the scale (and their siblings, the flatted and natural second degrees) is exposed first in clearly tonal surroundings, then in wider-ranging relations with the tonic. A similar but simpler procedure can be heard in *Lohengrin* I, 2, where the striking tonicization of the Neapolitan, A, within a closed period in A♭ expands to broader conflicts between A and A♭ in the ensuing pages, before providing the model for the modulation into A at Lohengrin's arrival.[25] In the *Tristan* analysis below, I suggest that the re-

---

[25]This is a splendid use of the symbolic powers of a tonal relationship—here clearly coordinated with the musical-formal use and clearly presented to our ears. JOSEPHSON (1979, fn. 25) mentions *Lohengrin* as an example of Wagner's love of half-step contrasts, but does not discuss how they are made symbolic for us there, or how they are worked out musically.

peated linear emphasis on the downward approach to the dominant from the sixth degree, in increasingly protracted and intense versions, serves both to articulate a large form and to help relate a heterogeneous and tonally unfocused group of motives to a single central tonic.

One of Wagner's boldest and surest techniques for projecting large forms through tonal contrast does not require the maintenance of a continuous sense of a single tonal center, either through traditional functional chord progressions or through techniques of linear prolongation. The contrast between tonal stability and tonal instability alone—a contrast amply exploited in the Viennese classical style—could in itself shape large forms through tonal means. In Wagner the contrast, freed from its relatively standardized disposition in the sonata form (instability in introductions, transitions, and development sections; stability in first and second and closing thematic groups) is used to shape all sorts of musico-dramatic forms. It becomes perhaps the most powerful element in defining large-scale tonal forms in Wagner.

We shall see shortly that in *Siegfried* III, 1, it is used to design a musical arch form passing from stability to instability and back (and to imply, through musical metaphor, the nature of a musico-dramatic conflict between decisive clarity on the one hand and indecisive lack of direction on the other). The overall tonal design of *Tristan* II, 2, for example, is the opposite. Although the scene is surrounded by tonally stable units on both sides (scene 1 and King Mark's Lament in scene 3), its fundamental design is the passage from tumultuous, forward-tumbling instability to peaceful, suspended stability and back to tumultuous instability.

Even some largely unstable sections, dependent mainly on other than tonal factors for their shape, are in some sense shaped by the contrast between stable and unstable tonality. Erda's successive speeches in the center of *Siegfried* III, 1, for example, are roughly shaped by what I have called a musical procedure—by passing from tonal stasis and functional incoherence, through an increasing tonal (and metric sense of motion and direction, to rela-

tive tonal (and metric) coherence. The gradual progression from recitative to aria style in *Walküre* II, 2 is created partly by a similar progression in tonal coherence and stability.

In this last instance, the progression from the tonally unclear recitative language of Wotan's *"Lass ich's verlauten"* to the tonally clearly formed language of his *Tonstück "Nur einer könnte"* is the one attenuated remainder of the direction-giving power of functional tonality. In any more specific sense than this, *Walküre* II, 2 cannot be said to be tonally shaped—which allows me to touch back once again to Dahlhaus's (and my) assertion that some of Wagner is not continuously functionally tonal. Although this point of view need not exclude all other views of the operation of tonality in Wagner, still it is an important one. It should help to discourage the kind of analysis that would present *Walküre* II, 2 as a movement from an E-major dominant at the beginning of the scene to an A-minor tonic at the end of the *Tonstück* and again at the end of the scene. For on such an interpretation the analyst will find himself in deep trouble when he tries to cope with the music in between. As the projection of a continuous functional-tonal design, the tonal events within the scene are not only unclear, they are hopelessly various and confusing. We can only conclude that Wagner's intent was not to project such a design. As I have said above, the scene as a whole, even much of it after the arrival of the *Tonstück*, is recitative writ large. The local illustrative and referential powers of tonality are here supreme over its syntactic, direction-giving powers. To overlook this is to minimize the variety of tonal technique in Wagner.

VI

In the following, I discuss three complete Wagnerian formal units of increasing length, by means of which I hope to demonstrate the interaction of the several points sketched above, with an emphasis on two points concerning tonality. First, even in those sections where the traditional chord connections of functional tonality are much clouded, a continuous relationship to a single central tonic is often maintained by linear means. And second, the contrast between stable and unstable tonality is a stronger tonal shaping force in some units than any sense of pull against and return to a single central key.

Die Walküre II, 1: Fricka's Lament

As a first, relatively simple example, I have chosen Fricka's Lament from *Walküre* II, 1 (S 92/2–95/4, Eu 298–313; "*O, was klag' ich um Ehe und Eid*"), principally because it has been discussed, or at least touched on, by two of the best of the modern Wagnerian analysts (DAHLHAUS 1971/79, 124–25, KUNZE 1970, 127–28). A strong reaction against the methods of Lorenz has led many recent German analysts to underplay and even ignore the overall tonal build of a Wagnerian unit. Both Kunze and Dahlhaus do so in this case, and as a result they miss some aspects of the unit's shape and expressivity.

Dahlhaus's is the more general treatment. He approaches the entire Lament as an aria-like musico-dramatic unit, and sees its form in terms of musical rhetoric—as two rhetorically parallel initial sections, followed by an antithesis and a peroration. The adoption of rhetorical concepts to interpret the musical shapes here is certainly illuminating. Fricka's conclusion ("*So fuhr es denn aus . . .*") is very like a concentrated peroration. And there is indeed an internal contrast, although the way it is introduced seems too subtle to allow us to call it an antithesis, and Dahlhaus has misplaced its actual point of introduction—principally, I think, because he has failed to pay proper attention to the tonal structure of the unit. Finally, the parallelism of members functions less powerfully between the first two sections, as Dahlhaus would have it, than within the third.

As I hear this unit, it proceeds as follows. The first section (through "*höhnend krankest mein Herz*") is fairly traditional in harmonic and metrical terms. Ending on the dominant, it suggests itself as the first member of a parallel antecedent-consequent pair, a suggestion which is reinforced when the second section (from "*Trauernden Sinnes*") begins like the first. Within this second section, however, we hear a small but typical example of those shifts of formal implication referred to above. The section begins like the first—and we are tempted, like Dahlhaus, to accept it as a parallel member to the first. As the section proceeds, however, it moves sharply away from the first course of action, and ends by establishing the principal contrast of the aria-like unit. This surprising shift in formal design is defined for our ears with typical Wagnerian thoroughness: the contrast, which arrives with Fricka's "*Denn dein Weib noch scheutest du so . . .*" (S 93/4, Eu 306/1), involves rhythm, instrumentation, style, and tonality. The traditional, easily audible tonal contrast between the tonic minor and its relative major is both the strongest and the most important for my point here. A coherent, clear and traditional modula-

tion tells us, when we arrive at the end of the second section ("*in Gehorsam der Herrin du gabst*"), that we have left the musical point of departure and reached somewhere new.

As is usual with Wagner, this musical contrast is reinforced by a dramatic one. Toward the end of the second section of the text, Fricka arrives at the one ray of consolation in her generally despairing assessment of Wotan's treatment of her. He had, she observes, at least cared enough for her prestige to make the Valkyries answerable to her. This wistful moment of recollection, this parenthetical aside in her tirade is made the dramatic justification for the needed musical contrast.[26]

With the third section of text, the dramatic situation reverses itself. As Fricka's mind snaps back to Wotan's present attitude, ("*Doch jetzt . . .*"), she moves back toward the angry, accusing tone of the opening of the aria. Thus while this reversal is sharp enough to be called an antithesis, it is not an antithesis to the opening section (or pair of sections), as Dahlhaus says. Musical and dramatic elements together tell us rather that it is an antithesis to the internal contrast—in dramatic terms the beginning of a move back to the original mood, in musical terms the beginning of a retransition.

Like the second section, this retransition section is characterized and shaped musically in various ways: by instrumentation, rhythmic figuration, melodic peaks, and tonality. Of these, tonality is to my ears again the most decisive, even though tonality, at the beginning of the section at least, is conveyed primarily by linear means. The two three-measure phrases at the beginning of the section (augmented triads in half-step ascending sequence) are functionally anomalous. Nonetheless, the linear progression in the bass, from the third degree through the sharped third degree to the arrival of the subdominant and finally the dominant functions, is such a strong and traditional bass-voice movement in tonal music that any temporary lack of clarity in local harmonic vocabulary is overcome by the clarity of the linear design. To present the section as a text-determined, non-functional sequential chain, or *Kettenstruktur*, as in KUNZE 1970, 127–28, under-

179

---

[26]If we were to listen carefully back over the first section, we might notice that Wagner, with typical care in preparing contrasts and smoothing transitions, had at the end of the first section prepared the ground musically for the contrast at the end of the second—tonally by the prolongation of the dominant of the relative major for five measures as an internal harmony in the first section (from "*lugte lüstern dein Blick*") before the arrival at its cadential dominant, and instrumentally by the simultaneous lightening of the wind band and introduction of a melody-carrying (as opposed to a figuration-carrying) group of strings. This subtle preparation of the musical contrast seems to have been a purely musical decision; one can find little justification in the text.

estimates the tonally binding force of the guiding bass line.

Kunze's interest in emphasizing the non-traditional elements here leads him also to stress in this section an aperiodic, text-determined rhythmic build far removed from the Viennese classical style. I should like to take the opposite tack, and suggest that much of the dramatic and musical effectiveness of the section comes from the way that it plays with the expectations of classical periodicity. This play is partially suggested by the parallel members of this section of text. As a projection of Fricka's path toward the heightened despair of the concluding section, Wagner built rhetorical parallelisms into the text ("*Doch jetzt . . . ; jetzt . . . ; jetzt . . . !*"). But when he came to set the text to music, he felt the need for an even more precisely crafted design of parallel members. He had failed to build into Fricka's speech here the device he would later use in Erda's climactic speech in *Siegfried* III, 1: a kind of periodic rhetorical crescendo, an expansion of the successive parallel units to convey swelling anger. Since the musician wanted such expanding units for his periodic design, he had either to rewrite the text or ignore its design on the detailed level. He chose the second course. He first separated the initial member of the text ("*Doch jetzt, da dir neue / Namen gefielen, / als 'Wälse' wölfisch / im Walde du schweifest*") into two distinct and parallel musical units (the sequencing augmented triads), a separation nowhere implied in the text. Then the second member of the text ("*jetzt, da zu niedrigster / Schmach du dich neigtest, / gemeiner Menschen / ein Paar zu erzeugen*"), now set as a whole, could appear longer and weightier than the first. Finally, he expanded the declamatory values of the shortest, last member of the text ("*jetzt dem Wurfe der Wölfin / wirfst du zu Füssen dein Weib!*") and appended to it an upward-surging instrumental extension of the dominant chord before the return. All this gave the retransition section as a whole progressively longer phrases of 3 + 2 + 4 + 6 measures—a use of periodicity that would not surprise us in a retransition by Haydn or Beethoven.

This overall periodic design is defined primarily by harmonic rhythm, and this, too, Wagner manipulates in traditional fashion to produce an effect of mounting tension. After the two sequential three-measure phrases moving from B to C in the bass, the fourth degree (C♯) is prolonged in the four-measure phrase first as a IV$_4^6$ chord and then, after the middle of the phrase, as a Neapolitan $\frac{4}{2}$ chord in alternation every halfnote with a V$_5^6$.[27] This pattern of alterna-

tion is then expanded in the final six-measure phrase (whose musical-metaphorical point is expansion, swelling) to a single, large instance of the progression N$_2^4$–V^7.

Tristan und Isolde II, 2: Love Duet

Fricka's short Lament is a closed, continuously tonal formal unit in four sections, moving from the minor tonic to the relative major and back. For only a brief moment near the beginning of the third section does it step outside the restrictions of traditional functional chord connections, and even there the linear control from the bass voice is simple and direct.

The central love duet from *Tristan* II, 2 (S 162/5–169/2, Eu 550/2–569) likewise maintains continuous reference to a single, central tonic, but here over a much larger span of time. The method again involves a strong controlling linear bass movement, which is a prolongation of a fundamental tonal degree or progression. Harmonic successions above these linear prolongations, often extremely difficult to explain by functional labels, give the desired impression of mysterious *Ausweichung*. But the tonality is not truly "wandering" (to follow Schoenberg and DAHLHAUS 1974/80) or "centrifugal" (to follow Kurth and DAHLHAUS 1965). The whole passage is quietly—it was perhaps even intended to be imperceptibly—controlled from below.[28]

In analysing this unit, I should like to make two points. 1) The unit is felt as formally distinct and closed; and, in spite of the non-traditional chord connections, this feeling is communicated primarily by tonality, through the linear direction of the bass line. 2) Important motivic evolutions within the unit are related to each other and given precision by what I have called a pitch reinterpretation (see p. 53), which also helps to locate a new wide range of harmonies in a single central tonality.

Each strophe of the piece sweeps from tonic to dominant to tonic. The prolongations between initial tonic and penultimate dominant are rich in contrast and quite complicated—especially those of the second strophe. The first strophe begins with a static tonic pedal (under the first two couplets of text). At "*Verloschen nun*" (S 164/2, Eu 554) there begins the first of the stepwise bass prolongations that control the motion from initial tonic to cadential dominant in each strophe. This first prolongation is clear in direction, moving from A♭ down an eleventh to low E♭ (at "*all Gemahnen*"). The E♭ introduces a deceptive cadence before a second tonic, then a second dominant pedal.

---

[27]This N$_2^4$ chord gives the occasion for the return, in midphrase and before the tonal return, of the motive of Fricka's anger, which had dominated the first section of the unit—a detail that serves as an example of the lack of synchronization of form-defining elements by which Wagner is wont to blur the edges of his forms and keep them unstably moving forward.

[28]I can think of no sizeable passage in Wagner where the primacy of the bass voice is challenged (cf. CONE 1960, 43), as it is in Debussy and sometimes even in Berlioz. What one does hear in a passage such as this one from *Tristan* II, 2 is what Cone elsewhere has called a state of tension between sound and syntax (CONE 1974, 21–24).

180

Over the second tonic pedal ("*Heil'ger Dämm'rung*") the upper voices (both vocal and orchestral) stress the pitches subject to reinterpretation in the unit, F and F♭ in relation to E♭. F–E♭ had echoed languorously near the start of the duet (S 163/4–164/1, Eu 552). Now the voices reach above the fifth degree, first repeatedly to the flatted sixth degree (F♭), then to the natural sixth (F) for a climactic dominant ninth chord over the second dominant pedal. With this sonority the strophe begins and ends.

An authentic cadence on the tonic is a primary element in marking the beginning of the second strophe ("*Barg im Busen uns sich der Sonne*"—S 166/1, Eu 559/1). The vocal line here is a varied, more active version of the rising vocal line of the beginning of the first strophe.[29] Harmonically the second strophe at once moves faster and farther, and its bass-voice prolongation of the progression I–V is considerably more complicated; in this strophe we hear a bold version of Wagner's definition of tonality through linear means. While the F♭⁶ chord that began the prolongation in the first strophe came after sixteen measures of tonic pedal, it arrives here after three measures (now respelled enharmonically as E⁶) and sets off the complicated reinterpretation and prolongation outlined in diagrammatic fashion below:

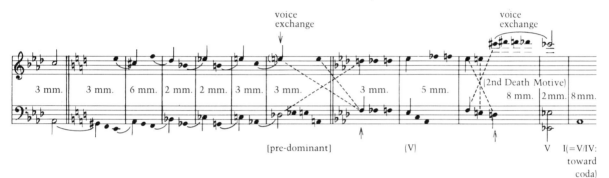

Example 1: *Tristan* II, 2, S 166ff., Eu 559ff.
Graphic Representation of the Guiding Linear Prolongations

The upward chromatic sequence moves fairly regularly in the bass from the first to the fourth degrees. But this arrival is not accompanied by the expected F in the top voice (at the point marked by the upper arrow in ex. 1). As a way of calling attention to the attainment of the natural sixth degree, so crucial in terms of tonality and expressivity, the vocal parts continue to bump against a ceiling of E (F♭) until a voice exchange occurs with the bass (at the change of signature to four flats. Note that the bass voice foreshadows the voice exchange by repeatedly moving from D♭ to E (F♭) in the measures immediately preceding.) The structuring bass voice now takes over the F and approaches the dominant from above, through the motivic natural and flatted sixth degrees, before sinking in a very gentle and lightly orchestrated deceptive cadence through the third degree to the first degree.

From this deceptive cadence begins a much expanded and more heavily orchestrated repetition of the pre-cadential approach to the dominant in the bass. The first move is from F to E♮—only half the motivic area F–E–E♭. At this halfway point, another voice exchange occurs (see the second arrow under ex. 1). The bass voice finally reaches the D that it was approaching when the previous voice exchange occurred. The upper voice, using the opening melody of this second strophe, takes over the E of

the bass and pushes it up to an F♯ in extreme register.

With this second voice exchange, Wagner adds a climactic element to his motivic descent from the natural sixth degree through the flatted sixth to the fifth degree. Over the (slightly elaborated) bass movement from fourth degree to fifth degree, he introduces the impressive second Death motive, first stated just before the beginning of the central duet (S 161/5, Eu 545). The high woodwinds bring out a chromatic voice that caps the descending motive with one higher pitch: f♯'''–f'''–e'''–e♭''' (at "*Liebe heiligstes Leben*"). Thus the f–f♭–e♭ movement is repeatedly returned to and reinterpreted within the texture—first as a chromatic inner-voice detail, then as a climactic upper-voice detail in the first strophe, then in the second strophe as a striking detail in the controlling bass voice, brought to the fore through a voice exchange before

---

[29]The variant, typically, is prepared in the midst of the previous strophe by the oboe at the arrival of the first low dominant in the bass—an example of the use of the motivic techniques of developing variation to smooth motivic joints.

being finally expanded by one more chromatic pitch in the upper voice of the short coda, prior to Brangaene's warning. The statements of this melodic motive are always explicitly connected to each other by functional tonality; they are all chromatic approaches to the cadential dominant, which is defined by the clear linear design of the controlling bass voice. Pitch reinterpretation and linear design thus work together to clarify tonal shape in a unit where the chordal connections are extraordinarily wide-ranging.

Siegfried III, 1: WOTAN AND ERDA

The libretto of *Siegfried* III, 1 went through several stages on the way to the final version set in 1869, stages thoroughly documented in STROBEL 1930. The surgery that took place in those stages left some wounds that healed imperfectly, particularly as concerns Wotan's motivation at a couple of moments. But the broad structure and idea of the scene remained as it was initially conceived—a typical structure for a dialogue scene in Wagnerian music drama. First, there is an opening definition of position on the part of both characters—in this case Wotan, vigorous, active, and wanting information; and Erda, sleepy, passive, and not inclined to tell. There follows a quickening dialogue in which positions are modified. Here Wotan loses some of his clarity of direction and Erda approaches Wotan's level of activity; both get angry and enter into quick interaction. Finally comes a re-solidification of position. In some dialogue scenes, this re-solidification brings ecstatic agreement, as in *Walküre* I, 3 or *Siegfried* III, 3; in others, it brings continuing modified opposition, as in the present scene, or *Walküre* II, 1 and III, 3.

Such a dramatic structure clearly suggests some kind of musical arch structure, and this is in fact what results here. But to label the scene musically as an arch is too simple. The architectural analogy of the arch suggests more symmetry than is appropriate for this strongly end-weighted scene, and the final accent of weight is produced here, as we shall see, by purely musical processes, for which the visual arts can provide no analogy.

There are in fact many kinds of formal process at work in *Siegfried* III, 1, none of them complete or unambiguous. In addition to the suggestion of arch form, there are aspects of ABA form, and aspects of variation and refrain procedures. As in classic ABA form, the flanking sections of the scene are clearly analogous, the moment of reprise is clearly defined, and there is a central section that contrasts in some clear way with the other sections. But we move into the central section gradually, without the sharp definition of the central contrast normal in an ABA form. In fact, the clearly stated elements of contrast in the scene proceed more by musical alternation of Wotan material and Erda material, recalling a kind of alternating variation procedure. And even this alternation is modified by the dramatic and musical

dominance of Wotan; one has the sense of a refrain form organized around Wotan's initial material. The scene as a whole is a fine example of the musically hybrid character of Wagner's musico-dramatic forms—in this case part arch form (from the overall structure of the dialogue), part alternating variation form using two themes (from the alternation of strongly contrasted Wotan and Erda material), part refrain form, (from the strength of Wotan's recurring material), and part end-accented apotheosis (from the final transformation of Wotan's refrain).

Let us proceed through the scene. The Act III prelude functions as a true introduction, dramatically and musically. It has a clear relation to the scene yet stands outside it formally, performing the function Wagner called "*Ahnung*" in *Oper und Drama* (GS IV, 186–90, 221). Dramatically it prepares us for the principal characters or moods of the ensuing scene; musically it foreshadows some of its principal motivic ingredients.[30] The initial picture is of Wotan, riding vigorously across the heavens, but consumed by the sense of anxiety that had descended on him in the first two scenes of *Walküre* II. The structuring of the first two phrases around the motive of the Need of the Gods, first generated in *Walküre* II, 2, reminds us directly of this crucial dramatic precedent for the present scene. Then, in music of a strongly projected periodicity, we are presented with the more forceful, self-confident Wotan who will dominate *Siegfried* III, 1. The broad two-measure units of pulse suggest the giant steps of the superhuman god, and the contrary motion between the Treaty motive at the bottom of the texture and the upward-moving chromatic line at the top suggests Wotan's almost explosive energy in the ensuing scene. The contrapuntal density and energy of this texture, unprecedented in the *Ring*, projects musically a Wotan quite different from the one whom Wagner had ride away from Fafner and Alberich in 1857.

These opening measures of the prelude (mm. 1–22) have other purposes, more accessible to musical than hermeneutical explication. They set up an expectation of metrical regularity on the two-measure level, which will be contradicted later in the prelude to make an important musical point. They give the listener a strongly centered assertion first of G minor and then of its dominant, in har-

---

[30]It does not erect new thematic pillars which, recurring only after large musical and dramatic spaces, will define large arches. In this respect the prelude to *Siegfried* III is like that to *Walküre* I rather than that to *Tristan* II, for example, which first states the Day motive, which recurs as the principal motive of the center of the second scene of the act, and then states the upward welling motive of Isolde's expectant waiting, which recurs at the end of the first scene of the act as a means both of rounding it off and moving into the second scene.

182

monies whose clear functional tonality will be a fundamental part of the scene to come.

In mm. 23 ff. Wagner calls upon previously existing material both to set the dramatic scene and to establish musical patterns. The most crucial dramatic references are to Erda's prophecy from the end of *Rheingold* (esp. S 194/1–2, Eu 632), and to the Twilight of the Gods motive that had accompanied it there. This rising and falling motivic complex is laid over the four-chord series of harmonies called the Wanderer Chords, which accompanied Wotan's first appearance in his guise of Wanderer in *Siegfried* I, 2. This harmonic series, by now well known to us, unrolls in a leisurely, almost regal metrical unit of six measures, the whole isolated and confirmed by sequential repetition (mm. 23–28, 29–34). The regular periodicity of the units is clear, although the harmonies do not function in a traditional sense. Then the harmonic pattern is repeated, but, in order to raise the sense of urgency and motion, the period is tightened to four measures. The basic metrical pulse of two measures is still unchallenged. Next comes the surprise, a bit of material that breaks sharply from the harmonic and metrical patterns so strongly established in mm. 23–38. Two three-measure groups propose the harmonic change A♭⁶–A and repeat it, the alternation of the two chords decked out in the striking colors of alternating brass choirs. This half-step shift (it is between the flatted second and the second degrees, although one may not realize that here) will become the principal tonal preoccupation of Wotan's refrain and of the ensuing scene.

Having not very subtly called our attention to this striking harmonic gesture, Wagner proceeds rapidly through a varied set of Wanderer Chords to a climax on what here sounds like the motive of Alberich's Servitude from *Rheingold* 3. The first chord of this motive (m. 51) will later appear in a new functional guise as the pivotal chord in the unstable portion of Wotan's refrain (cf. m. 77). The prelude subsides rapidly from its climax, turning Wotan's expanding gestures into Erda's tired, downward sliding chromatics in a lightening-quick transition of some four measures, during which the curtain rises. The end of the prelude foreshadows Erda's two motives in the scene, both of which have of course been heard previously: the Magic Sleep chords from *Walküre* III, 3 and the Fate Question from *Walküre* II, 4 (mm. 60–63, 64–65).

At this point the prelude has fulfilled its task. The two sharply contrasting characters whose alternation will in some sense structure the scene have been exposed, and some aspects at least of the thematic material and the tonal preoccupations of the scene have been foreshadowed. Wotan strides onto the stage. After two quick alternations between his striding Treaty motive and Erda's rhythmically inactive Fate Question, we move back toward the clear metrical and tonal structures of the opening of the prelude. With this we are thrown headlong into Wotan's exposition of the form-defining thematic material of the scene.

That the scene itself is articulated principally by motive and by tonality should come as no surprise in the music of one who studied the music of the Viennese classicists with as much passion and admiration as did Wagner. Still, as I have said, both motive and tonality are used differently by Wagner than by his mentors. Particularly important is the distinction between structural and referential use of motives, discussed above. The principal structural motive of the scene is Wotan's initial phrase, which, in varying degrees of completeness, serves as a refrain (mm. 74–89: S 242/2–243/2, Eu 784–90, esp. mm. 76–77: "*Wala, erwach'!*"). Erda's Sleep chords and Fate Question are also used for secondary structural articulation, but without much variation—as a static, retarding type of structural punctuation. The numerous other motives are mainly illustrative, referring to complexes of meaning outside of the scene—e.g., the Wanderer Chords have referential, not structural function here; the same is true of the Ring motive.

As I have said, Wagner does not always use traditional functional chord connections, relating each tonal contrast by its function to a central tonic. Although naturally there are some traditional passages in the present scene, the principal tonal contrast here, the contrast between Wotan and Erda, is of another kind. It is the contrast between functionally centered, stable tonality on the one hand, and nonfunctional, unstable tonality on the other. Wotan speaks the first language; it contributes much to his forceful, clearly directed musico-dramatic personality. Erda speaks the second, and derives from it something of her inactive, undirected personality. The tonal contrast shaping the altercation between these antagonists is not the contrast between any specific two (or three) keys; it is between Erda's tonal style, wherever it may occur, and Wotan's. In the central, dialogue portion of the scene these two tonal styles are brought together in conflict. Erda, pulling herself together around a couple of stable keys (mostly referential) or highly directed tonal procedures, assumes something of Wotan's tonal clarity. And Wotan sometimes loses his clarity of direction. Especially at the end of the central portion, at the height of their argument, both Wotan and Erda speak in a tonally unstable though highly active language. Wotan regains his feet, so to speak, when he makes his decision after "*Weisst du, was Wotan—will?*" (S 256/2, Eu 845).

That the return here is to the tonic key is of secondary importance in our perception of tonal shape. The return to the original tonal style, reinforced thematically by a return to the original refrain, and introduced by a broadly paced functional tonal cadence (S 256/2–3, Eu 845–46), tells us that we have arrived back home. The articulating forces of thematic material, cadential preparation, and contrast of stable and unstable tonal styles make clear to us a tonal shape that we might not have been able to follow without them.[31]

The tonal shape of *Siegfried* III, 1, in purely structural terms is, as I have said, roughly an arch. This arch can also serve as a dramatic metaphor, and is almost inevitably heard so. A clearly audible contrast between two distinct ways of moving tonally is set up at the outset of the scene. The central dialogue portion of the scene brings the two styles closer together in greater tension, as the antagonists draw dramatically closer in active discourse. The conflict is resolved in favor of the original tonal style (Wotan's) not by a long, organized retransition, but by a single dramatic stroke, when Wotan pulls himself together after his *"Weisst du, was Wotan— will?"* during the *"langes Schweigen"* (I have heard no conductor or singer take this direction as seriously as the musico-dramatic moment warrants). The important point in feeling the full musico-dramatic effect of this moment in the overall shape is that Wotan's return is from miles away—the centrifugal forces had nearly won, and they were overcome by a single great flexing of his will. Wagner projects this feeling of sudden return from afar in every way possible—by dynamics, rhythm, instrumentation, and register, as well as by harmonic vocabulary. With all this, a perception of what key we have been in counts for little.

Although the principal tonal contrast of *Siegfried* III, 1, is not strictly speaking a functional one—that is, between a tonic key area and another well-defined key area or areas serving as prolongation of a non-tonic function within the tonic key—still, functional tonal progressions carry a great structural and dramatic weight on another level. For they control Wotan's statements in the initial section of the scene. They define functional tonal tensions there that are used to make convincing the apotheosis of Wotan's decision in the final section.

Within Wotan's tonally clear statements at the beginning and end of the scene, the half-step tension between the flatted and the natural forms of the second and sixth degrees (A♭ and A, E♭ and E), first presented in the striking three-measure phrases of the prelude, is developed systematically to a climax and resolution. We must trace this rather complicated development through several steps: first within the initial exposition of the refrain itself (the beginning of Wotan's first speech), then in the continuation of Wotan's first speech and in his second speech, then rather more subtly in the central section of the scene, finally most clearly and dramatically in the final section.

1. Wotan's refrain, the principal structural thematic material of the scene, is exposed in a classically clear antecedent-consequent period of 8 + 8 measures at the outset of the scene (mm. 74–89; all references to measure numbers are counted from the beginning of Act III). Not only the metric but also the harmonic (and motivic) design of the period is in its outline traditional: both the first phrase (which ends on V) and the second (which ends on I) begin with the same motivic material, moving from I to a chord subdominant in function, here ♭II⁶₅. This seemingly innocent Neapolitan seventh chord immediately introduces a form of the half-step shift emphasized in the prelude; and instead of being allowed to slip past as a quick subdominant function, the Neapolitan chord is prolonged with its own dominant, an E♭ major ninth chord. This constitutes the kick-off point for a two-measure unit, *"Wala, erwach'!"*, the melodic and emotional climax of Wotan's refrain, that will be extracted from the complete period and used to represent it in the center of the scene.

From this dominant ninth (m. 76) forward—for four measures in the center of both antecedent and consequent phrases of the refrain—we are treated to a somewhat complicated chromatic prolongation of the dominant of A♭, which is never allowed to function as a dominant, but finally resolves (mm. 79–80) as an augmented sixth chord in G minor.[32] The prolongation is accomplished by chromatic voice-leading, in which the E♭ of the bass voice is first led up to E, then back down to E♭ and finally to D:

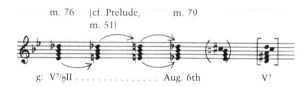

m. 76   (cf. Prelude,   m. 79
         m. 51)

g: V⁷/♭II . . . . Aug. 6th   V⁷

Example 2:
Siegfried, III, 1, mm. 76–79, S 242/3, Eu 784–86
Chromatic Prolongation of V/♭II in Wotan's Refrain

The half-step conflict around A♭–A and E♭–E, introduced in the prelude, is given a new harmonic guise here. Although the clear functional context is a prolongation of the Neapolitan and its dominant in G minor, the chromatic alteration chords within the prolongation do not, strictly speaking, behave functionally.

184

[31]Compare the lack of feeling of tonal return, even of false tonal recapitulation, produced by the relatively large block of G minor in the center of the dialogue section of the scene (S 250/4–251/4, Eu 825–28). The arrival at the tonic as a key alone has almost no articulative power.

[32]These four measures are an example of the tonally ambiguous harmonic structures that Kunze (1970) and Dahlhaus (especially 1974/80) stress in Wagner's harmonic language. Here, however, this language is clearly located tonally through a small example of what I have called pitch

2. After the exposition of the refrain, at Wotan's "*Erda! Erda!*" (S 243/2, Eu 790), Wagner defines a clear contrast, both of theme (the Erda motive) and of rhythm and emotion (smoother rhythms, more supplicating choice of words). Tonally he then immediately returns to the Ab–A, Eb–E conflict, now restating it in the harmonic form of the three-measure phrases on Ab–A from the prelude (in case we had missed this connection), then following these with a slight variation on Eb–E (mm. 107–110). By thus defining a central section with a clear contrast, Wagner sets up an expectation of an ABA form; but he chooses to leave this incomplete. He rounds off this first speech with a sharply incomplete reprise of the refrain (from S 244/1, m. 5, Eu 796, m. 2), leaping in at its third measure (the Eb⁹ chord), and proceeding only as far as a foreshortened version of the half cadence at the end of the first phrase.

In the midst of this cadence, the treaty motive sweeps the texture clean from top to bottom to prepare the musical contrast associated with Erda, which is reinforced visually as her eerily glowing torso rises on the stage. The decisive element of the tonal contrast here is the local impression of sinking. Erda's first speech begins with a clearly stated slump from the dominant D to C♯, but one cannot say that her speech is in C♯. It is in no key. These defining tonal elements of sinking and tonal lack of focus are confirmed at the beginning of Erda's second speech (S 247/4, Eu 813–14), where Wagner repeats and extends the gesture. An astonishing whole tone series descends to a C-major chord, which is certainly not functional—not C as subdominant of G, but C reached by the same path as at the beginning of Erda's previous speech, only proceeding one half step further.

But my point here is not the nature and presentation of Erda's tonal contrast, but rather the working out of the Ab–A and Eb–E tonal conflict within Wotan's functional language. This language returns after Erda's short parentheses, in a second speech for Wotan, which in many ways explicitly parallels his first. Yet Wagner again uses formal incompletion in

order to create ever greater formal openness as he moves toward the fluid center of the scene. He omits any initial statement of the refrain, instead moving directly to what had been the contrasting central section of the previous speech, stating the Ab–A and Eb–E progressions immediately in direct juxtaposition and in shortened two-measure phrases. Although the music of this previously central section is now considerably expanded, with the development of a number of referential motives (Wanderer Chords, Nature Figure), the tonal language remains clearly focused far into the speech. We hear another Eb–E progression in the clear context of G, now decorated by the Nature Figure (S 246/2–3, Eu 807–8), before this speech, like the first, again closes with the incomplete refrain.

3. At this point we move into what I have called the central dialogue area of the scene as a whole (S 247/4–256/2, Eu 814–45).[33] Across this central section, the overall control of a single tonality becomes much less clear. Successions of chords and keys do not always present themselves in a clear functional context, even in Wotan's speeches. There continue to be references to the Eb–E conflict, references which we certainly hear as examples of the familiar half-step shifts within Wotan's refrain. We may not be able to locate these half steps functionally as before, but it is not crucial that we do so. The half-step shifts connect with the tonal motives proposed by the prelude and by Wotan's refrain. The contrast between stable and unstable tonality provides the clear overall sense of tonal departure and return.

Let us trace the references to the half-step shift. Erda's first moment of tonal coherence is in E major, as she talks of the Norns (S 248/1–3, Eu 814–15); her second is in Eb, as she talks of Brunnhilde (249/4–250/1, Eu 821–22). Wotan's articulating refrain motive is here stated for the first time over E instead of Eb (S 249/2, Eu 819, the end of his third speech). Then the pitch level clearly sinks a half step as the refrain motive is transformed into the Ring motive. Similar clearly stated local half-step relations continue across the center of the scene, reaching a climax in the quick exchange of accusations at the end of the central section ("*Du bist nicht, was du dich . . .*"). At Wotan's "*Du bist nicht, was du dich wähnst*" (S 255/4, Eu 843), his refrain motive appears again over E, and leads rapidly to a cadence in Eb, which swirls immediately up to a big dominant-like articulation on E (this last half-step shift uses the

reinterpretation. The four-measure passage, introduced as a dominant of the Neapolitan, remains focused around the conflict between Eb and E, and closes with the reinterpretation of the dominant of the Neapolitan as an augmented sixth chord. This kind of local tonal parenthesis in the functional cadence, created by a momentary prolongation and reinterpretation of an unstable scale degree, was by no means uncommon in the Viennese style at the end of the 18th century (cf. Mozart, Quintet in C, K. 515, first movement, mm. 48–54). In the center of *Siegfried* III, 1, the four measures (or sometimes only part of the four measures), now extracted from their original tonal surroundings, lose their functional position and become more like the nonfunctional structures that Kunze and Dahlhaus describe, blending freely into the constant harmonic flux that characterizes Wagner's unstable style.

[33]To pick a single point of demarcation in a transition as fluid as this is inevitably to falsify it somewhat. Again, shifting formal implications contribute to this fluidity. Erda's second speech begins as if it were going to be the second statement of the second theme in a double variation procedure. Only as the speech continues do we realize that we are being led further and further into new material, and that we are on our way to a distinct central section.

harmonic motive of Alberich's motive of Servitude from the climax of the prelude). The E-major dominant is followed at the moment of Wotan's decision by C minor, with its prominent Eb. Now the decision is made, and the C-minor chord sweeps home to a functional cadence in G minor. The nonfunctional half-step vacillations of the center of the scene are over; a stable tonal center has been re-established.

4. The return of Wotan's firmly functional language reminds us once more (if we have lost track) where the half step vacillations are actually located. After the constant rubbing between A and Ab in the grand cadence of *"Dir unweisen / ruf' ich's ins Ohr, / dass sorglos ewig du nun schläf'st"* (S 256/3, Eu 846), the original conflict of pitches is put forth again in simplest functional terms, in an expanded restatement of the opening refrain, each of whose chords is retained aperiodically under a declamatory vocal line. Counting from the cadence, mm. 1–3 are the first chord of the refrain, mm. 4–8 the second chord, m. 9 the third chord (too active to be stopped?), mm. 10–13 the fourth, and m. 14 the fifth—at which point the equivalence is broken. The prolongation of Eb does not resolve as an augmented

sixth, as it did in the original refrain. Instead the chord is allowed to function as it was approached—as a dominant of Ab. The emphasis on bII and bVI throughout the traditionally tonal sections of the scene is finally allowed to realize itself, and the local progressions by half step are given their grandest realization in the modulation to Ab at *"führe frei ich nun aus"* (S 257/3, Eu 850). The move upward by half step here achieves through careful and complex tonal preparation its intended effect of ecstatic elevation.

The tonal effect does not have to stand alone. It is reinforced by a motivic transformation as subtle as the resulting motive is grand. The World Inheritance motive is presented, when first introduced at this Ab cadence, as the expanded realization of a particular rhythmic-melodic characteristic of the Refrain motive (the third and fourth measures of Wotan's refrain, ex. 3a below)—a characteristic that had lain fallow until Wagner began to call our attention to it across the central section of the scene. In this central section a group of motives began to be insistently related by the association of a common feature of their beginnings: an emphatic, marcato, downbeat-afterbeat pattern with the afterbeat longer than the downbeat, set to a falling melodic gesture:

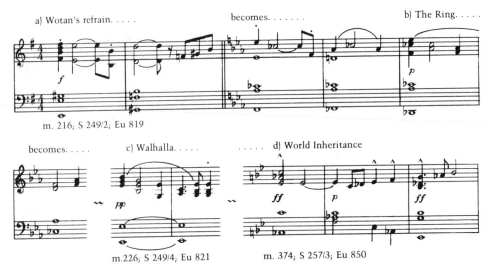

Example 3: *Siegfried* III, 1
Motivic Connections Leading to the World Inheritance Motive

Rapid switching from one to another of these motives, emphasizing similarities of rhythm and contour, is especially common in Wotan's and Erda's third speeches (S 248/3–250/1, Eu 815–22) and returns at the end of the central section (*"Du bist nicht, was du dich nenn'st ..."* S 255/3, Eu 841). There follows, as we have seen, a rhythmically expanded repetition of the original refrain at the beginning of the concluding section of the scene (S 256/3ff., Eu 846ff.). This repetition breaks its

chord-by-chord equivalence with the original refrain after the original refrain's fifth measure, and turns surprisingly back to the dominant function in the key of bII. Here (S 257/3, m. 1, Eu 849, m. 4) first the voice with its F'–Eb' then the cellos in the next measure on the same pitches emphasize the falling downbeat-afterbeat contour once more. Then this rhythmic-melodic idea is given its most expansive guise of all as the World Inheritance motive (S 257/3–4, Eu 850): the quarter-note pulse becomes a half-note pulse, the falling interval becomes a sixth (ex. 3d). Thus tonal and motivic tendencies come together at this point to project the feeling that the material of the scene is finally realizing its own destiny, just as Wotan is foreseeing the realization of Siegfried's destiny. The effect is both musically logical and splendidly dramatic.

The motives of example 3, with their stately, sarabande-like openings, are an expression in this scene of Wotan's proud self-confidence and his own self-realization through the love of Siegfried and Brünnhilde.[34] The last resonance of this family of motives, and of Wotan's mood of confidence and pride that accompanies it, is the motive called *Vaterfreude* by Wolzogen, which is connected with Wotan at the beginning of the following scene (S 265–67, Eu 883–90):

Example 4: *Siegfried* III, 2, S 267/2, Eu 890
The "*Vaterfreude*" Motive

---

[34]The connection of the refrain motive (Ex. 3a) with the Love motives of *Walküre* I is made explicit by Wagner in the coda to *Siegfried* III, 1 (S 259/2–3, Eu 859–60). STERNFELD 1913 offers an exegesis of the motivic ancestry of Wotan's refrain, but does not discuss its treatment in *Siegfried* III, 1 or its relation to the World Inheritance motive. COOKE 1979, 49–63, gives a long and perceptive analysis of the development of this Love motive, castigating WOLZOGEN 1876 and NEWMAN 1949 for their misunderstanding of it. Curiously enough, he fails even to mention the occurrence in *Siegfried* III, 1 (though it would have been grist for his mill), and hence does not see the family of motives that are grouped around Wotan's refrain in this scene.

The World Inheritance motive was conceived well before the composition of *Siegfried* III, 1, and apparently was not initially thought of for the *Ring*. (See BAILEY 1979, 333 and GLASENAPP, vol. II, part 2 [in some editions vol. III], p. 119. The transcription of the sketch fragment in WESTERNHAGEN 1976 is inaccurate.) This makes no difference to my point here, for, as I have said in section IV, 4 above, the local relations that Wagner wants us to hear between motives and that he draws forcibly to our attention in a particular scene are the relations important to the effect of the motive in that scene. Wagner brings together the downbeat-afterbeat, melodically falling motivic family, grouped around a single affect and a pair of musical characteristics, to fulfill a specific purpose in *Siegfried* III, 1–2. Then the family dissolves. When the same kind of rhythmic-melodic shape appears, for example, in the Gibichung motive of *Götterdämmerung* I, Wagner does not bring together the same motivic family. The rhythmic-melodic shape no longer has the same meaning; it is connected to different motives and to a different affect.

5. The grand large-scale modulation up by half step at the introduction of the World Inheritance motive leaves its mark on the rest of *Siegfried* III, 1, which never completely recovers its G-minor center. After the big cadence on A♭ comes one on E♭ (S 258/2, Eu 853). Only later do we get weaker, deceptive cadences to D (S 260/1, Eu 862) and G (S 260/3, Eu 866). With the visual and motivic rounding off of the scene, as Wotan's refrain motive (ex. 3a) disappears through the bottom of the texture and Erda's glowing torso sinks out of sight, we are swept into the beginning of scene 2—in A♭.

The entire final section of scene 1 is thus a large-scale example of Wagner's use of formal incompletion and shifting formal implications to keep the whole flowing forward. The section begins like a triumphant return home, implying a recapitulation of the initial material. But this recapitulation is never fulfilled, and the section is never properly closed, because the refrain never completes itself, and no strong, masculine cadence in G follows the one that begins the section. Tonally, then, the thematic and dramatic climax of the scene (the introduction of the World Inheritance motive) is part of a coda or transition to the following scene. The cadences on D and G near the end of the section, though they incorporate the New World Inheritance motive, are feminine, deceptive cadences built on the centrifugal end of the motive, rather than masculine authentic arrivals at the strong opening gesture of the motive as the A♭ cadence had been. They round off the scene tonally in one sense, but in another they do not, for they are unable to balance the weight of that vigorous arrival on A♭. The effect is of a tonal elision; the same section, the same set of harmonic moves, serves both to end G minor and to introduce A♭ major.

6. Before leaving *Siegfried* III, 1, I should like to look back briefly at the central section of the scene, in which I have said that the traditional connections of functional tonality are not continuously maintained. If neither the syntax of functional chord connections nor a strongly directed linear prolongation is present to guide us through the non-functional harmonies and far-flung tonal reminiscences of this section, what does give it shape and direction?

One answer lies in the returns to the E♭–E area of pitch reinterpretation sketched above. Another lies in a group of other musical factors, primarily metaphors for dramatic process. Prominent among these is the growth both of rhythmic activity and of metrical and harmonic coherence in Erda's speeches, as a projection of her rising anger and involvement. This impression of a directed dramatic process is reinforced by Wagner's musical control of elements in her dramatic delivery. Notice the tempo of her speeches: her first speech is marked *Bedeutend langsamer* (in relation to Wotan's *Lebhaft* and *Belebt*), her second *Langsamer*, her third *Mässig*; her fourth begins *Etwas zurückhal-*

187

tend and rises *allmählich belebend* to a climax of
rage; her last speech takes over Wotan's tempo
without alteration. Notice also the timing of her entrances: at first she is very slow to speak, leaving
long instrumental buffer-zones between her
speeches and Wotan's, but as the scene progresses
she loses her reticence, finally leaping right in on
Wotan's heels. Notice finally the rising tessitura of
her voice, most apparent in the free sequence of S
253/2–254/1, Eu 832/2–834, which translates into
musical procedure each step of the rhetoric of the
angry outburst in her fourth speech.[35] All this uses
musical technique to project dramatic process, at
the same time giving shape to the music by a simple
dramatic process: Erda is awakened, dragged up to
Wotan's level of activity, and finally goaded into
anger.

The process reaches its climax in the final measures of the central section (S 255/3, Eu 841, "*Du bist
nicht . . .*"). Erda takes up Wotan's tempo unaltered;
she follows him with scarcely an eighth-note interval, at the top of her range. And she contradicts him
directly, not only textually but melodically, trump-
ing his high E with her F. Not only the outlandish
intervals of her vocal line, but also the breathless,
stammering rhythms of her interjection "*störischer
Wilder,*" notated with Hugo Wolf-like exactness,
convey her outrage and excitement. Wotan then
gives her exactly the same treatment, but over-
trumps her F with his F♯, before pulling in the reins
rhythmically and melodically in order to announce
his decision.[36] To realize how Wagner the musician
uses control over tempo, timing, and pitch of delivery to project a dramatic development here is to understand more specifically what he had in mind in
his prose writings around 1870, when he stressed the
theatrical elements in opera, characterizing it as a
mimetic-musical improvisation.[37] I hope it is also to
understand more specifically what I meant in section II above, when I talked of the possibility of deriving a model for the shape of a section of music
from a familiar dramatic process or procedure.

188

---

[35]Here Wagner, when he set the text in 1869, rewrote the
rhetorical parallel members towards the end of Erda's
speech in order to get the larger final unit which reflects
Erda's swelling anger. (The speech remains as originally
written in WAGNER-GS VI, 155.) Compare the similar moment in the third section of Fricka's Lament, discussed
above, where he did not rewrite the text, but set it musically as if he had.

[36]The libretto of *Siegfried*, as printed in WAGNER-GS VI,
155, contains three further lines in Erda's last speech.
Wagner cut these when he set the poem in 1869, presumably to maintain the ever quicker alternations that characterize this central dialogue up to its interruption by Wotan's decision.

[37]See *Über die Bestimmung der Oper* (1871), WAGNER-GS
IX, 142–51, especially 148–50.

VII

The flanking sections of *Siegfried* III, 1, are
given overall shape principally by the chord
connections of functional tonality and by
motivic evolution; the central dialogue is given
overall shape principally by the projection,
through musical but not traditional functional-tonal means, of a dramatic process.
The alternation and interaction of the two
techniques is of basic importance in Wagner's
forms. Lorenz far overemphasized the former,
to the virtual exclusion of the latter. Modern
analysts such as Dahlhaus seem to take the opposite tack, failing to consider the linear prolongations and chord connections of functional
tonality as valid in Wagner over sizeable
stretches of music. Yet we misrepresent
Wagner if we fail to discuss him as a composer
in the tonal tradition, and we ignore his
greatest virtue if we fail to discuss his ability to
give powerful and coherent shape to vast
stretches of musical time. What the analyst
and critic of Wagner must now do is to strike a
balance between these two extremes. Against
the temptation to group motives and keys into
abstract formal and tonal patterns we must
place an insistence on how musical events actually happen in time—how one motive is
drawn out of or juxtaposed to another, how one
tonal area is connected to or contrasted with
another.

We must also admit that the essence of
Wagnerian form lies in its ambiguity and incompleteness. The character of his forms is
often falsified by the assertion that they *are*
this or that form, with sectional divisions occurring on this measure or that. In fact, the
forms are constantly becoming something else
as we move through them in time, and their
ends and beginnings are elided with great care.
It is to the appreciation and illumination of
this art of blurred edges, this characteristically
Wagnerian *Kunst des Übergangs*, that we
should dedicate ourselves. We only obscure
it—we blur it in an uncharacteristic, un-
Wagnerian way—by imposing upon it our convictions about clear edges
and formal closures.

ADLER 1904	Guido Adler, *Richard Wagner* [lectures delivered in Vienna, 1903–04], (Munich, 1923).
BAILEY 1969	Robert Bailey, *The Genesis of 'Tristan und Isolde' and a Study of Wagner's Sketches and Drafts for Act I* (Ph.D. diss., Princeton University, 1969).
BAILEY 1977	—, "The Structure of the *Ring* and its Evolution," *19th-Century Music* 1 (1977), 48–61.
BAILEY 1979	—, "The Method of Composition," in *The Wagner Companion,* ed. Peter Burbridge and Richard Sutton (New York, 1979), 269–338.
BORETZ 1972	Benjamin Boretz, "Meta-variations, Part IV: Analytic Fallout," *Perspectives of New Music* 11 (1972), 146–223.
BRINKMANN 1972	Reinhold Brinkmann, "'Drei der Fragen stell' ich mir frei': Zur Wanderer-Szene im 1. Akt von Wagners 'Siegfried'," in *Jahrbuch des Staatlichen Institute für Muskiforschung* 5 (Berlin, 1972), 120–62.
CONE 1960	Edward T. Cone, "Analysis Today," *Musical Quarterly* 46 (1960), 172–88; cited from reprint in *Problems of Modern Music,* ed. Paul H. Lang (New York, 1960), 34–51.
CONE 1961	—, "Music: A View from Delft," *Musical Quarterly* 47 (1961), 439–53.
CONE 1967	—, "Beyond Analysis," *Perspectives of New Music* 6 (1967), 33–51.
CONE 1974	—, "Sound and Syntax: An Introduction to Schoenberg's Harmony," *Perspectives of New Music* 13 (1974), 21–40.
CONE 1977	—, "Three Ways of Reading a Detective Story—or a Brahms Intermezzo," *Georgia Review* 31 (1977), 554–74.
COOKE 1979	Deryck Cooke, *I Saw the World End* (London, 1979).
DAHLHAUS 1965	Carl Dahlhaus, "Wagners Begriff der 'dichterisch-musikalischen Periode'," in *Beiträge zur Geschichte der Musikanschauung im 19. Jahrhundert,* ed. Walter Salmen, Studien zur Musikgeschichte des 19. Jahrhunderts, vol. 1 (Regensberg, 1965).
DAHLHAUS 1967	—, "Eduard Hanslick und der musikalische Formbegriff," *Die Musikforschung* 20 (1967), 145–53.
DAHLHAUS 1969	—, "Formprinzipien in Wagners 'Ring des Nibelungen'," in *Beiträge zur Geschichte der Oper,* ed. Heinz Becker, Studien zur Musikgeschichte des 19. Jahrhunderts, vol. 15 (Regensburg, 1969), 95–129.
DAHLHAUS 1970[a]	—, "Zur Geschichte der Leitmotivtechnik bei Wagner," in DAHLAHUS 1970[c], 17–40.
DAHLHAUS 1970[b]	—, "Soziologische Dechiffrierung von Musik: zu Theodor W. Adornos Wagnerkritik," *International Review of Music Aesthetics and Sociology* 1 (1970), 137–47.
DAHLHAUS 1970[c]	—, ed. *Das Drama Richard Wagners als Kunstwerk,* Studien zur Musikgeschichte des 19. Jahrhunderts, vol. 23 (Regensburg, 1970).
DAHLHAUS 1971	—, *Wagners Konzeption des musikalischen Dramas,* 100 Jahre Bayreuther Festspiele, vol. V (Regensburg, 1971).
DAHLHAUS 1971/79	—, *Richard Wagners Musikdramen* (Velber, 1971); citations from the English edition, *Richard Wagner's Music Dramas,* trans. Mary Whittall (Cambridge, 1979).
DAHLHAUS 1972	—, "Wagners dramatisch-musikalischer Formbegriff," *Analecta Musicologica* 11 (1972), 290–303.
DAHLHAUS 1973	—, "Grenzen der musikalischen Analyse" and "Ist die formale Analyse veraltet?," editorials in *Neue Zeitschrift für Musik* 134 (1973), 73 and 406.
DAHLHAUS 1974	—, "Wagners 'Kunst des Übergangs': Der Zweigesang in 'Tristan und Isolde'," in *Zur musikalischen Analyse,* ed. Gerhard Schuhmacher (Darmstadt, 1974), 475–486.
DAHLHAUS 1974/80	—, *Zwischen Romantik und Moderne* (Munich, 1974); *Between Romanticism and Modernism,* trans. Mary Whittall (Berkeley and Los Angeles, 1980).
DAHLHAUS 1975	—, "Some Models of Unity in Musical Form," *Journal of Music Theory* (1975), 2–31. Cf. DAHLHAUS 1977.
DAHLHAUS 1977	—, "Zur Theorie der musikalischen Form," *Archiv für Musikwissenschaft* 34 (1977), 20–37; a revised version of DAHLHAUS 1975.
DAHLHAUS 1978	—, "Satz und Periode," *Zeitschrift für Musiktheorie* 9 (1978), 16–26.
DANUSER 1975	Hermann Danuser, *Musikalische Prosa,* Studien zur Musikgeschichte des 19. Jahrhunderts, vol. 46 (Regensburg, 1975).
FLECHSIG 1970	Irmtraud Flechsig, "Beziehungen zwischen textlicher und musikalischer Struktur in Richard Wagners Tristan und Isolde," in DAHLHAUS 1970[c], 239–57.
GEORGE 1970	Graham George, *Tonality and Musical Structure* (New York, 1970).
GLASENAPP	Carl Friedrich Glasenapp, *Das Leben Richard Wagner's.* The edition available to me was the 3rd, in 3 vols. (Leipzig, 1894–99). In the 4th edition (1904–11), vol. II, 2 is called vol. III and vol. III becomes vol. IV. Vols. V and VI appear only as part of the 4th edition.
HALM 1916	August Halm, "Über Richard Wagners Musikdrama" in *Von Grenzen und Ländern der Musik* (Munich, 1916), 1–78.
HONOUR 1979	Hugh Honour, *Romanticism* (New York, 1979).
JOSEPHSON 1979	Nors Josephson, "Tonale Strukturen im musikdramatischen Schaffen Richard Wagners," *Die Musikforschung* 32 (1979), 141–49.
KUNZE 1970	Stefan Kunze, "Über Melodiebegriff und musikalischen Bau in Wagners Musikdrama dargestellt an Beispielen aus *Holländer* und *Ring,*" in DAHLHAUS 1970[c], 111–44.
KURTH 1923	Ernst Kurth, *Romantische Harmonik und ihre Krise in Wagners 'Tristan',* 3rd ed. (Berlin, 1923; rpt. Hildesheim, 1968).

189

LEVARIE 1979 Siegmund Levarie, "On Key Relations in Opera," *19th-Century Music* 3 (1979), 88–89.

LEWIN 1969 David Lewin, "Behind the Beyond," *Perspectives of New Music* 7 (1969), 59–72. A response to CONE 1967, with a brief answer from Cone.

LORENZ 1924 Alfred Lorenz, *Das Geheimnis der Form bei Richard Wagner*, vol. I: *Der Ring des Nibelungen* (Berlin, 1924; rpt. Tutzing, 1966).

MANN 1933 Thomas Mann, "Leiden und Grösse Richard Wagners," [radio address, April 1933]. Cited from Thomas Mann, *Wagner und unsere Zeit*, ed. Erika Mann (Frankfurt, 1963).

MARCO 1979 Guy A. Marco, "On Key Relations in Opera," *19th-Century Music* 3 (1979), 83–88.

MILLER 1968 J. Hillis Miller, *The Form of Victorian Fiction* (Notre Dame, 1968).

MITCHELL 1967 William J. Mitchell, "The Tristan Prelude: Techniques and Structure," *Music Forum* 1 (1967), 162–203.

NEWMAN 1949 Ernest Newman, *The Wagner Operas* (New York, 1949; rpt. 1963).

PETERSEN 1977 Peter Petersen, "Die dichterisch-musikalische Periode: Ein verkannter Begriff Richard Wagners," *Hamburger Jahrbuch für Musikwissenschaft* 2 (1977), 105–24.

POOS 1971 Heinrich Poos, "Zur Tristanharmonik," in *Festschrift Ernst Pepping*, ed. Heinrich Poos (Berlin, 1971), 269–97.

PORGES 1896 Heinrich Porges, *Die Bühnenproben zu den Festspielen des Jahres 1876* (Leipzig, 1896); also published serially in *Bayreuther Blätter* 3, 4, 7, 9, 13, 19 (1880–96).

ROSEN 1971 Charles Rosen, "Ornament and Structure in Beethoven," *Musical Times* 42 (1971), 1198–1201.

SERAUKY 1959 Walter Serauky, "Die Todesverkündigungsszene in Richard Wagners 'Walküre' als musikalisch-geistige Achse des Werkes," *Die Musikforschung* 12 (1959), 143–51.

STEPHAN 1970 Rudolph Stephan, "Gibt es ein Geheimnis der Form bei Richard Wagner?," a lecture of 1962 reprinted in DAHLHAUS 1970ᶜ.

STERNFELD 1913 Richard Sternfeld, "Wotans Lebenstrieb im musikalischen Symbol," *Richard Wagner Jahrbuch* 5 (1913), 233–48.

STROBEL 1930 Richard Wagner, *Skizzen und Entwürfe zur Ring-Dichtung*, ed. Otto Strobel (Munich, 1930).

SUPIČIČ 1970 Ivo Supičič, "Matter and Form in Music," *International Review of Music Aesthetics and Sociology* 1 (1970), 149–58.

VOSS 1977 Egon Voss, *Richard Wagner und die Instrumentalmusik*, Taschenbücher zur Musikwissenschaft, vol. 12 (Wilhelmshaven, 1977).

VOSS 1979 —, "Noch einmal: das Geheimnis der Form bei Richard Wagner" in *Theaterarbeit an Wagners 'Ring'*, ed. Dietrich Mack (Munich, 1979), 251–67.

WAGNER-
BRAUNE BUCH Richard Wagner, *Das Braune Buch: Tagebuchaufzeichnungen 1865 bis 1882*, ed. Joachim Bergfeld (Zurich, 1975); trans. George Bird (London, 1980).

WAGNER-GS Richard Wagner, *Gesammelte Schriften und Dichtungen*; all citations in this essay are to the second German edn. (Leipzig, 1883), or any subsequent one.

WAGNER-LISZT *Briefwechsel zwischen Wagner und Liszt*, 2 vols. (Leipzig, 1887).

WAGNER-UHLIG Richard Wagner, *Briefe an Theodor Uhlig, Wilhelm Fischer, Ferdinand Heine* (Leipzig, 1888).

WAGNER-
WESENDONCK *Richard Wagner an Mathilde Wesendonck* (Berlin, 1904).

WENK 1976 Arthur Wenk, ed., *Analyses of Nineteenth-Century Music: 1940–1975*, MLA Index and Bibliography Series, 15 (Ann Arbor, 1976).

WESTERNHAGEN
1973/1976 Curt von Westernhagen, *Die Entstehung des 'Ring'* (Zurich, 1973); *The Forging of the Ring*, trans. Arnold and Mary Whittal (Cambridge, 1976).

WOLZOGEN 1876 Hans von Wolzogen, *Thematischer Leitfaden durch die Musik zu Richard Wagner's Festspiel 'Der Ring des Nibelungen,'* 2nd rev. edn. (Leipzig, 1876).

190

Music in the theatre
(à propos of *Aida*, act III)

PIERLUIGI PETROBELLI

To Nicola LeFanu

In opera, various 'systems' work together, each according to its own nature
and laws, and the result of the combination is much greater than the sum of
the individual forces. In this essay I wish to discuss the interaction of the
three main systems – dramatic action, verbal organisation and music. The
dramatic action unfolds the events of the plot, the verbal organisation,
structured most of the time in lines and verses, offers support and definition
to the action, and the music interprets and transforms, in its own terms,
both action and text; I may add that by 'music' I do not only mean the
musical declamation of the text, but also the orchestral part(s) along with it.
Musical theatre involves the interaction of these three systems. But how
does the chemical compounding take place? And what is the nature of the
bonding?

Rather than expound abstract theories, I prefer to allow the basic principles to emerge from a specific example, and shall consider the first part of
the third act of *Aida*; only at the end of this essay I shall suggest some
conclusions – which I shall offer for discussion and development.

Let me start by summarising the situation at that point in the opera.[1] It is
night time on a bank of the Nile. Amneris, daughter of the Pharaoh, and the
high priest Ramfis enter on a barge. Amneris is betrothed to Radamès, a
young but already victorious Egyptian captain, and she has come to pray at
the temple on the eve of her wedding. Aida is an Ethiopian princess held in
slavery by the Egyptians; she is in love with Radamès and is afraid of being
abandoned by him. She dreams of Ethiopia, but fears that she will never see
it again. Her father King Amonasro is, in disguise, also a prisoner of the
Egyptians: he is planning revenge and wants Aida to obtain from Radamès
the secret of the Egyptian plan to attack Ethiopia. Aida is forced to yield by
the psychological violence inflicted on her by her father, who then hides
himself so that he may spy on the lovers.

This part of the plot is articulated in three distinct episodes: the entrance
of Amneris and Ramfis, Aida's monologue, and the exchange between Aida
and her father. These episodes, however, do not have equal importance.
Underlying the entire opera there are some basic conflicts: one between the

191

feelings and the aspirations of the individuals, and the interests of the state and religious establishment; the other within each of the two protagonists (Aida and Radamès) between their mutual love and the love for their own country. Because of these conflicts, not only are Aida and Radamès in the end crushed, but Amneris as well. These conflicts explain why, in the scenes we are analysing, Aida weeps over her country rather than her lover; and the reason why Amneris and Ramfis do not take part in the action here, but are absorbed in the Nile landscape until the end of the act: none of the conflicts concerns them at this point of the dramatic action. Aida is in a totally different situation; she is alone and motionless, but her inner conflict and especially her desperate longing for her homeland will set this part of the tragedy in motion.

All this is clearly discernible in the structure of the lines created by Ghislanzoni, the author of the libretto, under Verdi's watchful eye.[2] While the dialogue between Amneris and Ramfis is in plain, traditional recitative metre – eleven- and seven-syllable lines freely alternated – the episode in which Aida expresses the basic 'affect' of the situation consists of two quatrains of eleven-syllable lines alternately *piani* and *tronchi*[3] and with alternate rhymes:

192

> O cieli azzurri ... o dolci aure native
> Dove sereno il mio mattin brillò ...
> O verdi colli ... o profumate rive ...
> O patria mia, mai più ti rivedrò!
>
> O fresche valli ... o queto asil beato
> Che un dì promesso dall'amor mi fu ...
> Ahimè! d'amore il sogno è dileguato ...
> O patria mia, non ti vedrò mai più!   (lines 21–8)

The dialogue between Amonasro and Aida, on the other hand, is articulated in various sections; each of them is a well-calculated step forward in the crescendo of dramatic tension, and the verbal structure is clearly differentiated with respect to metre and rhyme; it can be summarised as follows:

a) Amonasro informs Aida that he knows all her feelings, and he lists them: love for Radamès, rivalry with Amneris, pride in her royal origin, longing to return to their country (lines 29–38).
Eleven- and seven-syllable lines are freely alternated in recitative style and concluded with a *rima baciata* (lines 37–8), the usual device in the libretto technique to indicate the closing of a section. After this recitative the duet proper begins.

b) Amonasro: 'Aida will be able to see her country again' (lines 39–46).
There are two quatrains of eleven-syllable lines with alternate rhymes

piane and *tronche*, each of them stemming from a couple of lines to Amonasro, immediately echoed by a couple to Aida:

Amonasro	Rivedrai le foreste imbalsamate . . .
	Le nostre valli . . . i nostri templi d'òr! . . .
Aida	Rivedrò le foreste imbalsamate . . .
	Le nostre valli . . . i nostri templi d'òr! . . .
Amonasro	Sposa felice a lui che amasti tanto,
	Tripudi immensi ivi potrai gioir . . .
Aida	Un giorno solo di sì dolce incanto . . .
	Un'ora di tal gaudio[4] . . . e poi morir!

c) 'The cruel Egyptians have invaded and soiled our beloved country' (lines 47–54).

Again, there are two quatrains of eleven-syllable lines, with the same structure as the two previous ones, a quatrain to Amonasro (47–50) and a quatrain to Aida (51–4), which echoes that of Amonasro:

Amonasro	Pur rammenti che a noi l'Egizio immite
	Le case, i templi e l'are profanò . . .
	Trasse in ceppi le vergini rapite . . .
	Madri . . . vecchi e fanciulli ei trucidò.
Aida	Ah! ben rammento quegli infausti giorni!
	Rammento i lutti che il mio cor soffrì . . .
	Deh! fate o Numi che per noi ritorni
	L'alba invocata dei sereni dì.

d) 'The time of revenge has come; everything is ready, but for the discovery of the military secret' (lines 55–8).

There is a quatrain of eleven-syllable lines to Amonasro, alternately *piani* and *tronchi*:

Amonasro	Non fia che tardi – In armi ora si desta
	Il popol nostro – tutto pronto è già . . .
	Vittoria avrem . . . Solo a saper mi resta
	Qual sentiero il nemico seguirà . . .

Sections b), c) and d) form a unity in themselves since they all stem from quatrains of eleven-syllable lines, each line being alternately *piano* and *tronco* with alternating rhymes. It is the very same structure of metre and rhyme scheme as Aida's monologue (lines 21–8). The 'affect' expressed there, the longing for her country, is structurally brought forward and the dramatic function is developed to a maximum.

e) Amonasro finally reveals his scheme: it is up to Aida to get from Radamès the military secret; Aida refuses violently (lines 59–62).

There are four eleven-syllable lines of recitative, *liberi*.

f) Amonasro: 'Let then the Egyptians come to destroy our country'; Aida is terrified (lines 63–72).

There are two quatrains of six-syllable lines (*intrecciate* thus: a *rima piana*

193

at the second and sixth lines, and a *rima tronca* at the fourth and eighth
lines), plus a couplet of six-syllable lines, the second rhyming with the
previous *rima tronca*:

Amonasro	Su, dunque! sorgete
	Egizie coorti!
	Col fuoco struggete
	Le nostre città …
	Spargete il terrore,
	Le stragi, le morti …
	Al vostro furore
	Più freno non v'ha.
Aida	Ah padre! …
Amonasro	Mia figlia
	Ti chiami! …
Aida	Pietà!

g) 'The Egyptians will raid Ethiopia' (lines 73–8).
A sestet of seven-syllable lines, alternately *sdruccioli* without rhyme and
piani with rhyme, is concluded by a *verso tronco*:

194

Amonasro	Flutti di sangue scorrono
	Sulle città dei vinti …
	Vedi? … dai negri vortici
	Si levano gli estinti …
	Ti additan essi e gridano:
	Per te la patria muor!

h) 'The ghost of Aida's mother will come to curse her' (lines 79–84).
Again a sestet of seven-syllable lines, but with the second and third lines
rhyming *a rima baciata* ('affaccia' / 'braccia') and the fourth and sixth
lines connected by assonance to the *rima tronca* of the previous sestet
('muòr' / 'levò' / 'Ah! nò'):

Aida	Pietà! …
Amonasro	Una larva orribile
	Fra l'ombre a noi s'affaccia …
	Trema! Le scarne braccia
	Sul capo tuo levò …
	Tua madre ell'è … ravvisala …
	Ti maledice …
Aida	Ah! no! …

i) 'You are just the Pharaohs' slave!' (lines 85–6).
Two *quinari doppi* without rhyme for the *parola scenica*:[5]

Aida	Padre …
Amonasro	Va indegna! non sei mia prole[6] …
	Dei Faraoni tu sei la schiava!

j) Aida is doomed; she will do what her father requests, in order to rescue
their country. Amonasro hides himself (lines 87–94).
Two quatrains of *quinari doppi*, with the rhyme scheme ABBC DCEC
(the rhyme C being a *rima tronca*):

Aida	Padre, a costoro schiava io non sono ...
	Non maledirmi ... non imprecarmi ...
	Tua figlia ancora potrai chiamarmi ...
	Della mia patria degna sarò!
Amonasro	Pensa che un popolo, vinto, straziato,
	Per te soltanto risorger può ...
Aida	O patria! o patria ... quanto mi costi!
Amonasro	Coraggio! ei giunge ... là tutto udrò ...

As a whole, then, the duet is articulated in three distinct parts, each of them
characterised by its metre and rhyme scheme, in turn determined by their
dramatic content and function. The two 'bridges' in recitative style between
the three parts do not function as links; they serve to emphasise the *parola
scenica* and isolate it from the symmetry of the musical discourse. In any
case, for dramatic purposes Verdi rejects in this duet the conventional
organisation in four parts which had been customary in Italian opera from
the time of Rossini: *allegro, cantabile, allegro* and *cabaletta*.[7] He does not
hesitate to return to it, for instance, when the drama requires it in the scene
immediately following, the Aida–Radamès duet.

The verbal structure, therefore, implies the musical structure in its points
of articulation. The position of the set pieces, and their internal organisation, are results of the overall conception of the musical drama; in giving
binding instructions to Ghislanzoni, Verdi refuses or accepts, according to
the needs of the drama, the conventions of nineteenth-century Italian
opera. The duet has the form of an arch, whose culminating point coincides
with the *parola scenica*: 'Dei Faraoni tu sei la schiava!'; but its articulation
can be understood only if considered in the economy of the entire act, and of
the opera as a whole. All this becomes even clearer if we compare the text of
the libretto with the *programme*, or scenario written by Mariette Bey, which
has only recently been published. The main difference between the two
texts lies in the dramatic coherence (and resulting tension) given by Verdi
to that succession of events, logically understandable but rather ineffective
and poorly organised from a dramatic point of view:

The set represents a garden of the palace. On the left the oblique façade of a
pavilion, or tent. At the back of the stage runs the Nile. On the horizon the
Libyan mountains, vividly illuminated by the sunset. Statues, palm trees,
tropical bushes. As the curtain rises, Aida is alone on stage. Radamès is in her
thoughts and heart more than ever. The trees, the sacred river which runs at
her feet, those distant hills – where the ancestors of her beloved rest – all this is
witness of her constancy and fidelity. She is waiting for him. May Isis,

195

protector of love, lead him to her, who wants to be only his. But it is not Radamès who comes, it is Amonasro. [Here follows a description of Amonasro's appearance.] He informs his daughter that Ethiopia has again lifted the flag of revolt, and that Radamès will again march against it. In a moving speech he reminds her of the land where she was born, of her desolated mother, of the sacred images of their ancestors' gods. But the love inspired by Aida in Radamès has not escaped his fatherly intuition (or premonition). She should take advantage of this love to seize from Radamès the secret plan for the Egyptian troops' march. Radamès will be taken during the battle, and led as a slave to Ethiopia, where eternal bonds will ensure forever their happiness. Won by her father's supplications, by the remembrance of her childhood, by the joy at the idea of being united to her beloved – away from a land where she has suffered all too long the tortures of slavery – Aida promises.[8]

If the dramatic structure and the verbal organisation already contain the essence of the episode, what then is the function of music? In my opinion, it is twofold: not only does it characterise in its own terms the elements of the dramatic discourse, but – and this is its crucial function – it determines its temporal dimension, its duration. These durations should not therefore be valued in abstract and absolute terms (indeed the same is true for the characterising musical elements); on the contrary, they should be related to the other durations which determine episodes, scenes, acts, the entire opera.

By shifting from the purple light of the sunset, as in the *programme*, to the dark night of the libretto, Verdi created the possibility of characterising the entire opening scene with the simplest of all 'musico-dramatic signs' – to use the terminology of Frits Noske[9] – a simple note, G.[10] This pitch repeated at different octaves by the violins, and around which unfolds also the 'exotic' melody entrusted to the flute, is further defined by the particular colour the composer gives it by using the overtones in the divided cellos; the sonority of G is – so to speak – 'wrapped' with these overtones, which give it an unmistakable character. This G is sustained in the orchestra throughout the chorus – off stage – of priests and priestesses, thirty-four bars altogether *Andante mosso*;[11] it is interrupted at the beginning of the dialogue between Amneris and Ramfis, and it starts again on the last sentence of the high priest, continuing further for fourteen bars, during which the material of the introductory chorus is repeated 'telescoped' both in its components and with the melody entrusted to the flute.[12] Through this dove-tailing of the sonority of G onto the recitative, and with the recapitulation of the opening material, the dramatic point is perfectly established, and Amneris and Ramfis are 'absorbed' into the night, cold and impassive as is the chanting of the priests. All this is realised dramatically by Verdi not with musical gestures, but with the very absence of them: the dramatic situation is defined by the static persistence of just one pitch.

Both the stage direction in the score and the *disposizione scenica* ask at this point for an 'empty stage for a few moments',[13] but Aida's arrival is announced by the motif which characterises her throughout the opera, and her few sentences of recitative lead directly into the two-verse *romanza*.[14] In contrast with Mariette Bey's *programme*, in which Aida, like a Metastasio heroine, calls on surrounding nature as witness of her fidelity to her beloved, the libretto emphasises just one 'affect', a desperate longing for her home country; and in the score all this is carried to the extreme. Verdi takes the last line of the first quatrain, 'Oh patria mia, mai più ti rivedrò', and transforms it into a true leitmotif of the *romanza*. The melodically passionate declamation of this line is preceded by an instrumental 'figure', entrusted to two oboes, two clarinets in C and a flute, modally articulated, which concludes first on F (four bars) and then on E (six bars).[15] This modal contour and this instrumental colour have an important structural function in the economy of the act; they return later, during the Aida–Radamès duet, when Aida mentions the 'novella patria' to her beloved, her own country where they will take refuge.[16] The *romanza* is articulated in two verses which are parallel also from a musical point of view; the second verse opens with the repetition of the *second* phrase (six bars long)[17] of the instrumental 'figure', and it is varied, in comparison with the first verse, only in the figurations of the accompaniment and in its scoring, and it is three bars shorter; a small coda, a sort of cadenza, repeats the Leitmotif – both instrumental 'figure' and melodic line[18] – thus sealing the dramatic function of the *romanza*: it is only because of this longing for her home country that Amonasro can bend Aida to his will. The musical articulation of all the 'signs' which characterise Aida's 'affect', especially their duration, is determined by their dramatic function. It was necessary first to state them, and then to prolong them for sixty bars *Andantino mosso*. Only by being given a pertinent temporal dimension can they acquire the necessary weight in the economy of the drama.

The duet between Aida and Amonasro opens with a quick recitative, given almost exclusively to 'that proud and cunning king', as Verdi puts it:[19] twenty-eight measures *Allegro vivo*, just to sketch the ancillary events, and then back *in medias res*.[20] The three stages through which Amonasro pushes his daughter into the trap prepared for her have in common the same metrical structure (eleven-syllable lines alternately *piani* and *tronchi*), as well as the same rhyme scheme. This tripartite articulation unified by common elements is perfectly matched at the musical level.[21] The musical metre is the same, 4/4, in the three sections, as is the key signature, five flats; but the relationship between these sections is a dynamic one, since the tension is gradually increased through the modification of common 'signs':

197

a) a semiquaver ostinato in the violas

moves to the cellos in the second section and becomes

and finally, in the third section, is entrusted to the first violins:

b) the melodic phrase given to Amonasro, at the beginning relaxed and *cantabile*,

198

becomes

where the rhythm remains the same, but the melodic shape becomes tense and moves to the relative minor; in the third section the vocal part becomes a sort of declamation, dissociated from the movement in the orchestra:

c) the first section is in D flat major, the second in the relative minor, B flat minor, moving to B flat major at the intervention of Aida; the third section again in B flat minor;

d) the crescendo concerns the agogic as well, from *Allegro giusto* (MM. 100 at the crotchet) in the first two sections to *Poco più animato* (MM. 116 at the crotchet) in the third section. Furthermore, the first section is seventeen bars long, the second twenty, the third only eight.

The musical crescendo is the direct result of the dramatic situation, the cruel trap into which Aida is led without her realising it. It is important also to notice that each of these sections, from the point of view of the harmonic rhythm,[22] is very static at the beginning, while their second part is richer in changes of harmony. In other words, Verdi first states and then develops the 'signs' of his dramatic language, and clearly distinguishes between static and dynamic durations.[23] The last section, as we have seen, is by far the shortest and it is dove-tailed with the recitative. Notice how the figuration

becomes

punctuating the crescendo of Amonasro's insinuating questions. The gradual thinning of the texture in the orchestra points in the same direction, as does the sequence of the cellos' motif:

199

Aida finally understands, refuses horrified, and Amonasro explodes.

The central part of the duet is subdivided, as is the first part, into three sections, both at the verbal and at the musical level. As in the first part, each section is linked to the following by common musical features.[24] The metre, 6/8, is the same, and the three sections are connected by a harmonic relationship, though by no means a 'classical' one: C minor, A flat major, E minor. Actually, these keys are neither established nor developed through cadential or even tonal movements; rather than keys, they are better regarded as tonal levels, and indeed one follows the other without clear-cut cadential caesurae, and they are more and more unstable as the dramatic tension grows. Each of these sections is subdivided, as are the previous sections of the duet, into two parts: one part, in which the main musical 'sign' is asserted,[25] is harmonically static; in the other the 'sign' is elaborated and developed in musical terms.

The *parola scenica* central to the duet, 'Non sei mia figlia! Dei Faraoni tu sei la schiava!', exploits the highest register of the baritone voice and, at the same time, almost completely dispenses with the orchestra. The contrast between elements of dynamics and of texture, on which the crescendo in dramatic tension is built up from the previous pages, reaches at this culminating point its extreme and most elementary form. The dramatic climax coincides with the barest use of language.

200

The third part of the duet, *Andante assai sostenuto* (MM. 76 at the crotchet), lasts thirty-one bars and is identified and unified, as are the previous parts, by common musical 'signs': first of all by the rhythmic pedal in the violins

which is extended through its entire duration, a musical transfiguration of Aida's inner sighing. This part is also in one key only, D flat major, the key of the opening section of the duet. Here also a first section, characterised by the repetition of the rhythmic pedal on the dominant – A flat – and corresponding to Aida's broken utterances *molto sotto voce e cupo*, [26] is followed by its dynamic counterpart, in which the syncopated pedal moves, always in the violins, upwards stepwise for the span of no less than two octaves, and where the harmonic rhythm undergoes different subtle fluctuations. Considering the first bar as introductory, the border-line between the two sections of this part of the duet is placed exactly half-way through, that is at the sixteenth bar, in correspondence with the beginning of the second quatrain of *quinari doppi* and, dramatically, with Amonasro's hypocritical 'consoling' intervention.

A more detailed and thorough analysis would certainly reveal other symmetries and relationships between the various components of the musico-dramatic language of this episode. On the basis of what has been said about this one example, I would like now to identify some of the general principles which govern the unfolding of the dramatic 'language' of opera. They can be summarised as follows:

1) The articulation of the musical language is already present in the organisation of the libretto. In other words, the verbal structure is determined by the musical structure, and is governed by dramatic principles. From this it follows that every analysis on the purely musical level of an opera score is bound to be incomplete and in the end to fail in its essential purpose; such an analysis grasps only one aspect of the musico-dramatic language, and constantly risks missing the essential point.

2) All the elements of the musical language can be used as 'signs'; they may be articulated as 'themes', and have a complex organisation defined by key, rhythm, melodic shape, harmony, timbre. They may, however, be just sonorities, or simple pitches used *per se*, without articulation, and yet be by no means less effective dramatically. Indeed, the simpler the musical 'sign', the more complex and articulated its dramatic function.

3) The articulation of these musical 'signs' is directly related to their duration, i.e. to their temporal dimension. A 'sign' which is not characterised by an appropriate duration, becomes unrecognisable, and ceases to be a 'sign'.

4) The articulation of a musical 'sign' can be static; the 'sign' is sustained, or repeated without modification throughout its duration. But it can also have a dynamic temporal dimension, during which it is developed, modified, and related to other 'signs', albeit always recognisable in its identity. One can find also both static and dynamic articulations of the same 'sign' – static articulations to assert it, dynamic articulations to qualify its function during its temporal dimension.

5) The value and the function of a musico-dramatic 'sign' can in no way be evaluated in abstract, by taking the 'sign' in isolation as an absolute musical element. Instead, one must always take into consideration its position, its articulation through well-defined durations, not only within the episode in which it appears, but also – and especially – as a part of a larger dramatic structure, as a structural factor in a scene, in an act, as a constituent element of the entire opera.

201

NOTES

1. The original Italian text of the libretto is available, besides the current Ricordi edition, in L. Baldacci (ed.), *Tutti i libretti di Verdi* (Milan: Garzanti, 1975), pp. 449–71. For the present study, however, I follow the libretto printed for the first Italian performance: *Aida*. Opera in quattro atti. Versi di A. Ghislanzoni. Musica di G. Verdi. R. Teatro alla Scala. Carnevale-Quaresima 1871–72 (Milan, Naples, Rome, 1872). The layout of the print in this edition clearly

reveals the poetic structure. The edition also contains some very interesting variants from the text as it appears in the score. I will indicate these variants in the corresponding places. For an English translation of the Italian libretto, see W. Weaver, *Seven Verdi Librettos ... with the original Italian* (New York: Norton, 1975), pp. 343–415.

2. The known Verdi–Ghislanzoni correspondence is published in G. Cesari and A. Luzio (eds.), *I copialettere di Giuseppe Verdi* (Milan, 1913), pp. 635–75. A few of the letters have been published in English translation in E. Istel, 'A genetic study of the *Aida* libretto', *The Musical Quarterly*, 3 (1917), 34–52, and in Charles Osborne (ed.), *Letters of Giuseppe Verdi* (London: Gollancz, 1972), pp. 155–67. The most comprehensive collection of documents concerning the birth of *Aida* and its early years is H. Bush (ed.), *Verdi's 'Aida' – The history of an opera in letters and documents* (Minneapolis: University of Minnesota Press, 1978). It is, however, absolutely essential to consult also Philip Gossett, 'Verdi, Ghislanzoni and *Aida*: The uses of conventions', *Critical Enquiry*, 1 (1974), 291–334: in this important essay not only is a correct chronology of the extant correspondence established, but also basic compositional conventions – especially for the duets – are identified; these conventions determine the overall as well as the detailed structure of the libretto, and they are typical of nineteenth-century Italian opera. For Aida's *romanza*, see the letter of Verdi to Ghislanzoni of 5 August 1871 (Cesari and Luzio, *I copialettere*, pp. 674–5: Bush, *Verdi's 'Aida'*, pp. 196–7; Istel, 'A genetic study', p. 47).

3. For the English-speaking reader a brief outline of the peculiarities of the Italian accent and verse system is perhaps in order here. Italian words are *tronche* (truncated) when the accent falls on the last syllable; they are *piane* (plain) – most of them – when the accent falls on the penultimate syllable; they are *sdrucciole* (slippery) when it falls on the syllable before the penultimate. A line takes its name from the position of the accent in its last word: thus, we have a *verso tronco*, a *verso piano*, and a *verso sdrucciolo*. Furthermore, the number of syllables in a line is calculated taking the *verso piano* as a standard measure: thus, 'O cieli azzurri ... o dolci aure natìve', an eleven-syllable line ending with a 'plain' word, is an *endecasillabo piano*, while 'Fiumi di sangue scòrrono' is a *settenario sdrucciolo*. A line or a group of lines can also take its name from the rhyme scheme adopted; consecutive rhymes are called *rime baciate* (AA BB CC DD...); alternate rhymes are called *rime alterne* or *alternate* (AB AB CD CD...); recurring rhymes are *rime incatenate*. *Verso libero* is a line without matching rhyme. For a detailed analysis of the Italian metrical organisation as applied to opera, see R. A. Moreen, *Integration of Text Forms and Musical Forms in Verdi's Early Operas* (Ann Arbor, Michigan, and London: University Microfilms International, 1979), and J. Budden, *The Operas of Verdi 2: From 'Il Trovatore' to 'La Forza del destino'* (London: Cassell, 1978), pp. 17 ff.

4. In the score: 'gioia'.

5. With this term Verdi indicates 'the word which cuts (*scolpisce*) the dramatic situation and makes it clear and evident': letter to Ghislanzoni of 17 August 1870; see Cesari and Luzio, *I copialettere*, p. 641; Osborne, *Letters of Verdi*, p. 159 (a pale and imprecise translation). Bush, *Verdi's 'Aida'*, p. 50, gives another translation. The above is mine.

6. In the score, Verdi destroys the metrical structure by changing the line into a much more direct and effective: 'Non sei mia figlia!' (You are not my daughter).

7. See Gossett, 'Verdi, Ghislanzoni', pp. 300–6.

8. J. Humbert, 'A propos de l'égyptomanie dans l'oeuvre de Verdi: attribution: à Auguste Mariette d'un scénerio anonyme de l'opéra *Aida*', *Revue de Musicologie*, 62 (1976), 229–56. The passage quoted here is on pp. 250–1 (text in French and in Italian; the translation is mine).

9. Frits Noske, *The Signifier and the Signified – Studies in the operas of Mozart and Verdi* (The Hague: Nijhoff, 1977); this book is a landmark in research on musical drama; it is the first attempt to apply systematically the principles of semiotics to the problems of opera, seen as the meeting point of different systems of communication. Particularly important, from a methodological point of view, is Appendix 1, 'Semiotic devices in musical drama', pp. 309–21, from which I take the following definition: '*Musico-dramatic sign* [...] – A musical unit which stresses, clarifies, invalidates, contradicts or supplies an element of the libretto. The sign is semantically interpretable and discloses dramatic truth' (p. 316).

10. On the dramatic function of single sonorities in Verdi's operas, see my essays 'Osservazioni sul processo compositivo in Verdi', *Acta Musicologica*, 43 (1971), 125–42, especially pp. 140–2, and 'Per un'esegesi della struttura drammatica del *Trovatore*', *Atti del 3° Congresso Internazionale di Studi Verdiani* (Parma, 1974), pp. 387–400, especially pp. 392–5.*

11. G. Verdi, *Aida*. Opera in quattro atti. Libretto di A. Ghislanzoni. Partitura d'orchestra [Milan], G. Ricordi, s.a., n. ed.le P.R. 153, pp. 265–7. The reader is kindly urged to consult the orchestral score while reading the following pages.

12. Orchestral score, pp. 269–70.

13. Orchestral score, p. 271; G. Ricordi, *Disposizione scenica per l'opera 'Aida'*. Versi di A. Ghislanzoni. Musica di G. Verdi, compilata e regolata secondo la messa in scena del Teatro alla Scala da G. R. [Milan, Naples, Rome], G. Ricordi, s.a., n. ed.le 43504, p. 40.

14. Verdi calls Aida's solo a *romanza* (and not an *aria*), no doubt because of the basically strophic nature of the piece, as opposed to the structure of a regular *aria*, where a *cantabile* is followed by a *cabaletta*. On the use of the term *romanza* in Verdi's operas, see M. Chusid, 'The organization of Scenes with Arias: Verdi's Cavatinas and Romanzas', *Atti del 1° Congresso Internazionale di Studi Verdiani* (Parma, 1969), pp. 59–66, especially pp. 61–2 and 66.

15. Orchestral score, p. 273.

16. Orchestral score, pp. 316–17.

17. Orchestral score, p. 275, last system.

18. Orchestral score, p. 278, second system.

19. Letter to Ghislanzoni of 7 October [1870]. See Cesari and Luzio, *I copialettere*, p. 650; Bush, *Verdi's 'Aida'* ..., p. 75.

20. Orchestral score, pp. 279–80.

21. In the orchestral score the first section (*Allegro giusto*, MM. 100 at the crotchet, rehearsal letter I) spans from the beginning of p. 281 to the penultimate bar of the second system, p. 283; the second section, starting from this bar, ends on the first chord of p. 288 (rehearsal letter J); finally, the third section (*Poco più*

203

animato, MM. 116 at the crotchet) runs up to the third bar in the first system of p. 289, but the musical flow continues without break in the ensuing recitative.

22. This term commonly signifies the rhythm created in a musical composition by changes in the harmony.

23. For instance, the static dimension is created by the absence of harmonic rhythm, emphasised by an A flat pedal distributed between three instruments: oboe (top A flat held for seven and half bars), violas, which repeat the figuration of the first music example on p. 136 above, and the basses (cellos and double basses), which repeat the pitch (at different octave levels) on the rhythm

24. The first section (*Allegro,* dotted crotchet 96, rehearsal letter K) goes from p. 292 to the first bar of p. 296; the second from this bar to the first bar of p. 298 (rehearsal letter L); the third section from this bar to the last bar of p. 300; as in the first part of the duet, there is no break with the following recitative.

25. Here again the static dimension is realised above all by the absence of harmonic rhythm: in the first section, by the persistence (six bars) of the C minor chord; in the third, by the pedal on top B in the first violins (ten bars).

26. The extraordinary expressive power of this page, one of the highest and most moving moments in Verdi's music, derives from the contrast between the *ostinato* pedal in the violins and the melody entrusted to the violas, cellos and one bassoon, playing in unison *ppp con espressione.* This melody is articulated, both in detail and at the overall level, following the principles of the poetic quatrain in nineteenth-century Italian opera, in consequence of which the first and second lines have the function of asserting a situation, the third of developing the tension to its maximum, and the fourth of concluding the episode (see L. Dallapiccola, 'Parole e musica nel melodramma', *Quaderni della Rassegna Musicale,* 2 (Turin, 1965), pp. 117–39, definitive version in *Appunti, incontri, meditazioni* (Milan: Suvini Zerboni, 1970), pp. 5–28; English version: *Words and Music in Italian XIX Century Opera* (Dublin: The Italian Institute, 1964)). In the melody we are considering, the poetic line has its equivalent in a melodic fragment one bar long, the quatrain in a four-bar phrase. Significantly, Aida sings in unison with this melody only from the beginning of the third quatrain ('Ancor tua figlia . . .'), and the climax of the episode – corresponding with the highest pitch of the melodic line – lies in the second 'line' of the fourth 'quatrain', at the words 'della *mia* patria'.**

*English trans.: "Towards an Explanation of the Dramatic Structure of *Il Tro- vatore*," *Music Analysis,* I (1982), 129–41.

**See also Luigi Dallapiccola, *Parole e musica,* ed. Fiamma Nicolodi (Milan, 1980), pp. 66–93; English trans. in *The Verdi Companion,* ed. Martin Chusid and William Weaver (New York, 1979), pp. 193–215.

Verdi, Ghislanzoni, and *Aida:* The Uses of Convention

Philip Gossett

I should like nothing better than to find a good libretto and with it a good poet (we have such need of one!), but I cannot hide from you that I read with great reluctance the libretti that are sent to me. It is impossible, or almost impossible, for another to sense what I want. I want subjects that are *new, great, beautiful, varied, bold* . . . and bold to the core, with *new forms,* yet at the same time appropriate for music. . . . When someone tells me: "I did it this way because that is how Romani, Cammarano, etc., did it," we no longer can understand each other. It is precisely because those great men did it so that I wish it done differently.[1]

Thus did Giuseppe Verdi write to a Neapolitan friend in 1853, shortly before the premieres of *Il Trovatore* and *La Traviata*. The quest for a good libretto and poet was to consume Verdi, and as his artistic needs matured he composed fewer and fewer operas rather than renew his frustrating search.

Compelled to accept mediocre texts in order to compose at all, Verdi

I wish to express my appreciation to the John Simon Guggenheim Memorial Foundation for the fellowship awarded me in 1971–72. This study derives from work done in Italy during that year.

1. Alessandro Luzio, ed., *Carteggi verdiani,* 4 vols. (Rome, 1935–47), 1:16. The letter, dated January 1, 1853, is addressed to Cesare De Sanctis. All translations from the Verdi correspondence are my own. Felice Romani was the most important and prolific librettist of the early nineteenth century, particularly famous for his collaboration with Vincenzo Bellini (see Patrick J. Smith, *The Tenth Muse* [New York, 1970], pp. 199–206). Salvatore Cammarano, a Neapolitan writer, prepared several libretti for Verdi, including *Alzira* (1845), *La battaglia di Legnano* (1849), *Luisa Miller* (1849), and *Il Trovatore* (1853), which was completed after Cammarano's death in the summer of 1852 by Leone Emanuele Bardare.

cajoled and bullied his librettists so as to transform their wares into a state approaching his ideal. To Cammarano, after the latter had submitted a scenario for what was to become *Il Trovatore,* Verdi wrote:

> I have read your scenario, and, as a man of talent and very superior character, you will not be offended if I, in my small way, take the liberty to remark that if this subject cannot be treated on our stage with all the novelty and bizarre quality of the Spanish drama, it would be better to abandon it.[2]

If he faulted Cammarano's scenario for lack of novelty, Verdi considered Antonio Somma's proposed libretto for the ill-fated *Re Lear* to have the opposite defect:

> I have received the remainder of the first act; I will say nothing to you of the verses, which are ever beautiful and worthy of you, but, with all the respect I have for your talent, I will say that their form does not lend itself easily to music. No one loves novelty of forms more than I, but they must permit a musical setting. Anything can be set to music, true, but not everything will be effective. To make music, one needs stanzas for cantabile sections, stanzas for ensembles, stanzas for largos, for allegros, etc., and all these in alternation so that nothing seems cold and monotonous.[3]

Somma's libretto, with many new forms and extended dialogues, did little to excite the composer's musical imagination.[4]

The existence of extensive written communications between Verdi and his librettists should have prompted scholars to prepare editions of the correspondence and to analyze its meaning and implications. Only rarely can we participate directly in the formative stages of an opera, and available material such as the correspondence between Richard Strauss and Hugo von Hofmannsthal is invaluable.[5] Obeisance, at least, has been

2. Letter of April 9, 1851, in Gaetano Cesari and Alessandro Luzio, ed., *I Copialettere di Giuseppe Verdi* (hereafter referred to as *Cop*) (Milan, 1913), p. 118. The source of the opera to which Verdi refers is the Spanish play *El Trovador* (1836) by Antonio García Gutiérrez.

3. Letter of August 30, 1853, in Alessandro Pascolato, *Re Lear e ballo in maschera: Lettere di Giuseppe Verdi ad Antonio Somma* (Città di Castello, 1902), p. 53.

4. Leo Karl Gerhartz discusses the nature of Somma's *Re Lear* libretto in his article, "Il Re Lear di Antoni Somma ed il modello melodrammatico dell'opera verdiana: Principi per una definizione del libretto verdiano," in *Atti del I° Congresso Internazionale di Studi Verdiani* (Parma, 1969), pp. 110–115.

5. Willi Schuh, ed., *Richard Strauss—Hugo von Hofmannsthal: Briefwechsel,* 4th ed. (Zurich,

---

Philip Gossett is the general editor of the critical edition of the works of Rossini and author of numerous articles on Renaissance music, Italian opera, Beethoven, and musical theory.

done to Verdi's correspondence. Alessandro Luzio calls the letters of Verdi to Antonio Ghislanzoni, "versifier" of *Aida* (we shall return to this formulation in a moment), "the most marvelous course in musical aesthetics in action."[6] Yet, for no opera do we have available a complete edition of the surviving letters between Verdi and a librettist.[7]

The fault lies only partially with Verdi scholars. Many important primary sources, letters to him, drafts of the letters he sent, working copies of the libretti, musical sketches for all the operas after *Luisa Miller,* manuscripts of entire compositions not included in definitive versions of his operas, remain in the possession of his heirs, and access to them has often proved difficult. As a result, perhaps, even much easily available material has been examined superficially.

The history of *Aida* is a case in point. The grandest of all grand operas celebrated its one-hundreth birthday in 1971 with festivities throughout the world. Many publications were devoted to the opera and its background, new recordings were released, and opera houses vied to produce the largest menagerie of elephants, giraffes, ostriches, and Nubian slaves for the grand triumphal march. Largely lost in the tumult were the real problems still surrounding the opera:

1. The absence of a proper critical edition of the score, reflecting authentic sources and unencumbered by a spurious appeal to "tradition."[8]

2. The existence of several unpublished compositions for *Aida,* omitted from the definitive version but of enormous historical and perhaps even musical interest. One manuscript, a complete overture, lies dormant at St. Agata.

3. The need for a complete and accurate edition of the correspon-

207

1970). An English edition, made from an earlier German edition with many omissions, was published as *A Working Friendship: The Correspondence between Richard Strauss and Hugo von Hofmannsthal,* trans. Hans Hammelmann and Ewald Osers (New York, 1961).

6. Luzio, 4:22.

7. For a general survey of the present state of research and publication of the Verdi correspondence, see my review of Charles Osborne, *Letters of Giuseppe Verdi* (New York, Chicago, San Francisco, 1971), in *Musical Quarterly* 59 (1973): 633–39.

8. Indeed, no opera by Verdi has been published in a critical edition, and the editions used for modern performances are often corrupt. The situation is worse for Bellini and Donizetti. Modern editions of their operas are appallingly inaccurate. The only nineteenth-century Italian opera currently available in anything approaching a reliable text is Gioachino Rossini's *Il barbiere di Siviglia,* in the edition by Alberto Zedda (Milan, 1969). The Fondazione Rossini, in cooperation with the Casa Ricordi, is about to publish the first volumes in a projected critical edition of the works of Rossini.

dence between Verdi and Antonio Ghislanzoni, letters in which the composer and versifier hammered out each detail of the libretto, with all that implies about the music.

It is this last problem that will concern us here.

Verdi first worked with Ghislanzoni during the winter of 1869, when the poet capably provided the verses necessary for the Milanese revision of *La forza del destino,* the original librettist, Francesco Maria Piave, having been struck down by a paralytic stroke some years earlier. Verdi must have been satisfied with Ghislanzoni's abilities, for on June 2, 1870, in his first communication concerning *Aida* with his publisher, Giulio Ricordi, he specifically asked whether "Ghislanzoni could prepare the libretto for me."[9] Verdi had himself received a synopsis of the plot only a few weeks before,[10] but the prehistory of *Aida* stretches back to August 9, 1869, when Verdi wrote to the director of the Cairo theaters:

> I am not unaware that a new theater is about to open in Cairo, during the forthcoming celebrations for the completion of [the canal through] the isthmus of Suez.
> While being cognizant that You, Monsieur le Bey, wished to do me the honor of considering me to write the hymn which will mark the day of the opening, I must regretfully decline this honor, both because of my numerous current tasks and because I am not accustomed to compose occasional music.[11]

The theater at Cairo opened on November 1, 1869 with a performance of Verdi's *Rigoletto,* but without his participation; later that month, on November 17, the long-sought direct sea route to the East became a reality.

Nothing seemed able to induce the composer to exercise his craft again, although there was no dearth of requests. The most insistent voice belonged to Camille Du Locle, co-librettist with Joseph Méry of Verdi's latest opera, the French *Don Carlos,* produced at the Paris Opéra on March 11, 1867, and now director of the Opéra Comique in Paris. Hoping to obtain a new Verdi opera for his theater, Du Locle fired off a barrage of letters offering Verdi play after play for his consideration as possible operatic subjects. The composer rejected them all. In one, "the part of the woman is necessarily odious";[12] for another, "I will receive

9. The letter is given by Franco Abbiati, *Giuseppe Verdi,* 4 vols. (Milan, 1959), 3:367.

10. It was sent to him by Camille Du Locle from Paris on May 14, 1870.

11. Saleh Abdoun, *Genesi dell'Aida,* no. 4 in the *Quaderni dell' Istituto di Studi Verdiani* (Parma, 1971), p. xv.

12. Letter to Du Locle, October 6, 1869, in Abbiati, 3:322. The play referred to is *Patrie!* (1869) by Victorien Sardou.

this play tomorrow, but it is a waste of time, since I shall hide it away";[13] while for a third, "one neither weeps nor laughs. It is cold, and does not seem made for music."[14]

But in a letter dated May 26, 1870, Verdi reacted quite differently to a scenario in French sent him earlier that month by Du Locle:

> I have read the Egyptian scenario. It is well done, splendid in its stage effects, and there are two or three situations which, if not completely novel, are certainly most beautiful. But who wrote it? There is in it the trace of an expert hand, versed in the craft, who knows the theater well.[15]

The "Egyptian scenario" was a four-page printed outline for an opera, prepared by the famous French Egyptologist, Auguste Mariette. Mariette, a friend of Du Locle's, had convinced the Egyptian khedive to commission an opera on an Egyptian theme for the new Cairo theater, and Du Locle was instrumental in having Verdi approached first. Wagner and Gounod were also under consideration, as Du Locle revealed to Verdi, hoping this information might nudge his friend to accept the commission.[16]

The proposal was ultimately accepted by Verdi, a contract was drawn up, and the composer set to work.[17] His immediate task was to have the four-page scenario transformed into a viable libretto. On June 18, he wrote to Du Locle:

> I can hardly wait to see you, first for the pleasure of seeing you again, then because I think we will quickly agree about the modifications which, in my opinion, should be made in *Aida*. I have already reflected about this, and will offer you my ideas.[18]

13. Letter to Giulio Ricordi, late November or early December 1869, in Abbiati, 3:323. The play is *Frou-frou* (1869) by Henri Meilhac and Ludovic Halévy.

14. Letter to Du Locle, May 26, 1870, in Abbiati, 3:371. The play is *El tanto por ciento* (1861) by Adelardo López de Ayala.

15. Letter to Du Locle, May 26, 1870, in Abbiati, 3:371.

16. See Mariette's letter to Du Locle, April 28, 1870, which Du Locle forwarded to Verdi on May 14 together with the scenario. The letters are printed in Ursula Günther, "Zur Entstehung von Verdis *Aida*" (*Studi Musicali* 2 [1973]: 15–71, see esp. pp. 43–44 and 46).

17. The prehistory of *Aida* is traced with exemplary care by Ursula Günther in her article cited above, in which she prints many documents for the first time. Saleh Abdoun's study (n. 11) reproduces important letters from the collection in Cairo. Professor Hans Busch of Indiana University is currently preparing for publication an English translation of an extensive collection of documents pertaining to *Aida*. Many of these have never been published before. I wish to thank Professor Busch for his kindness in allowing me to refer to his collection prior to its publication by the University of Minnesota Press.

18. A complete text of this letter is found in Günther, p. 56.

Du Locle had already left Paris for St. Agata, and in a week of inten-
sive discussion they prepared an extended prose draft in French of the
entire libretto.[19] On June 25, Verdi reported the progress of *Aida* to
Ricordi:

> Du Locle immediately came here [. . .], we studied together the
> scenario, and together made modifications we believed necessary.
> Du Locle has left [. . .] with the modifications to submit them to the
> powerful and anonymous author. I have restudied the scenario,
> and I have made and am still making new changes. Now we must
> think of the libretto, or, rather, of making verses, because all that is
> needed now are the verses. Could and would Ghislanzoni do this
> work for me? It is not an original work, explain this well; it is only
> to make verses.[20]

Ghislanzoni accepted and, together with Ricordi, visited St. Agata early
in July. Verdi had some qualms about the poet, which emerge in a letter
to Ricordi of July 10, shortly after the visit:

> I continuously reread the scenario of *Aida*. I see some observa-
> tions by Ghislanzoni which (just between us) frighten me a bit. I
> would not want that, in order to avoid imaginary dangers, some-
> thing were said which is inappropriate for the situation or the
> scene; and likewise I would not want *parole sceniche* to be forgotten.
>
> By *parole sceniche* I mean those words which carve out a situation
> or a character, words whose effect on the public is always most
> powerful. I know well that sometimes it is difficult to give them a
> select and poetic form. But . . . (pardon the blasphemy) both poet
> and musician must sometimes have the talent and the courage to
> make neither poetry nor music. . . . Horror! horror!
>
> Enough: we shall see. In any case, you can intervene if
> necessary.[21]

On July 15, Verdi gave a progress report to Du Locle:

> I did not write to you earlier because Giulio Ricordi was here
> with the poet who will versify *Aida*. We came to agreement about
> everything and I hope soon to receive the verses of the first act, so
> that I can begin working myself.[22]

The declaration of war by France against Prussia, on July 19, marking
the outbreak of the Franco-Prussian war, with the fall of the Second

210

19. This important document will be published for the first time in Professor Busch's
forthcoming book.

20. Abbiati, 3:368.

21. Abbiati, 3:348. The letter is undated in Abbiati, but Hans Busch supplies the date in
his article "(signed) G. Verdi" (*Opera News*, April 1, 1972, p. 9).

22. Abbiati, 3:376.

Empire, siege of Paris, and disastrous French defeat, effectively halted communication between Verdi and Du Locle during the months in which the music for *Aida* was composed.

Fortunately, thirty-five letters from Verdi to Ghislanzoni concerning *Aida*, almost all he probably wrote, survive. In them Verdi discusses the libretto in the greatest detail, piece by piece, often suggesting specific modifications. Most of the letters fall between August 12 and November 13, 1870, while Verdi was actually composing *Aida* in sketch form. A few later letters refer to isolated points which arose while he orchestrated the score and made some revisions. Only excerpts from Ghislanzoni's letters, presumably preserved at St. Agata, have been published. Without his part of the correspondence, some of Verdi's remarks remain obscure. Still, even those critics who have proclaimed Verdi's letters to be "the most marvelous course in musical aesthetics in action" have dealt with them only superficially. Indeed one wonders whether they have ever been read with any attention to their meaning.

All but one of Verdi's letters to Ghislanzoni were published by Gaetano Cesari and Alessandro Luzio in the appendix to their edition of Verdi's *Copialettere,* copy books for letters.[23] On the basis of this publication, Edgar Istel wrote a lengthy article entitled "A Genetic Study of the *Aida* Libretto." Franco Abbiati, in his mammoth four-volume biography of the composer, republished most of the letters. Charles Osborne, in a recent book of translations from the *Copialettere,* rendered a group into English. They were all translated into German by Renate Heckmann, with an explicatory essay by Klaus Schlegel. Many others have cited them extensively.[24]

No one seems to have observed, however, that the order in which the letters are printed in the *Copialettere* is patently wrong. Read in the sequence in which they were first printed and have been reprinted, translated, and discussed, they make no sense whatsoever. Indeed, the chronology is often absurd. The chief difficulty is that many letters are supplied only with days of the week. But given three letters dated November 2, Sunday, and November 4, a perpetual calendar easily re-

211

---

23. *Cop,* pp. 638–75. The additional letter, dated August 6, 1871, is given in Abbiati, 3:465. It has been found among Luzio's papers and was previously published, together with a facsimile of the autograph, in Giuseppi Stefani, *Verdi e Trieste* (Trieste, 1951), pp. 127–28.

24. Edgar Istel, "A Genetic Study of the *Aida* Libretto," *Musical Quarterly* 3 (1917): 34–52; Abbiati, 3:381–405; Charles Osborne, pp. 156–67; Renate Heckmann, trans., "Giuseppe Verdi: Fünfunddreissig Briefe zu 'Aida,' " and Klaus Schlegel, "Bekenntnis zum Ungewöhnlichen: Verdis Mitarbeit am AIDA-Libretto," both in *Jahrbuch der Komischen Oper Berlin* 9 (1969): 51–108 and 109–18; Dyneley Hussey, *Verdi* (New York, 1949), pp. 175–83, passim.

Table 1
The Letters from Giuseppe Verdi to Antonio Ghislanzoni

Published Order (*Cop,* etc.)	Postulated Correct Order
1870	
a. August 12*	1. August 12 (=a)
b. August 14*	2. August 14 (=b)
c. August 16*	3. August 16 (=c)
d. August 17	4. August 17 (=d)
e. August 22*	5. August 22 (=e)
f. August 25*	6. August 25 (=f)
g. Martedì*	7. September 8 (=h)
h. September 8*	8. Ca. September 13 (=dd)†
i. Undated (*Cop:* September 10)*	9. Ca. September 14 (=i)
j. September 28	10. September 27 (=g)‡
k. September 30	11. September 28 (=j)
l. October 6	12. September 30 (=k)
m. October 7	13. October 7 (=m)
n. October 8	14. October 8 (=n)
o. October 16	15. October 9 (=l)§
p. Martedì*	16. October 16 (=o)
q. Sabato*	17. October 17 (=r)
r. Lunedì*	18. October 18 (=p)
s. Martedì*	19. October 22 (=q)
t. Mercoledì*	20. October 25 (=s)
u. Giovedì*	21. October 26 (=z)
v. Sabato*	22. October 27 (=u)
w. November 2*	23. November 2 (=w)
x. Domenica*	24. November 4 (=y)
y. November 4	25. November 5 (=v)
z. Mercoledì*	26. November 9 (=t)
aa. Sabato	27. November 12 (=aa)
bb. Undated*	28. November 13 (=x)
cc. December 28*	29. Mid-November (=bb)
dd. Undated (*Cop:* December 31)*	30. December 21 (=ee)
. . .	31. December 28 (=cc)
1871	
ee. Mercoledì (*Cop:* January)*	32. January 7 (=ff)
ff. January 7*	33. January 12 (=gg)
gg. January 12*	34. August 5 (=hh)
hh. August 5*	35. August 6 (=ii)
ii. August 6‖	. . .

*These letters are now in the collection of the Pierpont Morgan Library, New York. The location of the other letters is unknown.
†This letter is in response to a letter from Ghislanzoni dated September 11 (in Abbiati [3:387]; and, in a fuller text, in Busch [forthcoming]). The following letter is a further response, referring also to a letter Ghislanzoni promised and presumably sent the next day (i.e., September 12).
‡This date is conjectural. September 20 is also possible.
§Despite the date of October 6 given in *Cop,* it seems almost certain that this letter follows the letter of October 8.
‖This letter is given in Abbiati (3:465–66).

veals that November 2 fell on Wednesday in 1870 and November 4 on Friday, so that a letter dated "Sunday" could not conceivably belong between them, even if connections between the letters made sense, which they don't. Yet the force of printed "fact" was so great that Abbiati simply declared Sunday to be November 3.[25] The location of the autographs of the letters had been unknown for many years, when recently a group of twenty-five were acquired by the Pierpont Morgan Library in

25. Abbiati, 3:403.

New York.[26] Though inspection of the originals gives no further clues for dating, in some cases the dates in *I Copialettere* prove to be inventions of the editors. Often, furthermore, the text of the published editions is faulty.[27]

Table 1 offers a list of the letters as published in the *Copialettere,*

Table 2
The Composition of *Aida:* After Verdi's Letters to Ghislanzoni

Acts 1 and 2

July 15, 1870: Ghislanzoni sends Verdi act 1 (see letter from Ghislanzoni to Ricordi's secretary, Eugenio Tornaghi, in Busch [forthcoming]).

July 26: Ghislanzoni sends Verdi revisions for act 1, with the exception of the Finale, presumably in response to Verdi letter(s) now lost. (Letter from Ghislanzoni to Verdi in Busch [forthcoming].)

August 12: Verdi works on act 1: Introduzione, Aida aria. He receives poetry from Ghislanzoni for act 1 finale (revision?); also act 2 opening chorus with Amneris and duet Aida-Amneris.

August 14: Verdi discusses problems with act 1 finale.

August 16: Discusses act 2 chorus with Amneris.

August 17: Discusses act 2 duet Aida-Amneris.

August 22: Receives revision of duet; also act 2 finale. Discusses again act 1 finale.

August 25: Invites Ghislanzoni to St. Agata to complete work on acts 1 and 2.

(Late August, early September: Ghislanzoni in St. Agata; Verdi completes act 1.)

September 8: Verdi works on act 2 finale.

September 13–14: Verdi completes act 2.

(September 15–28: Verdi touches up acts 1 and 2. By September 28 at the latest he receives from Ghislanzoni act 3.)

Act 3

September 28–30: Verdi criticizes the text of act 3; asks for revisions.

October 7–9: Verdi receives Ghislanzoni's revisions for act 3; discusses them.

October 16–18: Verdi composing act 3, asks for further changes.

October 22: Verdi discusses problems at the end of act 3.

October 27: Verdi has finished the music for act 3.

Act 4

October 16–17: Verdi offers suggestions for the duet Amneris-Radames.

October 25–27: Verdi receives and criticizes the duet.

Late October, early November: Verdi receives the text of the scena del giudizio and the finale.

November 4: He discusses the scena del giudizio; requests revisions.

November 5: He receives the revision of the duet and approves it.

November 9: He receives the revision of the scena del giudizio and asks for further alterations.

November 12: He approves the revised scena del giudizio.

November 12–13: He discusses the finale at length and requests revisions.

Ca. November 13: Verdi finishes act 4. Rather than wait for Ghislanzoni to revise the text, he uses his own rough draft.

(Mid to late November: Ghislanzoni comes to St. Agata for final adjustments.)

December 13: Verdi leaves St. Agata for Genoa.

December 21, 1870–January 12, 1871: Verdi asks Ghislanzoni for changes in details in the act 2 finale.

August 5: Verdi proposes a major revision of the opening of act 3.

August 6: Verdi requests a few additional verses for the end of act 3.

26. I wish to express my thanks to the Pierpont Morgan Library, and particularly to Mr. Herbert Cahoon, who on many occasions has generously assisted me at the Library.

27. Professor Busch independently has arrived at similar conclusions. His collection of *Aida* documents will include all these letters, rendered into English, based on the original texts where possible and agreeing in the main with the chronology proposed here.

213

together with my rearrangement of them. Table 2 offers a broad summary of their content.

Rather than merely justify the new order, for which a careful reading of the letters would suffice, I prefer to concentrate here on what we can learn from them.

Analysis of Verdi's operas rarely moves beyond plot summary. Of many recent studies, only Julian Budden's excellent *The Operas of Verdi: from Oberto to Rigoletto*[28] explores in depth those qualities which distinguish Verdi's music from that of his contemporaries. In particular, Budden seeks to demonstrate the relation of Verdi's musical and dramatic forms in his earlier operas to the Italian operatic conventions of his time. When the planning between composer and librettist occurs through correspondence, Verdi often makes quite explicit statements about these conventions. Although Budden quotes many extracts from the correspondence, he does not pursue their implications. *Aida* is one of Verdi's last operas; indeed for about ten years he considered it to be his last. The letters to Ghislanzoni help us penetrate Verdi's own understanding of the work, and the resultant picture is in many respects startling.

Since so much of the dramatic action of *Aida* unfolds in direct confrontation between characters, we shall focus on the duets in the opera. These include duets for Aida and Amneris, Aida and Amonasro, Aida and Radames, and Amneris and Radames. The last finale is also essentially a duet for Aida and Radames. In his correspondence with Ghislanzoni, Verdi discusses each composition at length. With five duets to compose, he obviously sought to achieve variety. To appreciate the extent of his compositional problem, we must turn back to the beginning of the nineteenth century and the operas of Gioachino Rossini.

Eighteenth-century *opera seria* tended to minimize ensembles. Under the influence of comic opera, they gradually infiltrated the design, until by 1800 ensembles within each act and lengthy finales were normal. As Rossini matured, during the second decade of the century, the number of solo arias in his operas decreased, until they played a relatively minor role in his later works. Some of his ensembles are primarily lyrical, short compositions in a single section expressing a common emotion or state of mind. But the main problem for Rossini and his librettists was to perfect an approach to the ensemble which offered characters opportunity for lyrical expression while focusing on their dramatic confrontation and interaction. We cannot assert with confidence that Rossini in-

28. Julian Budden, *The Operas of Verdi: From Oberto to Rigoletto* (New York and Washington, 1973).

214

vented any particular formal design, since little of the music of his contemporaries is known, but his operas so dominated every theater in Italy and wherever else Italian opera was performed that it was unquestionably from them that a coherent set of formal procedures entered the compositional vocabulary of every Italian opera composer through Verdi. The procedures were compelling because they fused in a simple, yet satisfactory manner the urge for lyrical expression and the needs of the drama.

The duet for Arsace and Semiramide, "Ebben, a te, ferisci," from Rossini's last Italian opera, *Semiramide* (1823), is a fine example of the fully developed Rossinian duet. The text is given in Example 1.

Example 1

Duet for Semiramide and Arsace from *Semiramide* by Rossini (1823) (translation adapted from the translation of the libretto by Peggie Cochrane from the London recording of the opera [A 4383; OSA 1383]. ©1966 The Decca Record Company Limited, London. Exclusive U.S. Agents, London Records, Inc., New York, New York 10001. Reprinted through the courtesy of London Records, Inc.)

215

Section 1:

Sem: Ebben, a te, ferisci!   Sem: Well then . . . go on—strike;
      Compi il voler d'un dio!   Fulfill a god's behest!
      Spegni nel sangue mio   Extinguish in my blood
      Un esecrato amor!   An abominable love!
      La madre rea punisci: Punish your guilty mother,
      Vendica il genitor!   Avenge your father.

Ars: Tutto su me gli dei   Ars: Let the gods vent upon me
      Sfoghino in pria lo sdegno;   All their wrath first;
      Mai barbaro a tal segno   Never shall a son's heart
      Sarà d'in figlio il cor!   Be so barbarous!
      In odio al Ciel tu sei,   You are hateful before heaven,
      Ma sei mia madre ancor.   But you are still my mother.

Sem: M'odia, lo merto.   Sem: Hate me . . . I deserve it.
Ars: Calmati.   Ars: Calm yourself.
Sem: Io già m'abborro, ah! Svenami!   Sem: I loathe myself now. Kill me.
      Figlio di Nino!   Nino's son!
Ars: Misera.   Ars: Unhappy woman.
      Ah, tu mi strappi l'anima,   You wring my heart.
      Ti calma, per pietà.   Calm yourself, for pity's sake.
Sem: Tu piangi, la tua bell'anima   Sem: You weep? Your tender heart
      Ha ancor di me pietà.   Yet has some pity for me.

Section 2:

à 2:	Giorno d'orrore!	à 2:	Day of horror . . .
	E di contento!		And of joy!
	Nelle tue braccia,		In your arms
	In tal momento,		At this moment
	Scorda il mio core		My heart forgets
	Tutto il rigore		All the rigor
	Di sua terribile		Of its terrible
	Fatalità!		Fate!
	E dolce al misero		It is sweet for the unhappy one
	Che oppresso geme		Who groans, overwhelmed,
	Il duol dividere		To share his grief,
	Piangere insieme		Weep with another
	In cor sensibile		And find sympathy
	Trovar pietà.		In a feeling heart.

Section 3:

Ars:	Madre, addio!	Ars:	Mother, farewell!
Sem:	T'arresta, oh Dio!	Sem:	Stay, Oh god!
	Senti . . . e dove?		Hear me . . . oh, where?
Ars:	Al mio destino . . .	Ars:	To confront my fate . . .
	Alla tomba, al padre, a Nino.		To the tomb, to my father, Nino.
Sem:	Ei vuol sangue.	Sem:	He will have blood . . .
Ars:	E sangue avrà.	Ars:	And blood he shall have.
Sem:	E qual sangue . . .	Sem:	And whose blood . . .

Section 4 (cabaletta):

Ars:	Tu serena intanto il ciglio,	Ars:	Be serene, meanwhile, mother
	Calma, o madre, il tuo terror.		Calm your fears.
	Or che il Ciel ti rende il figlio		Now that heaven restores your son
	Dei sperar nel suo favor.		You must hope for its favor.
	Vo a implorar per te perdono		I go to ask pardon for you . . .
	A punire un traditor!		To punish a traitor.
	Dal terribile cimento		From the terrible ordeal
	A te riedo vincitor!		I will return victorious to you!
Sem:	No, non so di qual periglio	Sem:	I know not what presentiment
	Fier presagio agghiaccia il cor!		Of peril chills my blood!
	Or che a me rendesti il figlio		Now that you have restored my son
	Ciel, lo salvi il tuo favor.		Heaven, protect him from harm.
	Ah sperar non so perdono,		I cannot hope for pardon
	Troppo giusto è il suo furor!		His wrath is all too just!
	Dal terribile cimento		From the terrible ordeal
	A me riedi vincitor!		Return victorious to me.

216

The text is constructed, typically, in four parts, beginning with a confrontation which dramatically motivates the entire composition. The plot is a conglomeration of the Oedipus and Orestes legends. Semiramide has murdered her husband Nino. She loves Arsace, but as the duet begins she has just discovered he is actually their son. She tells him to strike, to punish her; he recoils and tries to calm her. The initial confrontation in the typical Rossinian duet is presented in parallel poetic stanzas, which Rossini normally sets to the same or very similar music. Here Semiramide's stanza is set in two parts: a more declamatory phrase over a characteristic orchestral figure for the first four lines (moving harmonically from E minor to its dominant), and a more lyrical passage for the final tune (in E major) (see Example 2).

Example 2
Semiramide, Duet Semiramide-Arsace

a) Section 1, opening phrase:

217

etc.

b) Lyrical passage in section 1:

Arsace's stanza parallels Semiramide's, but the first section modulates to
V of V, and the lyrical passage is therefore in B major. With their
positions stated, the characters can now interact in dialogue over the
orchestral theme from the opening of the formal stanzas. This dialogue,
which is also punctuated by a restatement *à 2* of the lyrical phrase, leads
to a new key, and with it the second section.

218   This internal *cantabile* is a lyrical contemplation of the dramatic situation. Though characters may have different or similar views, they express them in concert, singing together in simple harmony or presenting
the same lyrical phrase with parallel texts in a primitive canonic fashion.
Here Semiramide and Arsace reflect on their reunion, a day of both
horror and joy (see Example 3).

Example 3

Semiramide, Duet Semiramide-Arsace, Section 2

Typically for Rossini, the *cantabile* is in flat III (G major) of the tonic of the entire duet (E major).

In the third section, which often recalls music from the opening, action is taken, new positions are defined. The music freely follows the events in an arioso style, dominated by short melodic phrases and a simple, often chordal, orchestral background. Arsace prepares to follow the wishes of his dead father, to descend into Nino's tomb, and there to seek his revenge. But, Semiramide cries, as the music veers back to V of E major, whose blood will you have?

Musically and dramatically, the third section prepares the final one, known as a *cabaletta*. The *cabaletta* is the lyrical conclusion of a multipartite composition; *cabalettas* are found in arias, duets, ensembles, even finales. In an aria, it consists of a lyrical period, often concluding with exuberant coloratura, a middle section, which may also involve the chorus, and a repetition of the opening period, during which the singer could take the flattering option of ornamenting the melody. Cadential material would conclude the piece.[29] There are several ways in which the *cabaletta* could be adapted to the duet. Normally, each protagonist would sing the entire melody in turn, followed by a middle section, and a repetition of the theme, now sung by both together. In the *Semiramide* duet, a different technique is used: the *cabaletta* theme is shared. This decision to alternate the voices was clearly Rossini's, since the parallel stanzas could easily have accommodated a more formalistic solution. In the *cabaletta* the characters reflect on their new positions, shout out new challenges, etc. Here, Arsace seeks to reassure his mother, but she fears the worst (see Example 4).

219

Example 4
Semiramide, Duet Semiramide-Arsace, Section 4

29. Typical *cabalettas* within arias include: "Ah! perchè non posso odiarti" in Elvino's aria "Tutto è sciolto" from Bellini's *La Sonnambula* (1831); "So anch'io la virtù magica" in Norina's *cavatina* (i.e., entrance aria) "Quel guardo il cavaliere" from Donizetti's *Don Pasquale* (1843); "Di quella pira" in Manrico's aria "Ah sì, ben mio" from Verdi's *Il Trovatore* (1853). It is extremely important to realize that the normal vision of the *cabaletta* as quick, with a simple melody and sharp rhythm, as in "Di quella pira," does not begin to account for the stylistic diversity we find during the sixty years in which *cabalettas* reigned supreme in Italian opera.

Her fears are more than grounded. When Arsace does descend into his father's tomb, his mother is hiding there, ostensibly to protect him from her coconspirator, Assur; unaware of this, Arsace kills her.

Formal conventions can easily degenerate into formula. Though Donizetti's melodic style is very different, and much less florid than Rossini's, formally much of his music simply accepts Rossinian models. As we have seen, Verdi, by the time of *Rigoletto*, was actively seeking not only new subjects but also new forms. Yet his librettists continued to offer him texts which largely paralleled the conventional schemes. The most vulnerable part of the duet was its opening movement. Even many of Rossini's duets seek alternative means of setting the parallel stanzas. By the middle of the century, often only two more formal musical sections remain: the slow and lyrical *cantabile*, section 2, and the *cabaletta*, section 4. The opening becomes freer both in text construction and musical setting; the third section keeps its character while enlarging its role in the design. Still, considering the gap of thirty years, a piece such as the duet for Violetta and Alfredo in the last act of *La Traviata*, the text of which is given in Example 5, parallels the Rossinian model in most respects.

Example 5
Duet for Alfredo and Violetta from *La Traviata*, Act 3, by Verdi (1853) (translation adapted from the translation of the libretto by William Weaver in *Verdi Librettos* [New York: Anchor Books, 1963]. ⓒ by William Weaver)

Section 1:

ALF:	Colpevol sono . . . so tutto, o cara . . .	ALF:	I'm to blame . . . I know all, my dear . . .
VIO:	Il so che alfine reso mi sei!	VIO:	I know that at last you've been restored to me!
ALF:	Da questo palpito, s'io t'ami impara, Senza te esistere più non potrei.	ALF:	See how I love you from my heart's beating, I could exist no longer without you.
VIO:	Ah s'anco in vita m'hai ritrovata, Credi che uccidere non può il dolor.	VIO:	Ah, if you've found me still alive, You must believe that grief cannot kill.
ALF:	Scorda l'affanno, donna adorata, A me perdona e al genitor.	ALF:	Forget your grief, adored woman, Forgive me and my father.
VIO:	Ch'io ti perdoni? la rea son io: Ma solo amor tal me rendè.	VIO:	I, forgive you? I'm the guilty one: But it was love alone that made me so.
à 2:	Null'uomo o demon, angiol mio, Mai più dividermi potrà da te.	à 2:	No man or demon, my angel, Will even again separate me from you.

Section 2:

Alf: Parigi, o cara, noi lasceremo,
     La vita uniti trascorreremo . . .
     De' corsi affanni compenso avrai,
     La tua salute rifiorirà . . .
     Sospiro e luce tu mi sarai,
     Tutto il futuro ne arriderà.

Vio: Parigi, o caro, noi lasceremo,
     La vita uniti trascorreremo . . .
     De' corsi affanni compenso avrai,
     La mia salute rifiorirà . . .
     Sospiro e luce tu mi sarai,
     Tutto il futuro ne arriderà.

Alf: We will leave Paris, O beloved,
     We'll spend our life together . . .
     You'll be rewarded for your past sufferings,
     Your health will bloom again . . .
     You'll be my light, my breath,
     All the future will smile on us.

Vio: We will leave Paris, O beloved,
     We'll spend our life together . . .
     You'll be rewarded for your past sufferings,
     My health will bloom again . . .
     You'll be my light, my breath,
     All the future will smile on us.

Section 3:

Vio: Ah non più . . . a un tempio,
     / Alfredo andiamo,
     Del tuo ritorno grazie rendiamo.
Alf: Tu impallidisci! . . .
Vio: E nulla, sai?
     Gioia improvvisa non entra mai,
     Senza turbarlo, in mesto core.
Alf: Gran Dio! . . . Violetta!
Vio: È il mio malore!
     Fu debolezza . . . Ora son forte . . .
     Vedi! sorrido . . .
Alf: (Ahi cruda sorte!)
Vio: Fu nulla! . . . Annina, dammi a vestire.
Alf: Adesso? . . . attendi . . .
Vio: No! Voglio uscire.
     Gran Dio! Non posso!
Alf: (Cielo! che vedo!)
     Va pel Dottore . . .
Vio: Ah! digli che Alfredo
     È ritornato . . . all'amor mio . . .
     Digli che vivere . . . ancor vogl'io . . .
     Ma se tornando non m'hai salvato,
     A niuno in terra salvarmi è dato.

Vio: No more . . . to a church . . . Alfredo, let us go,
     Let us give thanks for your return.
Alf: You're pale! . . .
Vio: It's nothing, you know.
     Sudden joy never enters
     A sad heart, without upsetting it.
Alf: Oh God! . . . Violetta!
Vio: It's my illness!
     Weakness . . . Now I'm strong . . .
     You see? I'm smiling . . .
Alf: (Alas, cruel fate!)
Vio: It was nothing! . . . Annina, give me my clothes.
Alf: Now? . . . Wait . . .
Vio: No! . . . I want to go out.
     Good God! I can't!
Alf: (Heaven! What do I see!)
     Go for the Doctor . . .
Vio: Ah! Tell him . . . that Alfredo
     Has come back . . . to my love . . .
     Tell him . . . I want to live again . . .
     But if, by coming back, you haven't saved me,
     Then no one on earth has the power to save me.

221

Section 4 (cabaletta):

Vio: Gran Dio! morir sì giovine,
     Io che penato ho tanto!
     Morir sì presso a tergere
     Il mio sì lungo pianto!
     Ah! dunque fu delirio
     La credula speranza!
     Invano di costanza
     Armato avrò il mio cor! . . .

Vio: Great God! . . . to die so young,
     I who have suffered so much!
     To die so close to drying
     My many, many tears!
     Ah! So my credulous hope
     Was delirium!
     I've armed my heart
     With constancy, in vain!

ALF: Oh mio sospiro e palpito,
      Diletto del cor mio!
      Le mie colle tue lagrime
      Confondere degg'io!
      Ma più che mai, deh! credilo
      M'è d'uopo di costanza . . .
      Ah tutto alla speranza
      Non chiudere il tuo cor!

VIO: Oh Alfredo, il crudo termine
      Serbato al nostro amor!
ALF: Ah! Violetta mia, deh! calmati.
      M'uccide il tuo dolor.

ALF: Oh, my breath and pulse,
      Delight of my heart!
      I must mingle
      My tears with yours!
      But more than ever, believe me,
      I need your constancy . . .
      Ah, don't close your heart
      To hope entirely!

VIO: Oh, Alfredo, the cruel end
      Destined for our love!
ALF: Ah! My Violetta, please be calm!
      Your grief destroys me.

222

The two principal lyrical moments are presented in parallel stanzas, at "Parigi, o cara" and then at the *cabaletta,* "Gran Dio! morir si giovine." The poetic meter of sections 1 through 3 is the same, but the character of the sections is already visible in the text. In the first section, the characters alternate lines of text within three four-line stanzas; in the second, the characters have essentially the same six-line stanza; in the third, there is no stanzaic structure at all. Rhymes come instead on successive lines, and the poetry splits the dialogue irregularly.[30] Only in the final section does the meter change, and here there are two parallel stanzas.

The text, then, has already forced Verdi's hand. The structure of the piece is perfectly clear, and Verdi need only ring out his incomparable melodies to achieve the duet (see Example 6).

Example 6
La Traviata, Duet Alfredo-Violetta, Act 3
a) First section:

30. Modern "editions" of the librettos, even such fine ones as the collection with English translations by William Weaver (*Verdi Librettos* [New York, 1963]), completely obscure the structure of the text.

b) Second section:

c) Third section:

223

d) Fourth section, *cabaletta*:

The opening section is organized into an extended musical period in dialogue (Example 6a). The second section is quasi-canonic: Alfredo first singing the tune, then Violetta, with some background from Alfredo (Example 6b). The two come together into a conventional cadential phrase which Verdi gives character by differentiating Alfredo's rather suave and beautiful line and Violetta's more hysterical counterpoint. The third section is quite free, the music following each gesture of the dialogue, adopting too an occasional lyrical line (Example 6c). The *cabaletta* is completely standard. Violetta takes the tune; Alfredo repeats it exactly; a short middle section in dialogue leads to Violetta's repetition of the theme, with accompanying lines for Alfredo (Example 6d). Cadences conclude the piece.[31]

Though Verdi did not always respond so docilely in his middle period to the "demands" of the text, he was constantly offered dramatic situations in the same molds. We can better understand, then, why Verdi wrote just before the premiere of *La Traviata* that he sought subjects "bold to the core, with *new forms*, yet at the same time appropriate for music. . . ." His favorite librettists, Piave and Cammarano, provided texts largely divided into numbers internally constructed in conventional molds. Verdi could and did protest, could and did bully. But the press of his commitments, the recalcitrance of his librettists, and his own artistic beliefs often lead him to adopt the texts given and to do with them what he could. Nowhere is this attitude clearer than in his correspondence about *Aida*. Verdi was the undisputed master of Italian opera in 1870, yet the complaint he raised in 1853 persisted. His relationship to the old models, however, whether he adopted, adapted, or rejected them, was curiously ambivalent. Selective and out-of-context quotation from his correspondence has effectively obscured this fact.

Example 7 gives the definitive text of the Amneris-Radames duet in act 4. Before following its earlier stages, we might analyze the final product in terms of the established model.

Example 7

Duet for Amneris and Radames from *Aida*, Act 4, by Verdi (1870–72) (translation and copyright as noted for Example 5)

Section 1:

AMN: Già i sacerdoti adunansi
  Arbitri del tuo fato;
  Pur dell'accusa orribile
  Scolparti ancor t'è dato;
  Ti scolpa, e la tua grazia
  Io pregherò dal trono
  E nunzia di perdono,
  Di vita a te sarò.
	AMN: Already the priests are meeting,
	  The arbiters of your fate;
	  And yet against the horrible charge
	  You can still defend yourself.
	  Defend yourself, and I will plead
	  For your pardon from the throne,
	  And for you I will be the messenger
	  Of forgiveness and life.

31. Notice that the duet no longer has tonal closure so typical of Rossini's practice earlier in the century. This permits more fluid tonal design in the opera as a whole while also blurring the outlines of some formal "numbers." "Gran Dio! morir si giovine" was originally written in Db major, with the close of section 3 correspondingly different. Verdi lowered the *cabaletta* to C major in his revision of the opera in 1854. On all counts the original key is better: it gives a more coherent conclusion to the duet (whose *cantabile* section is in Ab major) and a more effective transition to the final scene (the concluding "Db" becoming the melodic "C♯" in the ensuing A major chord). The transition Verdi penned to get from C major to A major is surely one of the most awkward passages in all his operas.

RAD: Di mie discolpe i giudici
Mai non udran l'accento;
Dinanzi ai Numi, agli uomini
Nè vil, nè reo mi sento.
Profferse il labbro incauto
Fatal segreto, è vero,
Ma puro il mio pensiero
E l'onor mio restò.

AMN: Salvati dunque e scolpati.
RAD: No.
AMN: Tu morrai . . .
RAD: La vita
Abborro; d'ogni gaudio
La fonte inaridita,
Svanita ogni speranza
Sol bramo di morir.

Section 2:
AMN: Morire! Ah! tu dei vivere! . . .
Sì, all'amor mio vivrai;
Per te le angoscie orribili
Di morte io già provai;
T'amai, soffersi tanto . . .
Vegliai le notti in pianto . . .
E patria, e trono, e vita
Tutto darei per te.

RAD: Per essa anch'io la patria
E l'onor mio tradia . . .

Section 3:
AMN: Di lei non più . . .
RAD: L'infamia
M'attende e vuoi ch'io viva?
Misero appien mi festi,
Aida a me togliesti,
Spenta l'hai forse . . . e in dono
Offri la vita a me?
AMN: Io . . . di sua morte origine!
No! . . . vive Aida . . .
RAD: Vive!
AMN: Nei disperati aneliti
Dell'orde fuggitive
Sol cadde il padre . . .
RAD: Ed ella?
AMN: Sparve, ne più novella
S'ebbe . . .
RAD: Gli Dei l'adducano
Salva alle patrie mura,
E ignori la sventura
Di chi per lei morrà!
AMN: Ma, s'io ti salvo, giurami
Che più non la vedrai . . .

RAD: The judges will never hear
A word of self-defense from me;
Before the Gods and men,
I do not feel base or guilty:
My impulsive lips revealed
A fatal secret, it's true,
But my thoughts and my honor
Remained pure.

AMN: Save yourself, then, and defend yourself.
RAD: No.
AMN: You will die . . .
RAD: I hate
Life; the source of all joy
Has dried up,
All hope vanished,
I long only to die.

AMN: Die! Ah! You must live! . . .
Yes, you will live, for my love;
I have already experienced
Death's horrible anguish because of you;
I loved you, I suffered so . . .
I lay awake nights in tears . . .
And country, throne, my life,
All I would give for you.

RAD: For her I too betrayed my country
And my honor . . .

AMN: No more of her . . .
RAD: Dishonor
Awaits me, and you want me to live?
You made me completely wretched,
You took Aida from me,
Perhaps you have killed her . . .
And you offer me life as a gift?
AMN: I . . . cause of her death!
No . . . Aida is alive . . .
RAD: Alive!
AMN: In the desperate race
Of the fleeing hordes
Only her father fell . . .
RAD: And she?
AMN: She vanished, nor was there news
Of her . . .
RAD: May the Gods lead her
Safely to her native walls,
May she never know the misfortune
Of him who will die for her!
AMN: But, if I save you, swear to me
That you will not see her again . . .

225

RAD: Nol posso!

AMN: A lei rinunzia
      Per sempre . . . E tu vivrai!

RAD: Nol posso!

AMN: Anco una volta
      A lei rinunzia . . .

RAD: È vano . . .

AMN: Morir vuoi dunque, insano?

RAD: Pronto a morir son già.

Section 4 (cabaletta):

AMN: Chi ti salva, sciagurato,
      Dalla sorte che t'aspetta?
      In furore hai tu cangiato
      Un'amor ch'egual non ha.
      De' miei pianti la vendetta
      Or dal ciel si compirà.

RAD: È la morte un ben supremo
      Se per lei morir m'è dato;
      Nel subir l'estremo fato
      Gaudii immensi il cor avrà.
      L'ira umana più non temo,
      Temo sol la tua pietà.

RAD: I cannot!

AMN: Give her up forever
      And you will live!

RAD: I cannot!

AMN: Once more
      Give her up . . .

RAD: It's useless . . .

AMN: You want to die then, madman?

RAD: I am already prepared to die.

AMN: Who will save you, wretch,
      From the fate that awaits you?
      You have changed into fury
      A love that has no equal.
      Now revenge for my weeping
      Will be taken by heaven.

RAD: Death is the supreme boon,
      If I am to die for her;
      In submitting to my final destiny
      My heart will have immense joy.
      I fear human wrath no longer,
      I fear only your pity.

226

The duet begins with two parallel stanzas for Amneris and Radames, each eight verses long with identical rhyme schemes and a final masculine ending in common. This exactly parallels the typical Rossinian opening. They continue in dialogue, with Radames singing several successive lines, until a masculine ending brings this "stanza" of six lines to a close. Amneris then has an entire stanza to herself; Radames begins another, but it is broken off by Amneris. The parallelism is nonetheless inherent, and we may suspect that with Amneris's full stanza we arrive at the second section of the duet, the lyrical internal section. The preceding six-line stanza, then, would represent a freer preparation for this lyrical moment. The verses which follow this lyrical section, while maintaining a similar poetic structure, are freer in design, divided between the characters with the meaning carried over from line to line. This must give rise to a more directly dramatic musical setting, with the possible exception of the short passage beginning "Gli Dei l'adducano," which might call forth a more lyrical phrase. The dialogue continues through Radames's "Pronto a morir son già." Now, for the first time in the duet, the structure of the verse changes, and in place of seven-syllable lines we find eight-syllable lines, organized into two parallel stanzas of six verses each, with masculine endings on lines 4 and 6. This certainly looks like an invitation to a *cabaletta.*

The text in its final form, then, parallels closely the typical Rossinian duet structure. Did Verdi fight against this text? What were the primitive versions like? In setting it, ultimately, does he follow the dictates of tradition, or does he reinterpret them? The letters to Ghislanzoni, even in the absence of the latter's responses, are extremely instructive.

Verdi first refers to the duet in a letter dated October 16, before Ghislanzoni had sent any text for act 4. He observes that the scene has great possibilities, and adds:

> Develop this situation then as you think best, and let it be well developed, and have the characters say what they must without concerning yourself in the least about the musical form.[32]

This sounds like Verdi the progressive, who cares nothing about convention; but he continues:

> Of course if you send me a recitative from beginning to end, I would be unable to create rhythmic music, but if you begin directly with some rhythm and continue it until the end I will not complain at all. Just perhaps it should be changed so as to make a little cabalettina at the end.

This is very different. Free verses or verse forms, that is, "recitative," would be unacceptable. Verdi wants a single rhythm from the beginning, changed only at the end to make a *cabaletta*. He is asking for a piece constructed rhythmically exactly as was the duet from *La Traviata*. This negates in large part his prior remark that Ghislanzoni should not worry "in the least about the musical form."

The next day, Monday, October 17, Verdi examined the *Aida* scenario and found the prose text of the duet worked out with Ghislanzoni in July. He copied it out for Ghislanzoni, adding annotations concerning the musical form. This scenario parallels in prose most of the verses of the finished text. Amneris's opening remarks are followed by those of Radames. Amneris does not interrupt him, however, entering again only at "Morire." Verdi feared that Ghislanzoni might put these opening speeches into freer verse, recitative, and he adds a note beside them:

> Beginning with a recitative, it might be difficult to find a place to attack the *cantabile*. It seems to me we could begin immediately with lyric verses, of whatever meter, and continue with the same meter until the end.

This echoes his remark of the previous day.

32. Quotations are from the original manuscripts when these are at the Pierpont Morgan Library; other letters follow the texts given in *Cop*. Dates follow the Postulated Correct Order shown in table 1. All translations are my own.

Verdi continues with the speech for Amneris beginning "Morire!" and the ensuing dialogue, adding alongside the text for Radames which corresponds to "Gli Dei l'adducano" of the final version:

> Much sentiment in this aside: so that a beautiful melodic phrase can be developed.

At the end, alongside Amneris's final speech, Verdi writes:

> Here alone it would be good to change the meter, and make a stanza of four or six verses for a short cabaletta.

He marks Radames' stanza "Idem." The prose corresponds to the text I have called a *cabaletta* in the completed version.

By Tuesday, October 25, Verdi had received Ghislanzoni's verses, and he was not pleased. In particular, Ghislanzoni seems to have ignored Verdi's advice about the opening, having begun with recitative, postponing the lyrical, metric poetry until "Morire!" Verdi makes this brief observation in his letter of October 25:

> . . . it seems to me that the duet should begin directly with a lyrical form. In this opening of the duet there is (if I am not mistaken) something elevated and noble, especially in Radames, that I would prefer to have sung. A melody *sui generis;* not the melody of romances or cavatinas, but a declaimed melody, sustained and lofty. The meter can be as you wish; even break up the dialogue if you think that will be more lively.

He then proceeds to comment on some of Ghislanzoni's verses. Amneris's opening stanza, in this primitive version, began: "Morir? che parli? ah misero!" Other lines included "te spento anch'io morrei" and "Com'io t'ho sempre amato." Verdi finds that:

> . . . in the lyrical verses for Amneris there are two or three which weaken the character a bit,

and he cites these. Keep "Morir!" he adds, but dispense with "che parli? ah misero!" The composer clearly believes in this piece, and he concludes:

> If this duet can be given a good opening, you will see what importance it will have in the whole opera.

The very next day, Wednesday, October 26, he writes again:

> After having answered your letter yesterday, I set myself to study

at length the duet of the fourth act, and I am ever more convinced that it must be given, from the beginning, lyrical form. With the very words of the recitative I pieced together some seven-syllable verses, and saw it was possible to make a melody. It might seem strange, a melody on words that seem to be spoken by a lawyer. But under these legal words, there is the heart of a woman desperate and burning of love. Music can succeed splendidly in depicting this state of mind and saying, in some way, two things at once.

Now, Verdi lays out the beginning exactly as he wants it. Amneris's opening remarks are to consist of a

> Stanza of eight verses: verses to be sung: And arrange them so that the melody can be expanded on the words: "Pregherò il Re" and "Spero nel perdono." If eight verses are too few, make 16.

This stanza is to be followed directly by one for Radames:

> Another stanza like that of Amneris. Here too let the last verses be made so that an expansive melody can be written . . . "expansive," not "shouted."

229

The text Verdi provides incorporates only the material in Radames' stanza in the final version. He also sketches out the remainder of the opening, now for the first time with Amneris's intervention, and adds:

> And here another stanza of 4, 6, or 8 verses, as you like, in dialogue, with whatever words you think best.

This opening is to be followed by:

> . . . the stanza of Amneris with the rest, as it is.

He adds some particular observations but assures Ghislanzoni that he should

> . . . do it as it best succeeds. Only be sure not to write verses which say little. In this duet, every verse, indeed every word must have *meaning*. [. . .] I repeat again, this duet must be sustained and lofty in its verse as in its music. In short, nothing common.

Verdi has now dictated the structure of the start of the duet, just as before he had dictated its conclusion. Despite his "In short, nothing common," despite his telling Ghislanzoni not to "worry in the least about the musical form," he has forced Ghislanzoni to construct the beginning and end of the composition in a manner that parallels exactly the most conventional approach to the duet text in nineteenth-century Italian opera.

On Thursday, October 27, the next day, he returns again briefly to this piece. He had been working hard on the music and seems particularly disturbed with the dialogue. Almost petulantly he complains:

> The verses are too broken up, and there is no way of making a melody, not even some long melodic phrase.

But his most interesting objection is:

> . . . the cabaletta, for the situation, is long. Ah! these cursed cabalettas, that always have the same form and all resemble one another! Let's see a bit if it is possible to find something more novel.

One wonders how Ghislanzoni must have reacted to this, since Verdi had dictated the presence of the *cabaletta* from his first letter. Finally, Verdi sums up this correspondence:

> As for the beginning of this duet, I really think it would be best to proceed as I wrote yesterday. A lovely melody, calm, long, extended for Amneris; another of the same for Radames; then some verses of dialogue to arrive at the other solo of Amneris as in your original text, changing a few verses, however, to arrive with the original text at "Or s'io ti salvo." Do not fear that these lengthy stanzas will seem cold. Let the verse be sustained and beautiful, as you know how, and have no doubts about this duet.

In this series of letters, then, Verdi led Ghislanzoni into casting the confrontation between Amneris and Radames completely in the Rossinian mold.

On November 2, Verdi says that he awaits "with anxiety" the opening duet of the fourth act. On November 4 he repeats:

> I have not yet received the changes for the first duet (Act IV).

The next day, Saturday, November 5, the text arrived, and he writes to Ghislanzoni:

> But it is just lovely this duet! lovely, lovely, lovely! After that of the third act between Aida and Amonasro, this seems to me the best of all. If you could find a form somewhat more novel for the cabaletta this duet would be perfect. In any case, we can adjust this by changing some verses. . . . And try a bit to make a long verse and then a short one; for example, one of eight syllables and one of five; or one of eight and one of seven; or one of seven and one of five; or one of ten and one of seven. Let's see what the devil will emerge.

Ghislanzoni apparently had no desire to accommodate Verdi here; the *cabaletta* text remained stolidly eight-syllable verses, six to a stanza.

Largely through his own doing, then, Verdi was faced with a totally conventional text, and it is hardly surprising that his musical response was dependent on earlier models. The opening stanzas are set to two identical musical periods (Example 8); they differ only in key and slightly at the concluding cadence.

Example 8
Aida, Duet Radames-Amneris, Act 4, Section 1

a) Amneris opening period:

231

b) Radames parallel stanza:

Even the orchestration is identical. A section more *arioso* in quality leads to the central lyrical section, Amneris's "Morire! Ah! tu dei vivere." Verdi effectively includes the word "Morire!" as part of the preceding section, beginning the *cantabile* with "Ah! tu dei vivere." The vocalization on "Ah!" that results (for there are now not enough syllables for the melody) is somewhat awkward (Example 9), but the effect of "Morire!" coming before the *cantabile*, a true *parola scenica*, more than compensates.

Example 9
Aida, Duet Radames-Amneris, Act 4, Section 2

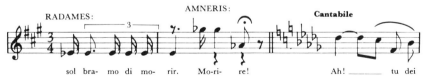

The central lyrical section includes the *cantabile* for Amneris, with Radames, to a fuller orchestration, repeating the cadential phrase, reminding Amneris that what she consciously offers him is what he, unconsciously, did for Aida. She stops him cold, and the section continues in dialogue. Verdi begins by returning briefly to the theme of the opening section (a technique characteristic of many Rossini duets) and continues in *arioso* style. The dialogue centers around Amneris, and her melodic line gradually rises from a low Eb up to B natural (see Example 10).

Example 10
Aida, Duet Radames-Amneris, Act 4, Section 3

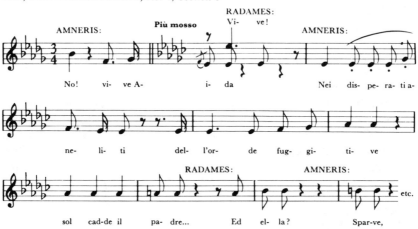

Picking up this pitch, Radames sings a lyrical period at "Gli Dei l'adducano." (Recall that Verdi had intended to place one here from the start.) But Amneris will not be put off. Beginning again on the same pitch, B, her line gradually moves chromatically up to Eb, with Radames following each step. Finally at "È vano," he takes the lead, moving the line to E natural; at "Morir" she brings it up to F; and at "Pronto a morir son già" he goes to the high G, which functions as the dominant for the ensuing *cabaletta*. This dialogue is simply but extremely well organized, the tension ever increasing until it explodes at the start of the *cabaletta*, "Chi ti salva, sciagurato."

Having himself set up the *cabaletta*, Verdi added, "Let's see a bit if it is possible to find something more novel." The conventional musical gesture here would be to set Amneris's stanza to a *cabaletta* theme. Radames would repeat the theme, a short middle section would lead to a final repetition of the theme, with both voices participating. Such a structure would be eminently possible with this text; Radames' text fits Amneris's music perfectly (see Example 11).

Example 11
Aida, Duet Radames-Amneris, Act 4, Section 4: *Cabaletta* Theme (Amneris), with Hypothetical Parallel Stanza for Radames

233

But Verdi's desire for new forms, and the obvious difference in the sentiments his characters express, Amneris's revenge and Radames' joy at being able to die for Aida, inspires him to search for an alternative procedure. His solution is simple enough. Amneris sings her full strophe in C minor. When she concludes, Radames begins, but instead of repeating her phrase he has a new phrase of his own, in C major, at a slightly slower tempo (see Example 12).

Example 12
Aida, Duet Radames-Amneris, Act 4, Section 4: Actual *cabaletta* Theme for Radames

234

The contrast is telling. Since at the fifth line of his stanza he turns from his abstract consideration of death to a challenge directed at Amneris, Verdi uses only the first four lines of the stanza for the lyrical period. Then he repeats the close of Amneris's theme, a gesture that fits the situation well but which derives directly from the *cabaletta* tradition. Only in the final cadences do we hear Radames' last lines together with the last two lines for Amneris. The voices are clearly in opposition, until the final cadence when they sing forth their mutual scorn in unison.

During a final orchestral section, Radames is led out by guards. Verdi uses this concluding passage to modulate out of C minor and to prepare the key of the following *scena del giudizio*. However effective, it remains an external gesture, in no way providing real continuity. Such transitions hardly break down divisions between numbers. Mozart did similar things in *Don Giovanni;* Rossini's operas are filled with them.

The statements most often quoted from Verdi's letters to Ghislanzoni are those in which he asks the librettist for new forms, inveighs against *cabalettas*, seeks peculiar combinations of verses, etc. But Verdi's attitude toward form was really much more ambivalent. Aware of the conventions, raised in them, working with a librettist also nurtured by them and unable to proffer anything truly new and yet musical, Verdi's bullying was by no means consistently along "reformist" lines. In this duet, at least, the most conventional aspects spring directly from the composer.

It need hardly be emphasized, however, that observations concerning the presence or absence of conventional forms are not at all equivalent to aesthetic judgments concerning the quality of the music.

A similar ambivalence pervades the other duets. The text for the Aida-Amneris duet in act 2 arrived by August 14, and on August 17 Verdi wrote about it at length to Ghislanzoni. The duet begins with several stanzas, one for Aida, a parallel one for Amneris, and then another, in a different meter, for Amneris. Verdi sets the parallel stanzas contrapuntally, with Aida's melody clearly in control. Amneris's metrically contrasting stanza balances the opening period so that the confrontation typical of the duet remains present. Then, as Verdi says, "the action warms up." Here Verdi objects to the strict stanzas Ghislanzoni sent. He wants instead more "parole sceniche." Instead of Ghislanzoni's:

> Per Radames d'amore
> Ardo e mi sei rivale.
> —Che? voi l'amate?—Io l'amo
> E figlia son d'un re,

Verdi suggests:

> Tu l'ami? ma l'amo anch'io, intendi? La figlia dei Faraoni è tua rivale! AIDA: Mia rivale? E sia: anch'io son figlia . . .

Adding:

> I know well what you will say to me: And the verse, the rhyme, the stanza? I don't know what to say; but when the action demands it, I would abandon immediately rhythm, rhyme, stanza; I would make irregular verses so as to be able to say clearly and precisely everything the action demands. Unfortunately, for the theatre it is sometimes necessary that poets and composers have the talent to make neither poetry nor music.

Verdi clearly liked that line. He had used it already in a letter to Giulio Ricordi of July 10. But this must be understood in context. Verdi is talking about dialogue, traditionally handled freely in the music. Even when Ghislanzoni supplies rhythm, rhyme, and stanza (as in the Amneris-Radames duet), Verdi sets it as so much prose. In this duet, the heart of the dramatic action comes between the initial section and the lyrical middle section instead of between the latter and the *cabaletta*. Despite this reversal, all traditional parts of the standard duet are present. The verses remain free until Aida's "Pietà ti prenda del mio dolor," where two parallel stanzas for Aida and Amneris are worked into a lyrical duet. Aida sings first, Amneris takes a contrasting phrase, and Aida's tune returns at the end, with Amneris singing counterpoint.

235

The remainder of Ghislanzoni's text presumably resembled Example 13.

Example 13
Duet for Aida and Amneris from *Aida,* Act 2, *Cabaletta* (Original Version) (translation and copyright as noted for Example 5)

Coro:	Su! del Nilo al sacro lido	Coro:	Hasten to the Nile's sacred shore
	Sien barriera i nostri petti;		Let our breasts be shields;
	Non eccheggi che un sol grido:		Let a sole cry echo forth:
	Guerra e morte allo stranier!		War and death to the foreigner!
Amn:	Alla pompa che s'appresta	Amn:	You, slave, will attend with me
	Meco, o schiava, assisterai;		The triumph that is being prepared;
	Tu prostrata nella polvere,		You, prostrate in the dust,
	Io sul trono accanto al Re.		I on the throne, beside the King.
	Vien . . . mi segui, apprenderai		Come . . . follow me. You will learn
	Se lottar tu puoi con me.		Whether you can compete with me.
Aid:	Ah! pietà! che più mi resta?	Aid:	Ah! Pity! What have I left?
	Un deserto è la mia vita:		My life is a desert;
	Vivi e regna, il tuo furore		Live and reign, I will soon
	Io tra breve placherò.		Placate your fury.
	Quest'amore che t'irrita		This love that annoys you
	Di scordare lo tenterò.		I will try to forget.

The off-stage chorus, the returning armies, sing a reprise of their war hymn from act 1, followed by parallel stanzas for Aida and Amneris. Verdi writes:

> The duet finishes with one of the usual cabalettas, and even too long for the situation. Let's see what can be done in the music. In any event, I don't think it good for Aida to say:
> > Questo amore che t'irrita
> > Di scordare lo tenterò.

In the final version, Ghislanzoni changed the last line to read "nella tomba spegnerò." Again faced with a *cabaletta* design, Verdi did not ask Ghislanzoni to alter either the structure or content of the poetry. Instead, he sought another way to accommodate the traditional *cabaletta,* and succeeded particularly well. The reprise of the chorus, instead of functioning as a mere introduction to the *cabaletta,* becomes an integral part of it, with Amneris singing over the chorus. Aida's lines are then set to different music, and the protagonists can interact briefly, before the duet and reprise of the hymn conclude simultaneously (see Example 14).

Example 14
Aida, Duet Aida-Amneris, *Cabaletta*

If we take Verdi's letter literally, Ghislanzoni's duet finished here.[33] In a sublime, yet simple touch, Verdi keeps Aida on stage after Amneris's departure and has her sing a short reprise of her first-act aria, "Numi, pietà del mio martir." It is a telling and beautiful gesture, but we must be careful to recognize it as the external gesture it is and not pretend that the duet to which it is appended becomes any less an obvious development of classical procedures because of it. On August 22, Verdi received and approved the corrections. Ghislanzoni presumably responded to the composer's remarks about *cabalettas,* and Verdi answers:

> Have no doubt, I do not abhor cabalettas, but wish only that there be an appropriate subject and pretext.

Verdi returned to the problem of *cabalettas* on September 28, when he received the text of act 3.

> I see you are afraid of two things: of some, shall I say, theatrical *boldness,* and of *not making cabalettas!* I remain of the opinion that cabalettas must be used when the situation demands them. Those of the two duets [in act 3—between Aida and Amonasro and then Aida and Radames] are not demanded by the situation. In the duet between father and daughter, it seems especially out of place. Aida is in such a state of fear and moral depression that she cannot and must not sing a cabaletta.

Here the composer had his way. In Ghislanzoni's original text, Aida's part concluded with a stanza in which she enthusiastically agreed to

----

33. Indeed, in its primitive version the duet probably did conclude here. In a letter of December 2, 1871, just before the Cairo premiere, Verdi wrote to Giulio Ricordi (see Abbiati [3:515] for an incomplete text; the entire text is translated by Busch, whose translation I use for those parts not in Abbiati):

> I have made another change at the end of the Aida-Amneris duet in the second act. It is about the same as before, but the few changes made require it to be newly copied. So have patience once more; this version will remain. Please have it copied as quickly as possible, and send it immediately to Cairo so that it will be performed there, if it is possible.

And on December 7 (according to Busch; the date of December 17 given in *Cop,* p. 677, is surely incorrect), Verdi wrote to the conductor in Cairo, Giovanni Bottesini:

> I have made a change in the stretta of the duet for the two women in the second act. I sent it two or three days ago to Ricordi, who should already have forwarded it to Cairo. As soon as it arrives, I urgently request you to have the two artists rehearse it and to perform it. The original stretta seemed to me a bit common. The one I have redone is not and finishes well, provided that, when the motive of the scena from the first act returns, Pozzoni [the Cairo Aida] sings it while walking falteringly towards the back of the stage.

This seems to imply that the reprise of "Numi, pietà" was a change introduced in December 1871 and that the original version was even more closely dependent on inherited formal models than the piece we have today. It seems likely that a copy would survive preserving the original ending, but none has been referred to in the Verdi literature.

betray her beloved, beginning "Della patria il sacro amor." Verdi insisted this be changed, saying again:

> For my part, I would abandon forms of stanzas, rhythm; I would not think of having them sing and would render the situation as it is, were it even in verses of recitative.

Ghislanzoni sent a revision, and on October 7 Verdi continued his commentary. Though he was unhappy, Ghislanzoni finally sent Verdi what the composer wanted, and on October 16 Verdi writes:

> As for the duet between father and daughter, the changes prejudice nothing. Indeed, Aida, in my opinion, now says what she ought to say and is truly in character.

In this duet, Verdi fought the librettist not only about details but about the basic conception. Through his insistence he created a remarkable dramatic confrontation, which he clearly considered to be the finest piece in the opera.

239

But Verdi could not alone sustain such an attack on basic principles. Having said that the *cabaletta* in the Aida-Radames duet was also "not demanded by the situation," he nonetheless accepted it, though not without protest. On October 8, after Ghislanzoni had already revised the duet, Verdi writes:

> Let it be said once for always that I never intend to speak of your verses, which are always fine, but to give my opinion on the scenic effect. The duet between Radames and Aida is, for me, greatly inferior to the other between father and daughter. The cause may be the situation or perhaps the form, which is more common than the preceding duet. Certainly this succession of cantabiles of eight verses, sung by one and repeated by the other, is not going to keep the dialogue alive. Let me add, too, that the material between these cantabiles is rather cold.

But it was Verdi who, on September 30, had requested Ghislanzoni to write a stanza for Radames matching Aida's lyrical stanza, which begins "Fuggiam gli ardori inospiti" and continues with the lyrical "Là tra foreste vergini," so that he was directly complicit in arranging the internal lyrical section. As for the conclusion of the duet, where Radames and Aida decide to fly from Egypt together, its text is quite close in meaning to the internal lyrical duet, though more assertive and decisive. Already on September 30 Verdi had questioned its purpose:

> Why in this cantabile did you change the meter, saying almost the same things? It would perhaps have been better to repeat the

earlier stanzas. But now leave them as they are, and we'll see what can be done.

Verdi hardly had to ask "why." Ghislanzoni had changed the meter at the end to set up a *cabaletta,* and on October 16 Verdi asks the poet to add extra verses for Radames:

> . . . since we have entered the path of cantabiles and cabalettas, we must continue in that direction, and Radames should respond with eight verses to the eight of Aida. . . .

Verdi not only accepted the *cabaletta,* then, but had Ghislanzoni make it more standard by preparing a parallel stanza for Radames. Example 15 gives the cabaletta theme as sung first by Radames.

Example 15
Aida, Duet Aida-Radames, *Cabaletta* Theme

240

The tune is in the mold typical of early Verdi, a a¹ b a², and it is immediately repeated by Aida. The continuation quotes and now completes the theme Radames had tried to sing at the opening of the duet but whose enthusiasm Aida then could not share.

Despite this device, the conventional aspects of the duet were not lost on Verdi's contemporaries,[34] and the *cabaletta* in particular was singled out for scorn by "progressive," Wagnerian-oriented critics such as Filippo Filippi of Milan, who wrote:

> The cabaletta is of that genre no longer adapted to the tastes of the public. The public does not look well on cabalettas.[35]

To which sentiment Verdi responded in a letter to his friend Opprandino Arrivabene on April 27, 1872

> As you know, *Aida* went well and they wrote me that also the third and fourth performances were fine with a packed house. Leave in peace, then, the cabaletta that bothers you so. Certainly it is no masterpiece, but there are many, many others much worse. Only right now it has become fashionable to rail against and to want no cabalettas. This is an error as great as that of the time when nothing but cabalettas were desired. They scream so against conventions, and abandon one only to embrace another! Like fat, stupid sheep![36]

But on April 6 he had already announced plans to revise at least the orchestration of the *cabaletta*, writing to Giulio Ricordi:

> I would like only to revise the instrumentation of that so horrible cabaletta, which has brought me so much advice, so much wisdom, and so much benevolence from your critics! Send me, then, the original of that cabaletta.[37]

34. Though Verdi clearly conceived of the act as a series of formal numbers during its composition, he ultimately felt that the outlines were blurred enough so that he could write Tito Ricordi on August 26, 1871 (the letter is cited after the translation to be published by Professor Busch):

> Tell your copyist that the entire third act, although it includes a choral scene, a solo scene for Aida, a scene with her father, another scene with her lover, a little trio and a finale, forms but a single scene, and therefore a single piece. In the orchestral parts, copy everything consecutively as it is in the score; in order to facilitate performance at the rehearsals, we will put in the rehearsal letters with A, B, C, etc. I think I myself can put in these letters later on, when you send the score that must go to Cairo for my review.

It is certainly true that the third act has a remarkable unity, but it is hard to view it as a "single piece," and it is quite clear that Verdi did not so consider it while he was composing.

35. Quoted in Annibale Alberti, *Verdi intimo: Carteggio di Giuseppe Verdi con il Conte Opprandino Arrivabene* (1861–1886) (Verona, 1931), p. 145 n.

36. Ibid., p. 144.

37. Abbiati, 3:570. The date of this letter, missing in Abbiati, is supplied by Professor Busch.

In the absence of a critical study of musical sources for *Aida,* the precise nature of the revision remains undetermined.

The finale of *Aida,* essentially a duet, stands as a last example of Verdi's ambivalence to inherited convention. The entire text is given in Example 16.

Example 16
Finale (Duet) for Aida and Amneris, Act 4, Definitive Text (translation and copyright as noted for Example 5)

Opening section:

Rad: Morir! sì pura e bella!   Rad: To die! So pure and beautiful!
      Morir per me d'amore ...   To die, for love of me ...
      Degli anni tuoi nel fiore,   In the bloom of your years,
      Fuggir la vita!   To flee from life!
      T'avea il ciel per l'amor creata   Heaven had created you for love,
      Ed io t'uccido per averti amata!   And I kill you because I loved you!
      No, non morrai!   No, you shall not die!
      Troppo t'amai! troppo sei bella!   I loved you too much! You are too
                                                                  / beautiful!

Aid: Vedi? di morte l'angelo   Aid: You see? ... The angel of death,
      Radiante a noi s'appressa ...   Radiant, is approaching us ...
      Ne adduce a eterni gaudii   He leads us to eternal bliss
      Sovra i suoi vanni d'or.   On his golden wings.
      Già veggo il ciel dischiudersi   I see heaven opening already,
      Ivi ogni affanno cessa ...   There all pain ceases ...
      Ivi comincia l'estasi   There begins the ecstasy
      D'un immortale amor.   Of immortal love.

Middle section:

Priestesses: Priestesses:
      Immenso, immenso Fthà ...   Mighty, mighty Ptah!
      Del mondo spirito animator ...   Life-giving spirit of the world ...
      Ah! noi t'invochiam!   We invoke thee!
Aid: Triste canto!   Aid: That sad chant!
Rad: Il tripudio dei sacerdoti ...   Rad: The celebration of the priests ...
Aid: Il nostro inno di morte ...   Aid: Our hymn of death ...
Rad: Nè le mei forti braccia   Rad: Nor can my strong arms
      Smuoverti potranno, o fatal pietra. Move you, O fatal stone!
Aid: Invan! Tutto è finito sulla terra per noi ...   Aid: In vain! All is finished on earth for us ...
Rad: È vero, è vero ...   Rad: It is true, it is true ...

Cabaletta:

à 2: O terra addio; addio valle di pianti ...   à 2: O earth, farewell; farewell, vale of tears ...
      Sogno di gaudio che in dolor svanì ...   Dream of joy that vanished in grief ...
      A noi si schiude il ciel e l'alme erranti   Heaven is opening to us and our wandering
                                                                           / spirits
      Volano al raggio dell'eterno dì.   Fly to the glow of eternal day.
Amn: Pace t'imploro   Amn: Peace, I beseech you,
      Salma adorata ...   Adored corpse,
      Isi placata   May Isis, assuaged,
      Ti schiuda il ciel ...   Open heaven to you ...

242

After some opening recitative, the duet originally began with Aida's stanza, "Vedi? di morte l'angelo." Ghislanzoni had difficulty deciding how Radames could respond and asked Verdi's advice. On November 2 Verdi made some suggestions, but after having received the text on Wednesday, November 9, the composer wrote on Saturday, November 12:

> After the beautiful seven-syllable verses for Aida, nothing can be found for Radames; and I would give Radames eight seven-syllable verses before, on the words: "You to die! You innocent, so beautiful, so young. Nor can I save you. . . . Oh sadness. My fatal love causes your death, etc. etc."

Laying out the entire scene, he again specifies: "Eight nice, singable, seven-syllable verses," thus asking for a stanza parallel to that already prepared for Aida. The next day, Sunday, November 13, Verdi returned to this question:

> We must avoid monotony by looking for uncommon forms. Yesterday I told you to make eight seven-syllable verses for Radames before the eight of Aida. These two solos, even if I write two dissimilar melodies, would have approximately the same form, the same character; and here we are in the commonplace. The French, even in their stanzas for melodies, sometimes use verses which are longer or shorter. Why could we not do the same? This entire scene can and must be nothing but a scene of pure and simple melody. An unusual verse form for Radames would oblige me to search for a melody diverse from those commonly used for seven- and eight-syllable verses, and would further oblige me to change the tempo and meter for the solo (a kind of *mezz'aria*) for Aida.

Verdi then sketches out a text:

> Morire! Tu, innocente?
> Morire! Tu, sì bella?
> Tu nell'april degli anni
> Lasciar la vita?
> Quant'io t'amai, no, no'l può dir favella!
> Ma fu mortale l'amor mio per te.
> Morire! Tu, innocente?
> Morire! Tu, sì bella?

> To die! You so innocent?
> To die! You so beautiful?
> You in the April of your years . . .
> To leave life?
> How much I loved you cannot be said!
> But my love was fatal for you.
> To die! You so innocent?
> To die! You so beautiful?

243

and continues:

> You cannot imagine what a beautiful melody can be made with such a strange form; and how graceful the five-syllable line is after three of seven syllables; and what variety the two succeeding eleven-syllable lines provide; both of these, however, should be either masculine or feminine. See if you can get some verses from this, and preserve "tu sì bella," which works so well at the cadence.

How revealing this is; Verdi is aware that not only does the procedure of the Amneris-Radames duet, which begins with parallel stanzas set to the same music, fall into a common mold but that even the expedient of setting the stanzas to different music (as, in a modified form, in the Aida-Amneris duet) only barely disguises the model. Creating dissimilar stanzas moves Verdi another step away from the model, to be sure, but it is outlined so clearly in his consciousness that it returns almost oppressively to haunt him in piece after piece.[38]

Nor is the ending free from contamination. Ghislanzoni's original verses are given below:[39]

> RAD: Nè le mie forti braccia
>   Smuovere ti potranno o fatal pietra.
> AID: Io manco
> RAD: Aida!
> AID: Io ti precedo
> RAD: Attendimi!
>   Solo un'istante vivere
>   Senza di te poss'io?
> AID: Là nell'eterna patria
>   Ci rivedremo . . . addio!
>   Odi, dell'arpe pronube
>   È l'immortal concento . . .
>   Rivivere mi sento
>   Nel cielo dell'amor (*muore*).
> RAD: Aida! ah parla . . . guardami . . .
>   È morta . . . e vivo ancor!

>   RAD: Nor can my strong arms
>   Move you o fatal stone.
>   AID: I die
>   RAD: Aida!
>   AID: I precede you
>   RAD: Wait for me!
>   How can I live for one instant
>   Without you?

38. Dissimilar stanzas are already common in Verdi's earlier operas (see Budden, passim).

39. These verses are printed in Luzio's article, "Come fu composta l'*Aida*," in *Carteggi verdiani* (4:22).

> AID: There in the eternal realm
> we will meet again . . . addio!
> Hear, the sound of the harp,
> Music of heaven,
> I feel alive again
> In a heaven of love (*she dies*).
> RAD: Aida! speak . . . look at me . . .
> She is dead . . . and I still live!

Verdi at first said only that they were "somewhat cold" (November 2), but on November 12 he was more specific:

> At the end, I would dispense with the usual agonies and avoid the words "io manco; ti precedo; attendimi! morta! vivo ancor! etc." I want something sweet, vaporous, a very brief duet, an *addio alla vita*. Aida would fall gently into the arms of Radames. Meanwhile, Amneris, knealing on the stone above the tomb, would sing a *Requiescant in pacem*.

Verdi himself supplies the text:

> *à 2:* O vita addio; addio, terrestri amori;
> Addio, dolori e gioie . . .
> Dell'infinito vedo già gli albori,
> Eterni nodi ci uniranno in ciel!

> AIDA, RADAMES: Farewell to life, to earthly love,
> Farewell sorrows and joys . . .
> I see the dawn of the infinite . . .
> Eternal bonds will unite us in heaven!

And he specifies:

> Four beautiful eleven-syllable verses. But so that they may be singable, place the accent on the fourth and eighth syllables.

He also supplies two lines of a proposed four-line stanza for Amneris:

> Riposa in pace   Rest in peace
> Alma adorata . . .   Adored soul . . .
> . . . .
> . . . .

In the original form of this scene, Amneris does not appear at all. The program as published in the Milanese artistic paper *Il Trovatore* on September 8, 1870[40] does not mention her, nor is she found in the published extract from Ghislanzoni's draft.[41] The touch is Verdi's, and it is a

---

40. Facsimile in Abdoun, facing p. 144.

41. Professor Busch will show that Amneris does not appear in this scene in Du Locle's prose draft in French, worked out with Verdi at St. Agata in late June 1870.

brilliant one, the supreme irony for Amneris, who remains unaware that her Requiem is also being uttered for her rival.

Yet again, despite the acknowledged brilliance of this final tableau, we must not let ourselves lose sight of Verdi's model, for "O terra addio" is a full *cabaletta*. It is slow, to be sure, quite unlike "Sempre libera" or "Di quella pira," but there are many examples of slow *cabalettas,* such as the famous one that concludes the duet between Edgardo and Lucia at the end of the first act of Donizetti's *Lucia di Lammermoor,* "Verranno a te sull'aure" (Example 17).

Example 17
Lucia di Lammermoor, Duet Edgardo-Lucia, *Cabaletta*

Verdi matches the *cabaletta* structure exactly: Aida sings the melody (Example 18); Radames repeats it, with Aida providing accompaniment; priestesses pray to the gods during the middle section; and the theme is then repeated by both characters in unison.

Example 18
Aida, Final Duet, Radames-Aida, *Cabaletta*

ciel, ___ si schiu-de il ciel e l'al- me er- ran- ___ ti ___ vo- la- no al

rag- gio dell'e- ter- no dì.

The addition of Amneris at the close, as we have seen, is a tremendous theatrical stroke for which Verdi alone seems to have been responsible.

Each of the duets in *Aida* belongs, to a greater or lesser degree, to a tradition fully embedded in the history of nineteenth-century opera in Italy. At one end, the Amneris-Radames duet fulfills practically all the basic requirements of the Rossinian model; at the other the Amonasro-Aida duet consciously avoids them. But a reading of Verdi's letters to Ghislanzoni leaves no doubt as to their overwhelming influence on the composer and his work. Yet, from descriptions by modern critics, one would have no sense of this. Speaking of the Amneris-Radames duet, Francis Toye uses the word "Wagnerian" twice in five sentences and suggests too that Radames' "È la morte un ben supremo," his *cabaletta* theme, "might have been suggested to Verdi by *Tristan and Isolde* had he known the opera at the time."[42] Charles Osborne, in a recent book about Verdi's operas, describes the scene as being "expounded in a series of splendid tunes, each with its appropriate dramatic character."[43] Gino Roncaglia, quoting only the passages in which Verdi says there should be nothing conventional, adds: "And he succeeded perfectly."[44] Through all this, no one has troubled to understand the musical context in which the duet was written.

We have been too ready to take Verdi at his most-quotable word. Mary Jane Matz has shown how the composer consistently falsified the story of his youth.[45] Frank Walker has shown how the composer consistently distorted the true nature of his relationships with others, especially Angelo Mariani.[46] It is time to look beyond the more quotable aspects of Verdi's remarks concerning his operas. It is no slur on the composer to

247

42. Francis Toye, *Giuseppe Verdi: His Life and Works* (London, 1931; reissued, New York, 1959), p. 402.
43. Charles Osborne, *The Complete Operas of Verdi* (New York, 1970), p. 391.
44. Gino Roncaglia, *L'ascensione creatrice di Giuseppe Verdi* (Florence, 1951), p. 301.
45. Mary Jane Matz, "The Verdi Family of Sant' Agata and Roncole: Legend and Truth," in *Atti del I° Congresso Internazionale di Studi Verdiani* (Parma, 1969), pp. 216–21.
46. Frank Walker, *The Man Verdi* (London, 1962), see esp. chap. 7.

assert that, at least through *Aida,* they were written squarely under the influence of conventions that had dominated Italian opera since the time of Rossini. The true quality of a work depends on the particular exemplification of convention, not its presence or absence. We do Verdi no justice by ignoring the roots of his style. What Julian Budden has said of the early operas remains true as late as *Aida:* "Verdi prefers to transform the conventions of his time rather than to overturn them."[47]

Indeed, in a sense, Verdi alone could not overturn them. As long as librettists supplied him with texts which essentially articulated the drama in older musical-dramatic forms, he could do no more than protest. If he protested urgently enough, as in the Aida-Amonasro duet, he might get results. Most of the means for transformation, however, remained external: to add the reprise of "Numi, pietà" for Aida at the end of her duet with Amneris, to obscure the parallel opening stanzas in the final duet of the opera, and to bring Amneris in at the close. These transformations are often superb, but they do not strike at the heart of the conventions. Presented with a complete text, Verdi would have had to rewrite from scratch to alter the dramatic structure. Thus, paradoxically, as long as the composer felt compelled to bully his librettists, no amount of bullying could truly achieve his will. Only when Arrigo Boito supplied texts which went beyond conventional ways of articulating the drama could Verdi find a text "bold to the core, with *new forms,* yet at the same time appropriate for music. . . ." And only with his recognition, arising from their collaboration on the revision of *Simon Boccanegra* (1881), that in Boito he had found the poet longed for for so many years did Verdi come out of retirement to create *Otello* and *Falstaff.*

47. Budden, p. 41.

Edward T. Cone   **THE OLD MAN'S TOYS:**

VERDI'S LAST OPERAS

250

I

It is now clear that Verdi was one of the giants. Thanks to recent performances, new recordings, and reprinted scores, we can observe in detail the slow and steady growth from youthful rawness through the vigor of the middle period to the refined splendor of *Aïda*—an advance predictable enough for a composer of Verdi's obvious musical gift. The final step, however—to *Otello* and *Falstaff* —could have been taken only by an imaginative intellect of the highest order. But the praise which it is now fashionable to bestow on these works is often grudgingly qualified. The critic may not go so far as Stravinsky, who for his own obvious purposes sees *Rigoletto* and *Traviata* as representing the high point of Verdi's art; but he often agrees with Shaw that in *Otello* and *Falstaff* subtlety has replaced melodic inspiration, and he considers the latter opera, for all its beauties, a meaningless puppet show, written for an old man's amusement.

Verdi himself suggested this point of view. His letters[1] indicate

---

[1] The English translation of the letters is that of Franz Werfel and Paul Stefan in *Verdi, the Man in His Letters* (New York, L. B. Fischer, 1942). The chief Italian source is *I Copialettere di Giuseppe Verdi*, ed. G. Cesari and A. Luzio (Milan, 1913). All the letters quoted in this essay are to be found there, except the one to Cammarano suggesting the libretto of *Il Trovatore*, which is reprinted in Gino Marchese Monaldi's *Verdi* (2nd ed., Turin, 1921).

that he was so afraid of making any commitments which his advanced age might not allow him to fulfill, that he protected himself by pretending that *Falstaff* was "a mere pastime." To Boïto, his librettist, he writes: "Did you ever think of my huge accumulation of years? . . . I could be accused of great rashness, if I were to undertake such a task. And suppose I could not master my weariness? Suppose I could not finish the music? Then you would have your time and pains for nothing!" To the Mayor of Parma he admits, "I am writing *Falstaff*, it is true. But I am writing it in moments of absolute leisure, simply for my own amusement, and without any definite goal in view; and I do not know whether or when I shall finish it." The cat is out of the bag, though, when he confesses to Gino Monaldi that "for forty years now I have been wanting to write a comic opera, and for fifty years I have known *The Merry Wives of Windsor*." The old man's toy was the consummation of a half-century's desire.

Such long-range plans are not unusual with Verdi, and they indicate from almost the earliest days a seriousness of purpose which refutes the conception of the young composer as a mere tunemonger. They suggest also that we must respect the earlier works as rougher embodiments of the same musical and dramatic conceptions which are found, refined and freed of inessentials, in the later masterpieces. Verdi himself respected them; his careful revision of *Macbeth* for the Paris performance proves it. *Macbeth* had been written in 1847—even before *Luisa Miller*; the new version was prepared in 1865—three years after *La Forza del Destino*. Yet his correspondence at this period reveals the liveliest interest in the new production; he was determined that it should be as musically and dramatically effective as possible. More remarkable still is the rewriting of *Simone Boccanegra* after twenty-four years. Originally the product of his first mature period, it became an important link between *Aïda* and *Otello*, and marked the composer's first collaboration with the librettist of his last great works.

A real collaboration it remained, for no other composer since Mozart worked so intimately with his poets. Although he never wrote a libretto, Verdi was always a dramatist; and although he was no philosopher, his opera was from the beginning based on a sound aesthetic. If we fail to comprehend it, or even to admit its existence, we shall continue to be troubled by the apparent contrivance of *Otello* and the meaninglessness of *Falstaff*.

II

One approach to the understanding of what Verdi was trying to do is suggested by a consideration of the charge that the style of the late works is a result of waning inspiration, that artifice has replaced creativity. Shaw thought this was true already in *Aïda* and attributed the richness of that opera's orchestration to the composer's attempt to make up for "the inevitable natural drying up of . . . spontaneity and fertility."[1] But in actuality, what we find in these works is not less invention, but more. The melody, it is true, is contented with single periods or even phrases (Falstaff's "*Te lo cornifico, netto, netto,*" Ex. 1) where the melody of *Il Trovatore* would have demanded an aria; but what would have been the construction of such an aria?

Ex. 1

Te   lo   cor-ni-fi-co   net-to   net-to

Look at "*Di quella pira,*" at "*La donna è mobile,*" at "*Di Provenza,*" and you will find that one motif—a single detail—is elaborated by sequential repetition and simple modifications to fill out the entire form. Fundamentally, the pregnant vocal fragments which carry the burden of the music in the later works are equivalent to these arias, with all such obvious development suppressed. Instead, the phrases are now subjected to real development: they appear in constantly new relations and in ever more varied forms. The "*cornifico*" motif referred to above (*Falstaff*, Act II, Scene 1) is not dropped after its initial presentation by Falstaff; it is kept as a constantly recurring thought beneath Ford's ensuing monologue. Two purely orchestral

---

[1]George Bernard Shaw, "A Word More About Verdi," in the *Anglo-Saxon Review*, March 1901, reprinted in *London Music in 1888–89* (New York, Dodd, Mead, 16.37)

statements of it introduce the arioso. The first ends on a simple tonic according to Falstaff's version; but the second leads to a dissonant deceptive cadence as the import of Falstaff's words begins to affect Ford—"*È sogno? o realtà.*" A little later, with completely altered harmonization leading into dark, abbreviated, chromatic sequences, it is reduced to only three tones, which in turn are used to form the crescendo to the outburst "*O matrimonio: Inferno!*" The composer returns to the device of the deceptive cadence (in a more startling form) as Ford imagines the dreaded words "*Le corna,*" and from the original motif he derives the persistent triplet rhythm which remains throughout the rest of the passage. The fullest development is reached when, accompanying "*Prima li accoppio/E poi li colgo,*" the little melody ascends through four octaves to break out in a newly truncated version which produces the exciting effect of simultaneous stretto and diminution. This marks the last appearance of the "*cornifico*"; from here on it is present only by implication in the triplets of the accompaniment.

Such is the rich orchestral treatment Verdi affords a simple cadential phrase. Other melodies, destined for purely vocal expansion, display a flexibility of line, a variety of contour, and a rhythmic subtlety unknown to his earlier style. Beautiful as "*Di Provenza*" is (*La Traviata,* Act II), it consists of the unvarying repetition of a single rhythmic element, broken only at the final cadence (Ex. 2). Melodically, it outlines the simplest of stepwise motions, both in its

253

Ex. 2

individual phrases and in the relation of one phrase to the next. Against this, a fair example of its period, set Desdemona's opening appeal in Act III of *Otello* (Ex. 3). Here the second half of the initial phrase corresponds rhythmically to the first half, it is true; but the syncopation, serving to accent the climactic F sharp, adds new potential energy which is admirably discharged by the embellished cadence. Now this phrase as a whole, consisting as it does of two symmetrical halves, is answered in Otello's part by one of equal length, but indivisible. A short digression is offered by Otello's next phrase, one of only three measures in contrast to the regular four of the first two. Finally, rounding off the tiny song-form, Desdemona repeats her opening melody in still another variation. Thus, although the opening motif has been heard four times, it is never rhythmically the same.

Ex. 3

254

Melodically, the passage displays equal subtlety. In the opening figure the line is progressing simultaneously on two levels: from the opening G sharp up and from the high E down—both leading to the closing B. In the repetition of the figure, the sixth thus defined is expanded to an octave, widening the compass of the melody and allowing for a longer, more elaborate fall to the cadential note. The two lines continue their way throughout the second phrase, which effects a modulation to the dominant; only in the truncated middle section, contrastingly characterized by a simple scale-progression, are they merged. The concluding section, again in the tonic, restores the two original levels in the expected reprise of the opening. Once more the high F sharp receives emphasis, this time by a poignant, dissonant leap which makes the closing descent to the tonic E doubly welcome. Such complex relations as these (I hardly touch on the harmonic details) indicate a concentration of expression beside which the more extended linear beauty of the earlier aria seems superficial.

Concentration—that is the clue. The aria of *La Traviata* is compressed into the short arioso passage of *Otello*. Even Mozart could never have achieved this, for Mozart's arias were already highly concentrated. They are longer than Verdi's arias because they contain so much more music—so many more ideas; but they are as concentrated as possible, and so they cannot be compressed. But Verdi's diluted arias contain much less music than their own space—so he learns concentration.

III

Perhaps Wagner taught Verdi more than the latter realized: this concentration, for example, although it is sometimes hard to think of the long-winded German composer in this term. Yet his essential expression is one of highly charged detail; no one has ever packed more into a motif of two chords. Just here, though, one difference between the two musicians becomes clear: most of Wagner's expressive details are harmonic progressions; Verdi's are melodies. Even at his most nearly Wagnerian, in the "Kiss Motif" from *Otello* (Ex. 4), Verdi remains primarily a melodist. Striking as the chromatic chords are, the fragment must be characterized as a tune, complete and rounded off with a cadence. The other recurrent leitmotiv in the

255

Ex. 4

opera, that of "Jealousy" (Ex. 5), although shorter and more amenable to orchestral development, is not even harmonized upon its first appearance: the orchestra merely doubles Iago's vocal line.

Interested as he was in the expressive possibilities of harmonic color, it was natural that Wagner should come to think more and more in terms of the orchestra, and that often his vocal parts should seem to be distracting adjuncts. On the other hand, it was impossible that Verdi, recognizing that melody and song are one, should forget

Ex. 5

the primary importance of the human voice. "Opera is opera, symphony is symphony": the warning was directed toward Puccini; but in thus summing up his aesthetic Verdi clearly showed what he must have considered the basic fallacy of his great German contemporary as well.

This is not to say that Verdi's orchestra is only an accompaniment. Already in the earlier operas, some of his most telling scenes are constructed around a primarily instrumental line: the meeting of Rigoletto and Sparafucile, the gaming scene in *La Traviata*. But he carefully observes the conditions which prevent the submersion of the voice, and in the Sparafucile scene we can see what these are. The orchestration, with its single muted cello and double bass projecting an unnaturally high melodic line against a background of plucked strings and woodwinds, is striking; but it is simple and remains almost unchanged throughout the scene. Once the listener has grasped the pattern, he can continue to perceive it almost subconsciously while he devotes his attention to the voices and the action. The melody itself, based upon easily remembered figures, is developed in the most unassuming manner; true symphonic style would create a texture so interesting and self-contained that it would completely absorb the ear. The vocal parts, recitative-like, contrast with the formal melodic structure of the accompaniment; but they never conflict rhythmically, for the broken vocal phrases and the smooth instrumental ones coincide at the important cadences, such as those at Sparafucile's words "*un uom di spada sta*" and "*La vostra donna è là.*" At each of these points, the conclusion of an instrumental period is marked by a similar close in Sparafucile's part, further accented by an echoing interjection from Rigoletto. The voices thus become the irregular surface of a basically simple solid.

Verdi had only to refine this particular type of writing to achieve the miracle of Otello's "*Dio! mi potevi*" in Act III. In the declamatory opening, the musical burden is the orchestra's: the constantly varied reiteration of a single motif. The variations do not apply to the rhythm, however, where the rigidity sets off to advantage the free declamation of the vocal part. In the same way the subtle melodic changes of the orchestral figure contrast effectively with the voice's constant repetition of a single note. Each level—voice and orchestra —thus contains one static, monotonous element, as if to symbolize Otello's inability to free himself from his obsession. Three times Otello's part quits its reiterated A flat for a lower note; each time coincides with a cadential point in the accompaniment. Finally, as the motif disappears in a modulation effected by an unusual deceptive cadence, the voice too surprises us by rising to a startling C natural —and the recitative is over. Here is a point at which the earlier Verdi would have introduced an aria, for the orchestra has borne the weight of the melody long enough. The late Verdi also gives us an aria here—short, asymmetrical, interrupted by dramatic exigency (the entrance of Iago), but an aria which proceeds to a satisfying conclusion at "*Cielo! O gioa!*"

In Wagner, as in Verdi, when we expect an aria we are given one —but by the orchestra, not the singer. Such a place is Brünnhilde's plea in the last act of *Die Walküre*, where the tension of the dialogue beginning with "*War es so schmählich*" is finally released in the passage beginning "*Der diese Liebe.*" It is just at this point, however, that the orchestra achieves its greatest eloquence, and its transformation of the earlier tentative "Motif of Pleading" into a definitive major form (sometimes called "The Beginning of a New Life") requires our total attention.

Verdi helps his voices to maintain their supremacy by orchestration

257

which is transparent even at its most opaque; to do so he learns to produce the most startling effects by the most economical means. This tendency is already apparent in *Rigoletto*—in the Sparafucile scene described above, with its unearthly duet of cello and double bass, and in the last act, when the oboe interjects its solitary high tones over the empty fifths of the lower strings. Here is another aspect of the composer's desire for concentration: not of sheer mass, as in Wagner, but of what might be called orchestral attention. The entire effect of the instrumentation is focused in one salient detail, to which all others are subordinated.

Increased mastery of this technique leads to the glowing translucency of *Aïda*. The Nile scene is famous for its coloring; yet the score reveals nothing but a single flute accompanied by muted strings in the simplest of patterns. Even this economy is carried still further in *Otello*, where all the evil of Iago's character can be compressed into a single unison on the strings, and in *Falstaff*, where two simple harmonics on the violins transform Nannetta's village children into the actual fairies they pretend to be.

IV

Looking at the same material in a slightly different way, I should say that Verdi at all times adheres closely to the two human sources of music: song and dance. When the voice is not predominant the body is. Such passages as those analyzed in the preceding section, in which the orchestra temporarily usurps primary interest and attention, are characterized by easily grasped rhythms suggestive of physical motion and thus referring to the human characters on the stage.

The third source of music, the nonhuman one increasingly drawn upon by Wagner as he develops from *Das Rheingold* to *Parsifal*, is pure sound. This is a new ideal which becomes increasingly important during the nineteenth century, as interest focuses more and more on the coloristic motif, which in turn points the way toward the single, highly expressive chord. Although in Wagner, a product of the German symphonic tradition, such moments of emphasis are still tightly controlled in the total flux, the intrinsic value of each is more important than its contribution to the whole. It is only a step

258

further to Debussy, who isolates them against a colorful but static background. The detail has become disintegrative, and the musical line is lost.

Verdi, even in his last works, refused to yield to this, the great temptation of the late nineteenth century. As a writer for the stage, and therefore for human beings, he knew that the path of pure musical color, of overindividualized chord or motif, leads to dehumanization. Although the style of *Otello* and *Falstaff*, a style stripped bare of all but essentials, became at times one of expressive detail, the details remained primarily melodic and always constructive, contributing to the continuous progress of the musical line, which in turn, as context, gave meaning to the details.

It is therefore easy to see why the concept of the leitmotiv should remain foreign to Verdi, and why he should use it only rarely. For the Wagnerian leitmotiv is independent of its surroundings to the extent that it can be freely transplanted without losing its effect. Even when Verdi does invent a movable phrase, such as the "Oath" in *Don Carlo*, the "Kiss Motif" mentioned above, and the "*Reverenza*" figure in *Falstaff*, he introduces it sparingly. More frequently a motif will be used to characterize a single scene, never to reappear. Themes like these are meaningful in one context alone; they fit only one situation. In *Otello*, the "handkerchief" scene and the "*Credo*" of Iago furnish examples. Going one step further, Verdi occasionally places at a climactic point a short expressive figure which occurs once only—a detail which has found its unique place in the complete flow and which can be subject neither to repetition nor to development. A phrase like Desdemona's almost hysterical farewell to Emilia is poignant only because of its position in the complete structure of the scene (Ex. 6). The instrumental introduction and

259

Ex. 6

the "Willow Song" which precede it have vacillated between major and minor, between a clearly harmonic and a modal tonality of

F sharp; now Desdemona's outburst resolves all doubts in a perfect major cadence. Heard in isolation, and thus unable to perform its function of discharging the tension so long sustained in the previous passage, it sounds commonplace. In contrast, a much shorter figure like "Treachery by Magic" (Ex. 7) from *Die Götterdämmerung*— only two chords—can weave its spell in any context or in none. Its own sound is sufficient.

Ex. 7

It is Verdi's achievement of emphatic moment without sacrifice of temporal span which today attracts the attention of those composers for whom pure sound is no longer enough. Sheer sonority can neither organize a large-scale instrumental work nor present human action in terms of the human voice. The colorful detail must take its place in the complete musical phrase, and the phrase must contribute to the unfolding of the complete line. These are the principles, stated in the quartets and sonatas of the aging Beethoven, which were rediscovered two generations later, for a different medium, by the old Italian.

V

Hermann Broch, writing about Homer,[2] suggests that one of the characteristics of the "style of old age" is an apparent preoccupation with matters of technique. This preoccupation is only apparent, he insists, even though it may deceive the artist himself. "Although the artist's problem seems to be mainly technical, his real impulse goes beyond this"; the true goal is "the reaching of a new level of expression." Technique and expression—these terms are more suggestive than the familiar "form" and "content." Too often the latter encourage the picture of form as a handily constructed vessel into which

---

[2] In his introduction to Rachel Bespaloff's *On the Iliad* (New York, Pantheon, 1947).

the content can then be poured. Technique, on the other hand, implies the living development of expressive means; and expression indicates the activity of a total organism rather than a mere "containable" substance. The compression of Verdi's last period, like that of Beethoven's, is not of formal interest only; it allows the composer to achieve an intensity—a realism, if you will—impossible in a more relaxed style. It is this intensity, transferred by association from the music to the characters on the stage, which endows them with an almost terrifying vitality. They become real in a sense unknown to the spoken drama; for a music-dramatist is able to endow his creatures with a new dimension through a dual control of the temporal continuum in which they move: as a dramatist, he uses this time as a natural physical fact; as musician, he manipulates, even distorts it, to form a vehicle for psychological expression. In a word, he turns time into tempo.

I have called Verdi a music-dramatist rather than an opera-composer precisely because of this control of both verbal time and musical tempo. In discussing the expressive goals of his works for the stage, I might even go so far as to say that he always wrote his own libretti—not as Wagner did, completing the actual labor of versification, but as Mozart did, working constantly and intimately with a professional of the craft. The composer's early correspondence with the librettists Cammarano and Piave makes clear to what a great extent he was responsible for the choice and shaping of his own plays. *Il Trovatore*, for example, seems to have been first suggested to Cammarano in a note written by Verdi early in 1850: "The subject I should like and which I suggest is *El Trovador*, a Spanish drama by Gutierez. It seems to me very fine, rich in ideas and in strong situations. I should like to have two feminine roles. First, the gypsy, a woman of unusual character after whom I want to name the opera. The other part for a secondary singer." Over a year later, after having received Cammarano's sketch for the play, he writes him again, dissatisfied: "It seems to me, if I am not deceived, that several situations no longer have the force and originality they had, and above all, that Azucena has not retained her strange and novel character. It seems to me that this woman's two great passions, *filial love* and *maternal love*, are no longer present with all their original force.'' There ensues a detailed criticism of Cammarano's version, followed by a scene-by-scene sketch of Verdi's own conception of the proper treatment. Equally interesting in this regard are Verdi's letters to Cammarano and later to Somma outlining his plans for an opera on *King Lear*. Here the composer indicates not only the succession of act and scene, but the exact pattern of recitative, aria, and ensemble as well, with prescriptions of the proper poetic meters at important points.

Much as we owe to Boïto, then, for the specific form of *Otello* and *Falstaff*, we must not overestimate his contribution—Shaw again to the contrary; and in what follows, I attribute to Verdi the specifically dramatic content of the two works as unreservedly as their musical treatment. Nevertheless, he was fortunate in finding a librettist who, as a skillful opera-composer in his own right, had first-hand experience of the problems involved. As a result, Verdi was no doubt willing to entrust to Boïto details of the poetic composition which he would have felt bound to supervise in the case of men like Cammarano and Piave.

The books of the two works prove that Boïto was sensitive to the difference between the problems presented by each. In *Otello* a great opera is made from a great play; in *Falstaff* an equally great opera from an obviously inferior play. The translation into the new medium must in one keep as much of the original content as possible; in the other, a new content must be provided. The libretto of *Otello* is fundamentally an abbreviated version of Shakespeare; to a certain extent *Falstaff* is a new play.

Naturally, each presents the composer with difficulties, but in some ways *Otello* lays upon him the heavier burden. Most good operas have libretti which are comparatively barren of poetry, of imagery, and of philosophical content. The music is free to add the poetry, to create its own imagery, to imply its own meanings. A play like *Othello*, still a tightly poetic drama even in Boïto's denuded version, necessarily limits the possibilities of musical interpretation. Yet the boundaries are not too strict; the composer has after all at least as much freedom as the actor in his reading of the lines, and what

Verdi has done is once and for all to fix securely his own reading of the parts. Thus his version is susceptible of much less variety in performance than Shakespeare's play, a rule generally applicable to musical as opposed to spoken drama.

A single example should make this principle clear. Act III, Scene 2 in the opera is a condensation of Shakespeare's Act III, Scene 4 and Act IV, Scene 2. Verdi indicates, by returning at the end of the scene to the suave opening melody, that Otello tries to conceal his fury under a veil of mock politeness. The appearance of the dissonant chord and the rise of the voice to high C on the dreaded word "*cortigiana*" evince his momentary loss of control; but he recovers sufficiently to finish the phrase on a note of suppressed menace, his true desperation breaking out in the immediately ensuing orchestral passage. The details of the music force this interpretation, but the corresponding lines in the play allow varying ones. (Paul Robeson, for instance, delivered them in a bellow of uncontrolled anger.) Verdi's interpretation has the added advantage that it permits him to round off the scene formally by a return to the original theme as suggested in the libretto by Otello's reference to Desdemona's hand, echoing his opening line. This repetition does not occur in the original, where the scenes are too far apart for such a device to be effective; moreover, it is a technique suited rather to musical than to purely dramatic form.

The foregoing discussion applies to passages which are essentially similar in opera and play. Sometimes, however, the poetry of the original is reduced almost to a bare skeleton—or omitted completely. One or the other is necessary if the music is to be allowed to supply its own imagery; for if the composer tried to underline and intensify Shakespeare's already heavy-laden verse, the action would be slowed down to such a degree that the opera would become impossibly long. The only alternative—merely to set the words in a purely declamatory style—would be a surrender of the musician's function. So most of the poetry has to go out of the window—only to enter again through Verdi's door. No trace of Othello's long soliloquy before the murder of Desdemona remains in the libretto. Instead, the double basses introduce an orchestral recitative, short but eloquent, and

263

serving a similar purpose. The relation of "kiss" and "kill," put into words by Shakespeare in his last scene, is here already made apparent by Verdi in the subtle transformation of the ominous double-bass melody into the "Kiss Motif" from the love-scene of the first act. But even Verdi would have found it an impossible task to translate into his own language the constant play on the word "light" in the original. Any attempt to reproduce this image musically, within the time allowed by his operatic economy, would have been ludicrous; the speech had to be omitted.

The problem of translation, arising in an opposite sense, also helps explain the presence of certain passages in the opera which are not found in Shakespeare at all. It is an important principle of music-drama that every important motivation must at some point be translated into musical terms. It cannot merely be talked about, or acted: it must be heard as music. That is why Verdi requires a love-scene in his first act. What Shakespeare tells us through his poetry, and by the action of his own first act, Verdi must have a chance to convey musically. In the case of *Otello*, a fairly long scene is required; only with *Falstaff* does the composer learn to compress the love duet into fifty short measures.

Similarly, the famous 'Credo', an invention of Boïto's, is necessary in order to give the music a chance to express fully the chief dramatic motivation of the play: the character of Iago. The soliloquy which concludes Shakespeare's first act will not do; it is too complicated, mixing self-revelation, self-justification, and plot-development. It could be set only as a pure recitative, but the characterization would then be lost or only imperfectly translated into music. The Credo takes its cue from Shakespeare's last lines:

> Hell and night
> Must bring this monstrous birth to the world's light.

These it expands into a speech permitting a terrifying musical interpretation of Iago, one that gives him stature as one of the great operatic villains, all of whom have revealed themselves in similar monologues: the Queen of the Night, Pizarro, Kaspar, and Hagen.

In the examples just pointed out poet and composer have had to expand certain passages of the original in order to convey them adequately in musical terms. It has often been stated, on the other hand, that one technique peculiar to opera facilitates a condensation of dramatic expression: the ensemble. The concerted singing of several characters makes possible the simultaneous presentation of contrasting points of view which in a play can be made clear only successively. The septet with chorus near the end of Act III of *Otello* achieves an intensity unknown at the corresponding point of the original (Act IV, Scene 1), with the innocence of Desdemona soaring above the pity of her friends, the plotting of the conspirators, and the horror of the crowd. But unanimity of purpose is equally well adapted to this technique, as the oath-duet of Otello and Iago testifies. *Falstaff*, even more advanced than the earlier work, presents double and triple ensembles in which the unanimity of one group of characters is contrasted with that of another. The nine-part ensemble of Act I, Scene 2 divides itself into four (the women, rapid six-eight meter) plus four (the men, rapid two-two) plus one (Fenton, sustained two-two). The finale of the second act presents Nannetta and Fenton as one unit, the three plotting women together with Falstaff as another, Ford and the other men as a third, and the chorus as a fourth. The group-contrasts essential to both these passages are nicely resolved in the final fugue of the last act—probably the best formal device available to indicate general acceptance of the outcome without loss of the individuality of each character.

265

VI

What is this outcome, which all accept with the words "*Tutto nel mondo è burla*"?[1] Is it Verdi's final judgment that all are "*gabbati*"?[2] Most critics have taken him at his word and find in *Falstaff* a trivial comedy adorned with some exquisite music. But such an interpretation is not substantiated by the libretto as a whole, differing in so many important respects from the original farce. Furthermore, such

---

[1]Everything in the world is a joke.
[2]One of the closing lines of the opera i.e. "*Tutti gabbati*": All are taken in.

a point of view implies a misunderstanding of the nature of music-drama, comprehension of which cannot be derived from a reading of the book alone. In any opera, we may find that the musical and the verbal messages seem to reinforce or to contradict each other; but whether the one or the other, we must always rely on the music as our guide toward an understanding of the composer's conception of the text. It is this conception, not the bare text itself, that is authoritative in defining the ultimate meaning of the work. And the music of *Falstaff* suggests a great deal more than "he who laughs last laughs best."

In the first place, the terrifying reality of Ford's jealousy, as portrayed in his "*È sogno? o realtà*," is sufficient proof that Verdi did not regard his characters as mere puppets. This is the same music that Otello sings—and this same motive reaches far into Verdi's past. *Don Carlos, Un Ballo in Maschera, Aïda*—all turn upon sexual jealousy. Even earlier, jealousy enters into the motivations of *Ernani, La Traviata,* and *Il Trovatore.* But in the two late works the emotion has acquired a moral aspect: the husband's sense of right and wrong has been outraged by the supposed conduct of his wife. (To a certain extent this motive is foreshadowed in *Un Ballo.*) This dimension is natural in *Otello* because it is basic to the Shakespearean original, but it is surprising to find it contributing equal intensity to Ford's emotions. In either case, it would have been easy for Verdi to create effective melodrama without this added depth, but he goes further and thus makes a tragic hero of Otello—and almost of Ford.

The comparison of Ford with Otello suggests another apparent similarity between the two situations: the guiltlessness of the woman involved. But whereas Mistress Ford is a virtuous wife, Desdemona is innocent in the complete meaning of the word. The innocent heroine is a recurring character in Verdi's dramatic mythos. Untouched by evil, her chastity is usually symbolized physically by some sort of cloister. Gilda, who is eventually betrayed by her own ignorance of the world, is shielded by Rigoletto's garden wall. Leonora in *Il Trovatore* and her namesake in *La Forza del Destino* both find refuge in convents. Even Violetta, by no means innocent, tries to escape into a secluded village. Here I find the explanation of

266

the scene in *Otello* during which the village children sing and dance around Desdemona. The division of Desdemona in the courtyard from Otello and Iago in the house presents a visual separation of her innocence from their guilt; the presence of the children heightens the irony of the scene.

In *Falstaff* it is Nannetta who is the innocent one, and on two occasions physical objects symbolize her separation from the world around her: the groves which hide the lovers in the garden-scene, and the screen in the bedroom. It is noteworthy that Verdi, writing to his stage designer, makes special mention of these two details, even drawing sketches of the stage. "Lots of plants and bushes here and there, so that the people can hide themselves," he specifies; and "This screen, so to speak, takes part in the action and must be put where the action requires." But the bushes and the screen differ from all the other cloisters in an important respect: they hide, not just Nannetta, but Fenton as well. For once in Verdi youthful innocence is represented by a pair of lovers rather than by a lone maiden, and for once love is pursued to a happy ending.

The identification of this series of heroines is confirmed by the music they sing. Particularly do the Leonora of *La Forza*, Desdemona, and Nannetta seem to be successive incarnations of the same voice— a clear sustained soprano, rising above all the surrounding agitation. What Verdi hinted at in the earlier Leonora's counterpoint to the Miserere, he carried out in the second Leonora's "*Madre pietosa*," soaring against the chanting of the monks. A more complex form of the same technique is prophesied in the *Rigoletto* Quartet, to be fulfilled in the two great ensembles of *Otello*, where Desdemona detaches herself from the accompanying voices and creates her own melodic line in lonely beauty. In *Falstaff* Fenton takes this role in the first big ensemble; but in the bedroom-scene he is joined by Nannetta, and through all the succeeding hurly-burly the love-duet behind the screen proceeds undisturbed. In one other case Verdi contrasts united lovers with the outer world in this way—the finale of *Aïda*—but here the union is achieved only in death. In *Falstaff*, the old man, gentler, permits the lovers to escape into a world of their own making.

267

Let me carry this one step further—into the last act, when Nannetta appears as the Queen of the Fairies (a role assigned to Mistress Quickly in the original). The music that she sings here is not unlike that which has characterized her throughout, but lighter, daintier, less solid. Her separation from the real world, already prepared in the passages previously pointed out, is now complete; contrasting, earthly counterpoint is no longer present. She has become the fairy she is pretending to be, and the elves she summons are real elves. The magical orchestration of the passage insures the transformation.

It should be noticed in this connection that Nannetta herself takes no part in the pinching and beating of Falstaff, for she does not exist in the same world as the imps to whom this mission is entrusted. The latter are certainly only townspeople in disguise; and even Nannetta's band, after their leader's departure, are gradually drawn into the general fray. It is evidently in Nannetta alone that the power of transmutation inheres, and if the pretended fairies become temporarily real ones through her innocence, so too does the pretended wedding become a real one for her. Once more music reveals the truth: the gently solemn epithalamium is obviously not for Bardolfo and Cajus, but for Nannetta and Fenton. That is why it is heard again, a little later, when the young couple pleads for Ford's forgiveness. And though they may join in the fellowhip of the final " *Tutto nel mondo è burla*," they at least have not been "*gabbati*."

I have said little about the character of Falstaff himself and about the broad humor which is the opera's most obvious characteristic, not because they are inessential, but because they are fully treated in most criticisms of the work. What is not usually mentioned is that the complete content involves a basic contrast. On the one hand is the world of fighting and clowning, of appetites and revulsions, of plots and counter-plots. Its depths are indicated by the darkness of Ford's jealousy; but its true representative is Falstaff himself, for "*l'uom è nato burlone*." Exaggerated in size and exaggerated in his actions, Falstaff is nevertheless recognized by the others as a mirror of themselves; as Alice points out to Ford and Cajus, all of them are wearing horns. For this reason they accept him wholeheartedly, even after brutally punishing him; and quite properly he becomes their

268

leader in the final ensemble to proclaim that laughter is the only solution to his world's problems. But there is another world: that of Fenton and Nannetta, which they create for themselves. Its symbol is Nannetta's fairyland, and into its unreality the lovers are able, for a little while, to escape. But they recognize that even they must eventually come to terms with the others, that the claims of ordinary society are imperative: so they too carry their parts in the final fugue.

There is evidence that Verdi wanted to set *The Tempest*. Perhaps he did—in *Falstaff*. All that he had learned during his lifelong exploration of the darker side of human emotions and passions, he had compressed into the four concise acts of *Otello*; now at last, for the first time, he was able to give this knowledge its proper place in a larger view—much as Shakespeare had done in his own last play. But the resemblances between *The Tempest* and *Falstaff* extend even to details. The ugliness of the world opposed to the strange beauties of the fairy island, the secluded maiden united with her suitor by a kind parent, the contrasting scenes of buffoonery, the interpenetration of dream and reality: all these elements of the one Verdi was able to suggest in the other. Most important, the spirit of wise good humor is always present. The day of the premiere Verdi wrote to Bellaigue, the French critic, "I don't know whether I have hit the gay note, the true note, and above all the sincere note." It is clear today that he hit all three—or rather that all three are really one.

269

Tristan in the Composition of *Pelléas*

271

CAROLYN ABBATE

This study of the early drafts for Debussy's *Pelléas et Mélisande* grew out of earlier work with the surviving sources for Debussy's last opera, *La Chute de la maison Usher*, based on Poe's short story. The question concerning the *Usher* sources is: How nearly complete was the opera in its surviving form, "completeness" being understood as the stage of advancement of the known sources toward what would have been the final stage in the opera's composition, the writing of the full orchestral score? In other words, do the surviving sketches and drafts of *Usher* represent a relatively early or late phase of the composition? This question was stimulated primarily by practical considerations, for if the known sources could be shown to represent an advanced or even fixed stage, then it

should be possible to supply the single missing dimension—the orchestration—and come up with a performable edition in which the intrusion of the editor is kept to a minimum.

The *Usher* sources[1] can be measured against a model of working method represented by the autograph sources for Debussy's two

[1] Single pages representing various stages of composition survive, and the location and identification of *Usher* sources will doubtless continue for some time. Based on the model generated from *Pelléas* these sources can be identified as either preliminary (first) or developed (second, pre-orchestral) drafts. A summary of the manuscripts, including those for the librettos, is given in Robert Orledge, "Debussy's 'House of Usher' Revisited," *Musical Quarterly* 62 (1976), 536–57. To those mentioned by Orledge can be added a single page in the miscellany Add. 47860/3 of the British Museum, a sheet from the 1917 developed draft. The developed draft of the first scene and part of a second, nineteen pages in clean copy bound with two half sheets belonging to an earlier preliminary draft, is today in

0148–2076/81/030117 + 25$00.50 © 1981 by The Regents of the University of California.

117

earlier operas, *Roderigue et Chimène**(1889–93) and *Pelléas et Mélisande* (1893–1902). The former exists as an unpublished but nearly complete *particell;* the latter is of course the only one of Debussy's numerous operatic projects to be completed and performed during his lifetime. Thus what began as a project in the editing of *La Chute de la maison Usher* has necessarily had to be continued in a number of related studies, one of which was a closer examination of the *Pelléas* documents.

Apart from their usefulness as models against which to measure the later *Usher* drafts, these documents have suggested that there was a model for the composition of *Pelléas* in Wagner's operas, in *Tristan und Isolde* in particular. That idea is hardly new, of course, nor is the study of preliminary materials in order to demonstrate the evolution of a musical text. What the *Pelléas* drafts indicate further is how the model of a system of composition may be transformed and how an indebtedness to that system may be disguised or obscured. They call less for an analysis of the technical evolution of the text in a sealed system which begins and ends with *Pelléas,* than for an analysis of how a nascent text *in statu componendi* is made to take account of a second, fixed musical text which thereby becomes part of its historical past. It is usually easy to identify imitation, modelling, or mimicry in a finished work. What is impossible to identify in the finished work is the way in which mimicry has been tested and rejected. Mimicry

detected in a finished work may be dismissed as unconscious, but its manipulation in earlier stages may not be so dismissed, and if we must in part explain composition by the outward apparatus of method, then conscious deliberation is a convenient piece of testimony for the case.

II

Debussy's first work on *Pelléas* was immediately preceded by work on *Roderigue et Chimène,* which occupied him from roughly 1889 to 1893. The manuscript of Acts I and III of this opera is a combination of a *particell* in clean copy with text and partial orchestration, and a working draft, like the *particell* in ink, but generally lacking text and much more hastily drawn. Act II survives as a piano-vocal score in a clean copy furnished with instructions for the engraver; it was obviously intended as a *Stichvorlage.*[2] The librettist for the opera was Catulle Mendès, an avowed admirer of Wagner's music, and an essayist who had often expressed himself on the subject of French music after Wagner.[3] It is generally supposed that the collaboration between Debussy and Mendès was one which was distasteful to the composer, suffered only because Mendès financed the engraving of the *Fantaisie* for piano and orchestra (1890), and because Debussy had hopes of further assistance along those lines. Two biographers, Léon Vallas and Marcel Dietschy, have adduced as evidence for the composer's dissatisfaction with *Roderigue et Chimène* both Debussy's more or less public condemnation of his own work, and his lack of interest in its possible publication.[4] The latter point must be reconsidered, given the format of the manuscript for the opera's second act. That a *Stichvorlage* had been prepared for at least one part of the work suggests that the question

---

Paris (**F–Pn** Mus. ms. 9885). Two further pages of a preliminary draft have been published in facsimile, one in Edward Lockspeiser, *Debussy et Edgar Poe* (Monaco, 1957), appendix I, and one in Lockspeiser's biography *Debussy* (London, 1937), facing p. 52. Sketches for *Usher* and parts of a preliminary draft are contained in the manuscripts 17726, 17727, and 17730 (former collection of Madame de Tinan) in the Bibliothèque Nationale, Paris.
  The edition of *Usher* published recently by Juan Allende-Blin (Paris, 1979) contains no critical apparatus, and gives no indication exactly which sections are orchestrations of the 1917 developed draft in Paris 9885, which are reconstructed out of pages of the preliminary draft for earlier, discarded versions of the libretto, and which were generated out of sketches. My edition of *Usher* (an orchestration of the pages belonging to the 1917 developed draft) was performed at Yale University in 1977 and at Lincoln Center in 1978. The problem of a diplomatic edition for publication has yet to be solved.

[2]Currently in the collection of Robert O. Lehman on deposit in The Pierpont Morgan Library, New York. Debussy's heirs have refused permission for its edition or publication.
[3]See, for example, the well-known essay "Le jeune Prix de Rome et le vieux wagneriste," *Revue wagnerienne* 1 (1885), 131–36.
[4]Léon Vallas, *Claude Debussy et son temps* (Paris, 1932), pp. 110–12, and Marcel Dietschy, *La Passion de Claude Debussy* (Neuchâtel, 1962), pp. 82–86.

*The correct spelling is *Rodrigue et Chimène.*

of publication had indeed become a serious one.[5]

In April 1890 Debussy had finished the *particell* of the first act; the cover sheet for this act bears both that date and a dedication to his mistress Gabrielle Dupont. By January 1892 two of the three acts were at least performable, as Debussy reported in a letter to his friend Robert Godet.[6] The date given by Vallas for the abandonment of the project, 1892, is probably too early, for as late as October 1893, when just beginning *Pelléas*, the composer was still playing *Roderigue et Chimène* at private auditions.[7] It seems clear that it was ultimately the desire to continue with *Pelléas* that caused the earlier opera to be laid aside; what is not so clear is why *Roderigue et Chimène* itself had become unsatisfactory.

If any of Debussy's works must be labelled "Wagnerian" that distinction might be thought most justly accorded to *Roderigue et Chimène*. The opera was begun only a few months after Debussy's second and last Bayreuth pilgrimage, perhaps during that voyage. Mendès was a former friend of Wagner, and his wife Judith Gautier was connected in various ways with the composer.[8] It is to the supposed rejection of

Wagnerian elements that nearly all of Debussy's biographers have appealed when seeking a reason for the composer's reluctance to finish *Roderigue et Chimène*. But in fact, it is only the outward circumstances of Debussy's life at the time of the opera's composition which have justified regarding it as some sort of imitation of a Wagnerian model. The libretto, and its source, belong to quite another tradition. *Roderigue et Chimène* is derived from episodes in Corneille's *Le Cid*, which in turn was derived from a complex of stories about Don Roderigo Diaz de Vivar, the hero, especially from the seventeenth-century epic of Guillen de Castro. The central strain of the stories concerns the relationship between Roderigo and Chimène, whose fathers come to be sworn enemies. Roderigo eventually kills Chimène's father, and she must then choose between her love and her loyalty to her family. There were a great number of dramatic reworkings of the *Cid* story in the nineteenth century, especially in Germany, where there were five plays written between about 1810 and 1830, and seven operatic settings.[9] The proliferation of German adaptations can probably be attributed to Herder's popular *Nachdichtung*, based on Corneille and published in 1805. The best known of any of the operatic versions is that in French of Massenet (*Le Cid*, 1885), but Bizet had also worked on a *Le Cid* setting which he never finished.

Though the librettos based on the *Cid* complex were all put together from different combinations of the repertory of tales which make up that complex, they have two things in common. First, they can all be traced back

273

---

[5]The Act II vocal score is (so far as I know) unique among Debussy's autographs in being written out on paper of German origin, bearing the marketer's stamp "H. Litolff/ Braunschweig." The composer's last trip to Germany had been in the summer of 1889. The paper may, of course, have been bought then and used later, but as a rule Debussy used paper marketed by the Paris firm Lard-Esnault (see below, fn. 30). The manuscript for *Roderigue et Chimène* was described by Alfred Cortot, in *Inédits sur Debussy*, ed. Arthur Hoerée (Paris, 1942), pp. 12–16, and by Gustav Samazeuilh in *Musiciens de mon temps: Chroniques et souvenirs* (Paris, 1947), pp. 126–30. It was Cortot who assembled the three acts of the opera, obtaining Act I from Gabrielle Dupont, and Acts II and III from the estate of Emma Debussy.

[6]"Ma vie est tristement fiévreuse à cause de cet opéra, où tout est contre moi, et tombent douloureusement mes pauvres petites plumes dont vous aimiez la couleur. À ce propos, j'ai hâte de vous voir afin de vous faire entendre les deux actes faits, car j'ai peur d'avoir remporté des victoires sur moi-même." *Claude Debussy: Lettres 1884–1918*, ed. François Lesure (Paris, 1980), p. 32.

[7]See the letter of Paul Dukas to Vincent d'Indy cited in Dietschy, p. 85: "Il m'a joué également son opéra . . . vous serez très surpris, je crois, de l'ampleur dramatique de certaines scènes . . ." (letter dated 1 October 1893).

[8]For a summary of the careers of Mendès and Gautier see Elaine Brody, "La Famille Mendès: A literary link between Wagner and Debussy," *Music Review* 33 (1972), 177–89.

[9]The nineteenth-century operatic settings of the *Cid* story are (in German): *Der Cid* (F. L. Seidel; Berlin, 1806), *Der Cid*, "Romantische Oper" (Neeb; Frankfurt, 1843), *Der Cid*, "Oper" (L. A. B. Schindelmeisser; Pest, 1846); *Der Cid*, "Romantische Oper" (Peter Cornelius; Weimar, 1865), *Der Cid*, "Grosse Oper" (Willy Böhme; Dessau, 1887), *Don Roderigo Diaz de Vivar, Le Cid* (Emil Mayer; Linz, 1848), and *Roderigo und Ximene* (Johann Aiblinger; Munich, 1821). See Franz Steiger, *Opernlexikon*, I: *Titelkatalog* (Tutzing, 1975). There were three settings in Italian, by Luigi Salvi (Parma, 1834), Giovanni Pacini (Milan, 1853; libretto by de Lauzières), and R. Coppola (Cremona, 1884). To the setting in French by Massenet (libretto by Blau, Dennery, and Gallet) can be added the unfinished projects of Debussy and Bizet.

(through Herder in some of the German settings) to the classical model of Corneille. Second, and most important, they belong to the genre of historical or historicizing texts characteristic of the French operatic tradition in the nineteenth century. Like *Rienzi*, Wagner's "French" opera, they are dramas of political and social intrigue, where emotional entanglements are affected by the larger concerns of fidelity to an authority or political-religious ideology. They admit no intrusion of the supernatural, the mythical, or the imaginary, and little of speculative psychology. In this, they are wholly divorced from the German romantic tradition which was to remain at the core of Wagner's dramas.

Of the German operatic versions, that of Peter Cornelius is probably best known. *Der Cid* was written between 1860 and 1864, and performed at Weimar in 1865, almost concurrently with the first performance of *Tristan* in Munich. Cornelius was, of course, a close friend of Wagner, but also one who refused to become one of the sycophants surrounding the composer. Cornelius's own interpretation of the *Cid* libretto, and his choice of it, was communicated in a letter of 1864 to his brother Carl:

I wrote, back then, after my refusal of his [Wagner's] first invitation. In a state of enslavement, one doesn't write a *Cid*. And so it is . . . you have no idea what my *Cid* is—that there is something in it which, in a profound wholesomeness and temperateness, is exactly the opposite of Wagner's feverish provocation. Here there is no myth-making, and no Old German sentimentality.[10]

Cornelius was describing his reasons for refusing to join Wagner in Starnberg on the latter's invitation. Throughout the period during which he was composing *Der Cid*, Cornelius had made similar gestures of defiance, refusing, for example, to take Wagner's suggestions for

alterations in the libretto.[11] The letter to Carl suggests that the choice of the text was in itself a sort of turning upon the model of the Wagnerian libretto, or the mythological libretto.

It is also in Cornelius's perception of his own *Der Cid* that the measure of Mendès's *Roderigue et Chimène* is to be found. Mendès the *wagneriste* had turned to a French source and a French genre of operatic text in the writing of his libretto, no doubt attempting to fulfill his own famous dictum about the future of opera in France, ". . . le drame musicale en France serait une œuvre où l'inspiration française, profondement française, se développerait selon les lois empruntées au système wagnérien. . . ."[12] The inspiration, then, would presumably emanate from his own verse libretto, and the *lois* would be those prescribed. The quality of Wagnerism in *Roderigue et Chimène* would, however, have to be found first in the text; it is precisely there that is is lacking. Mendès's historical libretto, arranged in a series of set pieces and including large choral ensembles—*inspiration française*—was duly supplied to Debussy. But Debussy's setting of that libretto is hardly according to the *lois*. Meyerbeer intrudes into the work more strongly than his famous rival, and the musical language seems to have come neatly under the control of the structure, and the genre, of the text. Thus to identify Debussy's abandonment of his first opera as a turning away from the Wagnerian seems exactly contrary to what an examination of that opera suggests. In abandoning *Roderigue et Chimène*, he abandoned not Wagnerism but the French operatic tradition, text and musical language alike. By contrast, Maeterlinck's *Pelléas*, in which Debussy found his *inspiration*, was in essence a Wagnerian libretto which, as yet, lacked its musical setting.

III

The history of the composition of *Pelléas* can be approached from the manuscripts on one hand, and Debussy's correspondence on

---

[10]"Ich schrieb damals nach Ablehnung seiner ersten Einladung. Ein Höriger schreibt keinen Cid. Und so ist es . . . Du weisst nicht was mein Cid ist—dass etwas drinsteckt, was in einer tiefen Gesundheit und Gemütsstärke—gerade dem hektischen Nervenreiz Wagners ganz entgegen ist. Da ist keine Verhimmlung und altdeutsche Sentimentalität." Carl Maria Cornelius, *Peter Cornelius: Der Wort und Tondichter*, vol. I (Regensburg, 1925), pp. 423–24.

[11]Ibid., p. 371; Max Hasse, *Der Dichtermusiker Peter Cornelius* (Leipzig, 1923), pp. 82ff.
[12]Mendès, "Le jeune Prix de Rome," p. 135.

the other. There is more preliminary material for *Pelléas* than for any of the composer's other works. The manuscripts are scattered broadly over time, from summer 1893 to spring 1902, when the final alterations were made in the interludes after the first full technical rehearsals.[13] Aside from some isolated sheets[14] the four major manuscripts have long been known: the Meyer manuscript (Paris, private collection), the Légouix manuscript (The Pierpont Morgan Library, New York[15]), the Bréval manuscript (Paris, B.N. Mus. ms. 1206), and the complete developed draft of the opera in the New England Conservatory (hereafter NEC). The Meyer and Bréval manuscripts have recently been published in facsimile with a preface by François Lesure, *Les Esquisses de Pelléas et Mélisande* (Geneva, 1977).

The family relationships among these four can be, for the moment, briefly summarized. Meyer is a collection of preliminary drafts and sketches for Act I (fragments), Act II (scenes 1, 2, and 3), Act IV, scene 4, and Act V. These were written at various times between summer 1893 and summer 1895, and represent the earliest work done on those sections of the opera. Légouix was long held by a Paris dealer and reported "missing" since the late 1950s; it

resurfaced at a Paris auction in December 1979. It is a second draft for Act IV, scene 4, this time a developed draft, and is dated at the end September–October 1893.[16] Bréval was written in May 1895. It is a discarded *third* version of this same scene (i.e., a second developed draft) today bound with a single bifolio of the draft for the end of Act IV, scene 1. Until sometime after 1900, these two sections of Bréval had been part of the complete developed draft for the opera (NEC). Around that time, Debussy made further revisions and a new *fourth* version of Act IV, scene 4 was made; this is the one which is today bound with the NEC manuscript. The draft for this scene in Bréval is written on eight bifolios; three of these (fols. 6–11) were originally part of Légouix, and were lifted bodily from that draft to be spliced into the later reworking. The multiple date at the end of Act IV, scene 4 in Bréval, "*Septembre–Octobre 93. Mai 95,*" in this case indicates the actual physical age of the two layers of the manuscript.[17] The construction of the relevant sections of the three developed drafts for Act IV, scene 4 is summarized in table 1 (p. 122).

Even in this brief account, the repeated pattern of excision and substitution focuses attention on the scene which generated it, the fourth scene of the fourth act, "Une Fontaine dans le parc." As far as one can judge from the available sources, this was the only scene which was not simply written out once in developed draft and altered, if necessary, *in situ*. It required more extensive surgery. This is evident both in the circumstance of the two rejected developed drafts and in Debussy's comments on the scene in letters to his friends. This special quality, the quality of being set somehow apart, is strengthened by the position occupied by this scene in the chronology of the opera's composition. It was the first scene in *Pelléas* to be composed, and with one minor exception (Act IV, scene 3) the only scene to be composed "out of order" and separately from the others in the act to which it belongs.

---

[13]Three dissertations in progress, all dealing with some aspect of the *Pelléas* sketches, might be mentioned here: James R. McKay, *The Bréval Manuscript* (University of Chicago), David Grayson, *The Genesis of Pelléas et Mélisande* (Harvard), and Clà Vital, *Studien zu Debussys Skizzen zu Roderigue et Chimène und Pelléas* (Zürich). Published descriptions are given in Oswald d'Estrade-Guerra, "Les Manuscrits de *Pelléas et Mélisande,*" *Revue musicale* 235 (1957), 1–24, and in James R. McKay, "The Bréval Manuscript: New Interpretations," *Cahiers Debussy*, nouvelle série 1 (1977), 5–15.

[14]Several pages were exhibited in Basel in 1975; they are a section of the clean copy for the piano vocal score *Stichvorlage* of Act IV; see Tilmann Seebass, *Musikhandschriften in Basel: Ausstellung im Kunstmuseum Basel 31 Mai bis 13 Juli 1975* (Basel, 1975), pp. 78–79. A further section of the clean copy for the piano-vocal score *Stichvorlage* for Act IV is in Paris (**F–Pn** Mus. ms. 17683). The University of Texas at Austin has three pages discarded from the orchestral score of *Pelléas*, and another sheet which though listed in the catalogue of the collection as a "sketch for *Pelléas*" is probably one for *Usher*. More *Pelléas* documents will doubtless continue to appear.

[15]The Légouix manuscript is described by d'Estrade-Guerra, pp. 13–14, and in the catalogue for the sale at the Hôtel Drouot, *Manuscrits musicaux: Vente de vendredi. décembre 1979* (item 31 and plate 31).

[16]Too late for consideration here, the manuscript reappeared in the Lehman deposit at The Pierpont Morgan Library.

[17]See McKay, "The Bréval Manuscript," p. 6ff.

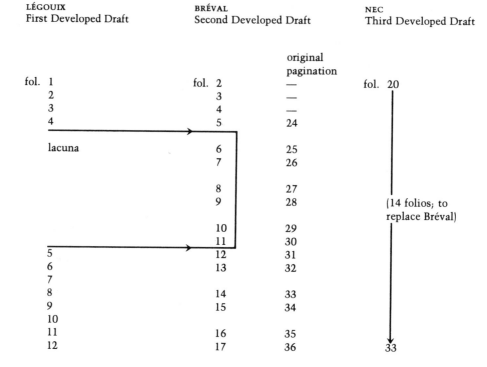

Table 1: Construction of the Three Developed Drafts: Act IV, scene 4

The chronology of the composition of *Pelléas* is on the whole unproblematic and is easily established in rough outline by the published correspondence, aided by the happy circumstance of Debussy's inscriptive dating of many of the sources. He began writing the opera in the summer of 1893, after having attended a performance of Maeterlinck's play in May that year.[18] Table 2 gives the inscriptions in the four major manuscripts, accompanied by a timetable for the opera's composition; the epistolary evidence which supports the chronology is self-evident, and can be conveniently reviewed in the preface of Lesure's facsimile edition of the Meyer and Bréval manuscripts.[19] These letters supply progress reports, the greatest number in the letters to Pierre Louÿs, who was absent from Paris for large

[18]A major error in some of the earlier biographies is the assignment of the first work on *Pelléas* to the year 1892. The misapprehension seems to have originated with two accounts by close friends of Debussy, Louis Laloy and Robert Godet. Laloy gave the date "summer 1892" in *La Musique retrouvée* (Paris, 1911), p. 61, and Godet stated that Debussy knew Maeterlinck's play in 1892 and began composition of the opera at that time; see "En Marge de la Marge," *Revue musicale* 7:7 (1926), p. 78. The correct date (1893) appears in Oswald d'Estrade-Guerra and Yvonne Tiénot, *Debussy* (Paris, 1961) and in Dietschy's biography. The year 1892 appears in none of the manuscripts for *Pelléas*, nor did Debussy mention the work in correspondence before fall 1893. In an account written in 1907, Debussy wrote "Ma connaissance de *Pelléas* date de 1893. Malgré

l'enthousiasme d'une première lecture, et peut-être la secrète pensée d'une musique possible, je n'ai commencé à y songer serieusement qu'à la fin de cette même année 1893"; cited in d'Estrade-Guerra, "Les Manuscrits de *Pelléas*," p. 7.

[19]Lesure gives excerpts from letters pertaining to the composition of *Pelléas* in his preface. From these he constructs a chronology which is accurate except for one small detail concerning Act II, scene 1. He takes a reference in a letter of April 1894, telling of a private audition of the "Scène de la fontaine," to indicate the best-known of the "Fountain" scenes, that which opens Act II, and hypothesizes that this scene was complete by spring 1894. Act IV, scene 4 was, however, also known by that title, and Act II was not written until late summer 1895. See Lesure, *Esquisses de Pelléas et Mélisande*, p. 8.

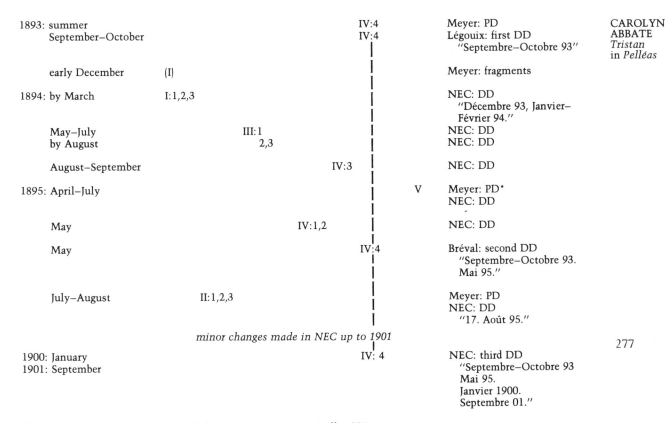

1893: summer				IV:4		Meyer: PD
September–October				IV:4		Légouix: first DD "Septembre–Octobre 93"
early December	(I)					Meyer: fragments
1894: by March	I:1,2,3					NEC: DD "Décembre 93, Janvier–Février 94."
May–July		III:1				NEC: DD
by August		2,3				NEC: DD
August–September			IV:3			NEC: DD
1895: April–July					V	Meyer: PD* / NEC: DD
May		IV:1,2				NEC: DD
May				IV:4		Bréval: second DD "Septembre–Octobre 93. Mai 95."
July–August		II:1,2,3				Meyer: PD / NEC: DD "17. Août 95."
minor changes made in NEC up to 1901						
1900: January / 1901: September				IV: 4		NEC: third DD "Septembre–Octobre 93 Mai 95. Janvier 1900. Septembre 01."

277

*Presentation inscription at the end of the entire MS: "Juin–Juillet 95"

Table 2: *Pelléas et Mélisande:* Chronology of the Composition
(PD = preliminary draft, DD = developed draft)

stretches of time during which Debussy was at work on *Pelléas*.[20]

Something more than straightforward announcements of time and place is to be drawn from remarks which the composer made during the writing out of Act IV, scene 4, and the problems posed by the task. On 7 September 1893, Debussy extended congratulations to himself in a letter to Ernest Chausson, explaining that he had finished the scene "Une Fontaine dans le parc."[21] The news was premature. In a second letter to Chausson, written about a month later, Debussy reported in a curious way that certain revisions had been necessary:

I was too hasty in crying victory over *Pelléas et Mélisande* because, after a sleepless night, the sort which brings counsel, I was forced to admit to myself that it wasn't right at all. It looks like the duet of Monsieur So-and-so, or it doesn't matter who, and above all, the ghost of old Klingsor, alias R. Wagner. He appeared at a certain measure; I tore everything up, and have started again in the search of a little formula made up of more personal phrases; I have forced myself to be both Pelléas and Mélisande; I

[20]Two sources for the Louÿs letters are *Correspondance de Claude Debussy et Pierre Louÿs 1893–1904*, ed. Henri Bourgeaud (Paris, 1945), and "Lettres inédits de Claude Debussy et Pierre Louÿs," ed. François Lesure, *Revue de Musicologie* 57 (1971), 29–39. For a selection, see Lesure's recent edition of *Lettres, 1884–1918*.

[21]*Lettres, 1884–1918*, p. 52.

have looked for music behind all the veils which it accumulates, even for its most ardent disciples.[22]

It is this second letter to Chausson which hints at the nature of the gesture which Debussy made in choosing this particular scene as a sort of trial case before taking up the remainder of the opera. It is a compositional test case because the close structural parallels between the Tryst scene in *Pelléas* and Act II of *Tristan* would have been unmistakable to Debussy's eye. Both have a certain sequence of events in common, beginning with the lyric rhapsodies of the waiting Isolde/Pelléas, continuing with the arrival of the other lover, the love duet, the warning of impending danger (Brangäne's Watch in one case, the sound of the castle gates being shut in the other), interruption, and finally a murderous attack upon the hero, this last a preparation for adumbration of a future and inexplicable death of the heroine.

In no other part of Maeterlinck's play is there a dramatic structure analogous to anything in *Tristan*, nor do the events of Acts I and III of Wagner's opera find any distinct echo in Maeterlinck's text. Put another way: it is in Act II of *Tristan*, and the Tryst scene of *Pelléas*, that the entire oft-noted parallelism of the *Tristan* and *Pelléas* librettos rests. It is the point of intersection between the two, and though Pelléas, going forward to meet Golaud without his sword, dies immediately, while Tristan, having thrown aside his sword to meet Melot, lingers in half-consciousness through another act, both have committed a symbolic act of suicide. Their acceptance of death occurs at the same point in the two similar sequences of events.

What the letter to Chausson also suggests is that, even at the earliest stage, Debussy

perceived that musical mimicry of some unspecified sort had gone too far. Whether *"tout déchiré"* is to be taken literally or metaphorically, the intent to avoid the recollection of Wagner was set out well in advance.

IV

So far, I have been referring to the four *Pelléas* manuscripts as "preliminary" and "developed" drafts without explanation of the terms. "Preliminary draft" refers to the type of draft in the Meyer manuscript. These are continuous drafts in pencil or ink, on two or three instrumental staves and one or more vocal staves. They are written without clefs, signatures, or text, except for a few words here or there, and are written for the most part on large upright sheets of thirty staves. "Developed draft" refers to the type of continuous draft in the Légouix, Bréval, and NEC manuscripts. These are in ink, often with corrections in many shades of pencil and crayon, also written on two to three instrumental staves, and fully supplied with text, accidentals, and generally also with indications for clefs, key and time signatures, and reminders for orchestration. All three were written out on large upright folios of thirty staves, mostly on bifolios. The musical text is confined to the rectos; versos are used for corrections. The information contained in this type of draft was sufficient to make the final stage—orchestration—in essence an application of the physical labor of writing out the full score to make a completed musical entity. Debussy considered *Pelléas* to be finished in 1895, though the orchestration was not finished until 1901.

This is not to say either that the orchestration was completely thought out in advance or, at the other extreme, that there was no role played at all by a preconceived or imagined orchestration in the first stages of the opera's composition. It is difficult, however, to locate the earthly traces of such a nebulous quantity as imagined orchestration. The Meyer drafts, rudimentary and hasty as they are, contain a number of orchestral cues—almost more of these than there are cues for the text. A most suggestive document belongs not to the *Pelléas* sources but to those for *La Chute de la mai-*

---

[22]"Je m'étais trop depêché de chanter victoire pour *Pelléas et Mélisande* car, après une nuit blanche, celle qui porte conseil, il a bien fallu m'avouer que ce n'était pas ça du tout, ça ressemble au duo de Monsieur de Tel, ou n'importe qui, et surtout le fantôme de vieux Klingsor, alias R. Wagner. Il apparassait au detour d'une mesure; j'ai donc tout dechiré, et suis repartie à la recherche d'un petit chimie de phrases plus personelles, et me suis efforcé d'être aussi Pelléas que Mélisande; j'ai cherché la musique derrière toutes les voiles qu'elle accumule, même pour ses dévots les plus ardents." Ibid., p. 55.

son Usher. This is a copy of Poe's story in Baudelaire's translation, owned by Debussy and containing his marginal annotations.[23] Most of the autograph additions take the unencouraging form of underlinings and exclamation points, but a single word—Poe's recurring refrain of *"la Peur . . ."*—was glossed in the margin with the indication *"c.a./alt.s.la.t./ cym."* (that is, English horn, violas *sur la touche* and cymbals). It was exactly this instrumental sound which Debussy used in the opera's prelude when he began the musical setting between 1908 and 1910, and which remained a constant in all later drafts up to the developed draft made in 1917.[24] In this case, the first musical motive in the conception of the work was not a melodic one—a collection of pitches in rhythm—but an instrumental sound which remained constant through its applications to various pitches and rhythms. It is, so to speak, an associative orchestration which belonged to the earliest stage of the opera's composition, Debussy's reading of the story with an eye to turning it into a libretto.

The terms "preliminary" and "developed" draft I have borrowed from the literature on Wagner's sketches and drafts, though the application there is to musical documents whose appearance and apparent function differs in many ways from those for *Pelléas.*[25] Nonetheless, the choice of this particular model was made not whimsically (if perhaps somewhat artificially) but in order to pinpoint those differences in the service of the dialectic I have set up between the two composers. Robert Bailey has characterized the preliminary draft for Act I of *Tristan und Isolde* as one in two essential voices, bass line and vocal part. Throughout his

analysis of the content of that draft runs the observation that it is the voice part that seems to take the dominant role in determining elements of design such as harmonic sequence and cadential patterning; from this vocal layer most of the contrapuntal detail would be generated.[26] It was in the developed draft for *Tristan* that Wagner worked out this detail, and the jump from developed draft to full score became a process that was notational rather than compositional.

By contrast, the preliminary drafts for *Pelléas* in the Meyer manuscript display no consistent number of voices. The musical text sometimes exists physically in the same range as it does in the developed drafts; that is, it occupies, and sometimes saturates, three instrumental staves, several registers, and varying degrees of harmonic fullness, from a single voice to six or more simultaneous pitches. An even greater contrast to *Tristan* is to be found in the treatment of the voice parts. In the preliminary drafts for *Pelléas* the vocal line is often completely omitted, and in at least one case added later to what began as a wholly instrumental draft, its pitch drawn from the preexistent instrumental display (see below, p. 129). In other cases, the vocal parts were written as stems without noteheads, the scansion of the text thus tracked with a purely rhythmic notation. This nonchalance toward the vocal parts as distinct melodic and rhythmic entities, coupled with an absence of text, also characterizes the preliminary drafts of works as far apart in time as *La Damoiselle élue* (1889) and *Usher* (1908–17).

One of the appositions often used descriptively of *Tristan* and *Pelléas* is the accordance of primacy to the orchestral substance in the former and the voice parts in the latter—Joseph Kerman's "symphony" and "sung play."[27] It is not by any means necessary to argue that a perceptible final result *need* be supported by the testimony of what is, in the end, a discarded

[23]Paris **F–Pn** Rés. Vm 41.

[24]Paris, **F–Pn** Mus. ms. 9885; see fn. 1.

[25]See Robert Bailey, "The Evolution of Wagner's Compositional Process after *Lohengrin*" in *Report of the 11th Congress of the International Musicological Society* (Copenhagen, 1972), I, 240–46, and "The Method of Composition" in *The Wagner Companion,* ed. Peter Burbridge and Richard Sutton (New York, 1979), pp. 269–338; J. Merrill Knapp, "The Instrumentation Draft of Wagner's *Das Rheingold,*" *Journal of the American Musicological Society* 30 (1977), 273–74, fn. 5; and John Deathridge, "The Nomenclature of Wagner's Sketches," *Publications of The Royal Musical Association* 101 (1974–75), 75–83.

[26]Robert Bailey, *The Genesis of Tristan und Isolde: Wagner's Sketches and Drafts for Act I* (Ph.D. diss., Princeton, 1969), pp. 60 ff.

[27]Joseph Kerman, *Opera as Drama* (New York, 1956), pp. 171–216.

witness. The converse is also admissible: one need not forbid the accretion of insights drawn from that discarded information to the critical construct. *Tristan* evidently began, at a certain stage in its history, with the vocal line which determined the structure of its accompaniment. In *Pelléas* the vocal line was extracted from, or laid over, an orchestral composition. Or, to reverse the construction: *Pelléas* is indeed a text spoken over an instrumental continuum, while *Tristan* is a symphony in which the voice lines determine the overall structure.

V

The Meyer manuscript, containing the preliminary drafts for *Pelléas*, is made up of 54 loose folios written out at various times, and is actually a miscellaneous assembly of those drafts. It contains fragments—sketches in the usual sense—for parts of Act I, a draft for roughly the second two-thirds of Act IV, scene 4, and complete drafts for all three scenes of Act II and for Act V. Since these latter two acts were the last to be written, the fact that they are the only ones to survive complete in their first stage suggests that the impulse to save the preliminary drafts for the opera came to the composer late, probably only in summer 1895.[28] The collection is inscribed and dated on the last page "*À Henri Lerolle/Claude Debussy/Juin–Juillet 1895.*" (The dates of the individual drafts range, of course, from summer 1893 for Act IV, scene 4 to summer 1895 for Act II.) The date of the final inscription is in fact somewhat odd; it gives the wide latitude of

two months, and is not the commoner sort of inscription which gives the day on which the presentation of the autograph was made. "June–July" 1895 may refer to the time during which the opera was finished with the composition of the preliminary draft for the second act. Debussy may have given the manuscript away at any time after he no longer had use of his first drafts—that is, after 17 August 1895. That is the date on the last page of the latest of the developed drafts, that for Act II in the NEC manuscript. It is also the only inscribed date in all of the four major manuscripts to give a day as well as the month and year. On the same day, Debussy wrote in a letter to Lerolle that the opera was complete,[29] and one senses that "*17 Août 95*" was considered more significant or ominous than any of the intermediate milestones.

The Meyer manuscript contains a mixture of bifolios and single sheets, the former predominating. Most of the drafts are written on 30-stave upright sheets bearing the blind stamp of the firm Lard-Esnault;[30] the final scene of Act II is written out on 20-stave paper of a smaller format. Two numberings of the sheets, neither in Debussy's hand, were added by later owners, and simply reflect the order in which the collector thought the sheets should be arranged. The order in which Debussy wrote out a given draft, or rather the proper sequential order of the sheets for a given draft, can be easily reconstructed from the musical text.

I have deliberately made a distinction between the "order in which Debussy composed the draft" and the logical order in which the draft is to be read through in sequence. This is because I think the two are not necessarily the same.

---

[28]The facsimile edition should be used with care since, in the interest of saving space, those folios in the Meyer manuscript which were blank were omitted from the edition, and many pages were not identified. In my discussion of the manuscript I have chosen to label the folios of the draft for Act IV, scene 4 as "folio 1, 2," and so forth, for that particular draft. This seemed less unwieldy than referring to the page numbers in the facsimile, which for this scene are rather confusing. For those who have the facsimile and wish to refer to it, the order is as follows: fol. 1^v=p. 53, 2^r=61, 3^r=60, 4^v=58, 5^r=54, 6^v=55, 7^r=57, 6^r (a recomposition of 5^r)=56, 4^r (three unidentified measures)=59. See table 3 for their arrangement. I am grateful to François Lesure and David Grayson for answering numerous requests for information about the manuscript, and to François Meyer for allowing me to examine it.

---

[29]Given in Lockspeiser, *Debussy* I, pp. 192–93.
[30]

Between 1898 and 1899, Lard-Esnault merged with another firm, that of Eduard Bellamy, and altered their mark. The Lard-Esnault-Bellamy stamp provides a *terminus post quem* of 1898–99 for the documents on which it appears. The NEC manuscript contains pages which bear both forms of the stamp; the third developed draft for Act IV, scene 4, for example, bears the newer mark.

A single example can be presented to illustrate the point. At the top of the last folio of the draft for Act V we find the final twelve measures of the opera, a cadence to C♯ major occupying about half the sheet. To this last folio were prefixed two folios which begin with the music accompanying Mélisande's death. Debussy ran out of room on the second of these folios, so he simply continued in the available space left on the last folio, below the final cadence in C♯, with Arkel's words ["*c'est au tour de la pauvre pe-*]*tite.*" In other words, the last twelve measures of the act were apparently written down before those which immediately precede them in the opera. Moreover, the whole of Act V appears to have evolved backwards from the final cadence. Within the draft for this act there are some sheets on which the musical text ends before all the available space has been used; there are others on which the

CAROLYN
ABBATE
Tristan
in *Pelléas*

(a) Physical Construction

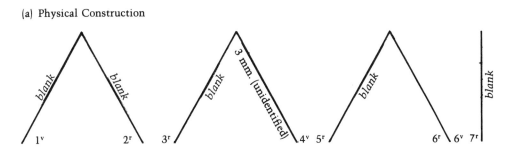

281

(b) Evolution

fol. 5ʳ: systems A–D
        systems E–H
        vocal part added to A–D

transition to Golaud's entrance
shutting of the castle gates

6ᵛ–7ʳ

Golaud's entrance to the end of the scene

1ᵛ–2ʳ–3ʳ–4ᵛ

Pelléas's song; dialogue; up to the shutting of the gates

6ʳ

recomposition of fol. 5ʳ:E–G and A

(c) Tonal Design

fol. 1ᵛ–2ʳ: Pelléas's song   F♯

2ʳ–4ᵛ: dialogue   F♯ / E♭

4ᵛ–5ʳ: shutting of the gates   G (V/V)

5ʳ: Pelléas moves into shadow C (V) shifts to C♯

6ᵛ–7ʳ: Golaud's entrance   to F♯

7ʳ: Pelléas's death   F minor

Table 3: The Preliminary Draft for Act IV, scene 4: Physical Construction, Evolution, Tonal Design

127

hand becomes more and more crowded, forcing the draft to overflow into the margins and remaining spaces on the following pages. In each of these cases, it is clear that a block of material existed at hand, and the section anterior to it was written down at some later time and spliced onto it.

This sort of retrograde accretion to the final cadence, as suggested by the appearance of the preliminary draft for this act, may in turn offer an explanation for Debussy's odd remark about Act V in a letter written to Louÿs in April 1895. "I really thought I would see you today," he wrote, "but I was surprised by the death of Mélisande, which disturbs me, and on which I am working, shaking all the while."[31] The remark seems enigmatic because the schedule established by the remainder of the correspondence indicates that work on Act V was mainly confined to June 1895. Why, then, did Debussy speak of working on the music for Mélisande's death—at the end of the act—in April, two months earlier? An explanation is suggested by the construction of the preliminary draft. *"La mort de Mélisande"* means quite literally the moment of her death. The music for it, even though it occurs at the end of the act, was the first music in the act to be composed, and therein, for Debussy, lay the quality of surprise.

A compositional habit which permits a complete scene to be assembled out of discrete blocks implies that the composer possessed in advance some structural plan which established the design that the separate units would form when put together. By choosing the Tryst scene (Act IV, scene 4) as a test case for analysis, as it was originally Debussy's test case for composition, I have chosen the scene which admittedly remained the most conservative harmonically. In it, however, an older and more rigid system of tonality can be observed in juxtaposition with a newer principle, that of an essentially text-determined harmonic de-

sign. It is in fact the latter, I will suggest, which represents Debussy's reading of what Mendès called the Wagnerian *lois.*

The draft for this scene represents a miniature display of the sort of out-of-order evolution observed in the draft for Act V. Table 3a gives, for orientation, a schematic diagram which shows the physical construction of the draft. The scene occupies seven folios (three bifolios and a single sheet) in the Meyer manuscript, forming a complete unit of about 200 measures. The musical text begins about one-third of the way through the scene with Pelléas's song *"On dirait que ta voix a passé sur la mer"* in F♯ major. It includes music for a long dialogue between Pelléas and Mélisande which Debussy cut in May 1895 when he made the second developed draft for the scene.[32]

In this case, the original core of music seems to have been about twenty-five measures, written on the recto of what is now the fifth sheet, and forming an orchestral transition to Golaud's appearance. That this passage was the first part of the scene to be written down is hinted at by the spatial arrangement of fol. 5ʳ, of which part is given in plate 1 and in example 1. Eight systems are drawn on the sheet, which can be labelled A through H. As soon as the missing text is supplied to the vocal part, it becomes apparent that E–G should be read before A–D (shown in plate 1 and ex. 1). The text at the bottom of the page, *"mon cœur bat comme un fou au fond de ma gorge,"* immediately precedes that which opens system A, *"Écoute, écoute, mon cœur est sur le point de m'étrangler."* Debussy apparently broke off after writing the fourth system, and added the cross as a cue to remind himself that what was to follow was a return of Golaud's motive in A♭ in the bass, referring back to the appearance of this motive in the third measure of system B. (Golaud had first sung this motive in the opera's first scene when he identified himself to Mélisande: *"Je suis Golaud, le petit fils d'Ar-*

282

[31]"Je pensais vraiment à te voir aujourd'hui, mais j'ai été surpris par la mort de Mélisande qui m'inquiète et à laquelle je travaille en tremblant." Bourgeaud, *Debussy et Pierre Louÿs,* p. 43.

[32]The text in question begins after Mélisande's *"Si, si je suis heureuse; mais je suis triste,"* to immediately before Pelléas's *"Quel est ce bruit?"*

kel, le vieux roi d'Allemonde.'') Fol. 5ʳ: A–D was first composed as a purely instrumental passage. Debussy left no space for a vocal staff, and the voice parts were later written in below the instrumental staves, in the blank staves which were normally left between systems. Moreover, Debussy did not provide enough music in systems A–D for the declamation of the available text. System H (transcribed as ex. 9, p. 140) is a four-measure phrase cued for insertion at m. 6 of system B, whose seven measures were thus expanded to eleven. It seems most likely that Debussy's second step had been the writing out of systems E–G, dovetailing the last measure of G with the first measure of A, and adding the text to A–D as he continued on. He later sketched out the music for Golaud's appearance and the end of the scene on fols. 6ᵛ and 7ʳ. (It is, of course, possible that 6ᵛ and 7ʳ were written down before 5ʳ: A–D; this would provide an alternate explanation for the anomalous arrangement of 5ʳ. At the very least, one must say that 5ʳ and 6ᵛ/7ʳ were written out at different times, separately from one another.)

The last part of the draft to be written down was the section occupying the first two bifolios, about one hundred measures extending roughly to the point in the text where Pelléas and Mélisande hear the castle gates being shut and realize that they are trapped outside. The music for this section begins at the top of fol. 1ᵛ, and continues through 2ʳ and 3ʳ, ending about two-thirds of the way through fol. 4ᵛ. This is the point at which it connects to the passage on system E of fol. 5; that it breaks off short indicates that the latter part of the scene was probably already written down.

Table 3b summarizes the apparent order of composition for the various subsections of the preliminary draft.

The information to be read from the actual appearance of the draft goes this far. The individual subsections seem to have fallen out according to the main events in the drama: Pelléas's rhapsodic hymning of Mélisande, the long dialogue between the two, then the closing of the castle gates, Pelléas's final resignation to entrapment, and at last Golaud's appearance and the catastrophe.

In a reading of the musical text itself, two things leap to the eye. First, each individual musical subsection begins strongly with a particular tonal focus, or cadences firmly in a particular tonal area. Secondly, and more curious: Debussy had begun the composition of *Pelléas et Mélisande* with an almost single-minded use of a system of metaphorical tonality—that is, by quite blatantly linking tonal areas with characters on the one hand, and textual imagery on the other. Example 2 shows the process at work in this crucial scene on a small scale and in unadulterated form. These five measures are transcribed from f. 2ʳ, and give Mélisande's first vocal entrance in this part of the scene. That entrance is signaled by the rubric "Fa♯," and her line is indeed set to a sudden shift to F♯ major. It was Debussy's occasional habit to thus mark a shift in tonal focus, but generally the cue was used as a substitute for writing out a change in signature. Here this is not the case; many of the required sharps are entered. As the dialogue between the two characters continues, the tonality of the musical setting on the local level alternates between F♯ when Mélisande speaks and E♭ when Pelléas responds, or (alternately) F♯ when Pelléas is speaking of Mélisande. The F♯ tonality thus appears not only when the "tagged" character speaks, but when she is spoken about, as she is in the rhapsodic episode which begins the draft. As subject or object, she provokes the same response, the same tonal association.

This particular symbol, established here from the first, resonated through the composition of the opera. In Act I, scene 1, for example, F♯ (as G♭) major is reached as a local tonic at the moment when Mélisande reveals her name to Golaud, singing its four syllables to the pitches D♭–D♭–B♭–G♭; thus both the gnomic tonality and the thing signified are distilled and stated in their purest forms, triad and name. E♭, on the other hand, is linked in the preliminary draft to the second of the protagonists; the melodic fragment generally identified as Pelléas's motive, for example, appears in the long dialogue between the two characters (fols. 2ʳ and 3ᵛ), and in E♭. Debussy's "Fa♯" (or my label "F♯") should not, however, be understood as necessarily standing for a tonic which exerts

283

284

Plate 1: Meyer Manuscript, fol. 5ʳ (part)
(Reproduced by permission from François Lesure, ed., *Les Esquisses de Pelléas et Mélisande*, 1977)

Meyer fol. 5ʳ/A–D (Lesure p. 54).

285

Example 1

Example 2

control over large stretches of music, or even necessarily as a single tonality, though it could be either. It is rather what I have been calling a "tonal focus," a potential collection of tonalities which work in the same harmonic sector (e.g., key signatures with five or six sharps). This collection may be contrasted, for example, with another tonal focus subsumed under the label "E♭," as it is in the preliminary draft.

I had remarked above that if a complete scene is to be assembled out of separate blocks, the plan for the ordering of those blocks must be established in advance. What the preliminary draft suggests is that Debussy linked certain textual elements with the appearance of certain metaphorical tonalities, and then constructed the scene by ordering these appearances into a skeletal pattern. The order and choice of tonalities—hence their position in relation to one another—may be made according to textual rather than functional harmonic exigencies. The transitional material which forms the link between the pre-established points of articulation is for the moment of secondary consideration; it may range from music of a traditionally "tonal" sort to a series of static sonorities without apparent direction. Both kinds of procedures appear in *Pelléas*, at one end of the opera's evolution in the preliminary draft, and at the other in the finished score.

Keeping all this in mind, it is possible to reconstruct the hypothetical design of Act IV, scene 4, from the preliminary draft. The last subsection (fols. 6ᵛ and 7ʳ forms a prolonged cadence to F♯/B, with the key of F minor interpolated abruptly at the end, at the moment of Pelléas's death (ex. 3). F♯ major was fixed as standing for Mélisande, both as a character in the drama, and as Pelléas sees her, the corporealization of his ideal of beauty. F minor, on the other hand, was being manipulated as a contrasting key, as attested to by its sudden and unprepared appearance at the catastrophe which closes the scene. Furthermore, an allied association was designed for its dominant C, for which an example may be drawn which again demonstrates the case for associative tonality in microcosm (see ex. 4). Here the transcription gives a section of the dialogue which was eventually cut from the scene. In the midst of an oscillation between F♯ and E♭, there is a striking shift to C major/minor, whose *raison d'être* apparently lies in the text, Pelléas's "*Tu es si belle qu'on dirait que tu vas mourir,*" and Mélisande's serene and disquieting reply, "*Toi aussi.*" There is a predictive element here—textually in Mélisande's simple statement, and musically in the momentary appearance of the dominant of the key which will close the scene. C major appears again somewhat later in the scene, not as an interpolation, but as the local tonic of one subsection, the transition to Golaud's entrance, on fol. 5ᵛ: A–D. I will return to this particular appearance below.

Table 3c summarizes the foregoing discussion of the harmonic design of the preliminary draft.

Example 3

Example 4

VI

At this point, before looking at one revision made *in situ* in the preliminary draft, it might be useful to turn to the scene in its final form—and not only in order to draw the foregone conclusion that many of the mappings of tonality and representation established in the first draft can be seen to have been retained in the final version. The play *Pelléas et Mélisande* is notorious for its admission of multiple interpretations. This quality could be identified as one common to symbolist drama, a genre which depends on the reader or listener bringing to the text a wealth of his own memories and recollections. The play may, in fact, perhaps only be considered complete when ornamented by such speculation. A musical reading of such a text necessarily draws in and narrows an originally wider range of interpretive possibilities. Perhaps it was the fear of such a constriction which led Mallarmé to insist in his review of the play *Pelléas* that the least musical intrusion would have shattered Maeterlinck's text, a comment which seems misconceived to a musical observer looking back after 1902.[33]

In his setting of *Pelléas* Debussy seems to have narrowed his attention and fixed it upon the symbol, split into pairs of opposite qualities, which recurs constantly in the text: vision/light and blindness/darkness. These symbols appear in every scene chosen by Debussy to use in his setting. The government itself, the principle of order in the play's world, is presided over by a blind king, Arkel. The blindness of order in turn manifests itself in the landscape, which is described as being almost constantly in darkness or shadow. Mélisande and Pelléas are set apart as the only characters who consistently search after some sort of light, the former more than the latter: it is Mélisande, for example, who is terrified of the dark, and who tells Golaud that she will die of being too long in the shadow of the castle. In Act II, scene 1, she drops her wedding ring into the "Fountain of the Blind." This event is often

interpreted as her symbolic rejection of her marriage: Mélisande is a young bourgeoise deliberately ridding herself of the mark of her condition. She loses the ring, however, because she has thrown it too high in the air and, blinded by the sun, allows it to fall. Disaster is the result not of the intention to misbehave, but of the inability to see.

Nonetheless, it is also to Mélisande herself that the double image is linked. It is the central metaphor for her own nature, which is compounded not only of innocence, but of destructiveness, and it represents a projection of that quality onto the physical world. The quality of destructiveness is seldom revealed, but it is present in the least of her actions—her lies to Golaud—and the greatest of them, her bringing of death to Pelléas, and to the kingdom, in her empty hands. The Tryst scene in Act IV is ostensibly a sort of seduction of Mélisande by Pelléas. It is in fact the case in reverse, Pelléas's *Verführung*; led astray, he is lost, and he dies. Only in this scene does Pelléas come to seek out darkness, or to prefer shadow to the light.

By speaking of interpretation of the text in advance, I have imitated the order of the composer's reasoning rather than that of the critic. The latter observes the musical setting and decides how it has been manipulated in service of the text, while the former begins with the text alone, and his reading of it. It has already been suggested how the principle of tonality as metaphor worked to establish certain key-sequences in the first draft for the Tryst scene. Table 4 gives an analytical reduction of the scene in its final form. The design of the preliminary draft can be seen to form the skeleton of the completed scene, which is divided roughly into three parts, separated by (a) the "declaration of love" at mm. 618–29 (in the Durand vocal score, p. 244, m. 3–p. 245, m. 6), and (b) the shutting of the castle gates at m. 692 vs, p. 255, m. 3). The harmonic structure of the scene is grounded in the opposition of two keys a semitone apart, F♯ and F, and their respective dominants. Part I shifts between these two dominants, C♯ and C. Part II, which begins with "*On dirait que ta voix a passé sur la mer,*" is centered in F♯ major, the key of that song. Part III is essentially a long cadence to F minor by way of V/V and the dominant.

[33]Stéphane Mallarmé, "Crayonné au Théâtre," *Divagations* (Paris, 1897). The review originally appeared in the *Reveil mensuel de litterature* of June 1893.

PART I

	tonal center
Introduction: Pelléas's monologue, vs 232, m. 11	(ambiguous)
Mélisande's entrance, vs 236, m. 6	Db/C♯
Mélisande's narration of her escape, vs 238, m. 5	C♮
Pelléas's reply, vs 239, m. 4	C♯
Declaration of love:	
Mélisande, "Je t'aime aussi," vs 244, mm. 3–4	C♮
Mélisande, "Depuis que je t'ai vu," vs 245, mm. 5–6	C♯

PART II

Pelléas's song: "On dirait que ta voix," vs 245, m. 7	F♯	(A)
Pelléas's search for ideal beauty, vs 248, m. 3	B	(B)
Pelléas, "Et maintenant je l'ai trouvée," vs 250, m. 5	F♯	(A')
Dialogue, vs 251, m. 3	f♯–F♯	(coda)
Pelléas, "Viens, dans la lumière," vs 252, m. 3	F♯	
Pelléas, "Il nous reste si peu de temps," vs 253, m. 1	(C♮)	

PART III

Shutting of castle gates, vs 255, m. 3	G♮
Pelléas, "Il est trop tard" Golaud's motive), vs 256, m. 12	G♮
Pelléas, "Ah! qu'il fait beau dans les ténèbres," vs 258, m. 12	C♮
Final cadence, iv–i, vs 267, mm. 20–23	f♮

289

Table 4: Tonal Design of the Final Version, Act IV, scene 4
(references are to page numbers in the Durand vocal score)

It is in the patterning of the shifts between C♯ and C in Part I that the first indication of Debussy's reading lies. The alternation between the tonal regions on the local level is designed to parallel the vocal entrances of the two protagonists. As Mélisande appears, or more exactly as Pelléas sees her, there is a shift to C♯/Db. Throughout the ensuing dialogue, Pelléas's vocal periods focus on C♯, while Mélisande's return always to the lower semitone key. There is therefore a fine subtlety in the distinction between Mélisande as she is seen, as opposed to Mélisande as her presence works its eventually disastrous effect, and in the tonal symbolism which mirrors it. When Mélisande, at the end of the first section, replies to Pelléas's declaration of his love, she says simply "Je t'aime aussi," sung to the pitch C♮. The contrast between this almost silent musical gesture and the complex musical *Nérvenreiz* of the analogous "declaration" in Act II of *Tristan* is notoriously used to point up the stylistic gulf between the two operas. How-

ever, given the metaphorical weight with which the pitch C (standing for the tonality) has been invested, Debussy's reduction of means can in the end hardly be taken as a piece of compositional simple-mindedness.

In Part III of the scene, the lower semitone key F minor is tonicized by the prolonged cadence. Golaud's motive appears in G in m. 709 (vs 256, m. 12: as Pelléas sings "*il est trop tard*") and marks the appearance of V/V. The dominant C is approached through an arpeggiation, and reached in m. 734 (vs 258, m. 12), at Pelléas's words "*Ah, qu'il fait beau dans les ténèbres.*" The symbolic acceptance of death implied by this turning-to-darkness is thus reached simultaneously with the structural dominant. The chain of resolutions V/V to V to i parallels the three major events in the latter part of the scene: the closing of the castle gates, trapping the two protagonists outside and making Pelléas's death inevitable, then Pelléas's resignation to that death, and finally his murder by Golaud.

135

VII

Once Debussy allowed textual imagery to control a pattern of tonalities, then the important subsequent revisions and recompositions, in all the drafts for the scene, took the form of defusing the reflexive, at times even trivial, musical responses to the text of the sort which have been identified above in the preliminary draft. Put another way: Debussy was obscuring the traces of the system.

I give here only a single example of a recomposition. One section of the draft for the Tryst scene was altered *in situ* in the Meyer manuscript. The new version was written out on the recto of the sixth folio. The section which was revised was that on fol. 5ʳ, from immediately after the shutting of the castle gates (systems E, F, and G) to the end of system A. The original version (see ex. 1) was constructed as a straightforward prolongation of G, followed by its resolution to the local tonic C at *"Écoute, écoute, mon cœur est sur le point de m'étrangler."* Both the original and the recomposition are given in example 5.

In the new version, two critical changes were made. First, the resolution V–I was interrupted by an arpeggiation to the tonality of ♭iii (E♭ minor). Secondly, the appearance of C major is delayed for four measures. The key still functions as a local tonic, and the harmonic purpose of the passage—preparing the eventual shift to F minor at the end of the scene—remains as originally established. What Debussy did was to narrow the focus of the tonality C major, by bringing the resolution to C to bear on Pelléas's words at the moment of its delayed appearance, the phrase *"Ah, qu'il fait beau dans les ténèbres,"* to which I have attached such symbolic significance above. Since, throughout the latter part of the scene, it has been Mélisande who has urged Pelléas to remain in the darkness, the recomposition of this passage suggests that the investiture of Mélisande with a dark side, and the consequent musical obfuscation, was already beginning to take shape in Debussy's mind.

VIII

Act IV, scene 4 of *Pelléas* is one where no great overt mimicry of Wagner is discernible on the surface of the final version even though—

or perhaps because—it is most nearly parallel to Wagner's *Tristan* on other levels. It is, so to speak, an interpretation of one aspect of Wagner's compositional technique made almost thirty-five years later by Debussy. This technique, which we have seen as it was put to use in the first stages of the composition of *Pelléas*, was a system of text-generated tonal organization, borrowed from the Wagnerian models with which Debussy was demonstrably familiar. That familiarity is attested to not only by visits to Bayreuth. It is more than coincidental that much of the composition of *Pelléas* should have intersected with Debussy's performances at *"séances wagneriennes"* during which he would play and single-handedly sing through entire operas. This was a money-making scheme which had occupied him from winter 1893–94 through 1895.[34]

Simple mimicry in *Pelléas* takes the form of direct quotation, and is present in abundance. Whether quotations can be convincingly identified depends both on the quickness of the critic's ear and the latitude of his reader's imagination. Richard Strauss saw *Pelléas* in 1907, and his behavior at the performance was reported by Romain Rolland:

After the first act he says, "is it like this, all the time?" "Yes." "Nothing more? There's nothing in it. No music. It has nothing consecutive. No musical phrases, no development." . . . He goes on listening, as much from a sincere desire to understand it as from consideration for me. But . . . the novelty of the work escapes him. On the other hand, he doesn't let a single instance of Wagnerian imitation go by without pointing it out, though not in admiration. "But that is all in *Parsifal*," he says at a certain passage.[35]

More recently, Laurence Berman has suggested a specific reference to the transition to the opening of Brangäne's Watch from Act II of *Tristan* in the transition to the return of the opening material in the *Prélude à l'après-midi*

[34]See the letter of Debussy to Chausson, "Correspondance inédit," 126. Robert Godet, speaking of his recollections of Debussy during spring 1895, wrote "On se souvient de l'avoir rencontré un soir, rue Royale, si pressé (il allait jouer *Tristan* on ne sait plus où) qu'il résista aux tentations d'une terrasse d'audiences apéritives et ne prit que le temps de jéter ces mots 'Pelléas est fini . . . de ce matin, pour être historique'" ("En Marge de la Marge," p. 79).
[35]Cited in Lockspeiser, *Debussy,* I, p. 89.

290

Example 5

291

Pelléas, Act II (opening of first interlude)

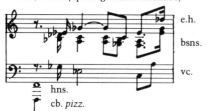

Pelléas, Act IV, Scene 4: scoring
of "Tristan" chord in m. 691

Pelléas, Act II (opening of second interlud

Die Meistersinger, Act III (at "Matt und
verzweiflungsvoll sieht er um sich")

Tristan: scoring in the Einleitung

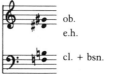

Tristan, Act III (opening measures)

Example 6   Example 7   Example 8

292

d'un faune. Berman also indicated a general family resemblance between Wagner's habit of disguising the four-measure period as transition and Debussy's similar blurring of the points of formal articulation in the Prélude.[36] An entire volume devoted to the identification of Wagner quotations in Debussy's works has recently been published,[37] though in this case the lines between actual quotation and the random occurrence of certain pitches have perhaps been too hazily drawn.

If the identification of quotation in Pelléas is a sort of game, nonetheless it is a game sanctioned and even secretly encouraged by the composer. The game is meant to be discovered, and its discovery changes the music for Pelléas into something more than an adequate—or exquisite—reading of Maeterlinck. The opera becomes a commentary on an earlier musical corpus, and the listener's knowledge of that corpus is in turn meant to enter into his own interpretation of Pelléas.

The Wagnerian quotations most often occur in the interludes; they were therefore sometimes entered into the opera at the latest

stage of its evolution, when the interludes were expanded in spring 1902. The most convenient source for the original, shorter form of the interludes is the first published vocal score (Paris: Fromont, 1902), from which the quotations can be identified as occurring either in the sections composed up to 1895, or in the later expansions. Of the latter sort is a quotation from Act III of Die Meistersinger, a single measure from the orchestral accompaniment to Beckmesser's long pantomime, which appears in Pelléas in the first interlude of Act II (ex. 6). The pitch content and rhythmic pattern of the two are nearly identical, and the orchestration of both reinforces the association horns sustain the low F, accompanied by an articulative pizzicato in the bass; the upper part are given over to strings or woodwinds. Finally the quotation was not made irrationally. In Die Meistersinger this particular measure is glossed with one of Wagner's careful bits of stage direction. Beckmesser has collapsed "Matt und verzweiflungsvoll sieht er um sich." Debussy uses this text—in this case direction for blocking—to refer to an even which is taking place off stage during this interlude in Pelléas. It is between scenes 1 and 2 of Act II that Golaud's horse has run against a tree; Golaud has been thrown and lies almost unconscious beneath the animal. Beckmesser's

[36]Laurence Berman, "Debussy's Summer Rites," this journal 3 (1980), 231ff.
[37]Robin Holloway, Debussy and Wagner (London, 1979).

despair and exhaustion are transformed to an abstraction of the despair of physical incapacity. The musical symbol for it can be stripped of the comic inflection in the context of *Die Meistersinger*, but retains its reference to the image; because it is a musical symbol its meaning is subject to a certain amount of purification.

The quotations from *Tristan* most often take the form of musical punning. The puns work on the aural identity of the name "Tristan" and the French word "*triste*," sad. The pitches F♮, B♮, D♯, and G♯, for example, recur with suspicious consistency when the word "*triste*" is sung by any of the characters. Even an alternative verbal construction such as "*pas heureuse*" suffices to generate the musical sound. In the latter case, what may have begun as a conjunction between two similarly sounding words retains its function even when the tagged word has been replaced by another with like meaning. The punning quotation can be seen, for example, in the Tryst scene, where Mélisande in a characteristically enigmatic way sings "*je suis heureuse, mais, je suis triste.*" As she does so, the pitches of the "Tristan" chord sound in the orchestra in the same register as they do in the Act I *Einleitung*. Again, the orchestration in *Pelléas* recalls that in the source (ex. 7).

A second quotation of this sort may be found in the expanded version of the second interlude in Act II. Here an allusion is made to the prelude to Act III of *Tristan*. The quotation is not at pitch, but a major third above, in A minor rather than F minor (ex. 8). The two have in common orchestration, and a repeated harmonic structure iv–i; the ascending melodic motive 2–3 (over iv) 4–5 (over i) is also discernible in the citation in *Pelléas*. This reference to the bleak Kareol music occurs as the beginning of the interlude, and might have been thought to be inspired by Mélisande's last words in the previous scene where, in reaction to Golaud's rage, she cries "*je ne suis pas heureuse.*" Actually, one need search no further than the autograph full score[38] to find the more immediate explanation for the allusion.

Here, an expressive direction—"Tristement"—is written above this measure in the interlude. It is a direction which does not appear in any of the published sources for the opera. Its omission may have been an oversight by the engraver, but it may also have been a deliberate excision on Debussy's part.

I have given only three examples of many, and have in these chosen quotations for which the case for deliberation is strong. They are at pitch, or similarly orchestrated, or obviously linked to the verbal "tag." In his study of Debussy and Wagner, Robin Holloway concluded that the large number of quotations which he identified seemed to have no meaning, that they were extracted from their source and used almost waywardly, or haphazardly, in a new setting where their original harmonic function has no logic.[39] While acknowledging the sensitivity of Holloway's ear in tracking down many of the Wagnerian allusions, I should prefer to turn the argument around, and start from the observation that many "quotations" may merely be the result of coincidental or vague affinities which arise whenever a common harmonic vocabulary is in use. Then at least we can clear away the bulk of such "quotations" and exonerate Debussy from the onus of their apparent pointlessness or dissimilarity to the "model." In this cleared field remain those quotations which were introduced for a purpose, albeit one which may indeed be completely unallied to the exigencies of musical composition. The "Tristan" chord has no structural harmonic significance in its context in the Tryst scene of *Pelléas*. But then, neither does the "Tristan" chord when it occurs in Act III of *Die Meistersinger*, in the well-known self-quotation at Sachs's "*Mein Kind, von Tristan und Isold / kenn' ich ein traurig' Stück.*" The purpose of the quotation in both cases is not musical at all. Rather, the composer has allowed a detail in the text to evoke a musical element which has no actual musical function or consequence.

---

[38]Paris, **F–Pn** Mus. ms. 962/II, fn. 75/3.

[39]Holloway, *Debussy and Wagner*, p. 125. Holloway does not mention the quotation from *Die Meistersinger*; he cites many quotations from *Tristan* but does not note the punning intent (see pp. 88, 127).

One of the most intriguing quotations from *Tristan* in *Pelléas* did not survive past the preliminary draft for Act IV, scene 4 in the Meyer manuscript. This musical passage was mentioned briefly above (p. 129). In discussing the physical arrangement of fol. 5ʳ of that draft, I referred to four measures of music added on the last two staves of that folio as "system H," and pointed out that these four measures were meant to be inserted into the second system on that page, as indicated by the cue. I also suggested that Debussy simply found that he needed to expand that particular section when he began to add the vocal line and noticed that he had too much text for the music at hand. Roughly thirty words would have had to be sung in the space of three measures:

MÉLISANDE: Il y a quelqu'un derrière nous . . .
PELLÉAS: Je ne vois personne . . .
MÉLISANDE: J'ai entendu du bruit . . .
PELLÉAS: Je n'entends que ton cœur dans l'obscurité . . .
MÉLISANDE: J'ai entendu craquer les feuilles mortes . . .

The four measures which Debussy composed to fill out the musical setting of the passage are a transformed, repeated statement of the "Tristan" chord (a diminished fifth below its pitch in the *Einleitung*) and its characteristic chromatic ascent (ex. 9):

Meyer fol. 5ʳ/H (Lesure p. 54)

Example 9

"*Il y a quelqu'un derrière nous*": Mélisande hears someone behind her, she hears the noise of the rustling of dead leaves, she hears Golaud's approaching footsteps. But stripped for the moment of their context, her words are an abstract description of the sensation of being followed, of "hearing someone behind" oneself in the dark. It is then the quotation which reveals the identity of the figure who is

"heard behind." By citing *Tristan*, Debussy evoked as this figure its creator, "*le phantôme de vieux Klingsor, alias R. Wagner.*" Symbolically, it was Wagner whom Debussy heard standing behind the composition of *Pelléas*, just as the aural memory of *Tristan* here stood so near to his own work.

The implications of Debussy's reading of this text might be turned outward to the entire opera. With the introduction of the *Tristan* quotation, there has been generated a momentary identification of the Golaud of Maeterlinck's drama with another figure, an association in parallel of Golaud/Wagner (hidden in the dark) and by extension Pelléas/Debussy. The catastrophe of the drama, Golaud's murder of Pelléas, is a manifestation of an archetype: the murder of a young man by an older man; that is, of a young man by someone born long before him. Debussy touched upon an interpretation of that archetype as a metaphor for the entire phenomenon of Wagnerism in the latter half of the nineteenth century, and its potential destruction of a composer born after 1859 should he come to embrace it. By excising the quotation from the version of this passage in the developed draft, he both erased the traces of the reading, and made a gesture towards avoiding the consequences of which it spoke.

IX

The question concerning supposed systems of text-generated tonal organization in opera is one which has generated a certain amount of controversy, most recently in earlier issues of *19th-Century Music*. Responding to Siegmund Levarie's essay on Verdi's *Un Ballo in maschera*, Guy Marco pointed out that

Opera composers have been no more helpful than critics in articulating such a theory, but of course it is not their task to do so. Wagner did not say how his poetical-musical periods were joined into patterns, nor even how to tell where one started and ended. Verdi's letters are a useful source of his ideas on relevant points, but they never speak to the details of large-scale structure.[40]

The drafts for *Pelléas* may be said to have—at

---

[40]Guy A. Marco, "On Key Relations in Opera," this journal 3 (1979), 84.

294

least partially—articulated the elusive theory, as it was understood by their author. If Debussy appeared to have used the theoretical system blatantly at first, as in the preliminary draft for Act IV, scene 4, the gradual obscuring of its traces was not only an act of criticism. It was also a decision made with the intent to disguise the indebtedness to a predecessor, though without disguising all traces of his presence.

I have, perhaps dangerously, attached a great deal of importance to evidence that Debussy's manipulation of the Wagnerian *lois* was conscious and deliberate, drawing from the text of the compositional draft signs of this deliberation. This is because I prefer to regard these discarded drafts neither as the accidental physical remains of the hypothetical works[41] which each one implies, nor even primarily as early versions of the published opera which testify to method, though the latter concern has obviously been taken into consideration. To me, their greatest significance lies in the fact that they are, so to speak, interpretations of Wagner. They illustrate a late nineteenth-century analysis of one aspect of Wagner's style with as much validity as might a contemporary critical essay.

Richard Kramer, discussing another delicate subject—the proper relevance of Beethoven sketches to Beethoven studies—has stated that "what in formal and substantive terms is excluded from the artifact (the finished work) is irrelevant to it, and, necessarily, to the criticism of it."[42] Kramer was herein disclaiming an "indictment of New Criticism" attributed to him by Douglas Johnson. But if Kramer will not indict New Criticism, then I will. I would not mind excluding consideration

of the *Pelléas* drafts from an analysis, though I would balk at an imposed requirement to do so. But by excluding, for example, consideration of *Tristan* from an interpretation of *Pelléas*, one would be willfully disregarding the main subtext of the opera for the sake of the formal critical principle. The drafts suggest how extensive the presence of that subtext is; the quotations are only its manifestations on the surface of the opera.

One might even suggest an apparent paradox: that the historically earlier work was being used to interpret the latter. After all, as listeners, or readers, we can hear or see *Tristan* not only behind *Pelléas*, but—encouraged in this by Debussy himself—between ourselves and that work. It was manipulated by the composer to become a sort of hidden commentary on *Pelléas*, and thereby became more than merely an obvious model for the later opera.[43]

The *Pelléas* drafts, on the other hand, may be thought of as one important reading of part of the Wagnerian system—or of *Tristan* standing for that system—and Debussy may be considered a Wagnerian commentator. He may even be judged a more distinctive interpreter of Wagner than the more familiarly post-Wagnerian German composers. He received from Wagner not only certain technical *lois*, but used allusion to the operas which were the source of that technique to fashion an interpretation of Maeterlinck's text, and to comment on his own musical reading of that drama. There are documents which should be added to the theoretical treatises, the critical essays, and the concert reviews in the making of a *Rezeptionsgeschichte* of the major monuments of nineteenth-century music. *Pelléas et Mélisande* is one of these documents.

---

[41]The term is borrowed from Richard Kramer's "Communication," ibid., p. 187.
[42]Ibid.

[43]See the discussion of *Rezeption* in Martin Zenck, "Entwurf einer Soziologie der musikalischen Rezeption," *Musikforschung* 33 (1980), 253–79. One *locus classicus* for discussion of the concept in literary criticism is Harold Bloom's *The Anxiety of Influence* (New York, 1973).

295

Winton Dean

THE TRUE 'CARMEN'?

French musicologists have shown so little interest in Bizet, and his operas have been so regularly and progressively corrupted in Paris, whether in print or performance, that the prospect of the *grande machine* of German scholarship getting to work on his masterpiece is bound to whet the appetite. Hitherto there have been two full scores of *Carmen*, one French, published by Choudens about 1877, and one German, edited by Kurt Soldan and published by Peters. Both contain Guiraud's recitatives in place of the original spoken dialogue, but both are based principally on the autograph and there are few material differences between them. Soldan replaced Bizet's cornets with trumpets, a solecism repeated in Dr Fritz Oeser's new edition.* It is surprising too to find a 'kritische Neuausgabe' giving Bizet's French tempo indications only in Italian and German.

The aims and the execution of this edition raise so many points of cardinal importance for the whole realm of musical scholarship that it demands examination in detail. Oeser lists seven major sources: Bizet's autograph score (A); the manuscript conducting copy used in 1875 (and later) (B); incomplete manuscript orchestral parts, also used in 1875 and later (C); the manuscript copy prepared in the summer of 1875 for the first Vienna performances in October (D); the first edition of the Choudens vocal score (E); the first edition of the printed libretto (F); and the manuscript rehearsal schedule of the Opéra-Comique during the winter of 1874-5 (G).

Of these sources, B, C and D are drawn on for the first time. D is not of primary importance since it was prepared after Bizet's death; but it yields one curiosity in a new end to the opera, supplied by some Viennese conductor, in which the melody of Escamillo's *couplets* rises to a final apotheosis after the manner of a Palm Court or military band selection. B and C are of great interest for the early history of the opera's composition. In several important movements Oeser has been able to reconstruct the various stages of the text in fuller detail than the present condition of the autograph allows. By the same token he has established the approximate date of certain cuts, insertions or alterations according to whether they appear in the conducting copy or the parts. Pigot's statement that the third entr'acte was composed for *L'Arlésienne* receives some support from the fact that it antedates the other entr'actes, which were not ready in time to be copied with the main body of the score. Oeser prints (not quite accurately) the *Grisélidis* sketch for baritone in C major that later became José's flower

song; but the even more interesting origin of 'Dût-il m'en coûter la vie' (Act 3 finale) in *La coupe du roi de Thulé* receives only a casual mention in the chapter on Felsenstein's German translation.

The steps by which a work of genius came into existence have a perennial fascination, particularly when we can watch a great dramatic composer reconciling the demands of words, music and action. In *Carmen* this process can be observed in all its stages from the first writing down of the full score (Bizet habitually made few preliminary sketches). Oeser's examination of B and C brings out two points of outstanding interest; both have been noted before, but the new evidence clarifies the picture. One is the great care Bizet expended on the finales, all four of which were repeatedly revised, the first, third and fourth as many as four times. The other is the much more lavish use of *mélodrame* in the original score. Bizet was clearly following up his very successful harnessing of this device in *Djamileh* and *L'Arlésienne*.

We already knew that the scene of the changing of the guard in Act 1, instead of being broken in two by dialogue (or recitative in the Guiraud version), originally comprised a single long movement with an orchestral middle section based on a canonic treatment of the street urchins' melody, against which Morales informed José of Micaëla's arrival. It was also known that the *mélodrame* in which Carmen makes insolent fun of Zuniga later in the act had been much longer. Oeser has discovered two further instances of this treatment. The arrival of Escamillo's torchlight procession in Act 2 consisted of three sections, an unaccompanied offstage chorus, an orchestral march (much expanded from its earliest version) with dialogue against it, and a short final chorus; of these only the third section and a fragment of the first were hitherto available.

Similarly José's offstage 'Dragon d'Alcala' song in Act 2, two unaccompanied stanzas separated by dialogue, was originally set to a different melody with light orchestral accompaniment and linked by a *mélodrame* quoting Carmen's motive. This version survives incomplete in the parts. Oeser makes the valid point that the *diminuendo* instrumental codas to several movements (some of them a good deal longer as first written) were intended to ease the transition from full musical treatment to spoken dialogue. Bizet was here following the example of Méhul's serious *operas-comiques* composed before the end of the 18th century, notably *Mélidore et Phrosine*, of which he possessed a full score.

Another discovery is the refrain of the original 6/8 habanera, rejected early in the rehearsals in favour of the modified Yradier melody. No trace of it remains in the autograph, but it survives pasted down in the conducting copy at the point where the female

Carmen. Kritische Neuausgabe nach den Quellen von Fritz Oeser (Alkor-Edition/Bärenreiter). 2 volumes, score and critical report, cloth £16, paper £12, vocal score 96s

chorus repeat it after Carmen has thrown the flower. It is an undistinguished and jaunty little tune from which we can rejoice to be delivered:

Ex 1

Oeser reconstructs with some plausibility the melody of the verse sections by piecing together incomplete orchestral parts in the cancelled finale of the act; for, as with the Yradier habanera later, Bizet brought it back just before Carmen trips José. This too is poor stuff.

The passages cut by Bizet before the score and parts were copied include the ineffective return of Escamillo's refrain accompanied by a single cello towards the end of Act 3 and Carmen's two references to the card scene in the third and fourth finales, which struck such a false note in the Sadler's Wells revival of 1961. Oeser is right to condemn Bizet's first idea here as unworthy of the heroine and the opera. His detective work on the early changes further establishes that the air with pantomime for Morales and chorus near the beginning of the opera, which was printed only in the 1875 vocal score and of which Bizet wrote three versions, was composed during rehearsals late in 1874. This happened when the baritone Duvernoy was cast as Morales; and at the same time the small part of an anonymous tenor officer (Andrès in the first draft of the libretto) in Acts 2 and 4 was transposed for him.

*

Thus far all is well. The earlier suppressed passages (with some exceptions to be mentioned later) are placed in the appendix. But the text of Oeser's score differs in innumerable particulars, great and small, from the older full scores. These differences are of two principal kinds. Oeser restores a large number of cuts, some of considerable length; and he removes an even larger number of what he terms 'retouches', which for the most part appear in the autograph but are attributed to various alien hands. These two issues, though interconnected and often involving the use of the same evidence, are best discussed separately.

It has been known for some time that many extensive cuts were made before the first performance (3 March 1875), probably during the prolonged rehearsals, which began in October 1874. Oeser confirms this, and ascribes most of them to late January 1875. How should an editor treat this reclaimed material? Now that *Carmen* is a classic he must surely print it all; but he needs to bear at least four considerations in mind. (i) He should distinguish clearly in the text between what was performed in March 1875—the only production during Bizet's life—and what was not. (ii) He should endeavour with the aid of all available evidence to determine

the composer's wishes. (iii) He should separate fact from conjecture and avoid *a priori* assumptions about the motives and intentions of everyone concerned in the production of the opera. (iv) Having adopted a policy as to what will be included in the main text, the notes and the appendices respectively, he should abide by it. On all four points this edition goes disastrously off the rails.

All that we know for certain about Bizet's attitude is that he ferociously resisted changes during rehearsals, and that he either initiated or agreed to all the cuts in the older full scores, with three possible exceptions. These are the three passages printed in the 1875 vocal score (Oeser's source E) but excluded from the subsequent full score: the scene for Morales and chorus in Act 1, the longer duel in Act 3, and the full coda to the first chorus of Act 4. E was published early in March 1875, almost concurrently with the first performance; it was advertised ('vient de paraître') in the weekly paper *Le Ménestrel* of March 14, and the legal deposit at the Bibliothèque Nationale was made by Choudens on the 18th. Bizet himself arranged the score and corrected the proofs, of which twenty pages (from his own library) survive. Oeser mentions them once, quite casually, and only to express a doubt whether the corrections are in Bizet's hand. They unquestionably are; but even if they were not, E represents the most important evidence we have as to the definitive form that Bizet wished his opera to assume. Its reading should be cited at every point where the text is in question, and only rejected for the very weightiest reasons. Oeser, though he has seen presentation copies signed by Bizet, has virtually ignored it; on the very rare occasions when he mentions its readings he attributes them to Guiraud, who had no more to do with it than the man in the moon. As the Court of Appeal has been known to remark when finding

Ex 1 p

L'a- mour est en- fant de Bo- hê- me, il n'a ja- mais con- nu de loi! Si tu ne m'ai- mes pas, je t'ai- me! Si tu m'ai- mes, tant pis pour toi! tant pis pas toi! tant pis pour toi!—

fault with a judge of first instance, he has so gravely misdirected himself on the relative value of the evidence that he has destroyed the foundations of his judgment.

He has assumed that all the rehearsal cuts (which number at least 30), and hundreds of other changes to be mentioned later, were made against Bizet's wish or better judgment. He begins his general introduction with the statement that a critical edition of *Carmen* 'must restore all those alterations that owe their origin to the dissensions of the first stage rehearsal, and present the authentic form of the work by opening the cuts'. This is to beg every possible question. There may have been dissensions at the first stage rehearsal (there frequently are with new operas—and old ones, for that matter), but we know nothing about them, and there is no conclusive evidence that a single cut originated on this occasion or was due to other than artistic considerations. Yet Oeser is so wedded to his preconceived theory, that all suppressed passages are essential to the integrity of the opera, that he waves aside every explanation except the stupidity of the producer, the inexperience of the chorus, the inadequacies of the Opéra-Comique stage, the hostility of du Locle (the director), and the general bafflement caused by an unfamiliar and shocking subject.

Now it is quite possible—though not susceptible of proof—that these considerations, or some of them, did play a part. They *could* account for some of the cuts, though certainly not for all. But to take this as an article of faith is unscholarly and perilous. Having assumed his premises, Oeser constantly asserts as facts (qualified now and then by words like 'sicherlich' or 'zweifellos') what are no more than guesses, some of them possible or even probable, but a great many unlikely or quite impossible. And, as we shall see particularly with the retouches, he is repeatedly led to denounce as sins against Bizet's style and dramatic vision changes that can be conclusively proved to originate with the composer himself. Indeed it is very lucky this is so; otherwise the score of *Carmen* might be permanently corrupted.

One of Oeser's principal scapegoats is Guiraud, whose treatment of Bizet's posthumous works certainly leaves him a good deal to answer for. But most of the charges against him in connection with *Carmen* fall to the ground. He and the 1883 producer are held responsible for beginning Act 3 with a tableau and a full stage, whereas Bizet, we are told, had the curtain raised before the end of the entr'acte on an empty stage, where the smugglers gradually assemble at the summons of one of their number sounding a horn. This was Bizet's first idea, but it was altered before performance, as the 1875 score proves. (This is one of the changes that could have been made for reasons of theatrical convenience, such as the difficulty of getting the chorus on stage in time; there is even a case for rejecting it in performance, since it leaves an inconsistency in the text.)

Guiraud is accused of shortening the Act 3 duel for Vienna in 1875, though Oeser tells us twice elsewhere that this was not done till the 1883 revival. That is certainly wrong: the Choudens full score and

two vocal scores dated 1877 and 1879 all give the shortened version. Moreover this cut—which removes the weakest music in the opera—could have been made by Bizet himself during the 1875 run, a point nowhere considered by Oeser. As we shall see, Guiraud's hand in the autograph was in almost every instance demonstrably obeying Bizet's wishes. Even his recitatives were fulfilling the composer's acknowledged intention, though Bizet would doubtless have carried it out differently. Oeser says that Bizet made a distinction between important and permanent corrections to the autograph, which he made in ink, and changes to serve temporary needs, which he wrote in pencil. There is no evidence for this supposition, which is more than once controverted by Oeser's own notes.

A very high proportion of the commentary is devoted to special pleading that can only be called tendentious. This is a dangerous frame of mind in an editor, since it predisposes him to make mistakes, both of omission and commission, and can lead to a wholesale queering of the pitch. The text of the score is a faithful and fatal reflection of this attitude. It is an arbitrary selection from almost every stage of Bizet's work; it includes versions abandoned at an early stage, others rejected later, and one or two never admitted at all, and it frequently rejects Bizet's final form. This might matter less if the sources were clearly distinguished. But they are not. It would take many hours—perhaps days— even with the aid of the commentary (which sometimes omits the most important evidence) to sort out what was performed in 1875 and what readings have Bizet's final authority. A busy conductor would never have time for this. Yet if he performed the score as printed here, he would in hundreds of places be resurrecting what Bizet specifically—and often for the clearest possible artistic reasons— rejected out of hand.

This elasticity of principle goes far beyond the restoration of passages cut during the later rehearsals. One whole character (Andrès), whom Bizet removed before the end of 1874, is put back throughout the opera. The choral repeat of Escamillo's refrain at his exit in Act 2 is included, though it was cut before the beginning of orchestral rehearsals; but the scene for Morales and chorus, which was sung and printed in 1875, is banished to an appendix. (Bizet could have cut this for dramatic reasons during the 1875 run, but again Oeser does not discuss the possibility.) We are given the rejected first form of Carmen's humming *mélodrame* in Act 1, and Guiraud's rehash with recitatives, but not the version performed in 1875, which on any reckoning deserves priority.

There are many changes to the words, early discarded versions being preferred to Bizet's improvements (for example in the seguidilla), and even more to the stage directions, some of which have no authority whatever. Oeser makes a great fuss about the shortening of instrumental codas, which he attributes to the first producer's *horror vacui* and other nameless sins, yet he marks as an optional cut one such passage (at the exit of the smugglers in Act 3) that Bizet never shortened. He admits that the original longer introduction to the cigarette girls' chorus is difficult to bring off convincingly in the theatre, but it does not occur to him that that may be why Bizet cut it; so back it goes into the text.

There are, when we look closely at the matter, several far more likely reasons for cutting than the *force majeure* postulated by Oeser, which contradicts all we know of Bizet's personality and temperament and (though Oeser does not appear to notice this) reflects on his integrity as an artist. He was a great dramatic composer, and an immensely practical one, as his letters reveal; but the implication that he never willingly modified a bar as a result of stage rehearsals is absurd. He is not likely to have shared Oeser's compulsive attachment to *Bogen* form, or bothered about the 'formally indispensable' elaboration of codas, if there was any question of interference with the dramatic action. Indeed he removed the 'Dragon d'Alcala' *Bogen* before rehearsals began. If, as is possible, the size of the Opéra-Comique stage or the difficulty of timing choral entrances and exits led to cuts, they are just as likely to have brought musical and dramatic improvements in their train, as in some cases they palpably did. One of the most striking features of Bizet's style is the care for dramatic concentration emphasized by his frequent revisions, especially in finales. Oeser is so far from appreciating this that he takes almost every opportunity of reversing the trend.

The most natural explanation of the cuts is the enormous length of the opera. Even as shortened, it lasted for 174 minutes (excluding intervals) on the first night. Act 1 alone, without the Prelude, took 58 minutes; Act 4 did not begin till after midnight. The Sadler's Wells revival, which restored some but by no means all of the cuts and considerably abridged the dialogue, demonstrated that Bizet had every reason for retrenchment. There is no need for Oeser's guess that the producer used what he calls the revolt of the chorus (who are known to have had difficulty with their parts) as an excuse for simplifying his own task. Oeser dismisses the idea that the object was to save time, on the grounds that only seven minutes would be involved (which is more than doubtful, and in any case no answer, since all depends on the context), and that this could have been made up by shortening the intervals—an argument that additionally ignores the habits and preferences of Paris audiences. He therefore prints the opera in three acts and opines that Bizet's conception can be understood only if it is played with a single interval after Act 2. This is to put the composer in his place with a vengeance. His definitive version was in four acts, with three intervals; and it had reached this form before the last entr'acte was composed.

It is certainly arguable that some of the cuts deprived us of good things, and there is everything to be said for having all the material in print (if only it were properly distinguished) so that it can be tested in the theatre. A case can be made on musical grounds for putting back the canonic *mélodrame* at the changing of the guard, the entry of Carmen in the middle of the quarrel chorus (with two motives combined in the orchestra) instead of at the end, the orchestral link between the seguidilla and the first finale, the fuller version of Escamillo's entry procession in Act 2, and perhaps the longer finale of that act. But this would slow down the action, and it is only a fraction of what Oeser declares to be indispensable.

He shows that the extended development of the Carmen-fate theme as it occurs in the Prelude was first composed for the moment when she advances on José and throws the flower. He guesses that it was shortened at the request of the librettists in order to clarify the dialogue. Yet the *second* version has one of the subtlest of those links with *mélodrame* on which he lays such stress elsewhere, and it makes its dramatic point far more economically. Do we really want the action to be arrested for 25 slow bars while Carmen manoeuvres around José and fixes him with a glance which for half that time he mutely returns? (This appears to be a refinement introduced by Oeser; Bizet makes clear that José does not look at her at all—'il est toujours occupé de son épinglette.') Above all, having transferred the passage to the Prelude, would Bizet have repeated it in exactly the same form (apart from the key and the scoring) so soon afterwards? From what we know of his ideas about dramatic concentration it seems unlikely. But Oeser, ignoring or misunderstanding Bizet's constant drive for clarity and compactness, would endow him with the leisurely symphonic elaboration of Wagner, which belongs to the opposite end of the operatic spectrum.

Oeser reasonably points to Bizet's several revisions of the first finale as overwhelming disproof of the thesis that the original version must at all costs be preferred. Yet he himself in practice comes very near to accepting the thesis that Bizet's final version must at all costs be rejected. In the same paragraph he claims to be able to distinguish firmly between the changes made by Bizet for artistic reasons and those to which he grudgingly assented. This temerarious assertion leads him to wreck the fabric of the third and fourth finales—arguably the most dramatic scenes in the opera—by printing versions which are not only immeasurably weaker than those finally adopted by Bizet, but were never at any time accepted by him. The former will be discussed later in connection with the retouches; the latter demands attention here.

From the point where José stabs Carmen Bizet composed at least four versions of this finale. The first comprises four bars of chromatic scales and tremolos against acclamations from the chorus offstage, a double cry of 'Carmen!' from José, Carmen's dying reference to the card scene, José's 'Ah! ma Carmen adorée!' in G♭ over tremolo strings (to the same phrase as in the last bars of the accepted score), the Toreador refrain in F♯ sung by the chorus off (but to different words), and a totally different end. Instead of the last 12 bars as we know them there were 24. Escamillo enters and sees Carmen dead (5 bars); José confesses and is arrested but does not sing 'Ah! ma Carmen adorée!'. The opera ends not with four orchestral bars but with 13, the fate motive being built up to a big climax and then dying away to a *pianissimo* close in D major.

Bizet's first change (before the parts were copied) was to remove José's repeated cry of 'Carmen!' and the reference to the card scene; about the same time or soon after he changed the words of the choral refrain. In the third version he rewrote the final bars as we now have them. Oeser suggests that this was because du Locle objected to the end, though it is not clear why he should have found the shorter version any less offensive; it was Carmen's murder on the stage to which he is supposed to have taken exception. (Other changes are conjecturally ascribed to pressure from du Locle; Bizet, it seems, cannot be left to make decisions for himself.) This revision left seven bars, including José's first cry of 'Ah! ma

Carmen adorée!' (which thus came twice to the same notes), between the stabbing and the F♯ chorus (Bizet does not appear to have cancelled the original stage direction, in which during the chromatic scales *Carmen tombe appuyée sur son bras gauche*):

Ex 2

His last revision removed these bars and substituted the octave fanfare on the note F♯:

Oeser objects to this last revision, and begins by throwing doubt on its authenticity. He guesses that it was the outcome of a hurried conference at rehearsal, in which Bizet presumably had no part, and condemns it as in many respects injurious to the context ('in mehrfacher Hinsicht schädlich')— musically on the pedantic ground that it makes Bizet follow tonic with tonic instead of dominant (a device employed with conspicuous effect on occasion by Beethoven), dramatically because it opened the way for the stage direction in the printed scores, which is attributed to the producer: *Il s'élance vers Carmen—Carmen veut fuir, mais Don José la rejoint à l'entrée du cirque—il la frappe—elle tombe et meurt. Don José s'agenouille auprès d'elle.*

This, declares Oeser, 'offends in the highest degree against Bizet's basic principles of musico-dramatic form'. But it is Bizet's own direction, as **E** (supported by the autograph) proves beyond dispute. Admittedly he changed his mind about the action here. Originally José was directed to stab Carmen just before 'damnée!' and during the chromatic scales she was to fall on her left arm and make the gesture of dealing the cards, dying before his cry 'Ah! ma Carmen adorée!' This was followed two bars later by the F♯ chorus.

In Bizet's ultimate version she dies while the chorus, with bitter irony, are singing 'Et songe bien en combattant qu'un oeil noir te regarde'. This is probably an echo of her death scene in Mérimée's novel, where José describes her last moments in these words: 'Je crois voir encore son grand oeil noir me regarder fixement; puis il devient trouble et se ferma'. It would be particularly effective if Escamillo were to emerge from the arena at that moment, but Bizet's directions are not explicit about this.

Oeser misses the double irony here and makes her die before the chorus begins. He then rewrites all the stage directions up to the end of the opera, restoring some that occur in Bizet's *first* version, where the music was quite different. But he is left with the seven extra bars of Ex 2, in which the words and music of José's last phrase are anticipated. He accordingly snips out these two bars and leaves in the text a broken-winded progression that never occurs in Bizet at all:

Ex 4

Three things must be said about Bizet's final revision (the substitution of Ex 3 for Ex 2). In the first place there can be no question about its authenticity, for it is in **E**. Secondly it is a palpable stroke of genius, since it brings José's loss of control, followed by the assault, right on top of the triumphant F♯ chorus—an electrifying moment in

the theatre. Thirdly it agrees with Bizet's procedure all through this finale, not only here but several times earlier, which is to simplify and concentrate: immediacy of impact was what he sought—not at the expense of musical sense, but certainly at the expense of musical elaboration at moments of decisive action. This is one of the qualities that make him a great musical dramatist, though not of the Wagnerian stamp. Yet Oeser religiously restores all these (mostly brief) cuts and simplifications, and waters down the whole finale.

There are illuminating examples at the two points where the duet is interrupted by offstage chorus and brass (the bullfighters' march on the first cornet, not the trumpet as printed here). In the earlier version (rejected by Bizet but restored by Oeser) the voice parts are rather more complicated and there are certain differences in the words, which at the second interruption describe the bullfight in detail. Oeser indignantly ascribes the change to 'Torschlusspanik', calls it 'a renunciation of [Bizet's] stylistic principle of absolute veracity' and (in another place) 'eine barbarische Gewaltkur' that Bizet would never have undertaken except under overwhelming pressure of circumstances. He assumes that the chorus could not cope with the music; yet it is not difficult to sing, and this is the one place in the score where they were not distracted by having to act and could even have read their parts. And it is easy to see why Bizet made the change. We do not require a running commentary on the finer points of tauromachy, which will not be heard in any case, to appreciate the parallel between the struggles inside and outside the bullring. Talk about the sublime conception of the finale being 'blotted out' by the change is preposterous. On the contrary, where the more complex version runs the risk of blurring the dramatic impact, the simpler strikes home as decisively as José's dagger. Even if an editor does not agree with this reasoning, it is no business of his—indeed it is the height of editorial impropriety—to assume that a sane composer did not intend what he left in his score.

*

The second declared aim of Dr Fritz Oeser's edition of *Carmen* is to search for and examine any alterations made by Guiraud and others after Bizet's death. The two most extensive of these have long been known: for the Vienna performances in October 1875 Guiraud composed recitatives to replace the spoken dialogue and inserted a ballet in Act 4, taking the music from *La Jolie Fille de Perth* and *L'Arlésienne* and rewriting the words of the first chorus to introduce it. Oeser prints both the dialogue and the recitatives throughout the opera, but he assesses their relative status fairly enough, and he properly damns the ballet. It appears that the shortening of the coda of this chorus, which is printed complete in E (the 1875 vocal score) and was so played until recent years at the Opéra-Comique, was the work of Guiraud when he attached the ballet.[1]

The other changes fall into a different category. Apart from Guiraud's recitatives, which are easily distinguishable, and many of the suppressed pas-

[1] I would therefore amend what I have written elsewhere on this point.

sages already discussed, the autograph contains numerous alterations to words, scoring, phrasing, note-values, accentuation, dynamics, tempo marks, stage directions, and occasionally to important themes. A fair proportion are in Bizet's hand, but some are doubtful and a good many were written by others, including Guiraud. The majority have been transferred to sources **B** and **C**, the conducting copy and parts. For a critical edition every one needs to be scrutinized with the greatest possible care in order to determine its provenance and authenticity.

For this purpose the prime source is E, Bizet's vocal score of March 1875. It is—or should be—well known that most composers constantly modify or retouch their work during rehearsal, and often withhold publication till after performance for that very reason. This applies particularly to opera composers, who have to make adjustments to fit not only musical exigencies but those of the theatre as well, which may be equally or more demanding. We should therefore expect Bizet to introduce changes at this stage, after the conducting score and parts were in use and when the autograph was in temporary retirement. He would not need to change the autograph; he would be unlikely to mark the conducting score and parts, the responsibility of the conductor; but he would certainly incorporate all the latest corrections in the vocal score, which he himself was arranging for publication. (This does not apply of course to details of orchestration or to every dynamic mark in the full score, but it affects all the other categories mentioned.) Now if the autograph has two readings, X altered to Y, and the 1875 vocal score has only Y, it is obvious that Y must be correct.

No retouch to the autograph, whether it is in the hand of Bizet, Guiraud, Antony Choudens, General de Gaulle or the Archbishop of Canterbury, can by any human possibility have got into the 1875 vocal score after Bizet's death or (barring misprints) without his approval. All such modifications to the autograph must have been made in conformity with Bizet's wishes as expressed in the vocal score.

In fact Guiraud and others made too few rather than too many changes of this kind. Bizet added certain refinements to E, especially in matters of tempo, that (if Oeser is correct) do not appear even in the conducting score and parts; nevertheless they are not to be rejected. E also contains his metronome marks, some of them modified or inserted in his hand in the surviving proofs—a point nowhere mentioned by Oeser, who prints them in editorial square brackets when he approves of them and silently omits them when he does not.

It is necessary to labour all this, since Oeser has ignored it completely. The consequences can only be described as catastrophic. Bizet made hundreds of alterations, many of them of crucial importance, between the first writing out of the autograph and the publication of the vocal score. Oeser, after remarking that the conducting score makes it easier to recognize 'Kapellmeister retouches or interferences by Guiraud', never quotes E on these points and constantly confuses it, under the word 'Erstdruck', with the full score, published after Bizet's death, with which Guiraud *was* concerned.

Indeed he says in his preface that the French vocal scores of *Carmen* have never been altered since the first issue (which is not true), without realizing that to the extent that this is a fact—for many of the plates seem to have been re-used—it automatically gives them the highest claim to authenticity.

In the event Oeser on page after page attributes Bizet's own retouches, the result of his experience in rehearsal, to Guiraud, the conductor or some other later or anonymous hand and ejects them without ceremony, even, on occasion, when he admits they are in Bizet's hand. The new score flatly and demonstrably contradicts the composer and debases the text of the entire opera far more grossly than the old Choudens and Peters scores, which when they conflict with Oeser are nearly always correct. And it would be rash to assume that Guiraud's not very numerous retouches to the scoring lack Bizet's authority. Only a few examples of each type of corruption can be quoted.

While changes in orchestration can seldom be detected in a vocal score, there are passages where Bizet thinned out or silenced the orchestra in order to let the words come through. One of them occurs in the duet after the flower song, where he removed most of the accompaniment (a heavy crescendo) to Carmen's vital sentence 'Oui, tu m'emporterais si tu m'aimais'. Oeser restores it, though it is not even in the conducting score and parts, and was therefore cut by Bizet very early on (he also removes Bizet's direction *con islancio*). When a few bars later, as José's resolution weakens, Carmen resumes her haunting 'Là-bas, là-bas tu me suivras' at a slower tempo (*Un peu retenu*, emphasized by a changed metronome mark) Oeser rejects this as a posthumous insertion particularly damaging to the climax of the duet, thereby showing a total misunderstanding of the whole episode.

There are literally dozens of wrong tempo marks, many of them in important and familiar pieces. Of the Introduction to Act 1 Oeser observes that Guiraud changed the original *Allegretto moderato* to *Allegretto* and established a false tradition of an excessively lively and marchlike pace; this change was made by Bizet. So was the 'falsification' of the tempo of the opening of the cigarette girls' chorus from *Allegretto moderato* to *Allegro*, and the division of the 6/8 bars in the chorus by means of dotted lines, with the direction 'Battez à 3/8'. At Carmen's first entry, where Bizet in close conformity with the drama has three changes of tempo in 22 bars (*Allegretto molto*, dotted crotchet 108—*Allegro moderato*, 92, the moment of her appearance with her motive in the orchestra—100), Oeser spoils this gradation by giving one tempo throughout (*Allegro moderato*, 100), sweeping aside the changes as due to the conductor.

Poor Guiraud is again saddled with creating a false tradition by debasing the tempo of the G major section of the José-Micaëla duet from *Andantino moderato* to *Allegro moderato*, another of Bizet's changes. We are told that all tempo modifications in the *Chanson Bohème* apart from the *Più animato* for the refrain of the second and third stanzas were supplied by Guiraud; *Andantino quasi allegretto* at the beginning, which Oeser accepts, is Guiraud

(Bizet's marking is *Andantino*), the *Presto* in the coda, which he ignores, is Bizet.

The most disastrous corruption of tempo occurs in the finale of Act 4 at the first *fortissimo* entry of the Carmen-fate motive in C major (last bar of p. 359 of current Choudens vocal score). This follows an A major chorus and fanfare offstage (*Allegro giocoso*, crotchet 116) saluting Escamillo's victory. At first Bizet continued both chorus and fanfare against the fate motive on the pit orchestra and wrote *Même mouvement*. Later, in deepening the contrasts of the whole finale, he cut short the chorus and fanfare and broadened the tempo to *Moderato*, confirming this with a metronome mark (crotchet 84) and restoring a fast tempo (*Allegro*, crotchet 126) at the renewed fanfare 19 bars later. The improvement should be clear to the most obtuse ears; yet Oeser—attributing it as usual to Guiraud and ignoring both metronome marks—not only restores the feeble original but argues that it is of particular importance for the architecture of the finale. Does he seriously suppose that *Allegro giocoso* is a suitable tempo for this shattering moment, and for the whole of the 3/4 section of the duet (based on the same motive) that follows? Even if he does, Bizet did not.

All Bizet's improvements to Escamillo's *couplets* are ruthlessly expunged. According to E the tempo should be *Allegro moderato*, but it is just possible that *molto* was omitted by accident. Oeser makes several changes to the music, both in the verse and the refrain, altering note-lengths, removing fermatas, replacing the baritone Morales with the ghost tenor Andrès, making Escamillo waste his breath by joining in the first four bars of the chorus, restoring a particularly inane two bars of till-ready accompaniment between the stanzas, and ejecting the appoggiatura c in Escamillo's final 'L'amour!' The latter, a clever touch of character, he damns as a melodically unmotivated insertion by Guiraud without any authority from the sources. In every case he is turning his back on Bizet—and he admits that one of the changes was written by Bizet himself in the autograph.

This sort of thing happens in almost every number, sometimes without editorial comment. (What for instance is the source of the grotesque accentuation of Example 5 instead of Example 6 in the fourth bar of the duet for José and Escamillo?

Could it have been adapted to fit the German 'Der Matador'?[2] The opening phrase of the José-Micaëla duet has its rhythm adjusted to the weaker first version, though Oeser once more allows that the change is in Bizet's hand. In the card trio a manifest improvement to the string ritornello is thrown out, and Bizet's expressive phrase to the words 'Je suis veuve et j'hérite' disappears, together

[2]Further inquiry has revealed the answer: Bizet wrote Ex 5 in the autograph, and substituted Ex 6 in the vocal score.

with his marking *retenez un peu*. The duet 'Si tu m'aimes' receives a wrong tempo mark and time signature (*Andantino 2/2* instead of *Andantino quasi allegretto 4/4*), and Bizet's alteration to the cadence is dismissed as without authority. In the final duet the obvious verbal improvement 'Entre elle et toi [entre nous] *tout est fini*' yields to the poor '*C'est fini*'; Carmen's high A♭ on '*Non*, je ne te céderai pas!' and the higher setting of her 'Je répéterai que je l'aime' are subordinated to lower originals rejected by Bizet; while José's top B♭ at 'Pour la dernière fois, *démon!*' is attributed to Guiraud humouring a singer and left out altogether.

The most conspicuous of the thematic changes concerns an important melody in Act 1. Immediately after Carmen has thrown the flower at José and run off, the orchestra plays a tune that returns in a different rhythm when José leads Carmen out of the factory under arrest (it also appears at Carmen's entry in the longer quarrel scene, a passage cut before performance). Its original form was:

Ex 7

During the rehearsals, after the quarrel scene was shortened, but before the publication of E, Bizet rewrote it thus:

Ex 8

E establishes the authenticity of the later form (which is entered in the autograph, though probably not in Bizet's hand); a glance proclaims its superiority. It does away with the poor symmetry between the second and sixth bars; the sudden upward leap at the end of the second is far more effective after the thrice repeated A. Oeser, ignoring the evidence, attributes the change to a late date and obscure provenance; the only explanation he can find is a possible resemblance between Ex 7 and a popular song of the day. It has been said that Ex 8 with its threefold A is incompatible with Bizet's style, a statement that can proceed only from ignorance; the Duke's love theme in *La Jolie Fille de Perth*, the most prominent motive in that opera, begins in exactly the same way:

Que vous ê - tes jo - lie,   quelle grâce accom - plie,
Près de vous on ou - blie   les beautés de la cour!

It is all too clear that a basic unfamiliarity with Bizet's whole style and personality lies behind more than one recent attempt to tinker with the score of *Carmen*. A little study of published work on the composer could have saved Oeser from disaster; it is symptomatic that he regularly mis-spells the names of Pigot and Mina Curtiss and cites the latter's book only in its mutilated French translation. It is most improbable that Bizet had the scenario of *Carmen* as early as June 1872, and inconceivable that Offenbach's soubrette Zulma Bouffar was his first choice for the heroine. It is possible, as Mina Curtiss has suggested, that the conception of Carmen owed something to Céleste Mogador, but to trace the habanera directly to her because she was singing another song by Yradier in 1865 is farfetched in the extreme (Bizet had several of Yradier's songs in his library); and the picture of Bizet at that date as a young man of rigorous moral principles (linked with his love for his mother, who had been dead four years), to whom Céleste would appear a being from a strange world, is grotesque to anyone acquainted with his personal life.

But his character as an artist matters more, and Oeser's attitude to this emerges from his conclusion that the quotation of the card scene at Carmen's death must have vanished before Galli-Marié caught a glimpse of the score, since she would never have allowed Bizet to cut it. Who does Oeser think was composing this opera? That he misunderstands the very kernel of the plot is clear from one extraordinary feature of this edition.[s] He is convinced that when Carmen in the quintet sings 'Je suis amoureuse à perdre l'esprit' she is thinking not of José but of Escamillo. It will be recalled that she has made a direct bid for José's love by throwing her flower in his face, and has come to Lillas Pastia's tavern to meet him on his release from prison. Escamillo on the other hand she has just met for the first time—and given him a cool brush-off. Yet at this point of the action Oeser can talk of the new, deeper and more passionate emotion that Escamillo has stimulated in her, in contrast to her transitory and vicarious feelings for José. (Is that why he gratuitously alters Bizet's marking at 'Je suis amoureuse' from *Très retenu* to *Un peu plus lent*, and attributes to the conductor Bizet's fermata immediately before it?) To such a theory the only adequate reply is that of the Duke of Wellington when someone accosted him in the street with the words 'Mr Smith, I believe?'—'Sir, if you believe that, you would believe anything.'

Unfortunately this is no laughing matter; the consequences are grave. In order to support this untenable thesis Oeser has in several scenes shamelessly cooked the stage directions by inserting passages for which he can claim no authority (some of them are flagrantly at variance with the score). At Escamillo's exit in Act 2 he adds *Carmen suit*

[s] A less important misapprehension, due perhaps to ignorance of the French language, concerns the change of José's rank from 'sergent' to 'brigadier' during the composition of the opera. This is not a promotion but the opposite; 'brigadier' means a corporal, not a sergeant-major. Still less does it correspond to the British rank of brigadier, as in a performance once broadcast by the BBC.

854

Escamillo longtemps des yeux. At his second exit in the third finale (refrain of his couplets on the orchestra in D♭) he goes one better with *Carmen, en extase, le suit des yeux*, and declares that Bizet's own stage directions contradict the message of the music (that the D♭ refrain reflects Carmen's idealized picture of Escamillo!) and destroy one of the strongest and most intimate moments in the opera—the link with Carmen's simpler and purer declaration of love in the last scene. There is no question of Carmen showing the remotest interest in Escamillo before the finale of Act 3; she is simply growing tired of José.

Oeser dredges up one further piece of 'evidence' in support of his hypothesis. This is the single word 'Escamillo' sung by Carmen to a commonplace phrase (a rising fifth and a falling tone) just after she has interrupted the duel. It occurs in Bizet's first version, and is clearly no more than a cry of recognition (she has only set eyes on the man once before). To Oeser however it is one of the most highly charged moments in the opera, and 'indispensable', since it indicates that Carmen has been in love with Escamillo for weeks. It certainly held no such meaning for Bizet, who cut it out *before the score was copied* and therefore before pressure of any kind could have been put upon him. Oeser himself tells us this (p.717), but that does not prevent him from later attributing the cut to Guiraud (p.765).

It is hardly surprising after this that the superb finale of Act 3 is reduced to something like nonsense by the wholesale rewriting of stage directions. When Micaëla tells José that his mother is dying he replies 'Partons! ah! partons!' and says to Carmen 'Sois contente . . . je pars . . . mais . . . nous nous reverrons!'. Between these sentences Bizet has the direction *Il fait quelques pas, puis, s'arrêtant, à Carmen.* Oeser cuts this (except for the last two words) as a mere instruction to the stage-manager. On the last syllable of 'reverrons!' the fate motive sounds in the orchestra, whereupon *Don José entraîne Micaëla; en entendant la voix d'Escamillo, il s'arrête hésitant.* This is Bizet, but it is not good enough for Oeser, who abolishes it as 'missverständlich und der Musik nicht konform' and inserts a preposterous *Micaëla entraîne Don José* on a *diminuendo molto* (*mf—pp*) chord for flutes and clarinets.

At bars 4-6 of Escamillo's offstage refrain Bizet has *Carmen veut s'élancer; Don José, menaçant, lui barre le passage.* Oeser makes José merely hesitate and go off tamely with Micaëla. Three bars later he restores a singularly limp and undramatic passage from an earlier version, with Escamillo's refrain extended for several bars at the cadence and José calling 'Micaëla, partons!' He refers to this cut as 'a very late measure of doubtful provenance'; it is nothing of the kind. Bizet clearly wanted a tableau at the end; he marked the cue for the curtain on Escamillo's final top F. Oeser kills the whole design by bringing down the curtain ten bars late, after José and Micaëla have disappeared and the smugglers begun to march off.

These are by no means the only places where Bizet's stage directions are suppressed, mangled, misplaced or otherwise disorganized: it happens at

the beginning of the first, third and fourth acts, the opening of the cigarette girls' chorus and the quarrel scene, Escamillo's first entry, the finale of Act 2 (where Zuniga is made to strike José, as in the printed libretto, instead of threatening him, as in Bizet's score), and elsewhere. Nor have anything like all the errors in notes, words or tempo marks been mentioned. But enough has been said to show that this score does Bizet no sort of justice. It is a bewildering amalgam of what he wrote, what he rejected, and what the editor thinks he ought to have written. Anyone performing *Carmen* as it is printed here is foredoomed to misrepresent it on several different levels.

It is no pleasure to point this out, especially as the score is beautifully printed and much labour has clearly gone into its production. But it is a necessity and a duty, for an issue far beyond the feelings of individuals is involved—the integrity of a great operatic masterpiece. The editor, no doubt unwittingly, has slighted Bizet's genius and treated him as a weak-kneed nonentity incapable of knowing what he really wanted or (if he knew) of standing up for it. It is a pervading sin of the artistic middlemen of our time, as a certain type of opera producer is never tired of demonstrating, to assume an air of bland superiority and debauch the work of the geniuses whom they claim to interpret. But a stage production does not remain in print. A critical edition that betrays its standards can do infinitely more damage, since it may be accepted for generations as the composer's last word. And the present climate of musical scholarship makes it an urgent necessity to illustrate the fearful dangers of an editor taking an autograph as his ultimate source when later printed scores appeared during the composer's life.

This edition carries a preliminary notice forbidding its use for performance and its sale in France. It is not clear whether the intention is to protect the French from corruption or from apoplexy; or is Bizet still copyright there? But if the nation that produced him (and has paid him less honour than Germany) wishes to take a bloodless revenge, let it do what it should have done long ago and undertake a complete critical edition of his works. Bizet is one of France's greatest composers; much of his music is still unpublished, and the versions of several of his operas on sale in Paris today are in far greater need of a drastic purge than the score of *Carmen.*

The **John Lyon School**, Harrow, opens its Music School on Dec 4 with first performances of John Gardner's Mass in C and Malcolm Macdonald's Chorale Fantasia for horn and orchestra, commissioned for the occasion.

The first public concert to be given at the **British Museum** took place in the King's Library on Oct 4, given by the Museum Choral and Orchestral Society under John Parkinson. The programme included Telemann's Psalm 117, and Brandenburg No 3.

The **Deal and Walmer Handelian Society**, conductor James S. Hall, will sing **Alexander's Feast** on Nov 25 at 7.30 at the Royal Marines Concert Hall, Deal.

The **Guild for the Promotion of Welsh Music** is organizing an international competition for violinists who will play the Violin Concerto by David Harris, first performed in 1964. Adjudicators: Yehudi Menuhin, Fredericke Grinke, Robert H. Masters. Prizes: £200 and a performance with the BBC Welsh Orchestra; £100 and £50. Finals at Cardiff on 2 July 1966. Details from Public Relations Services Ltd, 4 Gold Tops, Newport, Mon.

305

Wozzeck and the Apocalypse: An Essay in Historical Criticism

Leo Treitler

Among the central meanings in Büchner's *Woyzeck,* there is one that comes clear only when we read the play in the context of the history of ideas—specifically in the light of certain currents of thought about human history and eschatology. Aspects of the play's expression are thereby elucidated, that are forcefully brought forward through the organization and compositional procedures of Berg's *Wozzeck.*

Near the end of the long third scene of the opera, Wozzeck appears suddenly at Marie's window and alludes cryptically to the mysterious signs that had come to him in the field the scene before,[1] confiding to her that he is "on the track of something big." As those signs had first been presented through Wozzeck's eyes, they seemed like the imaginings and fears of a simple man about Freemasons and who knows what other objects of superstition. But now in the third scene he gives them a scriptural context, as though through a sudden insight: "Isn't it written, 'And behold, the smoke went up from the land, as the smoke from a furnace'?"

What Wozzeck has recalled here is a passage in the Book of Genesis, chapter 19: "Then the Lord rained upon Sodom brimstone and fire from the Lord out of heaven. . . . and, behold, the smoke went up from the Land as the smoke from a furnace. The image is repeated in the New Testament Book of Revelation (the Apocalypse), chapter 9: "And the fifth angel sounded, and I saw a star fall from heaven unto the earth;

---

1. For the reader's convenience I have provided a summary of the scenic order of Berg's libretto. See appendix.

251

and to him was given the key of the bottomless pit; and there arose a smoke out of the pit, as the smoke of the great furnace; and the sun and the air were darkened by reason of the smoke of the pit."

Both passages are about a holocaust visited by a wrathful God upon a corrupt and debauched people, and that is the idea that begins to form in Wozzeck's mind as he stands for the first time on the stage before his mistress. And he asks, "What will it all come to?" The answer to this thematic question lies in the strange unfolding of the drama, pressed forward by forces that lie, as Büchner had once put it, "outside of ourselves"[2] and by Wozzeck, who guarantees the outcome as he imagines himself becoming aware of what it must be.

The Book of Revelation comes to command Wozzeck's perception of his situation. But its imagery and atmosphere—and most of all its portentousness—are not confined to Wozzeck's mind. Attention to that fact provides the focus for an interpretation of Berg's drama that I now wish to advance.[3]

The point of departure is a reading of the libretto in the light of the Apocalypse. The following citations from the latter are most directly relevant.

> 6:12: And I beheld when the angel had opened the sixth seal, and lo, there was a great earthquake; and the sun became black as sack cloth of hair, and the moon became as blood.
> 16:1: And I heard a fearful voice saying to the seven angels, Go your ways, and pour out the vials of the wrath of God upon the Earth.
> 16:3: And the second angel poured out his vial upon the sea; and it became as the blood of a dead man; and every living soul died in the sea.
> 16:4: And the third angel poured out his vial upon the rivers and fountains of waters; and they became blood.

2. Letter to his family, February 1834: "I scorn no one, least of all because of his understanding or his education, for it lies in no one's power not to become a dumbbell or a criminal—because we have all become alike through like circumstances, and because the circumstances lie outside of ourselves . . ." Werner Lehmann, *Georg Büchner: Sämtliche Werke und Briefe* (Hamburg, 1971), 2:422.

3. It is the opera that is the principal subject of this essay, but in presenting my interpretation I shall sometimes refer to Büchner's play and to its philosophical context.

Leo Treitler, professor and chairman of the department of music at the State University of New York at Stony Brook, is the author of, among other works, "Dufay the Progressive" and "Homer and Gregory: The Transmission of Epic Poetry and Plainchant." His *About Music* is scheduled to appear in 1977.

16:18: And . . . there were voices and thunders, and lightnings, and there was a great earthquake.

17:1: And there came one of the seven angels . . . and talked with me, saying unto me, Come hither: I will show thee the judgment of the great Whore with whom the kings of the earth have committed fornication, and the inhabitants of the earth have been made drunk with the wine of her fornication.

17:16: And [she shall be made] desolate and naked and burned with fire.

In the opera these images begin to be displayed in the second scene. (In Büchner's fair copy that scene opens the play, and that rather substantiates the impression one has of it as a source.)[4] As Wozzeck moves through the field cutting brush, he believes that the earth is hollow and quaking beneath him. He perceives the brilliant twilight as a fire on the horizon, and that impression is still vivid in his mind in the third and fourth scenes of act 1 as he describes his visions to Marie and the Doctor, respectively. This, to him, tumultuous eruption of the second scene is followed by darkness and by deathly silence: "Still, Alles still, als wäre die Welt tot." In the third scene, as he relives it all for Marie, he says, "Und jetzt Alles finster, finster. . . ." In the fourth scene of act 3, as Wozzeck returns to the scene of the murder, it is no longer "as though the world were dead"; it is "Still, Alles still und tot." And at the end of the scene, as Wozzeck's drowning noises subside, the Doctor, taking the air with the Captain, says, "Stiller . . . jetzt ganz still." In the fourth scene of act 1, the darkness is on Wozzeck's mind as he tries to bring the Doctor to understand what he has been experiencing. And in the tavern scene of act 2, he expresses his agony at seeing the Drum Major paw Marie, pleading with God to bring down the darkness: "Warum löscht Gott nicht die Sonne aus?" To Marie, standing alone after Wozzeck's departure at the end of the third scene, the darkness is unnatural, and she is terrified by it ("Es schaudert mich").

    Berg provided the most explicit lighting instructions for the staging of the opera. After the second scene of act 2, the scene in which

309

4. See Lehmann, 1:338 ff. Berg's libretto follows the scenic order of the first edition by Franzos (see George Perle, "*Woyzeck* and *Wozzeck*," *Musical Quarterly* 53 [1967]: 206–219). In both versions the scene in the field is followed immediately by the scene that opens with Marie ogling the Drum Major. That fact seems most essential, for it is the latter act that initiates the chain of events which Wozzeck comes to interpret as the fulfillment of the prophecy revealed to him through the signs in the field. The question arises, What understanding can we have of the first scene if the essential process of the drama appears to begin in the second? The drama runs its course in two settings at once, really: the predatory external world of the first scene and the haunted world of Wozzeck's mind, introduced in the second. In the first scene Wozzeck is shown as the victim of conditions that are responsible for the state of his mind and for what unfolds subsequent to the second scene. The last scene of the opera, too, is outside the process that begins in the second. It is in a way the ultimate statement about the condition of the external world.

Wozzeck's suspicions become explicit, every scene is played in darkness of one sort or another: overcast day, night, candlelight, red moonlight. In particular the death scenes of Marie and Wozzeck are both illuminated by the appearance of a red moon. Marie describes it as red, Wozzeck sees it as bloody in his own death scene, and Berg confirms this, again in his lighting directions ("Der Mond bricht blutrot hinter den Wolken hervor"). And as Wozzeck descends into the water that will drown him he cries, "Das Wasser ist Blut." Only in the very last scene does the morning sun that shone on the first scene illuminate the pathetic figure of the lone survivor. Darkness is one of the means whereby a sense of foreboding is projected. The descent of silence and darkness on Wozzeck's world is a central process of the drama.

The tavern scene in act 2 forces upon Wozzeck the palpable evidence of what it had amused the Doctor and the Captain to insinuate in the second scene of act 2. The sight of Marie dancing lewdly with the Drum Major launches him permanently into a morose and fanatic state of mind. It is not an ordinary act of infidelity that he sees, but a symbolic act of depravity. It is, he says, as though the whole world were waltzing about in fornication, and it is the whole world he wants punished at that moment, crying for God to extinguish the sun. From the moment that the idea of Marie's adultery had first entered Wozzeck's mind, he had assimilated it in this symbolic way; in act 2, scene 3, he speaks to her of "a sin so great and foul that it might drive the angels from heaven." In Berg's text for the murder scene, Wozzeck kisses Marie and expresses the wish that he might often kiss her thus. "But I may not," he says—"Ich darf nicht."

All this suggests that in Wozzeck's tormented mind the killing of Marie is an act that he has been called upon to carry out. There seems to be a premonition of this even as early as the interview with the Doctor in the fourth scene of act 1 when Wozzeck speaks of a terrible voice calling to him. The murder seems more a ritual act of execution than a passionate act of vengeance. Such an interpretation is consistent with the mysterious course of Wozzeck's death. It never seems quite to the point to call it suicide, but it seems even further off to call it an accident. It just happens, and, like Marie's death, it is something to which events and circumstances seem to move ineluctably. Again Wozzeck senses it coming. After the second scene of act 2 he alludes repeatedly to his own death. At the same time, however, we cannot but see Wozzeck's hand, and behind it his perverse will, as active in both deaths.

This suggests a view of the complexities in the determination of events in the drama. First, there is a perfectly natural explanation based on circumstances and motives. Marie is weary of a bleak existence with Wozzeck. He works long hours, sleeps away from home, and when he turns up he can do no more than rave about his hallucinations; never mind that he does it all for her sake and that of their child. She betrays

310

him with a man who offers her some diversion, and when Wozzeck learns the truth he kills her. It is a common enough story, but a tragic irony emerges from the tension between that surface view of things and Wozzeck's perceptions. Although Marie, as an adulteress, and Wozzeck, as a murderer, have violated the moral order of their world, they are nevertheless presented to us as the only sympathetic inhabitants of that world, driven to their acts by the cruelty of circumstances and of their fellow men. There would be pathos enough were we able only to see Wozzeck under these circumstances strike out against all that he has in the world. But the pathos is far more intense than that. Wozzeck imagines that he follows a divine calling in acting as Marie's righteous executioner, and the world that he thereby destroys is not the inhuman world represented to us by the Captain and the Doctor—it is the essentially innocent and worthy world of his little family. He acts, fulfilling a prophecy that he himself has spun out of hallucinations and superstitions and messianic religious ideas. In his mind what happens must happen, and so he causes it to happen in reality. He has no possibility of understanding Marie's actions on a human scale. She hopes for forgiveness, after the example of Mary Magdalene;[5] but he sees her as marked for destruction, after the example of the Great Whore Babylon. He has assimilated her act, from the moment of its first glimmering in his mind, into a grotesquely paranoid mental construction in which there are no acts of will, no choices, only the inevitable, and in which individual events are understood always as signifying something larger. Marie too, but without any fanaticism, has resigned herself to the abandonment of choice. For when she yields to the Drum Major, she yields in utter despair: it makes no difference to her what she does.

Beyond any causal analysis of the action, and quite outside the minds of any of the characters, there is an atmosphere of foreboding and doom that hangs like a pall over the drama as it unfolds to its seemingly inevitable conclusion. The apocalyptic imagery is only the most concrete manifestation of that atmosphere; all of the main characters respond to it: Marie, standing in the darkness, terrified; the hysterical Captain, hiding his fear of the future behind his flippancy and callousness; the Doctor, desperately keeping himself under control through his compulsive rationalism. And Wozzeck.

The sense of doom—the sense that the things that happen were bound from the first to happen—is not only in Wozzeck's mind; it is an essential aspect of the drama's expression. We feel that most acutely of all in contemplating the fate of Marie's child, which is the ultimate fulfillment in the piece. He is left at the end, riding off into the world like the little child of which Marie had told at the beginning of act 3 (in Büchner's version, the tale of the Grandmother):[6] "Once there was a

5. I refer here to Marie's monologue in act 3, scene 1.
6. Lehmann, 1:427.

poor child that had no father and no mother, for everyone was dead, and there was no one in the world, and he starved and cried day and night." That is the answer to the question of meaning that the drama poses: there is no larger meaning; things move irresistibly forward, but to no greater purpose.

That idea belongs to the thematics and to the tone of the drama, and the impact of the tragedy depends on it. We can bring it more sharply into view if we enter into the philosophical context of Büchner's play.

In the tavern scene, just as Wozzeck has blurted out his apocalyptic curse, "Warum löscht Gott nicht die Sonne aus?" the drunken apprentice begins to preach a different view of things: "Wherefore is man? Verily, beloved listeners, I say unto you, everything is for the best. For how else could the farmer, the caskmaker, and the doctor earn their living if God had not created man? How could the tailor live if God had not implanted in man a sense of shame? How could the soldier and the innkeeper live, if He had not equipped man with the need to shoot people and to quench parched thirsts? Therefore most beloved, doubt not, since everything is lovely and fine. . . ." This burlesque of a theodicy is reminiscent of the prattling of Pangloss in Voltaire's *Candide:* "Observe how noses were made to carry spectacles, and spectacles we have, accordingly. . . . Our legs are clearly intended for shoes and stockings, so we have them. . . . Pigs were made to be eaten, and we eat pork all the year 'round." It is the teleological view of the world that is being ridiculed here. Everything is valued in terms of the purpose it serves or the goal toward which it moves, and since world history is seen as moving toward some higher good, everything is, in the long run, for the best.

Just a few years before *Woyzeck,* Hegel had lectured thus:

> Our intellectual striving aims at recognizing that what eternal wisdom *intended* it has actually *accomplished.* . . . Our method is a theodicy, a justification of God. . . . [The reconciliation of the thinking mind with evil] can only be attained through the recognition of the positive elements in which that negative element disappears as something subordinate and vanquished. This is possible through the consciousness, on the one hand, of the true ultimate purpose of the world and, on the other hand, of the fact that this purpose has been actualized in the world and that evil cannot ultimately prevail beside it.[7]

But *Woyzeck* and *Wozzeck* embody a refusal to be reconciled to the evil they portray, a rejection of the idea that everything is for the best. There is no higher good that justifies this tragedy. Wozzeck's struggles to find wider meanings in small things merely show him victimized by a way

7. *Reason in History,* trans. Robert S. Hartman, The Library of Liberal Arts (Indianapolis and New York, 1953), p. 18.

of thinking that has somehow filtered down to him. It is another of
Büchner's jabs of bitter irony to show his anti-hero fingering the crumbs
of a philosophy that would dismiss him as one of the "innocent flowers"
that must be trampled down by the juggernaut of history.

In 1836 Büchner was appointed to the Faculty of Medicine of the
University of Zürich. He began his inaugural lecture on the cranial
nerves by speaking directly to this very issue. "In the domain of the
physiological and anatomical sciences we encounter two mutually opposed views. . . . The first regards all manifestations of organic life from
the teleological viewpoint: it finds the solution to the riddle in the purpose of an organ. It knows the individual only as something that is to
fulfill a purpose outside of itself." This attitude Büchner identified as the
"dogmatism of the Enlightenment philosophers," and he opposed to it
his own insistence that "Everything that exists, exists for its own
purposes."[8]

Büchner had said elsewhere that in writing plays he regarded himself as a kind of historian, and in the domain of history the teleological
viewpoint was completely at odds with his attitudes.[9] Hegel had proclaimed that "Universal Law is not designed for individuals. . . . In
affirming that the Universal Reason *does* actualize itself, we have nothing
to do with the individual empirically regarded."[10] Kant had written that
the older generations must "pursue their weary toil for the sake of those
who come after them. . . . It is to be the happy fate of only the latest
generations to dwell in the building upon which the long series of their
forefathers have labored. . . ."[11] The Turkish philosopher in *Candide*
asks, "What does it signify whether there be good or evil? When his
Highness sends a ship to Egypt, does he concern himself whether the mice
on board are comfortable or not?"

The historiography of the Enlightenment arose out of reflection
over the same perplexity that plagued Wozzeck. The difference is only
in the grandeur of the formulation: How can sense be read out of the
history of human existence when history daily displays so much of senseless barbarism and suffering? How could so much misery be reconciled
with the idea of a rational and provident order? It could only be that the
meaning of history is to be found in mankind's future. The question
came to be formulated as a question about ultimate purposes; and the
answer was a doctrine of progress, a secular copy of the doctrine of
salvation, which decreed that the misery in individual lives must be suf-

313

8. Lehmann, 2:291 ff.

9. Letter to his family, 28 July 1835: "The dramatic poet is in my eyes nothing other
than a writer of history. . . . His highest task is to come as near as possible to history as it
really transpired." Lehmann, 2:443.

10. Hartman, pp. 46–47.

11. "The Idea of a Cosmo-Political History," trans. W. Hastie, in *Eternal Peace and
Other International Essays* (Boston, 1914).

fered for the sake of what was to come.[12] No one had put it more eloquently than Hegel:

> When we consider the spectacle of the passions; . . . when we behold individuals, with the deepest sympathy for their indescribable misery—then we can only end up with sadness over this transitoriness and, insofar as this destruction is not only a work of nature but of the will of men, even more with moral sadness, with the indignation of the good spirit over such a spectacle. . . . But even as we contemplate history as this slaughter bench on which the happiness of peoples . . . and the virtue of individuals have been sacrificed, our thoughts cannot avoid the question, for whom, for what final aim these monstrous sacrifices have been made.[13]

The answer was formulated in systems of history that were complacent about the inevitability of progress and ultimately callous about the quality of individual human lives.

Büchner was one of the growing number to whom that answer was no longer acceptable, and *Woyzeck* is a powerful statement of opposition.[14] It answers exactly to Hegel's sneering characterization of the "litany of lamentation that the good and pious often, or for the most part, fare ill in the world, while the evil and wicked prosper."[15] It reverses the historical view of the Enlightenment philosophers. Where they saw the inevitable progress of man in the ascendancy of reason, *Woyzeck* enlarges upon injustice and suffering as a continuing condition. Where they read meaning out of history on the grand scale, *Woyzeck* insists upon the contemplation of meaninglessness. And as for the idea that reason and progress characterize man's condition, Büchner took that only as the object of grotesque parodies.

There is a scene in the play that Berg did not incorporate in his

314

12. Regarding the interpretation of Enlightenment historiography as secularization of Christian doctrine, see Karl Löwith, *Meaning in History* (Chicago, 1949) and W. H. Walsh, " 'Meaning' in History," in *Theories of History,* ed. Patrick Gardiner (Glencoe, Ill., 1959).

13. "Die Vernunft in der Geschichte." The passage is trans. by Walter Kaufmann, in *Hegel: A Reinterpretation* (New York, 1965; paper reprint, 1966), p. 251. (See Kaufmann's bibliographical note, p. 383, regarding the relation between his text and Hartman's.)

14. I cite just one other contemporary declaration of despair with the religion of progress in order to show something of the climate of controversy: "From all the signs that have been staring us in the face during the past year, I believe it is safe to say that all progress must lead not to further progress, but finally to the negation of progress, a return to the point of departure. . . . Is it not very clear that progress, that is to say, the onward march of things, good as well as evil, has brought our civilization to the brink of an abyss into which it may very possibly fall, giving place to utter barbarism?" *The Journal of Eugéne Delacroix,* trans. Lucy Norton (London, 1951). The passage is cited in E. H. Gombrich, *The Ideas of Progress and Their Impact on Art,* a lecture delivered at the Cooper Union School of Art and Architecture, New York, 1971.

15. Hartman, p. 45.

libretto but that shares the tone of the sermon of the drunken apprentice. A barker, speaking with a French accent, stands in front of a carnival booth:

> ". . . Ladies and Gentlemen, step right up and see the astronomical horse and little canary birds—they're the darlings of all the potentates of Europe, members of all learned societies. They'll tell you everything: how old you are, how many children you have, what diseases you carry. [Pointing to the monkey.] He shoots a pistol, stands on one leg. It's all a matter of training; all he has is beastly reason, or rather a quite reasonable beastliness. He's no beastly-dumb individual like lots of people, present honored company excluded. Step right in. The commencement of the commencement will take its beginning at once.
>
> "See the progress of civilization. Everything moves forward, a horse, a monkey, a canary bird. The monkey is already a soldier—that's not much, the lowest level of the human race. Start the representation. Make the beginning of the beginning. The commencement of the commencement will take place at once."[16]

The issues over reason and progress are reflected again in the distorting mirror of the scene between Wozzeck and the Doctor: the Doctor, raving that the *musculus constrictor vesicae* is subject to the will, that in man alone individuality is exalted to freedom; Wozzeck, paying no attention, confiding to the Doctor his secrets about nature; the Doctor, losing himself in raptures over the progress of science and about his own immortality, then remembering that he mustn't lose his own self-control, assuring himself that it isn't worth aggravating oneself over another person—if it had been a lizard, that would have been something else again. (In the opera that callousness reaches its depth in the fourth scene of act 3 when the Doctor and the Captain hasten away from the sounds of Wozzeck drowning.)

The provocation of these issues was already at hand in the celebrated case of the real Woyzeck, which Büchner took as substance for his play. Woyzeck was condemned to death by the Leipzig tribunal for the murder of his mistress. On the petition of his public defender the case was reviewed by the privy counselor Clarus, with respect to the question whether Woyzeck, given the miserable conditions of his existence, could be held fully responsible for his act. In a long and thoughtful analysis Clarus argued that, inasmuch as Woyzeck was fundamentally in possession of his senses (he was embittered but not mentally ill) he must be held accountable for the exercise of his freedom of choice. It would be an unacceptable precedent and an intolerable example for the young if Woyzeck were granted his life after having followed his passions and not

16. Lehmann, 1:411.

315

his reason. Woyzeck was beheaded, and Büchner, to put it in the words of Berg's *Wozzeck* lecture, appealed the case to the public.[17]

Berg achieved an extraordinary operatic portrayal of the relentless progress of Wozzeck's entrapment between a murderous world and his own psychic disintegration. I wish to pursue in the remainder of this essay the most intense of the means by which he did so, the association and development of motivic ideas, which weave an ever more constraining and ever more clearly portentous network about Wozzeck and his family.[18]

The source is in the second scene. The scene-changing music following the first scene falls away quickly, leaving a sonority that develops in the first five measures as a motive based upon three chords. I call it motive *a* (ex. 1). It is recalled naturally enough in the third and fourth scenes, as Wozzeck tells Marie and the Doctor of his visions. But that it should be brought back in the barracks scene (act 2, scene 5) is a special idea. Wozzeck, plagued by nightmare recollections of the preceding scene in the tavern, is unable to sleep. To be sure, music from that scene returns to him eventually, but at the outset the atmosphere is set by those chords, moaned by the chorus of sleeping soldiers. In this way the music leads us to refer the tavern scene—which is in Wozzeck's consciousness—back to the scene in the field and suggests that the contents of the second scene are transformed from Wozzeck's unconscious, concretized as the episode on the dance floor, realized as the working out of what was portended. This interpretation will be substantially reinforced when I return to this scene near the conclusion of the discussion, and the role that the music here plays in projecting the penetration of the implicit or unconscious meaning of events in Wozzeck's mind onto their explicit, surface meaning will be exemplified in other connections.

Throughout the course of the opera the chords of motive *a* are unpacked, and their upper strand is transformed in stages into a number of distinct motivic identities. The moments in the action which these accompany are then always marked with the affect of their source in the second scene. More than that, those moments thereby fall together as the chain of consequents from that beginning.

17. The report of Clarus is printed in Lehmann, 1:487 ff. In March 1929 Berg presented a lecture on *Wozzeck* in connection with the performance of the opera in Oldenburg. About the scene-changing music between the fourth and fifth scenes of act 3 he said this: "From the dramatic standpoint it should be conceived as an 'Epilogue' to Wozzeck's suicide, as a declaration of the author who, stepping outside the action on the stage, issues an appeal to the audience, regarded as the representatives of humanity." Printed in H. Redlich, *Alban Berg: Versuch einer Würdigung* (Vienna, 1957), pp. 311–27.

18. This is not the first time that attention has been drawn to the motivic tautness of Berg's music. With respect to *Wozzeck,* see esp. George Perle, "Representation and Symbol in the Music of *Wozzeck,*" *Music Review* 32 (1971): 281–308 and "The Musical Language of *Wozzeck,*" *Music Forum* 1 (1967): 204 ff. From this point on the reader can best follow the argument by referring to a score and a recording.

Ex. 1.—1.2.201–6. Examples sound as written.

In the initial presentation of the *a* motive, the upper voice of the chords turns on an augmented second, A♭–B–A♭ (see the bracket in ex. 1).[19] In the second and third presentations, that interval is distinctly isolated. With just those pitches, it will constitute a kind of fixed tonal reference throughout.

Two new motives evolve from the augmented second: I shall refer to them as *b1* and *b2; b1* follows immediately upon the reiteration of the augmented second in the third presentation of motive *a*. It accompanies Wozzeck as he points to the mysterious sign above the toadstools (ex. 2); in the fourth scene it accompanies him as he asks the Doctor whether he has ever seen the toadstool rings (ex. 3); and it is recalled to Wozzeck by the cello as he lies sleepless and afraid in the barracks scene (ex. 4). After the introduction of *b1* in the second scene, the motive is picked up by the French horn, then by the English horn (ex. 5). The last phrase in the English horn is imitated in canon by the trombone, the harp, and the oboe. This is the moment in which motive *b2* evolves from *b1,* with Wozzeck singing about the mysterious disembodied head.

Ex. 2.—1.2.227.   Ex. 3.—1.4.554–55.   Ex. 4.—2.5.752–53.

Motive *b2* is recalled at pitch and in canon in the third scene as Wozzeck cites Genesis (ex. 6). It is recalled again in the barracks scene as the melody to which Wozzeck begins his recitation from the Lord's Prayer (". . . and lead us not into temptation," [ex. 7]). These musical associations carry the mystery and terror of that moment in the second scene ("Three days and nights later he lay in his coffin"), through the moment of revelation in the third scene ("Isn't it written . . ."), and ultimately to the moment in the barracks scene when Wozzeck, haunted by an unexpressed awareness of the significance of things, lies abed praying.

19. The upper voice of motive *a* is marked H in the score ("*Hauptstimme,*" or principal voice). That is the case with every strand of the motivic network I am describing here, something I take to be an indication of Berg's intentions with respect to the rank of these motives.

Ex. 5.—1.2.233–34.

motive *b 1*

motive *b 2*

318

Ex. 6.—1.3.443–47.

Wozzeck: Steht nicht ge-schrie - ben "Und sich es ging der
Is it not writ - ten: "Be - hold the smoke did

Rauch auf vom Land, wie ein Rauch vom O - fen."
rise from the land, as from out a fur - nace?"

Ex. 7.—2.5.754–58.

Wozzeck: Mein Herr und Gott,
          Lord and God,

und   füh - re uns nicht   in Ver - su - chung.
and   lead   us   not   in - to temp - ta - tion.

As motive *b1* evolves from *a*, and as *b2* evolves from *b1*, so *b2* repeatedly leads back to the substance and tone of *a*. The canon with *b2* rises to a phrase that peaks in the highest voice and quickly falls through a whole-tone line (exx. 6–8). In the scene with Marie, Wozzeck picks up the whole-tone descent for the recitation from Genesis (ex. 6). In the barracks scene he takes it for the recitation from the Lord's Prayer (ex. 7). The line is achieved through filling in of the upper voice of the chords of the *a* motive, which come back into focus each time at this point (cf. exx. 6–8 with ex. 1). This return to the point of origin assures our continued awareness of the source of these motives and of the links between their dramatic contents.

There is yet another strand in this network that contributes to the same result. In the third scene Wozzeck's biblical recitation is prepared by an arpeggio solo in the bassoon that eventuates in a tremolando on

Ex. 8.—1.2.241–44.

the notes A♭ and B (ex. 9), the same augmented second previously
mentioned. It is a sort of intonation for the coming passage which begins
with the same interval. The cello plays such an intonation in the fourth
scene, ending again with a tremolando on A♭–B. This time those pitches
prepare not the *b2* motive but Wozzeck's plaint, "Ach, Marie" (ex. 10).
That is of course one of the thematic motives of the opera, always an
expression of lamentation and of anxiousness for Marie or the child.
Marie sings it in the third scene with the words "Komm mein Bub." The
strings cry it out at the moment of Marie's death. In the third scene it is
heard a second time, in association with the equally thematic motive
"Wir arme Leut" (ex. 11). The associations among these motives rest on
two things: the place of the augmented second in them, and their introduction in association with one another. The dramatic significance of the
association seems clear. The motives of lamentation refer again and
again to the hard circumstances of Wozzeck's and Marie's life—there is
no getting away from that—but they have their musical source in the
mystery and terror of the imagined supernatural. These are then two
different manifestations—we might say material and spiritual, or external and psychological—of the forces that press in on Wozzeck and his
family. For Wozzeck the two blend into one in his perceptions of a
threatening world.

Ex. 9.—1.3.441–43.

Ex. 10.—1.4.534–40.

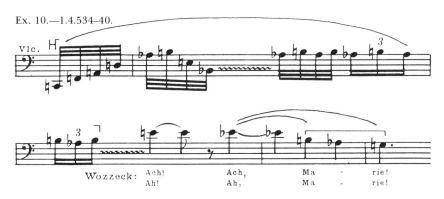

Ex. 11.—1.3.466–68.

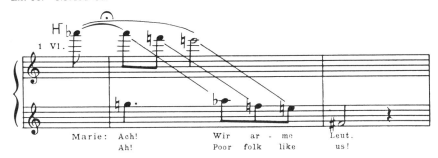

Something like that is expressed again in the melody of Marie's lullaby in the third scene, a moment of melancholy tenderness that falls between the march—which we may reckon as the beginning of the end—and the appearance of Wozzeck with his report about the second scene. The melody comprises two elements: a dotted figure that occurs in several folklike tunes (e.g., the accompaniment to Andres' hunting tune in the second scene [see ex. 12, the figure in parentheses], and motive *b2* [ex. 12]). On the surface, the melody has the qualities of a lullaby. Its full meaning, however, entails also the affect of the lamentation motives and the haunting portentousness that it receives from the the context of the *b2* motive.

Ex. 12.—1.3.372–73; (1.2.250).

This motivic complex has its final outcome in Wozzeck's death, and after that it is washed away, as we shall see. As the moon "breaks blood-red through the clouds" (act 3, scene 4), Wozzeck moans, "But the moon will give me away; the moon is bloody." The strings just then descend in a scale whose intervals derive from the *b2* motive, as is made clear by the

321

scoring. Those intervals are identical with the intervals of a six-note chord that pervades the entire scene just as the pitch B pervades the entire scene of Marie's death (ex. 13).

Ex. 13.—3.4.267–68.

Wozzeck wades into the water to wash the blood away but finds that the water has turned to blood, and he drowns. At that moment the strings rise chromatically, carrying up the six-note chord (ex. 14). The chord is sustained as the Doctor and the Captain stroll by and is left sounding to the end of the scene. At the very end it is resolved to the chord that begins that great outpouring of sympathy, the D-minor orchestral epilogue (ex. 15). The music of the second scene has run its course, just as we may say the prophecy of the second scene has run its ironic course, and it is wiped away, leaving us to contemplate once more that external world on which the first curtain rose.

Ex. 14.—3.4.284.

Ex. 15.—3.4.318–21.

But the six-note chord of this scene was first heard just after Marie's death. There is a moment's silence, then the orchestra in unison takes up the B that has been sounding throughout the murder scene, makes an enormous crescendo, and crashes down on the six-note chord (ex. 16). The germinal motive of the second scene has reached forward to link both deaths together as its own eventuation.

Ex. 16.—3.2.109–14.

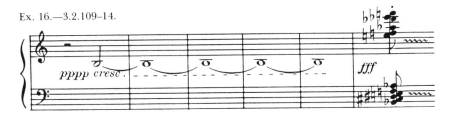

I want finally to describe two musical associations, involving different motivic material, through which meaningful links are established between moments in time and between levels of consciousness. At a certain point in the second scene (meas. 286) there begins a lengthy, detailed direction for lighting, with each effect marked exactly with respect to the beat on which it is to occur: "The sun is just setting. The last strong ray bathes the horizon in the most glaring sunlight, which is directly followed by a twilight with the effect of deepest darkness, to which the eye becomes gradually accustomed." What is important here is the immediate juxtaposition of brilliant light and sudden darkness. With the flash of the last strong ray Wozzeck screams, "Ein Feuer! Das fährt von der Erde in den Himmel." In the orchestra a pair of chords crashes up through successive octaves, then falls chromatically to the bottom again (ex. 17). This figure returns in the tavern scene of the second act, as Wozzeck, watching the dancing, screams, "Warum löscht Gott nicht die Sonne aus?" (meas. 517–22). The twilight that Wozzeck saw as a fire in the second scene now returns to his mind as the conflagration before the apocalyptic darkness that he is calling down. This is for him the moment that was foretold by those signs.

323

Ex. 17.—1.2.291–95.

Just before the great lighting display in the second scene, Wozzeck says to Andres, "Listen! Something down below is moving with us." The horns are the principal orchestral voice at that moment, and they rise quickly and hysterically to a climax (ex. 18). In the barracks scene, describing his nightmare visions to Andres, Wozzeck sings a development of that line. His words are "I keep seeing them and hearing the fiddles, 'Immer zu, Immer zu'" (ex. 19). With the words "Immer zu" Wozzeck is aping Marie and the Drum Major dancing and singing in the tavern (ex. 20). There the rhythm of those words had fallen right in with the waltz rhythms of the stage band. But now as Wozzeck recalls them, it is in the musical context in which they originated, that fearful moment in the second scene (cf. bracketed notes of exx. 18 and 19 with ex. 20). Now we recognize that the waltz has had implanted in it the germ of that earlier music and that the waltzing plays out in Wozzeck's mind what that music portended.

Ex. 18.—1.2.274–78.

Ex. 19.—2.5.746–49.

Ex. 20.—2.4.546.

Continuing with the description of his nightmare, Wozzeck sings on with the same music: "Then something flashes repeatedly before my eyes, like a knife, a great knife" (ex. 21). With that the first idea of what must be done enters his mind as the last step in a chain of associations which leads from the mysteries of the second scene, through their concretization, to their inevitable consequence. But it is not just an association of ideational contents that is accomplished here. It is a chilling musical projection of the conglomeration of contexts that give nightmares their disturbing character.

Ex. 21.—2.5.750–51.

This passage brings us about full circle, for it leads directly into motive *b1* in the cello (meas. 752) and thence to the recitation from the Lord's Prayer with motive *b2* (meas. 753). With all that has just been shown as crammed together in Wozzeck's mind, the prayer is understandable as the momentary refuge of a terribly frightened man. But with his relentless irony, the tune with which Berg saw fit to provide him is that one he learned in the second scene, singing about a disembodied head and the man who picked it up and was dead three days later.

Wozzeck is a marked man, ground down by the press of circumstances and by the machinations of his own mind. As we reflect on his story, these remarks of Büchner's about his own feelings upon studying the French Revolution become filled with meaning.

> Ich fühlte mich wie zernichtet unter dem grässlichen Fatalismus der Geschichte.... Der Einzelne nur Schaum auf der Welle, die Grösse ein blosser Zufall, die Herrschaft des Genies ein Puppenspiel, ein lächerliches Ringen gegen ein ehernes Gesetz, es zu erkennen das Höchste, es zu beherrschen unmöglich.... Das *muss* ist eins von den Verdammungsworten, womit der Mensch getauft wurde.[20]

20. Letter to his fiancée, after 10 March 1834: "I felt crushed under the monstrous fatalism of history.... The individual mere foam on the wave, greatness a matter of chance, the power of genius a puppet-play, a laughable bout against a law of brass. To comprehend it is the most we can do, to defeat it is impossible.... 'Must' is one of the curse-words with which man is baptized." Lehmann, 2:425–26.

Appendix

Wozzeck

Act/Scene	Place	Persons
1.1	Captain's rooms, morning	Wozzeck, the Captain
1.2	Open field outside of town, late afternoon	Wozzeck, Andres
1.3	Marie's room, evening	Marie, the Child, Wozzeck
1.4	Doctor's study, sunny afternoon	Wozzeck, the Doctor
1.5	Street in front of Marie's door, twilight	Marie, Drum Major
2.1	Marie's room, sunny morning	Marie, the Child, Wozzeck
2.2	A street in town, daylight	The Captain, the Doctor, Wozzeck
2.3	Street in front of Marie's door, overcast day	Marie, Wozzeck
2.4	Tavern courtyard, late evening	Crowd, Apprentices, Marie, Drum Major, Wozzeck, Andres
2.5	Barracks, night	Soldiers, Wozzeck, Andres, Drum Major
3.1	Marie's room, night, candlelight	Marie, the Child
3.2	Forest path near a pond, darkening	Marie, Wozzeck
3.3	A bar, night, weak light	Crowd, Margret, Wozzeck
3.4	The same forest path, moonlight as before	Wozzeck, the Captain, the Doctor
3.5	In front of Marie's door, bright morning, sunshine	Children, Marie's Boy

MOSES UND ARON:
SOME GENERAL REMARKS, AND
ANALYTIC NOTES FOR ACT I, SCENE 1

DAVID LEWIN

General Remarks

THE DRAMATIC idea of the work hinges on the paradoxical nature of God: the *Unvorstellbares* that commands itself to be *vorgestellt*. The musical metaphor that reflects (or better defines) the dramatic idea is the nature of the twelve-tone row and system as "musical idea" in Schoenberg's terminology. "The row" or "the musical idea" is not a concrete and specific musical subject or object to be presented for once and for all as referential in sounds and time; it is, rather, an abstraction that manifests itself everywhere ("allgegenwaertiger") in the work. And yet it can only be perceived, or realized, by means of an aggregation of specific *Vorstellungen*, even *Darstellungen*. Or, more exactly, the *composer* may perceive it as a sort of resonant abstraction, but it remains unrealized and unfulfilled until it is manifested through performance and communicated to an audience by means of material sounds, representing the idea in all its manifold potentialities.

In this connection, the multiple proportion—God: Moses: Aron: Volk equals "the idea" (row): composer (Schoenberg): performer: audience— is suggestive. Moses, like Schoenberg, perceives directly and intuitively a sense of divine ("pre-compositional") order. He cannot communicate this sense directly, however. As he suggests in Act I, Scene 1, he would much prefer to spend his life in simple contemplation of this order. But God commands him to communicate it ("Verkuende!") and he is powerless to resist.

God demands that His order be communicated to the Volk. Yet how can they be taught to love and understand the immaterial and *Unvorstellbares* (the true musical experience)? They will likely mistake this or that specific material manifestation of it (especially when brilliantly performed by Aron) for the idea itself. In fact, this is exactly what happens. To make matters worse, Moses is no performer, he cannot communicate directly to the Volk. As it turns out, he cannot even make himself understood by Aron, his sympathetic performer. This state of affairs

· 1 ·

is symbolized, of course, by Moses's Sprechstimme as opposed to Aron's coloratura tenor.

In sum, the following dramatic relationships are set up:

God loves the Volk (more than He loves Moses, as we gather from Act I, Scene 1) but cannot communicate with them directly, and they do not know or love Him.

Moses knows and loves God; he does not love the Volk, nor they him, though they fear him; he cannot communicate with the Volk.

Aron does not know God, but wants to love Him; he loves the Volk and is loved by them. Note that, in his love for the Volk, Aron is more like God than is Moses. He communicates easily with them.

Moses and Aron (the crucial link) love each other and think they know each other; as it turns out, they do not. The link breaks down, with tragic consequence.

Aron has dual allegiance: to Moses, whom he respects and tries, at first, to obey; and to the Volk, by which he gets carried away (just as the performer gets carried away by the audience even while intending to concentrate on the composer's wishes). Ultimately his infatuation with the Volk wins out. (And we must recall that, in his love for the Volk, Aron is closer to God than is Moses in feeling, if not in understanding. Note his "Israels Bestehn bezeuge den Gedanken des Ewigen!" in II.5, mm. 1007ff.)

To what extent the tragic breakdown is due to Moses's inability to communicate clearly enough to Aron, or to Aron's inability to suspect and resist his natural affection for the Volk—this remains an open question at the end of Act II. Schoenberg evidently meant to decide this question, in the third act, in Moses's favor. But the libretto is unconvincing to me. The problem posed by the drama is not whether Moses or Aron is "right," but rather how God can be brought to the Volk. If the triple-play combination of God to Moses to Aron to Volk has broken down between Moses and Aron, and if the Moses-Aron link cannot be repaired, then the catastrophe of the philosophical tragedy has occurred in Act II and the drama is over. If there is a personal tragedy involved, it is surely that of Moses, and he, as well as or instead of Aron, should be the one to die (which in a sense he does at the end of Act II).

Remarks on the Singing-and/or-Speaking Chorus, in General, and in I. 1

By opening the opera with the bush scene, Schoenberg first presents the singing-and/or-speaking vocal ensemble as the voice of God. It is important for us to have made this association *before* we encounter the Volk, who will constitute the same sort of vocal mass—singing or speak-

· 2 ·

ing or both together. The effect is to bind God and the Volk together in a special way which, so to speak, includes both Aron (singing) and Moses (speaking). *Both* Moses and Aron are necessary to realize God's plan. God's voice is a mixed speaking-and-singing mass, hence He seeks the Volk, who can realize the *Klangideal*. Neither Moses nor Aron, both being individuals rather than masses and vocally restricted to only speaking or only singing, is of real interest or importance to God except as "a tool," a means of focusing the two paradoxically coexistent facets of His nature. The speaking facet is identified with the "unvorstellbar" nature of God, the singing facet with His demand to be "verkuendet." (Note the absence of the Sprechchor under the text "verkuende" at m. 15 of the opening scene, and again at the end of the scene.)

Aron, the singer, is necessary for the "Verkuendigung," then. He can, for instance, pick up the tune of "Dieses Volk ist auserwaehlt . . ." (m. 71 of I. 1), without even having heard it, at the end of Act I (m. 898) and feed it to the Volk for a triumphal reprise of the *sung* part of "Dieses Volk" (mm. 919ff.). But he is unaware of the overwhelmingly powerful *spoken* element going with the sung chorus at m. 71. From the point where Aron takes over from Moses (m. 838), there is no speaking to the end of the act. This reflects Aron's unawareness of the "unvorstellbar" part of God, and the Volk's consequent lack of understanding of it. Aron's text from m. 838 on is a compendium of *material* ideas and promises; his *misreading* of the text of mm. 71ff. is also symptomatic and disastrous:

Voice of God, mm. 71ff.	*Aron, mm. 898ff.*
Dieses Volk ist auserwaehlt, vor allen Voelkern,	Er hat euch auserwaehlt, vor allen Voelkern
das Volk des einzigen Gottes zu sein,	das Volk des einzigen Gottes zu sein,
	ihm allein zu dienen,
	keines andern Knecht!
dass es ihn erkenne	Ihr werdet frei sein
und sich ihm allein ganz widme;	von Fron und Plage! (!)
dass es alle Pruefungen bestehe	
denen in Jahrtausenden der Gedanke ausgesetzt ist.	Das gelobt er euch:
Und das verheisse ich dir:	Er wird euch fuehren
Ich will euch dorthin fuehren	in das Land wo Milch und Honig fliesst, und ihr sollt geniessen
wo ihr mit dem Ewigen einig	leiblich was euren Vaetern
und allen Voelkern ein Vorbild werdet.	verheissen geistig. (!)
	(But cf. Exodus 3:17 . . . ! !)
	(following sung Volk chorus to the same text)

329

Aron here is surely the virtuoso performer, carried away in front of his audience, adding, as he thinks, expressive embellishments and "interpretation" to a piece he "knows"! Moses is, of course, the writhing composer in the audience at the concert.

In contrast, we immediately identify Moses, in I.1, with the speaking, "unvorstellbar" aspect of God. From a purely theatrical point of view, this involves our understanding those parts of I.1 in which the Sprechchor predominates over the solo singers as particularly intense for Moses. Thus: "Du muss dein Volk befrein" (m. 26) and the entire prophecy (mm. 67–85). It will be noted that these sections are those most crucially involving Moses's duty with respect to God's love for the Volk.

In I.1, Schoenberg uses a variety of means to shift the focus between the solo singers and the Sprechchor, most notably (i) relative dynamics, (ii) entry time with respect to text (who leads off, who follows), (iii) completeness vs. hocketness of text presentation.

Dramatic Structure of I.1

The scene glosses into four dramatic sections:

α): EXPOSITION (1–28). Moses encounters the bush. God commands him: "Verkuende!" (not yet specifically mentioning the Volk). Moses wants to demur, but God tells him he is not free to do so, and more specifically and forcefully commands "Du muss dein Volk befrein!"

β): AGON (29–66). Moses offers a series of objections, God counters them.

γ): THE PROPHECY (67–85) for the Volk.

δ): CODA (86–end). Transition back to the immediate situation, and "Verkuende!"

Serial Background for I.1

Example 1 shows the row and its hexachordally related inversion, S_0 and I_0. Hexachords, hexachordal "areas" will be denoted as follows: H_0 is the first (unordered) hexachord of S_0, the second of I_0; h_0 is the first of I_0, the second of S_0. A passage is "in A_0" when the hexachords involved appear as H_0 and h_0, or when rows used are S_0, I_0, R_0, RI_0, or when X and Y ideas (see below) appear at levels derived from S_0 and/or I_0, etc. A_1, A_2, etc. denote the corresponding transpositions of the entire complex A_0.

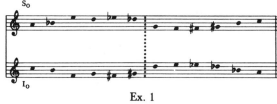

Ex. 1

· 4 ·

S_0 and I_0 have the same dyadic segments; also, the chromatic tetra-chord 3-4-5-6 of S_0 is the same as 7-8-9-10, reordered, of I_0. Textures reflecting these segmental structures emerge in the scene.

Schoenberg does *not* state any complete row-form in I.1 in a melodic linear way. The first such statement in the opera is reserved for Aron's entrance in I.2. At the prophecy, in I.1, we do get linear melodic statements of hexachords, at 0 level, and with periodic musical construction.

Up to that point, the principal thematic intervallic ideas are those indicated by Exx. 2 and 3. Example 2 is the chordal progression X_0 from the first to the last three notes of the row, with answering rx_0. As first presented, the relation sounds more variational than (retrograde) inversional. Later in the scene, as we shall note, when X appears against x rather than rx, Schoenberg makes the inversional relation aurally clear. In the sequel, I will speak of X chords or Xx textures, etc. pretty loosely. It will be noted that any X chord is sufficient to define the row and area in which it appears. This is aurally very helpful in the scene.

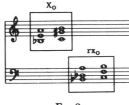

Ex. 2

Example 3 shows the melodic idea Y_0, notes 4 through 9 of S_0. The thematic idea has a preferred contour (as in Ex. 3) and rhythm, but is subject to some variation in these respects. It can also be split, symmetrically, in half. Note that y_0 (4 through 9 of I_0) is the same, linearly, as rY_1; analogously, $Y_0 = ry_{11}$. These relations can be used to pivot between areas related by 1-or-11 interval, and Schoenberg makes use of the property to do so in the scene (mm. 50 1/2–53 1/2, mm. 67–70, m. 85). In the passages just cited, A_0 is "inflected," in this way, by both A_1 and A_{11}; A_8 is inflected by A_7 . . . (presumably).

Ex. 3

The reason for "presumably" is that, although there is only one occurrence of $Y_8 = ry_7$ (so that it is not intrinsically clear which is accessory to the other), the area A_8 is very clearly one of the important secondary areas in the scene, and it is frequently preceded or followed by A_7 or A_9 (without the use of the Y-pivot).

· 5 ·

It will be noted that both the X and Y ideas contradict the hexachordal, dyadic and 3-4-5-6 vs. 7-8-9-10 articulations of the row. This abstract "tension of textures" is realized in the scene by the use of musical textures in the chorus that reflect the abstract one. Of course, the X and Y ideas are not only compatible, but serially complementary with each other, and are so employed in the music to a great extent. In the course of the scene, the chorus moves from X texture (with Y obbligato, representing Moses, in the orchestra) at the opening of the scene, to more dyadic textures approaching the prophecy, to linear hexachord statements with fairly dyadic accompaniment at the prophecy, and then returns to its original X texture in the coda.

Analysis of α Section (Exposition)

The chorus sings in A_0 up to the end of the section, where it breaks loose violently into A_5 at "Du muss dein Volk befrein!" (m. 26), generating energy for the following section. The Xx chords belong to the singers. They sing nothing else until "so kannst du nicht anders mehr" (m. 25), where we get a sort of "serial *Zug*" in the women's voices (passing through the row from the first X_0 chord to the second one), and x_0 linearized against y_0 in the men's voices. At m. 26, the singers return to X chords, but in A_5. Here x, rather than rx, is presented against X, bringing out the inversional rather than "variational" relation, as the A_0 area is left. (But all this is greatly covered by the Sprechchor dynamically and in the text-setting.)

The chorus is thus essentially a *static* musical element until the end of the section. This reflects its dramatic position. It is *Moses* who introduces tension into the scene. Correspondingly, Moses's music is very active in the section. He is never accompanied by A_0 row forms here, and he is very modulatory.

(We do not hear the Sprechchor until after we hear Moses speak. This may symbolize the notion that God is not "unvorstellbar" when He is singing to Himself, but only to *human beings*.)

The Y idea belongs to Moses. The characteristic slow, uneven, trudging rhythm laboriously wending its way through small intervals that is generally imposed on presentations of Y seems apt to depict musically the character that appears through Moses's self-descriptions. At Moses's first speech (mm. 8–10), Y_0 is presented melodically in the upper notes of the chords, arhythmic but with its characteristic contour. It is harmonized by 4-note chords from RI_1 and S_{10}. The function of neither the texture nor the row-forms is clear to me, but they certainly do introduce contrast, while presenting a melody which will "go with" the serial area of the chorus.

The melody is, in fact, picked up immediately by the orchestra, in A_0, as obbligato to the following choral statement; presumably this represents Moses listening to the bush.

The local connections into and out of Moses's first speech are smooth, hinging on the tritone E-Bb: that tritone plus D pivots from m. 7 to m. 8; the tritone plus A pivots from m. 10 to m. 11. Contrast, but little tension yet, as the text indicates.

However, Moses is much disturbed by "Verkuende." He launches into his longest and most structured speech of the scene, with very sharp harmonic contrast and quick "harmonic rhythm" (total-chromatic turnover). As we shall see at the end of this paper, the serial structure of this speech can quite suggestively be regarded as generating the large structure of the whole remainder of the scene; at any rate, it certainly introduces important areas and area relations that will figure later on.

This speech falls into two parts, dividing at m. 21 ("Ich bin alt"). The first part is, rhetorically, in form aba'b', with the apostrophising of God articulating the a and a':

a: "Gott meiner Vaeter . . ."
b: "der du ihrem Gedanken . . ."
a': "mein Gott,"
b': "noetige mich nicht . . ."

That form is supported by the music. a and a' correspond in texture. For a, we get a quick run-through of I_9 and R_8, coming to rest in A_5 at b, with a clear thematic texture, X and Y. At a', we get an analogous quick run-through of I_2, followed at b' by a return to A_5 in which the serial texture clears up again, this time into dyads in m. 20. In sum, Moses's gesture here is a twofold modulatory excursion, coming to rest in A_5 both times, first with X and Y texture, then with dyad texture.

(A nice psychological touch is provided by the "groaning" modulatory X chords alternating with awful, squashy-noise chords at the 9, 8, and 2 areas, depicting Moses's reaction to the implacable static A_0 X-chords of the chorus.)

N.B.: It will become clear later on that A_8 and A_5 are the two principal secondary areas of the scene, and that A_9 is "supposed" to inflect A_8 via the 1-relation of areas. Hence, the area progression: $9\ 8 \rightarrow 5,\ 2 \rightarrow 5$ may be "reduced," intellectually, to: $8 \rightarrow 5,\ 2 \rightarrow 5$. Thence it will be noted that there is an inversional balance which "motivates" the choice of A_2 to balance A_8 about A_5, "tonicizing" A_5. This idea seems to go nicely with all the previous analysis of the passage, and the actual rows involved, RI_8 and S_2, do have a harmonically inversional relation. Whether one is actually aware of this, or to what extent one is, at m. 16 3/4 and m. 19, is somewhat hazy, to say the least, but possible to my ear.

There is still a bit of "smooth" connection from m. 15 to !6̂: the texture hints at picking up the oscillating A and B from the chorus melody into the agitated opening of m. 16; these notes recurring as a harmonic pair at the bar-line of m. 17, and finally vanishing in effect as the 5-area sets in.

The second part of Moses's speech ("Ich bin alt . . .") begins with a distorted X and Y texture applied to S_8, and proceeds, in m. 22, to a straight run-through of I_9 and RI_9. Measure 21 picks up the F♯-C-F chord of S_8 from the second beat of m. 17, creating an aural link between the two 8-forms. Here, A_8 is the clearly and thematically textured area, just as A_5 was in the first part of the speech; important, since these will become the two principal secondary areas of the scene.

The pickup of the chorus at m. 23 is definitely "smooth," in view of the preparation of the C-F-B in m. 22 (see Ex. 4). The C-F appears to refer back to m. 21 also: while several elements carry over harmonically from m. 20 to 21, the striking sense of harmonic change (and local arrival) at m. 21 seems most strongly created by the conjunct move from the melodic E-B-F♯ of m. 20 to the chordal F♯-F-C of m. 21; thus the fourth C-F is what is moved to at that point. To this extent, Moses is setting up the chorus entrance (unconsciously?) at m. 23—or perhaps they are showing him that he can't escape.

Ex. 4

The turn of the chorus to A_5 at m. 26, then, picks up that area from the first part of Moses's preceding speech. Perhaps Moses had a premonition of this most unwelcome command, or perhaps they are hitting him in his vulnerable area. At mm. 26–27, Y and y forms appear in the orchestra as before, but now greatly distorted in contour (mirrorwise, as are the X chords in the chorus)—probably reflecting Moses's agonized reaction to the chorus's command.

Analysis of β Section (Agon)

Dramatically, the section divides in two at 48 1/2 ("Ich kann denken . . ."). Throughout, the chorus becomes very active in all respects (modulation, new textures, initiative for same). Up to 48 1/2, Moses becomes more and more passive, musically as well as dramatically: here he is not so much raising real problems as offering excuses and evasions. His speeches become shorter and shorter. At 35 1/2, 40 1/2, and 47 1/2, he accepts whatever serial area the chorus has left off on, and the chorus changes area with their replies (this serial situation is quite audible).

At 48 1/2, though, Moses finally articulates a real insight and problem: "Ich kann denken, aber nicht reden." Here, Moses becomes active again musically also. He returns to the original area A_0 "all by himself" (that is, from his own preceding A_9, which he had picked up from the chorus, rather than in response to any immediately preceding nudge from the chorus). The serial return is supported by a sort of reprise of mm. 11ff. This finally gives the chorus some pause; it has to stop and think during the modulatory orchestral interlude that follows. The remainder of section β consists of the chorus's answer to this real objection of Moses: first, they bolster his faith and reassure him ("Wie auf diesem Dornbusch . . ."), then they come up with a practical solution ("Aron soll dein Mund sein . . ."). The latter, of course, sets up the central problem of the drama.

(As later metric analysis will attempt to show, "Aron soll dein Mund sein . . ." carries a very big stress; it will be analyzed as *the* big A_8 arrival of the scene. In this respect, it is perhaps of note that when Aron enters, in I.2, he is singing in A_4, an area which is *antipodal* to A_8 with respect to A_0!)

While Moses soon becomes passive after the opening of section β, he is still musically active at m. 29. (Nevertheless, his speech covers only two measures, as opposed to his previous three-with-fermate and five-measure speeches.) Texturally, the gesture of m. 29 is similar to that of m. 19. The trail-off into quintuplets is a familiar aspect of Moses's complaints by now, and the I_9 form at m. 29 1/2 can be heard, to some extent, as recalling the I_9 of m. 22.

"On paper," the preceding S_7 (m. 29) balances the I_9 about the A_8 coming up in the chorus at m. 31. As will become clear in the sequel, this relation is "supposed to be" functional, as are the 1-and-11 area relations between 7-and-8 and 9-and-8.

An aspect of m. 29 that is very audible to me is the emergence of the 3-note chromatic "half-of-Y" motive as a musical carrier *across* an articulation, from mm. 26–28 *into* m. 29. (Ex. 5 shows what I mean.) Likewise, the same motive carries the B-C♯ trill of m. 30 into the middle C of m. 31, across an articulation. While there are also some binding common-tone relations involved at these moments, we are used to that situation; the *kinetic* use of the 3-note motive is new, very effective, and goes well with the activation of the Moses-chorus agon.

The speech of the chorus at mm. 31–35 sits in A_8. As noted above, this is the "balance point" for Moses's previous S_7 and I_9. A_8, of course, picks up the other main area Moses had already exposed, in the second

335

· 9 ·

Ex. 5

part of his long speech in section α. In fact, the chord on the last beat of m. 30 can be heard to pick up the relevant chords from that earlier section (2nd beat of m. 17, first half of m. 21).

The chorus now begins to sing the "inversional" X-against-x (as opposed to the "variational" X-against-rx), just as they did in A_5 ("Du muss dein Volk . . ."), and as they did *not* do in A_0. They do not complete the Xx idea though; instead, they become very active serially, running through hexachords, Y motives, etc. in more or less mirror fashion.

Moses's next question (m. 35 1/2) is supported by only one chord, a vertical h_8. While he appears to be taking the initiative rhetorically, by asking a question, the musical and serial treatment make it clear that he is really simply treading water, taking his cue from the chorus.

As before in section β, there is a strong kinetic sense about the interchanges between Moses and the chorus here. Moses's chord in m. 35 1/2 sounds "passing," via the Bb-Ab-F♯ in the upper register, mm. 35-37. (The serial rationale of the three whole-tones is not clear to me.) Also there is a 3-note chromatic carrier from the E-Eb within Moses's chord to the F-E in the men's voices at m. 36.

The chorus calms down at 36-40. (Why? There seems to be some sense of return to the texture preceding m. 8 here. I can't figure out what the idea might be.) They return to simple Xx chords in A_7. The Xx relation is inversional, as it always has been in secondary areas, rather than variational as in A_0.

The Ab of Moses's "passing" chord in m. 35 1/2 returns as neighbor to the F♯ of m. 37, and this relation is prolonged in register through Moses's subsequent extension of the chorus's A_7 area (again, in spite of his rhetorical "initiative"), up to another local stress (like m. 36 1/2) at m. 41 1/2. There, the chorus lands again on an X-chord, changing area back to A_5. Intensifying the situation of m. 30 3/4, we get here only a mere hint of "X-ness" before other serial textures set in.

The longish choral speech that follows is modulatory, from the familiar A_5 through A_8 (orchestra, m. 43), through A_3 and A_9 (mm. 44, 46). Two features seem to stand out strongly.

First, the chorus begins to pick up dyadic and chromatic-tetrachord (3-4-5-6 and 7-8-9-10 of the row) textures more and more. (N.B. already the line of the chorus bass from m. 36 to 42.) As pointed out in the "serial background" portion of this paper, these textures are incompatible with the X texture, and we may note again that (except for the mysterious sitting on that texture in mm. 36–40) there has been a progressive liquidation of X sounds in the chorus going on (noted in connection with the amount of X-reference at m. 30 1/4 and m. 41 1/2). There is some hint of X-sound in the female voices at mm. 44–45, but by 46 they have very definitely yielded to the dyads and chromatic tetrachords. This seems to have to do with God's turning to thinking about the Volk.

The second feature that stands out strongly in the chorus passage under discussion is that the B♭-A♭-F♯ idea which was introduced in mm. 35–37 gets picked up and developed here into E(38)-D(41 1/2)-C(42)-[C-B♭-B]-C(44)-D(45)-E(46 1/2). The medial C-B♭-B is, of course, our friend the 3-note "half-of-Y" motive. As I said before, I can't find any serial rationale for this three-whole-steps idea, but it does seem more than fortuitous in the music.

At m. 47 1/2, Moses begins another stock excuse, continuing the chorus area, as he did earlier at m. 35 1/2 and m. 40 1/2. (We might note that the three areas, in order, are A_8, A_7, and A_9. This might be viewed as a composing out of the already cited use of 7 and 9 areas as balanced "accessories" to the 8-area, noted in connection with mm. 29–31. Perhaps both of these are supposed to compose out the "half-of-Y" motive?) His opening chord and quintuplet texture recall the old story of his earlier I_9 statements as m. 22 and m. 29 1/2. But here we are in an *antecedent,* not a *consequent* part of his phrase, and there is a sudden and dramatic break texturally, dynamically, and serially, as he puts his finger on what is *really* troubling him: "Ich kann denken, aber nicht reden." The reprise here has already been mentioned. One notes also that Moses picks up the X and Y ideas that have just been abandoned by the chorus in favor of the dyads and chromatic tetrachords. If we recall that the latter gesture of the chorus was tied up with God's thinking on the Volk, the dramatic appropriateness of Moses's gesture here is clear, though hard to put into words. His X-chords make a particularly strong color contrast after the chords in m. 47 and the first half of m. 48.

There follows a modulatory orchestral interlude (mm. 50 1/2–53 1/2), involving extended chromatic wiggling à la "half-of-Y" or chromatic-tetrachord. The motion is from I_0 (RI_0?) to S_1 (R_1?), demonstrating $Y_1 = ry_0$ for the first time, and thence sequentially through I_7 and S_8, demonstrating the analogous relation $Y_8 = ry_7$. This suggests yet another rationale for the 7-and-9-surrounding-8 area relations already discussed: that it will be an analogous tonicization of the principal secondary area A_8 to the tonicization of A_0 surrounded by A_1 and A_{11} (and Schoenberg will make the latter very clear in the sequel, via the appropriate Y/y symmetries). In this connection, since mm. 52–53 is the only passage in the scene which explicitly links A_8 with A_7 or A_9 via a Y-symmetry, we might note that the X-chords that appeared in the chorus S_8 at m. 31 and I_7 at 36 1/4 are picked up in mm. 52-53. (Measures 31 and 36 1/2 were clearly paired by the text, recalling in both cases Moses's original "Einziger, ewiger . . ."—although Moses did not use those areas at that time.)

As mentioned before, the last choral speech of section β divides in two: bolstering Moses's faith (mm. 53 2/3–59 1/2) in A_5; then solving the practical problem via Aron (mm. 59 1/2–67) in A_8, inflected by RI_9 and R_7. A_5 and A_8 are, of course, the two principal secondary areas of the scene, originally exposed in Moses's speech at mm. 16–22. And the RI_9 and R_7 inflection of A_8 is by now an old acquaintance. The A_5 and A_8 of this chorus should be taken as the definitive "answer" to Moses's early speech, for Moses does not speak again, and, after this point, everything is very clearly in a basic A_0 (although the chorus does return to A_5 for a bit to begin its coda).

After an initial run-through of S_5, the remainder of the A_5 part of this choral passage is completely based on the dyads of A_5. (In fact the run-through itself is pretty dyadic, especially as accompanied.) All the more striking, then, is the return to inversional Xx chords for the A_8 section at m. 59 1/2. The Gb-C-F of the female voices is a familiar tag for recognizing A_8 (cf. 17 1/4, 21, 31, 43?, 52 3/4?); the chord is restated at m. 62, where we get overlapping presentations in run-through form of S_8, RI_9, R_7, and I_8. The powerful inversional Xx at m. 59 1/2 is the last time we shall hear such a clear X texture until the coda. Because of the great power of the inversional feeling at 59 1/2, and the symmetrical formal arrangement of rows in mm. 62–65, the chances of our hearing the RI_9 and R_7 as balanced inversionally about A_8 seem pretty good here, in spite of (or maybe to some extent even because of) the dense texture.

Analysis of Section γ (the Prophecy)

The prophecy is articulated musically, as in the text, into two parts, each beginning with a preliminary announcement of upbeat character: mm. 67, 71, 79, 81. Each part builds to a climax at its end. The second part is much more intense than the first in all musical respects.

I have a very clear sense of m. 81 being the "big downbeat" of the scene, rather than m. 71. I can't find any "tonal" reason for this. Other factors seem to indicate that 81 is a more crucial metric articulation than 71. For instance, the setting of "Und das verheisse ich dir" that precedes 81 is such as to make the text, with its built-in strong upbeat character, very clear. The rest that begins m. 81 and the purity and clarity of the sung sound in m. 81, after all the speaking static and noise preceding, create for me an enormous (negative) accent. Probably, too, factors of large-scale metric consistency are operative in my hearing here: as we shall see later, "Aron soll dein Mund sein," "Dieses Volk ist auserwaehlt . . . ," and "Ich will euch dorthin fuehren . . ." (mm. 59 1/2, 71, and 81) are metric articulations on the same level to my hearing, and I certainly hear "Aron soll . . ." as a *bigger* stress than "Dieses Volk . . . ," which is of course consistent with hearing "Ich will . . ." as also more stressed than "Dieses Volk. . . ." The drama supports the latter readings, I think. "Aron soll . . ." is the release (downbeat) for all the accumulated tension of the problem of Moses involving his inability to communicate. "Dieses Volk . . ." involves vision, but not action or decision, and the section has the character of God taking a very deep breath to come out with a decisive statement of resolve at "Ich will. . . ."

Measures 67–68 present A_0 with a complex texture: in the orchestra, we have X_0 progression in whole notes, Y_0 theme obbligato, and dyads from A_0. The chorus sings the dyads, but only one note from each of the X_0 chords. (As mentioned earlier, the chorus will not return to clear X_0 sound until the coda.) Measures 69–70 are in "sequence" with mm. 67–68, in A_{11}, displaying $ry_{11} = Y_0$ (and thus balancing the earlier A_0-A_1 relation at mm. 50 1/2–51, just as A_7 and A_9 have been balanced about A_8. An analogous A_0-A_1 will, in fact, return later.)

The connection from the orchestral I_8 at m. 66 to the choral opening at m. 67 involves not only the carry-over of the G in the bass, but also, to some extent, the common-tone function of the chromatic tetrachord D♯-C♯-D-E between m. 66 and m. 67. The latter relation is noteworthy, since it demonstrates, for the first time, a *segmental* (hence intrinsic serial) relation between I_8 and I_0 (also S_0); this provides a "natural" serial basis for a link between A_0 and the important secondary area A_8. (Cf. the dyads of A_0 that open I.2 and the segment G♯-F♯-G-F of S_4 at Aron's entrance—more specifically, m. 98 1/2 et al. and Aron's part at mm. 125 3/4–126. The analogous relation functions here between A_0 and S_4.)

The chromatic tetrachord is also used to slide kinetically into m. 71: F♯-E going to G-F at the bar-line in the orchestra.

The emergence of linear hexachords in the Hauptstimmen from mm. 71–76 was noted earlier; it seems to be the big serial event of the scene, after all the play with X textures, dyads, and chromatic tetrachords in the chorus textures. We are evidently getting close to "the idea," and, logically enough in terms of the sonorous metaphor of the opera, the Sprechchor begins to get very noisy and to take over the lead in presenting the text. The orchestra makes it clear that the accompanying voices are

339

basically derived from a dyadic texture, though various other hints occur, notably of X-chords at "wrong" levels in the choral bass part at mm. 71 and 74, and in the alto at m. 75.

At mm. 77–78, the serial texture is liquidated, hexachords alone more or less taking over, reflecting the change of character in the text.

Measures 79–80 make another big textual upbeat, with analogous texture to mm. 67–68 and mm. 69–70.

Measures 81–84 in the sung chorus and orchestra are basically an intensification of the texture of mm. 71–76. The relative dynamics of singers and orchestra versus (reinforced!) Sprechchor are disturbing here, but Schoenberg's conception is consistent, in terms of the musical metaphors: As the tonal texture becomes more and more complex, revealing and suggesting infinitely complicated relationships which one would have to strain to sort out under the most favorable conditions, the "unvorstellbar" static rises in a great swell to block Moses's (and our) perception of it.

As the Sprechchor drops out at m. 85, the area shifts to A_1, with mm. 67–68-type texture. The orchestral Hauptstimme demonstrates $rY_1 = y_0$, balancing the events of 69–70, which demonstrated $ry_{11} = Y_0$. The soprano link B-C, A-B$\flat$ over the bar-line into m. 85 is very neat: these are the sevenths associated with the rX_0 progression, and here they are demonstrated as combining to form a chromatic tetrachord!

Analysis of δ Section (Coda)

After having whipped itself into a frenzy of sublimity, the chorus suddenly remembers Moses, who is standing there, doubtless open-mouthed and utterly clobbered. It returns abruptly, without smooth tonal connection, to its misterioso pianissimo texture, to X-chords and then dyads, in A_5. Measure 86 evidently refers back specifically to 36 1/2, 87 3/4 to 41 1/2, and 88 1/2–89 to 55 (and thence 20), all of these being earlier A_5 moments. The idea is, I think, that the chorus is reminding Moses that all his objections were answered in section β.

I don't know exactly what the A_{10} is doing in m. 90—it certainly provides a fresh kind of contrast for the last return of A_0 at m. 91. A_{10} was used once (and only once) before: this preceding the first return to A_0 (m. 11). The analogy is intellectually attractive, but musically pretty thorny; the texture preceding m. 11 was so different (in fact, unique in the scene, and the 4-note chord texture does not reappear until the equally "unique" m. 208 of the second scene: "Reinige dein Denken...."). Nevertheless, there may be something in the fact that the common-tone transition from m. 10 to m. 11 was E-B$\flat$-plus-A, and that the same sonority appears at the return to A_0 in m. 91. (However, it is not conspicuous in m. 90.)

The concluding A_0 passage (mm. 91–97) presents X-chords and liquidates the Y-motive. I.e. the bush remains, *sicut erat in principio;* Moses leaves. Interesting are the harmonic tritones formed of the sixth and seventh notes of the rows that appear as a result of the Y liquidation in mm. 95 and 96. These tritones *bridge* the hexachords, and perhaps, in terms of the textures we have had so far in the scene, this has something to do with their pertinence as cadential sonorities.

Further Remarks on Some of the Textures

The X-texture seems to be generally associated with God as a mystery, as drawn into Himself. (This is not to be confused with His "unvorstellbar" aspect, which involves human reaction to Him and is pretty clearly identified with speech, rather than with any tonal idea.)

One can make a good case for the dyadic texture as going with God's desire to be "verkuendet," and His thinking of the Volk (which is essentially the same phenomenon). Thus, the first dyadic texture we encounter is at m. 20, under Moses's text: "...ihn zu verkuenden." The accompaniment textures for the prophecy (to the extent they are audible) are basically more dyadic than anything else, and here God is certainly thinking of the Volk. Similarly, the dyadic bias of the textures at mm. 43ff. appears to go with God's imagining Moses before the Volk. The opening of scene two, with its veritable orgy of dyads, seems suggestive here, as heralding and accompanying Aron, who is to accomplish the "Verkuendigung."

But here we run into trouble and inconsistency in our symbolism. For the *most* dyadic chorus texture certainly appears at mm. 53–58, where God is thinking about Himself communicating to Moses, not about Moses or Aron communicating to the Volk. And, along with this, we have the spectacular contrast of the X-texture, and *not* dyads, immediately following, at "Aron soll dein Mund sein . . . ." According to the reading of the previous paragraph, this seems completely, even perversely, inconsistent.

In sum, I can't make consistent symbolic sense out of the use of the textures. But it's a problem of interpretation that is certainly worth grappling with, since Schoenberg handles these textures so carefully and dynamically in the scene.

Summary and Speculative Metric Analysis of the Scene

The chart on page 17 attempts, first, to make sense of the area-structure of the scene, assuming that A_8 and A_5 are the main secondary areas (which is very clear), that A_1 and A_{11} are inversionally balanced accessories to A_0 (which also seems clear) and that A_9 and A_7 are analogous accessories to A_8 (which is at least intellectually convincing, in light of our preceding labors).

341

· 15 ·

The A_2 at m. 19 makes good intellectual sense, as mentioned earlier, if it is regarded as balancing A_8 about A_5, "tonicizing" A_5. The 1 and 10 areas at mm. 8–10 remain a puzzle (as does the passage itself—A_1 is certainly "accessory" to A_0 here only by a real stretch of the imagination). This is not too disturbing, since the melodic Y_0 at that point serves to prolong A_0. The 3 area at m. 44 and the 10 area at m. 90 also don't "fit in"; otherwise the area chart seems quite logical.

Additionally, I have attempted, largely "by ear," to articulate the scene into commensurate metric units at a fairly large level; I have indicated these articulations, which overlap the Greek-letter formal divisions of the scene, by dotted lines on the chart.

This metric reading seems by and large convincing and suggestive to me. It supports Moses's entries at m. 8 and m. 16, and then indicates how God takes over the important stresses up to Moses's articulation of his "real" problems at 48 1/2. Also, the reading seems to work well, in other respects, with the dramatic kinesis of the scene, and with the importance of A_5 and A_8 as secondary areas. (The mysterious areas at m. 8 and m. 90 are made more mysterious by the metric reading, but this, too, seems appropriate.)

Even a larger metric reading still seems suggestive: taking m. 81 as *the* big downbeat (as discussed earlier), the reading:

1 | 8 16 | 23 31 | 41 3/8 48 1/2 | 59 1/2 71 | 81 90

appears logical, and stimulates thought. Thus, after the anacrustic A_0 of m. 1, the big measure | 8 16 | is dominated by Moses and his tension against A_0. Measure 23 then provides the first A_0 big downbeat, releasing this tension, as God takes over.

The foreground push from A_0 to A_5 that God then introduces with "Du muss dein Volk befrein . . ." is covered with speech static locally, but works itself out in the large progression from A_0 at m. 23 to A_5 at m. 41 3/8 (the next "big big bar-line") through a subsidiary A_8 at m. 31. And this motion, from A_0 to A_5 through A_8, seems also to augment the progression of the opening of Moses's long speech (mm. 16–19, after the preceding choral A_0).

Moses's "Ich kann denken . . ." at 48 1/2 is an A_0 upbeat, on this metric level, to God's downbeat A_8 answer at m. 59 1/2, "Aron soll dein Mund sein." The latter, and the relative stresses at m. 71 and 81, were discussed earlier.

Thus, from the first A_0 big-big downbeat at m. 23, we have the following:

and, reducing this, we get:

$$
\begin{array}{cccc}
0 & 5 & 8 & 0 \\
23 & 41\ 3/8 & 59\ 1/2 & 81
\end{array}
$$

And this big progression makes excellent sense as an expansion of Moses's long early speech (mm. 16–22, together with the preceding A_0 and the following A_0 downbeat at m. 23).

It probably would be helpful to read over the analysis again at this point, following the chart.

α):

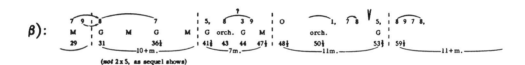

343

β):

γ, δ):

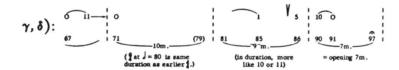

· 17 ·